OUR NATIVE TREES

Black Squirrel Books

BOOKS BY HARRIET L. KEELER

STUDIES IN ENGLISH COMPOSITION, WITH
LESSONS IN LANGUAGE AND RHETORIC
 with Emma C. Davis (1892)

THE WILD FLOWERS OF EARLY SPRING (1894)

OUR NATIVE TREES AND HOW TO
IDENTIFY THEM (1900)

OUR NORTHERN SHRUBS AND HOW TO
IDENTIFY THEM (1903)

HIGH SCHOOL ENGLISH: A MANUAL OF
COMPOSITION AND LITERATURE
 with Mary E. Adams (1906)

OUR GARDEN FLOWERS (1910)

THE LIFE OF ADELIA A. FIELD JOHNSTON (1912)

ETHICAL READINGS FROM THE BIBLE
 with Laura H. Wild (1915)

OUR EARLY WILD FLOWERS (1916)

THE WAYSIDE FLOWERS OF SUMMER (1917)

OUR NORTHERN AUTUMN (1920)

OUR NATIVE TREES

AND HOW TO IDENTIFY THEM

A Popular Study of Their
Habits and Their Peculiarities

By HARRIET L. KEELER

Introduction by
Carol Poh Miller

Foreword by
Anne Raver

The Kent State University Press
Kent and London

This facsimile edition was made from a scan of a first-edition copy of *Our Native Trees and How to Identify Them.*

©2005 by The Kent State University Press, Kent, Ohio, 44242
All rights reserved

Library of Congress Catalog Card Number 2004065757
ISBN 0-87338-838-0
Manufactured in the United States of America

Previously published by Charles Scribner's Sons, New York ©1900.

Library of Congress Cataloging-in-Publication Data
Keeler, Harriet L. (Harriet Louise), 1846–1921.
Our native trees and how to identify them : a popular study
of their habits and their peculiarities / by Harriet L. Keeler ;
introduced by Carol Poh Miller.
p.   cm.
Originally published: New York : C. Scribner's Sons, 1900.
With a new foreword and pref. Includes index.
ISBN 0-87338-838-0 (pbk. : alk. paper) ∞
1. Trees—North America—Identification. I. Title.
QK110.K438 2005
582.16'0973—dc22   2004065757

British Library Cataloging-in-Publication data are available.

TO THE MEMORY OF

PHYLLIS AND NICHOLAS

MY LOVING COMPANIONS THROUGH

FIELD AND WOOD

THIS VOLUME IS DEDICATED

CONTENTS

FOREWORD

BY ANNE RAVER

Harriet Keeler was one of those amateur botanists who was as at home with a calyx and peduncles as with the writings of Emerson and Shakespeare. I can imagine her teaching high school English, making sure, in her ladylike manner, that each student could diagram a sentence as well as understand Hamlet as he struggles to avenge his father's death: "is't not perfect conscience / To quit him with this arm?" And I suspect she took them on country walks to understand with their hearts what Thoreau was getting at in *Walden* when he wrote, "Instead of calling on some scholar, I paid many a visit to particular trees . . . , standing far away in the middle of some pasture, or in the depths of a wood or swamp."

In *Our Native Trees,* first published by Charles Scribner's Sons in 1900, she takes us by the hand to say, in her conversational voice, what is so engaging about the magnolia or the linden or, in the case of the pawpaw, what is not. Of the pawpaw's fruit, she writes, "Although credited in the books as edible and wholesome, one must be either very young or very hungry really to enjoy its flavor." (Hear, hear! The pawpaw, though a lovely tree, bears tasteless fruit with the consistency of pablum.)

Keeler's informal yet authoritative tone reminds me of Mrs. William Starr Dana's *How to Know the Wild Flowers,* which was published by Scribner's in 1893. But Frances Dana, in striving to write a book strikingly different from the botanical tomes of the day, kept botanical descriptions to the bare basics: shape of the leaf, height of the stem, color of the flower and fruit. This is part of what makes it so accessible and yet too easy, like a Golden Book for ladies who might not be up to the mental gymnastics of botanical language.

Keeler, however, strides right into the botany, as if to say that this is not a man's world, and she proceeds to parse a flower's parts matter-of-factly—just as she must have diagrammed those sentences on the blackboard. The linden's flowers, for example, she describes as "perfect, regular, yellowish white, fragrant, nectariferous, downy, born in cymous clusters, pendulous, with the flower-stalk attached for half its length to the vein of an oblong leaf-like bract as long as itself." Now, here is a technical description that I can actually picture! I might skip over it in order to read all the intriguing things she has to say about the linden, but it is there to refer to when I am out and about, sticking my nose into one of those nectariferous, cymous clusters.

Read on and you will find that the linden is unsurpassed by any native as a shade tree. It is often planted on the windward side of orchards to protect young trees. In winter it is "recognized by its deep red buds; and the delicate leaves which burst from them in the spring are a vivid green." (Here is the firsthand observer telling us what to watch for.) And then, the English teacher quotes Tennyson, observing the same tree: "A million emeralds break from the ruby-budded lime." She tells of a European linden reported to be 1,000 years old when it died and of Linnaeus's father, who took it for his name: "His father belonged to a race of peasants who had Christian names only, but having by his personal efforts raised himself to the position of pastor of the village in which he lived, he followed an old Swedish custom, common in such cases, of adopting a surname." And he chose the name Linné, which is Swedish for linden, the beautiful tree that grew near his home.

I had never heard of Harriet Keeler before Carol Poh Miller wrote asking me to read *Our Native Trees*. And I am grateful that Ms. Miller, a historian who seems to have the same observant eye as the woman who would become her subject, was intrigued by the little ode to her on a memorial plaque mounted on a boulder in a park near Cleveland. It is her scholarly detective work that has brought this lovely book back into print.

I think I would have liked Harriet Keeler. For one thing, she dedicated her book not to some beloved professor or husband (she didn't have one) but to her two dogs, Phyllis and Nicholas, who are pictured in a rather faded black-and-white photograph in the front of the book, accompanied by the words "my loving companions through field and wood."

And Ms. Miller pointed out another connection to me. Harriet Keeler graduated from Oberlin College in 1870, at a time when few women earned more than a high school education. I graduated from the same school 102 years later, and the small liberal arts school, the first in the country to accept women, changed my life. Somehow, it attracted the kind of quirky, idiosyncratic people—nerds, we called ourselves—who couldn't help but follow their own course. And some of us became friends for life.

I picture Harriet sitting in a long, sensible dress beneath the tall elms in Tappan Square, not just enjoying the color of the yellow leaves but examining their short petioles and fugacious stipules. (And had I taken a walk with her, she might have inspired me to have gotten more than a D in biology, which, in those days, covered plants.) I wonder if Keeler joined her fellow students on "Learning and Labor Day," a time-honored tradition at Oberlin when students, who are supposed to learn from physical labor, help their professors rake up leaves and so on. I remember doing just that at my English professor's house before we all retired to the living room to have a Rolling Rock and to talk about *The Golden Bowl.*

I think Keeler would have used her rake as energetically as she used her mind. Her presence is palpable in this friendly guide to native trees. There is no reason not to savor every moment while embracing the world in all its layers. And there is no excuse for not being accurate.

Keeler Memorial, Brecksville Reservation, Brecksville, Ohio.
Jim Mathews, Score Photographers.

INTRODUCTION

BY CAROL POH MILLER

I first discovered Harriet Keeler in 1974. At a trailhead in the
Brecksville Reservation, some fifteen miles south of Cleveland, I
came upon a memorial at once simple and enigmatic. Mounted on
a glacial boulder was a bronze plaque bearing, in relief, a woman's
profile and this inscription:

Harriet L. Keeler
Teacher—Author—Citizen
She Liveth as Do the Continuing Generations
of the Woods She Loved

Who was this woman who had inspired such tender remembrance?
Cursory research revealed that Keeler was an early graduate of Oberlin
College who had spent her career as an educator and administrator
with the Cleveland public schools. She was also an amateur botanist whose published works—*Our Native Trees, Our Northern Shrubs,
Our Garden Flowers,* and others—were said to have "inspired nature
study throughout the nation." The three-hundred-acre Harriet L.
Keeler Memorial Woods at Brecksville was meant to remind visi-
tors of this "eminent educator who loved Nature."[1] Nearly two decades would pass before I knew more.

In 1992 I was commissioned to prepare a small history of the Cleveland Metropolitan Park District on the occasion of its seventy-fifth
anniversary. As part of that work, I gathered biographical informa-
tion on Keeler and the nature trail created in her memory in coop-
eration with the then-nascent Cleveland Metropolitan Park Board.
A few years later I audited a class on local flora taught by the eminent botanist (since retired) Dr. George Wilder of Cleveland State

Harriet L. Keeler, senior class photograph, Oberlin College, 1870.
Oberlin College Archives, Oberlin, Ohio.

University. Keeler's books, which I had begun to collect, enriched what I observed in the field. Dr. Wilder, too, found her works on native plants—especially the present volume, first published by Charles Scribner's Sons in 1900—to be both authoritative and literate. With his encouragement, I determined to resurrect this notable woman.

It was not easy to flesh out the story of Harriet L. Keeler. Her personal papers, if they survive, have not been discovered, and so I have had to piece together the life of this intriguing subject from disparate sources.

Harriet Louise Keeler was born on July 28, 1844, in South Kortright, Delaware County, New York, the last of six children born to Burr and Elisbeth A. Barlow Keeler.[2] Her father was a prosperous farmer; from her grandfather, Martin Keeler, Harriet is said to have received her love of nature. Harriet attended the district school, leaving at age fourteen. After briefly teaching in Cherry Valley, New York, she entered the Delaware Academy in Dehli, a college preparatory school where Harriet was the only girl. A teacher there encouraged her to go to college—an unusual course for girls of that period. In the fall of 1867 Harriet Keeler enrolled as a sophomore in Oberlin College, and she received her AB degree in 1870. Of the thirty-six students in the College Department's senior class that year, Keeler was one of only five women.[3]

Following her graduation, Harriet Keeler moved to Cleveland, where she would spend her entire career as a teacher and administrator with the Cleveland public schools. Taking a room on Superior Avenue (she later moved to the Hollenden Hotel), Keeler taught geometry for one year at the old Central High School on Euclid Avenue. Between 1871 and 1878 she served as supervisor of primary grades. Then, in 1878, Keeler joined the faculty of the new Central High School, a great Gothic pile opened that year on Willson (East 55th) Street just south of Cedar. For three decades Keeler taught English and history there, her duties expanding by 1895 to include those of assistant principal.

By all accounts Harriet Keeler was a beloved and inspiring educator who made her strong individuality a part of her work. Her students might begin their class hearing Miss Keeler, with her clear, bell-like voice, read from Emerson's "Self-Reliance" or recite Lowell's "Pictures of Appledore." She eschewed the "vivisection" of literature (as one student would later put it) in favor of teaching students to read for knowledge and pleasure. A gentle counselor, Keeler might advise extravagant talkers to "avoid superlatives, my dears," or persuade a student to prune a wordy oration by asking, "How often have you heard a speech that was too long? How often have you heard a speech that was too short?" The Central High School Class of 1904 dedicated its class book to Miss Keeler "in appreciation of her valued service and unswerving fidelity to the school," describing her affectionately as "our good friend and teacher."[4]

In 1908, after thirty-eight years of service, Harriet Keeler retired from the Cleveland public schools. Four years later, in response to an unexpected vacancy during a period of disharmony within the school district, she was called back to serve as superintendent, a post she filled from January 7 until August 31, 1912.[5] Keeler was the first woman to hold that position. In reply to a message from Henry Churchill King, president of Oberlin College, congratulating her on her appointment, Keeler wrote: "I appreciate all the good wishes that are coming to me. Queer things happen in this life, and one of the queerest is that which has happened to me."[6]

With an open face, her hair loosely gathered into a high chignon, Harriet Keeler was said to have an "interesting" personality—calm, fearless, optimistic. She was known as a delightful conversationalist with an inexhaustible supply of stories drawn from her reading, writing, and travel. (By 1898 Keeler had been to Europe five times; in 1901 she traveled with her friend and mentor, Professor Adelia A. Field Johnston of Oberlin, across the continent to Alaska.) But above and beyond all mental gifts, friends recalled, Harriet Keeler possessed a generous heart and was ever ready to assist a friend in need. "Talking things over with her was sure to make the mists and darkness disappear," one wrote.[7]

Keeler was active in civic life. She was a founder of the College Club and a member of the Women's City Club and the Consumers League of Cleveland. She was the recipient of honorary degrees from Oberlin College and Western Reserve University, and, in 1915, the Oberlin College alumni elected her to a six-year term on the board of trustees.[8] Keeler had a strong interest in the betterment of women and was a staunch suffragist. When the Cuyahoga County Woman's Suffrage Association, founded in 1869 but long dormant, was reinvigorated at the hand of Elizabeth Hauser in 1911, Keeler—by then a nationally known author—lent her name to the campaign to win universal suffrage by state adoption, later becoming honorary chairwoman.[9]

In a pamphlet distributed by the Ohio Woman Suffrage Association, *The Question of Woman Suffrage as It Seems to Me*, Keeler penned her personal thoughts on the subject. Citing the social and industrial revolutions that had occurred in the previous half-century, and the millions of women that had since entered the work force, Keeler called suffrage "the outward and visible sign of respected citizenship, of self-respect and the power of self-protection; the only means by which intrenched injustice can be successfully attacked and permanently overcome." She gave no quarter to those women of wealth and social position opposed to suffrage, writing, "Their efforts are and must be in vain, for the world they seek to keep has already passed away." For Keeler the matter was simple: "Since women are compelled to live under government and obey its laws, they are therefore equally entitled with men to a voice in that government."[10]

While Harriet Keeler enjoyed a distinguished career as an educator and garnered encomiums for her civic work, it was as an amateur botanist and nature writer that she gained national recognition. "Her joy," one friend recalled, "was in botanical expeditions, acquiring and disseminating knowledge and pleasure from flowers and trees."[11] Keeler's first botanical work, *The Wild Flowers of Early Spring*, appeared in 1894. Subtitled *A Study of One Hundred Flowers Growing in the Suburbs of Cleveland and Throughout Northern Ohio*, it met with such favor that Keeler brought out a second edition three years later, this one illustrated by drawings "made directly from the plants" by Mary Keffer. *Wild Flowers* established the formula for Keeler's subsequent works. Relying on standard authorities, especially Gray's *Manual of the Botany of the Northern United States*,

Harriet L. Keeler, 1912.
Oberlin College Archives, Oberlin, Ohio.

and after consultation with the foremost experts, she was careful to employ scientific classification, nomenclature, and descriptions. To these she added her own field observations, together with literary references culled from her wide reading. Indexes of Latin and English names and a glossary of botanical terms enhanced the books' usefulness to the general reader.

Keeler had a sprightly and engaging style. Here, in *Wild Flowers,* she discusses *Arisaema triphyllum,* a member of the Arum family:

> The fancy of calling this flower Jack in the Pulpit seems to have arisen from a resemblance between the green canopy which waves over the club-like spadix and the ancient sounding board formerly placed over pulpits. . . . English children also call the plants, Lords and Ladies, the purple ones being the Lords and the green ones the Ladies.
> The greenhouse gives us two Arums, the Calla lily and the Anthurium, both of which are evidently poor Jack's fine relations.

Quoting Tennyson—"And the Marsh Marigold shines like fire in swamps and marshes gray"—of *Caltha palustris* she writes: "Its bright yellow flowers, borne in clusters on the leafy stem do, indeed, shine like fire, for they are buttercups intensified, larger and more brilliant."[12] Such vivid descriptions helped readers to easily identify what they observed outdoors.

Between 1900 and 1920 Charles Scribner's Sons published six books by Harriet Keeler: *Our Native Trees and How to Identify Them* (1900), *Our Northern Shrubs and How to Identify Them* (1903), *Our Garden Flowers* (1910), *Our Early Wild Flowers* (1916), *The Wayside Flowers of Summer* (1917), and *Our Northern Autumn* (1920). These volumes were well received at a time when America was rapidly urbanizing and public interest in conservation and the establishment of parks was growing. (In Ohio, legislation authorizing the appointment of county park boards was approved in 1911; the Cleveland Metropolitan Park District, now known as Cleveland Metroparks, was established in 1917.) At the same time, the increasing popularity of the automobile, the improvement of roads, and increased leisure time combined to stimulate interest in travel and sightseeing—and the need for nature guides.

Our Native Trees, Keeler's first book written for a national audience, was warmly received. The *New York Times* pronounced it "well-written and thoroughly interesting" and expressed special admiration for its logical organization and the author's reliance on respected authorities, including Charles S. Sargent of the Arnold Arboretum. The reviewer concluded: "The book . . . should add new interest to the coming summer for many to whom Nature is practically a sealed book, as well as heighten the pleasure of others to whom she has long been dear."[13] *Our Native Trees* quickly became a standard volume in libraries and proved so popular that Scribner's reprinted it more than a dozen times between 1901 and 1937.

The question naturally arises: where did Harriet Keeler conduct her fieldwork? From 1895 until about 1915, Keeler lived at 93 Olive (later East 59th) Street, just off Euclid Avenue, on Cleveland's East Side. There she shared the home of the newspaper editor John C. Keffer and his two daughters, Bertha and Mary.[14] (Bertha, a graduate of Vassar, also taught at Central High School; Mary, an art instructor at Lake Erie College in Painesville, would illustrate many of Keeler's books.) To observe the trees and plants about which she wrote, Keeler might easily have taken the streetcar to Wade or Rockefeller Parks (both established in the late nineteenth century) or to the Shaker Lakes in the upper Doan Brook Valley. Then, too, interurban rail lines brought most places in northern Ohio within easy reach during this period. There is no documentation of Keeler ever having owned an automobile; in a small self-profile written in 1898 for a collection of Oberlin class notes, Keeler alluded to her bicycle being "a somewhat 'skittish' but attractive steed."[15]

It is well, too, to recall that in Keeler's day Cuyahoga County outside of Cleveland was still largely rural. In 1910 the vast majority—88 percent—of Cuyahoga County's 637,425 people resided in Cleveland, and many fine old trees and woodlands were yet standing in the city's suburbs. Indeed, in her introduction to *The Wild Flowers of Early Spring,* Keeler defined the limits of her study area as "a territory which would easily be enclosed by a circumference drawn with a radius of ten miles, from the Court House [Public Square] as a center."[16] Thus, she did not have to go very far to gather her specimens.

Especially following her retirement, Keeler supplemented her local rambles with extended visits to other parts of the country. The December 1916 issue of the *Oberlin Alumni Magazine* reported that Keeler had spent the previous summer in the White Mountains of New Hampshire and elsewhere in New England, gathering material for *The Wayside Flowers of Summer*. The same magazine, in May 1920, reported that she had wintered at Buchanan, Virginia. And in the archives of the Cleveland Museum of Natural History lies the product of three winters Keeler spent in "tropical Florida": the unpublished manuscript of her last work, "The Changing Everglades."[17]

In the summer of 1920, Harriet Keeler moved with Mary Keffer into a rambling, clapboard-sided house at 195 South Professor Street in Oberlin. But her health already had begun to decline, and in November Keeler left Oberlin for the Clifton Springs (New York) Sanitarium. Learning of her confinement, Keeler's many friends kept flowers in her room. Before her death at age seventy-seven on February 12, 1921, she is said to have sent this message: "Tell my friends I died in the midst of flowers."[18] Funeral services were held in Cleveland, at the Amasa Stone Memorial Chapel on the campus of Western Reserve University, following which Harriet Keeler was buried in Oberlin's Westwood Cemetery beside her life-long friend Adelia Johnston.

On Friday, February 18, all Cleveland public schools suspended their activities for two minutes to remember Miss Keeler. The Bird Club of Central High School was moved to change its name to the Keeler Club and expand its activities to include "all nature work." Within a month of her death, a group of friends organized the Keeler Memorial Association and began a campaign to raise funds; cooperating in the project, the Cleveland Metropolitan Park Board set about acquiring what would become the Keeler Memorial Woods in the Brecksville Reservation.[19]

An obituary of Harriet Keeler in the *Oberlin Tribune* concluded, "She leaves a large circle of friends."[20] With this new edition of *Our Native Trees*, I trust that circle will grow larger and that this woman of quiet accomplishment will again become more widely known.

NOTES

1. William Ganson Rose, *Cleveland: The Making of a City* (Cleveland: World Publishing, 1950), 800.

2. The essential facts of Keeler's life come from two principal sources: the Harriet L. Keeler alumna file in the Oberlin College Archives (hereafter OCA), Oberlin, Ohio; and the Delaware County, New York, Genealogy and History Site, http://www.dcnyhistory.org. Her birth year is variously given as 1844 and 1846. I have used 1844, as given in South Kortright Presbyterian Church Baptismal Records, 1810–85, available on the Delaware County History Site.

3. *Catalogue of the Officers and Students of Oberlin College for the College Year 1869–70* (Cleveland, 1869), 9.

4. "Tribute of a Friend to the Memory of Harriet L. Keeler," *Cleveland Topics*, February 24, 1921, Harriet Keeler clipping file, History Department, Cleveland Public Library; *Class of '04—Central High School*, 11.

5. *Proceedings of the Board of Education of the City School District of the City of Cleveland, January 1, 1912, to December 23, 1912, Inclusive* (Cleveland: Board of Education, 1913), 33:5.

6. Harriet L. Keeler to Henry Churchill King, January 17, 1912, Henry Churchill King Correspondence, box 43, OCA.

7. "Tribute of a Friend."

8. Keeler received an honorary A.M. from Oberlin College in 1900 and an LL.D. from Western Reserve University in 1913. Keeler alumna file, OCA.

9. Virginia Clark Abbott, *The History of Woman Suffrage and the League of Women Voters in Cuyahoga County, 1911–1945* (privately printed, 1949), 15.

10. *The Question of Woman Suffrage as It Seems to Me* (Warren, Ohio, n.d.), 2, 6, 7. A copy of this pamphlet is located in the library of the Western Reserve Historical Society.

11. "In Tribute," undated news clipping, Keeler alumna file, OCA.

12. Harriet L. Keeler, *The Wild Flowers of Early Spring* (Cleveland, 1894), 55, 5.

13. *New York Times Saturday Review of Books and Art*, June 9, 1900, 378.

14. Cleveland city directories (various issues), History Department, Cleveland Public Library. With the adoption of a revised street-numbering system in 1905, 93 Olive Street became in 1953 East 59th Street. After serving as an editor of the *Cleveland Leader* and *Cleveland Herald*, John C. Keffer (1827–1906) became editor and publisher of the *East End Signal* (Cleveland). For a biographical sketch of the Keffer family, see Elroy McKendree Avery, *A History of Cleveland and Its Environs*, 3 vols. (Chicago: Lewis Publishing, 1918), 3:296–97.

15. "Class of 1870 in 1898 Oberlin," Keeler alumna file, OCA.

16. Keeler, *Wild Flowers,* iii.

17. Keeler alumna file, OCA; Archives, Cleveland Museum of Natural History.

18. "In Tribute," Keeler alumna file, OCA. In a letter to "Miss Wolcott," September 12, 1921, Mary Keffer reported the cause of death as "carcinoma of the cecum," or upper intestine. Keeler alumna file, OCA.

19. *Central High School Annual, Diamond Jubilee 1846–1921* (n.p.). A letter soliciting donations, signed by Mary E. Adams, chairman of the Keeler Memorial Committee, reads: "In furtherance of this living memorial, Miss Keeler's friends are planning to place a large boulder suitably inscribed, near the entrance of the woods, and to plant within them, specimens of all native trees and shrubs as yet not represented there." Mary E. Adams to President Henry King, Oberlin College, April 6, 1923, Henry Churchill King Correspondence, box 43, OCA. The monument and woods were formally dedicated on October 24, 1936. "Dedicate Memorial Woods in Honor of Harriet L. Keeler," *Cleveland Plain Dealer,* October 25, 1936, Harriet Keeler clipping file, History Department, Cleveland Public Library.

20. February 18, 1921, Keeler alumna file, OCA.

PREFACE

THE trees described in this volume are those indigenous to the region extending from the Atlantic Ocean to the Rocky Mountains and from Canada to the northern boundaries of the southern states ; together with a few well-known and naturalized foreign trees such as the Horse-chestnut, Lombardy Poplar, Ailanthus and Sycamore Maple.

It is hoped that this book will commend itself :

To amateur botanists who desire a more extended and accurate description of trees than is given by the botanical text-books in ordinary use.

To such of the general public as habitually live near fields and woods ; or whose love of rural life has led them to summer homes in hill country or along the sea-shore ; or whose daily walks lead them through our city parks and open commons.

To all those who feel that their enjoyment of out-door life would be distinctly increased were they able easily to determine the names of trees.

The author is glad to acknowledge her great indebtedness to the following books of reference ; Sargent's " The Silva of North America," Michaux's " North American Sylva," Loudon's " Arboretum et Fruticetum Britannicum," Emerson's " Report on the Trees and Shrubs of Massachusetts," Sach's " Physiology of Plants," Sach's " Text-Book of Botany," Le Maout and Decaisne's " General System of Botany," Britton and Brown's " Illustrated Flora of the United States and Canada," Dawson's " Geological History of Plants," Hough's " American Woods," Gray's " Manual of Botany," sixth edition, Vine's "Students' Text-Book of Botany," "The Check List of the Forest Trees of the United States," and the magazine *Garden and Forest.*

The extracts from the works of Lowell, Longfellow, Emerson, Whittier, Holmes, Thoreau, Burroughs, and Miss Thomas are used with the permission of and by special arrangement with the publishers Messrs. Houghton, Mifflin & Co., those from Wilson Flagg with the permission of the Educational Publishing Co., that from Bryant with the permission of the publishers, Messrs. D. Appleton & Co.

The quotations from the works of Professor G. Frederick Wright, Professor George Pierce, and Professor D. T. MacDougal are made by the kind consent of the authors. Especial acknowledgment is due to Professor Charles S. Sargent not only because in the preparation of this volume the Silva of North America has been the authority which has decided every case of doubt and because of his kind permission to quote from his writings, but also because of his kindly interest and his invaluable assistance in obtaining specimens for illustrations from the Arnold Arboretum. To Miss Anna J. Wright, Miss Charlotte Bushnell and Mr. Charles F. Pack especial thanks are due for valuable notes and suggestions ; also to the Director of the Missouri Botanical Garden for specimens kindly sent upon request.

The outline pictures are the work of Miss Mary Keffer of Cleveland, Ohio. The photographs for the illustrations were taken partly by Mr. Alfred Redher, of the Arnold Arboretum, partly by Mr. Charles H. Coit, of Glenville, Ohio, but principally by Decker, Edmonson & Co. of Cleveland, Ohio.

May 20, 1900.

GENERA AND SPECIES

DICOTYLEDONES

GENERA AND SPECIES

GENERA AND SPECIES

GYMNOSPERMÆ

ILLUSTRATIONS

ILLUSTRATIONS

ILLUSTRATIONS

GUIDE TO THE TREES

Leaves simple—1
Leaves compound—2
    1.—Leaves alternate—3
    1.—Leaves opposite—4
        3.—Margins entire—5
        3.—Margins slightly indented—**6**
        3.—Margins lobed— 7

5.—Oblong-ovate or obovate, large, thick...........*The Magnolias*
5.—Oblong, sub-evergreen at the south..........*Swamp Magnolia*
5.—Evergreen............................ { *Rhododendron* / *Mountain Laurel* }
5.—Obovate, 6′ to 10′ long...............................*Papaw*
5.—Oblong, thick, shining, 3′ to 5′ long...................*Tupelo*
5.—Oblong, tree occurring sparingly at the north........*Persimmon*
5.—Heart-shaped ....*Redbud*
5.—Leaves of three forms—oval, two-lobed, or three-lobed—
    frequently all three on one spray................*Sassafras*
5.—Thick, shining, willow-shaped................. { *Shingle Oak* / *Willow Oak* }
5.—Thick, shining, ovate, spines in the axils........*Osage Orange*
5.—Broadly oval or obovate, veins prominent, leaves
    usually in clusters at the ends of the branches. *Alternate-leaved*
                                   Dogwood
    6.—Obliquely heart-shaped.....................*The Lindens*
    6.—Obliquely oval.................................*The Elms*
    6.—Obliquely ovate..........................*The Hackberry*
    6.—Oval or ovate, doubly serrate .... { *The Birches* / *The Hornbeams* }
    6.—Repand with spiny teeth............................*Holly*
    6.—Coarsely-toothed, twigs bearing thorns.........*The Thorns*
    6.—Of quivering habit, petioles compressed......*The Poplars*

6.—Long, slender, finely serrate................ *The Willow*

6.—Coarsely crenately-toothed............ *The Chestnut Oaks*

6.—Obovate or oval—wavy-toothed............ *Witch Hazel*

6.—Serrate ....
$$\begin{cases} \textit{The Plums} \\ \textit{The Cherries} \\ \textit{Crab-Apple} \\ \textit{Sourwood} \\ \textit{June-berry} \\ \textit{The Silver-bells} \\ \textit{The Beeches} \end{cases}$$

7.—Lobes entire—8

7.—Lobes slightly indented—9

7.—Lobes coarsely toothed—10

8.—Apex truncate, three-lobed .... *Tulip-tree*

8.—Lobes and sinuses rounded...... *Oaks (White Oak Group)*

8.—Lobes rounded, lobes 2 or 3................... *Sassafras*

8.—Lobed or coarsely toothed, under surface covered with white down................... *White Poplar*

9.—Five-lobed, finely serrate........................ *Sweet Gum*

9.—Variously lobed, irregularly toothed........... *The Mulberries*

10.—Irregularly toothed, lobes bristle pointed.. *Oaks (Red Oak Group)*

10.—Leaf broad, lobes coarsely toothed.............. *Sycamore*

4.—Margins entire—11

4.—Margins serrate.......................... $\begin{cases} \textit{Sweet Viburnum} \\ \textit{Black Haw} \end{cases}$

4.—Margins lobed................................. *The Maples*

11.—Ovate, veins prominent............. *Flowering Dogwood*

11.—Heart-shaped, large .... *The Catalpas*

11.—Oval .... *Fringe Tree*

2.—Leaves pinnately compound—12

2.—Leaves bi-pinnately compound—13

2.—Leaves palmately compound .... $\begin{cases} \textit{The Buckeyes} \\ \textit{The Horse-chestnuts} \end{cases}$

12.—Alternate—14

12.—Opposite—15

14.—Margin of leaflets entire—16

14.—Margin of leaflets with two or three teeth at base.. *Ailanthus*

14.—Margin of leaflets serrate........
$$\begin{cases} \textit{The Sumachs} \\ \textit{The Mountain Ashes} \\ \textit{The Walnuts} \\ \textit{The Hickories} \end{cases}$$

16.—Leaflets oval, apex obtuse .... *The Locusts*

16.—Leaflets oblong apex acute. ....*Poison Sumach*

16.—Leaflets oval or ovate........................... *Cladastris*
16.—Leaflets ovate—three in number................. *Wafer Ash*
  15.—Margin of leaflets entire..................... *The Ashes*
  15.—Margin of leaflets serrate..................... *The Ashes*
  15.—Margin of leaflets coarsely toothed............ *Box Elder*
    13.—Margins of leaflets entire........ *Kentucky Coffee-tree*
    13.—Irregularly bi-pinnate, margins of leaflets
      entire, thorns on stems above the axils
      of the leaves .... *Honey Locust*
    13.—Margins of leaflets serrate, stems spiny. *Hercules Club*

Note.—It must be remembered that the typical leaves of a species are to be found upon mature trees, not upon young ones. The leaflets of a compound leaf can be distinguished from simple leaves by the absence of leaf-buds from the base of their stems. No guide has been prepared for the Conifers, as it is believed the illustrations will be sufficient.

SIGNS USED IN THIS BOOK

(´) Acute accent over a vowel marks the short sound.
(`) Grave accent over a vowel marks the long sound.
(°) The sign of degree is used for feet.
(´) When used with figures means inches.

DICOTYLEDONES

Flowering Spray of Swamp Magnolia, *Magnolia glauca*.
Leaves 4′ to 6′ long, 1½′ to 2½′ broad.   Flowers 2′ to 3′ across.

MAGNOLIÀCEÆ—MAGNOLIA FAMILY

SWAMP MAGNOLIA. SMALL MAGNOLIA. SWEET BAY

Magnòlia glaùca.

Magnolia was named by Linnæus in honor of Pierre Magnol, an eminent botanist who lived in the seventeenth century. *Glauca*, glaucous, refers to the under surface of the leaf.

A small tree, nearly evergreen, with slender trunk. In the Gulf States it reaches the height of seventy feet, with a trunk two or three feet in diameter, but at the north it is reduced to a shrub. Roots fleshy. Prefers swamps and wet soils. Ranges from Essex County, Massachusetts, to Long Island, from New Jersey to Florida, west in the Gulf region to Texas.

Bark.—Light brown, scaly ; on young trees light gray, smooth. Branchlets green at first, downy, later reddish brown ; bitter, aromatic.

Wood.—Light brown tinged with red, sapwood cream-white. Sparingly used in manufactures at the south. Sp. gr. 0.5035 ; weight of cu. ft., 31.38 lbs.

Winter Buds.—Terete, pointed, downy, formed of successive pairs of stipules, each pair enveloping the leaf just above. Flower-bud enclosed in a stipular, caducous bract.

Leaves.—Alternate, simple, feather-veined, subpersistent, four to six inches long, one and one-half to two and one-half inches broad, oblong or oval, rounded or pointed at base, entire, obtuse at apex ; midrib conspicuous. They come out of the bud conduplicate, pale green, covered with long silvery hairs ; when full grown are a soft leathery texture, bright green, smooth and shining above, pale, glaucous beneath, sometimes almost white. At the north they fall late in November, at the south the leaves remain with little change of color until pushed off by the new leaves in the spring. Petiole short, slender.

3

MAGNOLIA FAMILY

Flowers.—June. Perfect, solitary, terminal, cream-white, fragrant, two to three inches across ; enveloping bract thin, caducous.

Calyx.—Sepals three, obtuse, concave, shorter than the petals but resembling them, cream-white.

Corolla.—Petals nine to twelve, in rows of three, hypogynous, imbricated in bud, cream-white.

Stamens.—Indefinite, imbricated in rows upon the base of the long conical receptacle ; filaments short ; anthers adnate, two-celled, introrse ; connective fleshy, pointed.

Pistils.—Indefinite, packed together and covering the lengthened receptacle, cohering with each other and forming an oval mass. Ovaries fleshy, one-celled ; style short ; stigma long, yellow, turned back at the top ; ovules two.

Fruit.—Scarlet oval mass formed of the coalescent carpels, smooth, two inches long, containing many seeds. Seeds drupaceous, red, shining, aromatic. Suspended at maturity by a long thin cord of unrolled spiral vessels. September, October.

> Long they sat and talked together, . . .
> Of the marvellous valley hidden in the depths of Gloucester woods,
> Full of plants that love the summer, blooms of warmer latitudes,
> Where the Arctic birch is braided by the tropic's flowery vines,
> And the white magnolia blossoms star the twilight of the pines.
> —John G. Whittier.

A sheltered swamp near Cape Ann not far from the sea is thought to be the most northern habitation of this plant and until lately was supposed to be the only one in Massachusetts. It has recently been found at the distance of some miles in another swamp in the midst of deep woods in Essex.
—George B. Emerson.

Magnolia trees are among the finest productions of the North American forests. They are distinctively southern trees ; two species alone are indigenous to the northern states, and one of these may be looked upon rather as a survival, or a wanderer which has strayed across the border and forgotten to return, than as a resident to the manner born.

The Swamp Magnolia, or Sweet Bay, to the surprise of botanists is found growing naturally in a sheltered swamp on the peninsula of Cape Ann. That it can live there in so exposed a position without protection from man, proves that it can live elsewhere, in a climate equally severe, with such protection. As a matter of fact it is fairly hardy under cultivation throughout the north, but its leaves are not always evergreen nor will it remain in continuous bloom throughout the summer unless in a moist situation. It must have water in order to do its best.

The flowers appear in May, solitary, at the ends of the branches, cream-white, large as a rose and fragrant as a lily. Under favorable conditions they will continue to appear through the greater part of the summer, and the combination of these creamy blossoms surrounded by the dark shining leaves is beautiful indeed.

By midsummer the fruit has formed, a green oval mass, made up of many seed-vessels which have grown together. When ripe this becomes red and is about two inches long. The enclosed seeds turn a brilliant scarlet, and when released from their prison walls hang down for awhile on their slender white threads, and finally fall to the ground or are eaten by birds. In taste they are aromatic, pungent, and slightly bitter.

This charming little tree has a variety of common names, referring to its size or its habitat or its individual characteristics. Among these names is Beaver-wood, given because the fleshy roots were eagerly eaten by the beavers, who considered them such a dainty that they could be caught in traps baited with them. Michaux relates that the wood was used by the beavers in constructing their dams and houses in preference to any other.

The tree is easily propagated by layers which, however, root slowly ; but the preferred method is to graft it upon a root of the Cucumber-tree, *M. acuminata*, where it makes a stronger growth than upon its own roots. To obtain plants from the seeds they should be preserved in moist earth and sown very early in the spring in a moist situation.

Magnolia tripetala, the Umbrella-tree, frequently planted on northern lawns, is a southern species ranging from Pennsylvania to the Gulf. It may be easily recognized by its great leaves, twelve to eighteen inches long, and four to eight inches broad. These radiate from the ends of the branches in such a way as to suggest an open umbrella, whence its common name. Often it sprawls, a straggling bush. The huge, terminal, cream-white blossoms appear in May. They are from eight to ten inches across and exhale a disagreeable odor. The name *tripetala* refers to the three petaloid sepals.

The Magnolia shrubs found in northern gardens whose great white or pink flowers appear before the leaves are of Chinese or Japanese origin.

The science of Paleobotany is fragmentary as yet, but enough is already known to give us a wonderful outlook into the life history of our common plants. It is evident that immediately preceding the glacial period the polar regions were not covered with ice, but sustained a rich growth of vegetation, and plants flourished there which are now known only in warmer countries. The genus *Magnolia* to-day is sub-tropical. Its species are found only in southeastern North America, southern Mexico, and southern Asia. But the scientists tell us that once it flourished abundantly throughout America and Europe, and its fossil remains are found in the tertiary rocks of Greenland and elsewhere within the arctic circle.

Professor G. Frederick Wright, in " The Ice Age in North America," admirably presents the latest opinion in regard to the flight of the forests. He writes as follows : " The key applied by Professor Gray for the solution of this problem was suggested by the investigations of Heer and others, which had just brought out the fact that, during the Tertiary period, just before the beginning of the Ice Age, a temperate climate, corresponding to that of latitude 35° on the Atlantic coast, extended far up toward the North Pole, permitting Greenland and Spitzbergen to be covered with trees and plants similar in most respects to those found at the present time in Virginia and North Carolina. Here, indeed, in close proximity to the North Pole, were then residing in harmony and contentment, the ancestors of nearly all the plants and animals which are now found in the north temperate zone, and here they would have continued to stay but for the cold breath of the approaching Ice Age, which drove them from their homes, and compelled them to migrate to more hospitable latitudes.

Umbrella-tree, *Magnolia tripetala*.
Leaves 12′ to 18′ long, 4′ to 8′ broad.

" The picture of the flight and dispersal of these forests, and of their struggle to find and adjust themselves to other homes, is second in interest to that of no other migration. A single

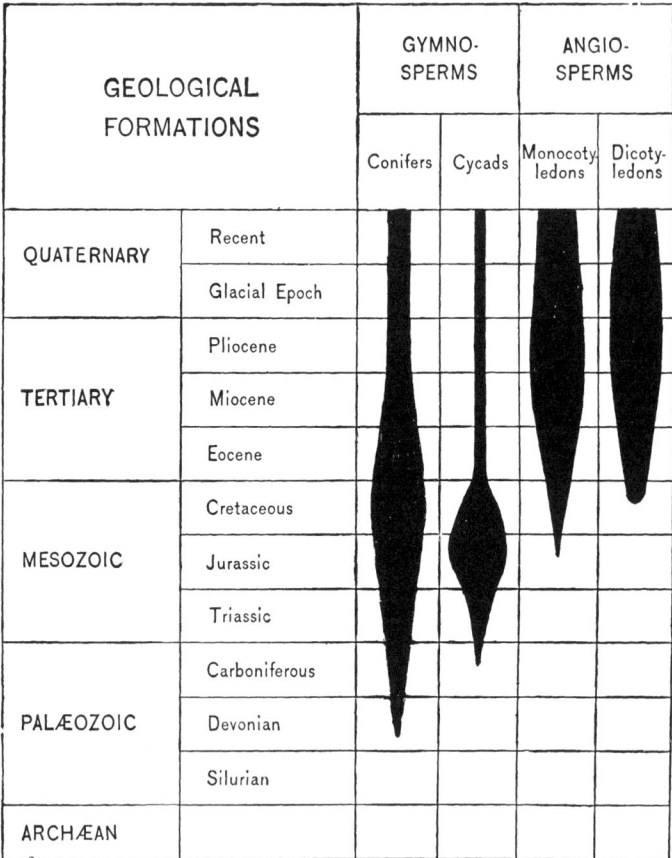

GEOLOGICAL FORMATIONS		GYMNO-SPERMS		ANGIO-SPERMS	
		Conifers	Cycads	Monocoty-ledons	Dicoty-ledons
QUATERNARY	Recent				
	Glacial Epoch				
TERTIARY	Pliocene				
	Miocene				
	Eocene				
MESOZOIC	Cretaceous				
	Jurassic				
	Triassic				
PALÆOZOIC	Carboniferous				
	Devonian				
	Silurian				
ARCHÆAN					

Chart Showing the Development of Vegetation during the Geological Ages.

tree is helpless before such a force as an advancing glacier, since a tree alone cannot migrate. But a forest of trees can. Trees can "take to the woods" when they can do nothing else, and so escape unfavorable conditions. There is a natural climatic belt to which the life of a forest is adjusted. In the present instance, as the favorable conditions near the poles were disturbed by the cooling influences of the glacier approaching from the north, the individual trees on that side of the forest belt gradually perished ; but at the same time that the favorable conditions of life were contracting on the north, they were expanding on the south, so that along the southern belt the trees could gradually advance into new territory, and so the whole forest belt move southward, following the conditions favorable to its existence. It is therefore easy to conceive how, with the slow advance of the glacial conditions from the north, the vegetation of Greenland and British America was transferred far down toward the torrid zone on both the Eastern and Western continent. Being thus transferred, the forest would be compelled to remain there until the retreat of the ice began again to modify the conditions so as to compel a corresponding retreat of plants toward their original northern habitat. Thus it is that these descendants of the pre-glacial plants of Greenland, arrested in their northward march, have remained the characteristic flora of the latitudes near the glacial boundary."

CUCUMBER-TREE. MOUNTAIN MAGNOLIA

Magnòlia acumináta.

Acuminata refers to the pointed apex of the leaves.

Of two forms ; in the forest it rises to the height of ninety feet with sturdy unbroken trunk for two-thirds its height ; when allowed sufficient space to develop, it becomes a cone with branches that sweep the ground. Prefers a moist, fertile soil, but will grow on rocky river-banks. Roots fleshy. Ranges from western New York to southern Illinois, south through central Kentucky and Tennessee to Alabama, and throughout Arkansas.

Bark.—Brown, regularly furrowed and scaly. Branchlets slender, red brown, downy, later becoming gray.

Wood.—Light yellow brown, sapwood almost white; light, soft, satiny, close-grained and durable. Sp. gr., 0.4690; weight of cu. ft., 29.23 lbs.

Winter Buds.—Terete, acute, downy. Terminal bud an inch long. Outer scales fall when spring growth begins, inner scales enlarge and become the stipules of the unfolding leaves. Flower-bud enclosed in a stipular, caducous bract.

Leaves.—Alternate or scattered, simple, feather-veined, seven to fourteen inches long, four to six broad, oblong, pointed or rounded at base, entire, slightly ruffled at margin, acute; midrib and primary veins prominent beneath. They come out of the bud conduplicate, green, covered with long silky hairs; when full grown are bright deep green, smooth above, paler and slightly downy beneath. In autumn they turn a bright yellow. Petioles an inch to an inch and a half long.

Flowers.—May, June. Perfect, solitary, terminal, bell-shaped, greenish yellow, three to four inches across.

Calyx.—Sepals three, greenish yellow, acute, an inch to an inch and a half long, soon reflexed.

Corolla.—Petals six, in two rows, greenish yellow, imbricate in bud, hypogynous, obovate, concave, acute, two to three inches long; inner row narrower than outer.

Stamens.—Indefinite, imbricated in many rows on the base of the receptacle; filaments short; anthers long, adnate, introrse, two-celled; connective pointed.

Pistils.—Indefinite, imbricated on the lengthened receptacles. Ovaries fleshy, one-celled; style short, recurved; ovules two.

Fruit.—A red cylindrical mass composed of coalescent carpels, smooth, two to three inches long, often curved, containing many scarlet drupaceous seeds, which when released hang down on slender white threads. September, October.

The struggle for life among the trees of the forest is quite as keen, the conflict as pitiless, and death to the weakest quite as certain, as in the higher ranks of life. The survival of the fittest is the law of the wildwood as well as of the creatures who live beneath its protecting cover. There is just so much space below, and just so much light above to be appropriated, and roots that can dig deepest and hold tightest, trunks that can rise the highest and then spread out their branches and bear their leaves into the air and sunlight have the best chance to survive. There is no time to loiter and grow fat, there is no time to indulge in the luxury of branches. Upward is the cry, and the race is given to the strong, not to

Cucumber-tree, *Magnolia acuminata.*
Leaves 7′ to 14′ long, 4′ to 6′ broad.

the weak. All trees that live in the forest learn this lesson, and this is the explanation of the well-known fact that in order to find out what the actual typical form of a tree really is, one must see it growing alone with ample space to develop after the law of its nature.

No tree shows the difference between free life and forest

Trunk of the Cucumber-tree.

life more clearly than the Cucumber, for it takes on two distinctly characteristic forms dependent upon its location. An individual which has attained its growth in the forest rises straight as a column to the height of thirty, forty, or fifty feet without a branch. When, however, a seedling starts in a clearing, or a sucker grows up from a decaying stump, the entire habit is changed ; the branches start low, become pendent, and by the time the tree is thirty feet high, the ends of the lower branches sweep the ground, making the contour a beautiful cone, a n d beneath the branches a perfect tent.

Flowering Branch of Cucumber-tree, *Magnolia acuminata.*

Such a tree having its branches tipped with pink fruit presents in September a unique and striking appearance.

The spray of the Cucumber, like that of all large-leaved trees, is coarse. The effect of the foliage, however, is singularly fine, for the leaves are of a clear bright g r e e n, arranged alternately along the branch and short petioled, so that they have little independent motion, and the branch sways as a whole when moved by the wind.

The flowers are not so beautiful nor so conspicuous as those of the other magnolias, for their greenish yellow color causes them virtually to be lost among the leaves.

The fruit is a cylinder-shaped bunch borne at the end of the branch, with a tendency as it matures to turn up. When

Cucumber-tree Fruit Discharging its Seed.

green this somewhat resembles a cucumber, whence the name of the tree. In September the little cucumber turns pink, finally the red berries within break through the skin of the covering, hang for a time on long white threads, and at length become food for birds. Within the red pulp is a shining black seed. Both fruit and bark are aromatic and somewhat bitter.

The Cucumber loves the mountain-side, the narrow valley, and the banks of streams, an atmosphere constantly moist, a soil deep and fertile. It is a magnificent tree for lawn planting, and thrives with but little attention. The only objection that can be urged against it is its tendency to drop its leaves more or less throughout the summer.

TULIP-TREE. YELLOW POPLAR

Liriodéndron tulipífera.

Liriodendron, from two Greek words meaning lily and tree.
Tulipifera, tulip-bearing.

One of the largest and most beautiful of our natives trees, known to reach the height of one hundred and ninety feet, with a trunk ten feet in diameter; its ordinary height, seventy to one hundred feet. Found sparingly in New England, abundant on the southern shore of Lake Erie and westward to Illinois. It extends south to Alabama and Georgia, and is rare west of the Mississippi River. Prefers deep, rich, and rather moist soil; is common, though not abundant, nor is it solitary. Roots fleshy. Growth fairly rapid. Typical form of head conical.

Bark.—Brown, furrowed; branchlets smooth, lustrous, reddish at first, later dark gray, finally brown. Aromatic and bitter.

Wood.—Light yellow to brown, sapwood creamy white; light, soft, brittle, close, straight-grained. Used for interior finish of houses, for siding, for panels of carriages, for coffin boxes, pattern timber, and wooden ware. On account of the growing scarcity of the better qualities of white pine, tulip wood is taking its place to some extent, particularly when very wide boards are required. Sp. gr., 0.4230; weight of cu. ft., 26.36 lbs.

Winter Buds.—Dark red, covered with a bloom, obtuse; scales becoming conspicuous stipules for the unfolding leaf, and persistent until the leaf is fully grown. Flower-bud enclosed in a two-valved, caducous bract.

Leaves.—Alternate, simple, feather-veined, five to six inches long, as many broad, four-lobed, heart-shaped or truncate or slightly

Tulip-tree, *Liriodendron tulipifera.*
Leaves 5′ to 6′ long.

wedge-shaped at base, entire, and the apex cut across at a shallow angle, making the upper part of the leaf look square ; midrib and primary veins prominent. They come out of the bud recurved by the bending down of the petiole near the middle bringing the apex of the folded leaf to the base of the bud, light green, when full grown are bright green, smooth and shining above, paler green beneath, with downy veins. In autumn they turn a clear, bright yellow. Petiole long, slender, angled.

Flowers.—May. Perfect, solitary, terminal, greenish yellow, borne on stout peduncles, an inch and a half to two inches long, cup-shaped, erect, conspicuous. The bud is enclosed in a sheath of two triangular bracts which fall as the blossom opens.

Calyx.—Sepals three, imbricate in bud, reflexed or spreading, somewhat veined, early deciduous.

Corolla.—Cup-shaped, petals six, two inches long, in two rows, imbricate, hypogynous, greenish yellow, marked toward the base with yellow. Somewhat fleshy in texture.

Stamens.—Indefinite, imbricate in many ranks on the base of the receptacle ; filaments thread-like, short ; anthers extrorse, long, two-celled, adnate ; cells opening longitudinally.

Pistils.—Indefinite, imbricate on the long slender receptacle. Ovary one-celled ; style acuminate, flattened ; stigma short, one-sided, recurved ; ovules two.

Fruit.—Narrow light brown cone, formed by many samara-like carpels which fall, leaving the axis persistent all winter. September, October.

Different species of trees move their leaves very differently. On the tulip-tree, the aspen and on all native poplars, the leaves are apparently Anglo-Saxon or Germanic, having an intense individualism. Each one moves to suit himself. Under the same wind one is trilling up and down, another is whirling, another slowly vibrating right and left, still others are quieting themselves to sleep. Sometimes other trees have single frisky leaves, but usually the oaks, maples, and beeches have community of interest. They are all active together or all alike still. —HENRY WARD BEECHER.

The Tulip-tree has impressed itself upon popular attention in many ways, and consequently has many common names. In the western states it is called a poplar largely because of the fluttering habit of its leaves, in which it resembles trees of that genus ; the color of its wood gives it the name White-wood ; the Indians so habitually made their dugout canoes of its trunk that the early settlers of the west called it Canoe-wood ; and the resemblance of its flowers to tulips named it the Tulip-tree.

The Tulip-tree in the forest reaches a size that may be

properly called magnificent, for it rises to the height of one hundred and ninety feet. The Tulip-tree, however, standing alone attains its finest development. The trunk rises like a Corinthian column, tall and slender, the branches come out symmetrically, and the whole contour of the tree, though somewhat formal, possesses a certain stately elegance.

Unfolding Leaves of Tulip-tree.

The leaves are of unusual shape and develop in a most peculiar and characteristic manner. The leaf-buds are composed of scales as is usual, and these scales grow with the growing shoot. In this respect the buds do not differ from those of many other trees, but what is peculiar is that each pair of scales develops so as to form an oval envelop which contains the young leaf and protects it against changing temperatures until it is strong enough to sustain them without injury. When it has reached that stage the bracts separate, the tiny leaf comes out carefully folded along the line of the midrib, opens as it matures, and until it becomes full grown the bracts do duty as stipules, becoming an inch or more in length before they fall. The leaf is unique in shape, its apex is cut off at the end in a way peculiarly its own, the petioles

Flower of Tulip-tree.

are long, angled, and so poised that the leaves flutter inde-
pendently, and their glossy surfaces so catch and toss the
light that the effect of the foliage as a whole is much brighter
than it otherwise would be.

The flowers are large, brilliant, and on detached trees numerous. Their color is greenish yellow with dashes of red
and orange, and their resemblance to a
tulip very marked. They do not droop
from the spray but sit erect.

The fruit is a cone two to three inches
long, made of a great number of thin narrow scales attached to a common axis.
These scales are each a carpel surrounded
by a thin membranous ring. Each cone
contains sixty or seventy of these scales,
of which only a few are productive. Loudon says that seeds from the highest
branches of old trees are most likely to
germinate. These fruit cones remain on
the tree in varied states of dilapidation
throughout the winter.

Fruit Cone of Tulip-
tree.

The Tulip is never abundant in the sense that oaks and
beeches and ashes are abundant, because it delights only in
deep, loamy, and extremely fertile soils, such as the bottom-
lands of rivers and borders of swamps. Its finest development is in the valleys of the rivers flowing into the Ohio. It
is recommended as a shade-tree, especially for the cities
where bituminous coal is burned.

The wood of the Tulip is known in the arts as the poplar
and the whitewood. Mechanics who use it have divided it
into the white and yellow poplar, judging from the color and
texture of the wood. There seem to be no botanic distinc-
tions sufficiently constant upon which to base a variety, and
the difference is believed to depend upon the character of
the soil.

The tree grows readily from seeds, which should be sown
in a fine soft mould, and in a cool and shady situation. If

sown in autumn they come up the succeeding spring, but if sown in spring they often remain a year in the ground. It is readily propagated by cuttings and easily transplanted.

The *Liriodendron* is now a genus of a single species. In the cretaceous age the genus was represented by several species, and was widely distributed over North America and Europe. Its remains are also found in the tertiary rocks. One species alone survived the glacial ice, and this is found only in eastern North America and western China—the well-known Tulip-tree of the western states.

ANNONÀCEÆ—CUSTARD-APPLE FAMILY

PAPAW

Asímina tríloba.

Asimina is formed from Asiminier, an early colonial name used by the French for this tree. Its meaning is in doubt. *Triloba* refers to the blossom.

A small tree, often a shrub. Its northern limit is the western part of New York, is abundant on the southern shore of Lake Erie. Occurs in eastern and central Pennsylvania, west as far as Michigan and Kansas and south to Florida and Texas. Rare east of the Alleghany Mountains, but in the low lands bordering the Mississippi River often forming dense thickets. Trunk straight, branches slender and spreading. Roots fleshy ; loves rich bottom lands and sometimes attains the height of thirty feet.

Bark.—Dark brown, blotched with gray spots, sometimes covered with small excrescences, divided by shallow fissures. Inner bark tough, fibrous. Branchlets light brown, tinged with red, marked by shallow grooves.

Wood.—Pale, greenish yellow, sapwood lighter ; light, soft, coarse - grained and spongy. Sp. gr., 0.3969 ; weight of cu. ft., 24.74 lbs.

Winter Buds.—Small, brown, acuminate, hairy.

Leaves.—Alternate, simple, feather-veined, obovate-lanceolate, ten to twelve inches long, four to five broad, wedge-shaped at base, entire, acute at apex ; midrib and primary veins prominent They come out of the bud conduplicate, green, covered with rusty tomentum beneath, hairy above ; when full grown are smooth, dark green above, paler beneath. In autumn they are a rusty yellow.

Petioles short, stout. Stipules wanting.

Flowers.—April, with the leaves. Perfect, solitary, axillary, rich red purple, two inches across, borne on stout, hairy peduncles. Ill smelling.

Papaw, *Asimina triloba.*
Leaves 10′ to 12′ long, 4′ to 5′ broad.

Calyx.—Sepals three, valvate in bud, ovate, acuminate, pale green, downy.

Corolla.—Petals six, in two rows, imbricate in the bud. Inner row acute, erect, nectariferous. Outer row broadly ovate, reflexed at maturity. Petals at first are green, then brown, and finally become dull purple and conspicuously veiny.

Stamens.—Indefinite, densely packed on the globular receptacle. Filaments short; anthers extrorse, two-celled, opening longitudinally.

Pistils.—Several, on the summit of the receptacle, projecting from the mass of stamens. Ovary one-celled; stigma sessile; ovules many.

Fruit.—Baccate, oblong, cylindrical, fleshy, from three to five inches long. Sometimes curved or irregular because of imperfect development of seeds. Edible. Seeds flat, oblong, rounded at ends, an inch long, half an inch broad, wrinkled. September, October. Cotyledons broad, five-lobed.

One of two things a forest tree must do, it must be able to reach the top and so enjoy the air and sunlight, or it must learn to grow in the shade. The Papaw has elected to grow in the shade. In its chosen home, which is the rich bottom lands of the Mississippi valley, it often forms a dense undergrowth in the forest; sometimes it succeeds in obtaining complete possession of a tract, and there it appears as a thicket of small slender trees, whose great leaves are borne so close together at the ends of the branches, and which cover each other so symmetrically, that the effect is to give a peculiar imbricated appearance to the tree.

Flower of Papaw.

The blossom is interesting rather than beautiful. It appears with the leaves, and at first is green as the leaves, but as the days go by it increases in size, darkens in color, and by way of greenish brown and brownish green it arrives finally at a rich, dark, vinous red. Part of the petals are honey laden, erect, gathered close about the stamens and pistils, and the others are open, spreading, finally reflexed. The flower appeals to the scent, the sight, and the taste, of the vagrant fly and the wandering bee.

The fruit is an unusual one for northern forests. The early settlers called the tree Papaw because of the resemblance of its fruit to the real papaw of the tropics ; it certainly suggests a banana. It is oblong in shape, nearly cylindrical, rounded, sometimes pointed at the ends, more or less curved and often irregular in outline ; the flesh is yellow and soft ; the seeds flat and wrinkled. Ripening in September and October, it is frequently found in the markets of western and southern cities, and although credited in the books as edible and wholesome, one must be either very young or very hungry really to enjoy its flavor.

Fruit of Papaw, 3′ to 5′ long.

The *Asimina* is the only genus of the great Custard-Apple family found outside of the tropics, and the Papaw is the most northern species of the genus.

TILIÀCEÆ—LINDEN FAMILY

LINDEN. BASSWOOD. LIME-TREE

Tìlia americàna.

Tilia is the ancient classical name retained by Linnæus. Basswood alludes to the use of the inner bark for mats and cordage.

A native of rich woods in the northern states and Canada, reaches its greatest size in the valley of the lower Ohio, becoming one hundred and thirty feet in height, but its usual height is about seventy feet. The trunk is erect, pillar-like, the branches spreading, often pendulous, forming a broad rounded head. Roots large, deep, and spreading. Juices mucilaginous.

Bark.—Light brown, furrowed, surface scaly. Branchlets terete, smooth, light gray, faintly tinged with red, finally dark brown or brownish gray, marked with dark wart-like excrescences. Inner bark very tough and fibrous.

Wood.—Pale brown, sometimes nearly white or faintly tinged with red; light, soft with fine close grain; clear of knots but does not split easily. It is sold generally under the name of basswood, but is sometimes confounded with tulip-wood and then called whitewood, and is largely used in the manufacture of wooden-ware, wagon boxes and furniture. Sp. gr., 0.4525; weight of cu. ft., 28.20 lbs.

Winter Buds.—Dark red, stout, ovate, acute, smooth.

Leaves.—Alternate, simple, feather - veined, obliquely heart-shaped, the side nearest the branch the largest, five to six inches long, three to four inches broad, unequally cordate at base, serrate, acuminate at apex; midrib and primary veins conspicuous. They come out of the bud conduplicate, pale green, downy; when full grown are dark green, smooth, shining above, paler beneath, with tufts of rusty brown hairs in the axils of the primary veins. In autumn they turn a clear pale yellow. Petioles long, slender. Stipules caducous.

Linden, *Tilia americana.*
Leaf 5′ to 6′ long, 3′ to 4′ broad. Fruit half-grown.

LINDEN FAMILY

Flowers.—June, July.   Perfect, regular, yellowish white, fragrant, nectariferous, downy, borne in cymous clusters, pendulous, with the flower-stalk attached for half its length to the vein of an oblong leaf-like bract as long as itself.   Flower buds densely coated with white tomentum ; bract pointed at base.

Calyx.—Sepals five, lanceolate, valvate in bud, hypogynous, downy within, hairy without.

Corolla.—Petals five, imbricate in bud, hypogynous, alternate with the sepals, spatulate-oblong, creamy white.

Stamens.—Numerous, polyadelphous ;   filaments thread - like, forked, collected into five clusters, with a petaloid scale placed opposite each petal ; anthers fixed by the middle, two-celled, extrorse.

Pistil.—Ovary superior, five-celled ; style erect ; stigma five-lobed ;   ovules two in each cell.

Fruit.—Nut-like, woody, tomentose, gray, ovoid or spherical, clustered on a long stem, about the size of peas.   October.

> Oh, who upon earth could ever cut down a Linden ?
> —WALTER SAVAGE LANDOR.

The Linden is to be recommended as an ornamental tree when a mass of foliage or a deep shade is desired ; no native tree surpasses it in this respect.   It is often planted on the windward side of an orchard as a protection to young and delicate trees.   Its sturdy trunk stands like a pillar and the branches divide and subdivide into numerous ramifications on which the spray is small and thick.   In summer this is profusely clothed with large leaves and the result is a dense head of abundant foliage.

In winter a branch of the Linden may be recognized by its deep red buds ; and the delicate leaves which burst from them in the spring are a vivid green.   Tennyson, who saw so many of the hidden beauties of nature, did not fail to observe this, as :

> A million emeralds break from the ruby-budded lime.

The characteristics of the linden family are the same whether the individual tree grows in America, Europe, or Asia.   The wood is light, soft, tough, and durable.   This makes it valuable in the manufacture of wooden-ware, cheap furniture, bodies of carriages ; it is also especially adapted for wood-carving. The inimitable carvings of fruit, flowers, and game by Grinling Gibbons, the famous English carver, were made entirely of linden ; no other wood could be relied upon to be so even of texture and so free from knots.

The leaves of all the lindens are one-sided, always heart-shaped, and the tiny fruit, looking like peas, always hangs attached to a curious, ribbon-like, greenish yellow bract, whose use seems to be to launch the ripened seed-clusters just a little beyond the parent tree. The flowers of the European and American lindens are similar, except that the American bears a petal-like scale among its stamens and the European varieties are destitute of these appendages.

The possible age of the Linden in America has not yet been determined. In Europe it is known to have reached the age of centuries. In the court-yard of the Imperial Castle at Nurembérg is a Linden which tradition says was planted by the Empress Cunigunde, the wife of Henry II. of Germany. This would make the tree nearly nine hundred years old. It looks ancient and infirm, but sends forth thrifty leaves on

Fruit of the Linden, *Tilia americana.*

its two or three remaining branches and is of course cared for tenderly. The famous Linden of Neustadt on the Kocher in Würtemberg was computed to be one thousand years old when it fell.

The Linden is loved of the bees. No matter how isolated the tree the bees are sure to find the fragrant nectar-laden blossoms. The excellence of the honey of far-famed Hybla

Trunk of the Linden, *Tilia americana.*

was due to the lime-trees that covered its sides and crowned
its summit. We read that in obedience to Amphion's music,

> The Linden broke her ranks and rent
> The woodbine wreaths that bound her,
> And down the middle, buzz ! she went
> With all her bees around her.

Homer, Horace, Virgil, and Pliny mention the lime-tree
and celebrate its virtues. As Ovid tells the old story of
Baucis and Philemon, she was changed into a linden and he
into an oak when the time came for them both to die.

Herodotus says : " The Scythian diviners take also the leaf
of the lime-tree, which, dividing into three parts, they twine
round their fingers ; they then unbind it and exercise the
art to which they pretend."

It is interesting to recall that Linnæus, the great botanist,
derived his name from a linden tree. His father belonged to
a race of peasants who had Christian names only, but having by his personal efforts raised himself to the position of
pastor of the village in which he lived, he followed an old
Swedish custom, common in such cases, of adopting a surname.

A very beautiful linden tree stood near his home, and being something of a botanist himself he chose Linné, the
Swedish for linden, and called himself Nils Linné or Nicholas
Linden. When his famous son Carl became professor of botany at the University of Upsala, his name Linné was lat-
inized into Linnæus, as we know it to-day. But when the king
of Spain conferred upon him a patent of nobility it was given
to him as Count von Linné or Count of the Linden tree.

Like the Magnolia the Linden belongs to an ancient and
northern race. *Tilia* appears in the tertiary formations of
Grinnell Land in 82° north latitude, and in Spitzbergen. Sa-
porta believed that he found there the common ancestor of
the lindens of Europe and America.

All the lindens may be propagated by cuttings and grafting as well as by seed. They grow rapidly in a rich soil, but
are subject to the attacks of many insect enemies.

LINDEN FAMILY

Tilia pubescens, the Downy Linden, or Small-leaved Basswood, is a southern species which makes its way as far north as Long Island. It is a small tree, nowhere common, but found at its best in South Carolina. The leaves are usually two or three inches long ; shoots and leaves and fruit covered with rusty down ; the fruit bract rounded at the base, the flowers smaller and the nutlets more spherical than those of *T. americana*.

Tilia heterophylla, the White Basswood, is a mountain species ranging along the Alleghanies from Pennsylvania to Tennessee. At its best it reaches the height of sixty feet. The leaves are large, very unilateral, six or seven inches long, four or five broad, light green or smooth above, silvery downy beneath. The fruit bract is pointed at the base, the flowers are larger than those of *T. americana*, the fruit is spherical and downy. The tree is not generally known, but Professor Sargent, in " The Silva of North America," says of it : " Few North American trees surpass it in beauty of foliage ; and the contrast made by the silvery whiteness of the under surface of its ample leaves as they flutter on their slender stems, with the dark green of the Hemlocks and Laurels on the banks of rapid mountain streams produces one of the most beautiful effects which can be seen in the splendid forests which clothe the valleys of the southern Appalachian Mountains."

Tilia europæa, the European linden, is distinguished from the American lindens by its smaller and more regularly heart-shaped leaves. Although the second midrib is present the leaf often becomes scarcely unilateral. The flowers are destitute of the petal-like scale among the stamens, which is so marked a characteristic of all American lindens, and the leaves are a little darker than those of our native species. Several varieties are in cultivation.

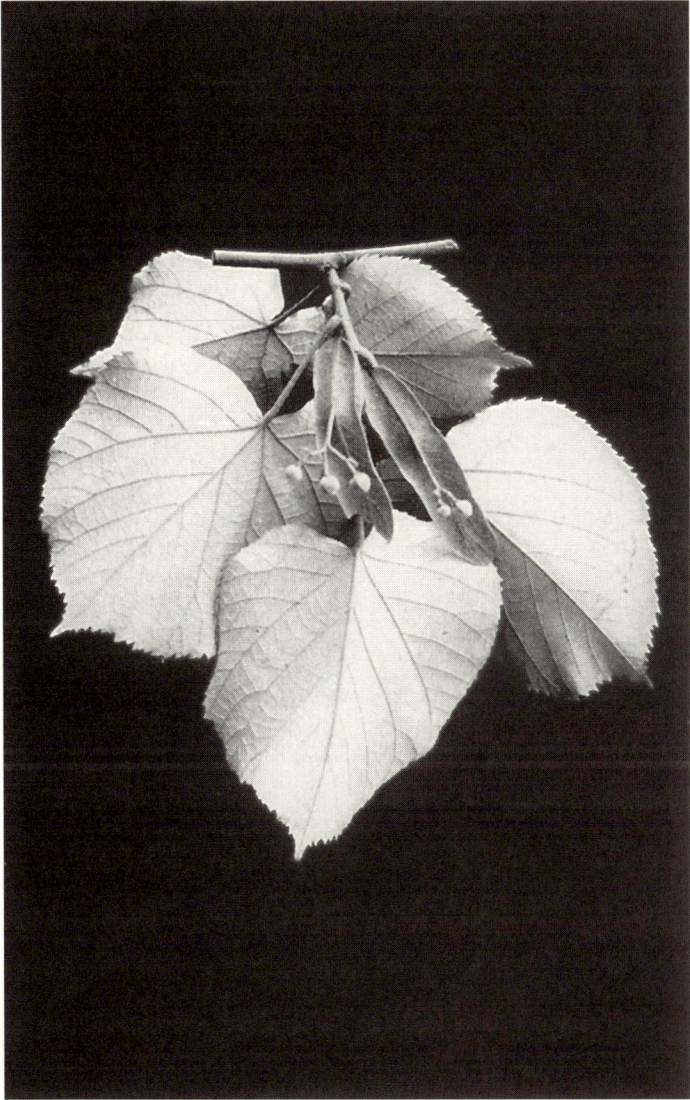

Underside of a Fruiting Spray of White Basswood, *Tilia heterophylla.*
Leaves 6′ to 7′ long, 4′ to 5′ broad.

RUTÀCEÆ—RUE FAMILY

WAFER ASH. HOP-TREE

Ptèlea trifoliàta.

Ptelea, of Greek derivation, is the classical name of the elm tree, which was transferred by Linnæus to this genus, because of the resemblance of its fruit to that of the elm. *Trifoliata* refers to the three-parted compound leaf.

A small tree, sometimes reaching the height of twenty feet, often a shrub of a few spreading stems. It makes part of the undergrowth of the forests of the Mississippi valley, and is found most frequently on rocky slopes. Has thick fleshy roots, flourishes in rich, rather moist soil. Its juices are acrid and bitter and the bark possesses tonic properties.

Bark.—Dark reddish brown, smooth. Branchlets dark reddish brown, shining, covered with small excrescences. Bitter and ill-scented.

Wood.—Yellow brown ; heavy, hard, close-grained, satiny. Sp. gr., 0.8319 ; weight of cu. ft., 51.84 lbs.

Winter Buds.—Small, depressed, round, pale, covered with silvery hairs.

Leaves.—Alternate, compound, three-parted, dotted with oil glands. Leaflets sessile, ovate or oblong, three to five inches long, by two to three broad, pointed at base, entire or serrate, gradually pointed at apex. Feather-veined, midrib and primary veins prominent. They come out of the bud conduplicate, very downy, when full grown are dark green, shining above, paler green beneath. In autumn they turn a rusty yellow. Petioles stout, two and a half to three inches long, base enlarged. Stipules wanting.

Flowers.—May, June. Polygamo-monœcious, greenish white. Fertile and sterile flowers produced together in terminal, spreading, compound cymes ; the sterile being usually fewer, and falling after the anther cells mature. Pedicels downy.

Calyx.—Four or five-parted, downy, imbricate in the bud.

Fruiting Spray of Wafer Ash, *Ptelea trifoliata.*
Leaflets 3′ to 5′ long, 2′ to 3′ broad.

Corolla.—Petals four or five, white, downy, spreading, hypogynous, imbricate in the bud.

Stamens.—Five, alternate with the petals, hypogynous, the pistillate flowers with rudimentary anthers ; filaments awl-shaped, more or less hairy; anthers ovate or cordate, two-celled, cells opening longitudinally.

Pistils.—Ovary superior, hairy, abortive in the staminate flowers, two to three-celled ; style short ; stigma two to three-lobed ; ovules two in each cell.

Fruit.—Samara, orbicular, surrounded by a broad, many-veined reticulate membranous ring, two-seeded. Ripens in October and hangs in clusters until midwinter.

The Wafer Ash is a tree in miniature ; no matter if only six feet high, it will assume the arborescent habit and produce a broad, rounded, spreading head, as much as to say " I can be a tree if I am small." Long ago, like the Papaw, it acknowledged itself vanquished in the struggle for light and elected to grow in the shade. Its northern limit is the north shore of Lake Ontario, its southern the mountains of Mexico, and in all that vast region it forms no inconsiderable part of the undergrowth of the forest.

Losing on many sides in the struggle for existence it has certainly gained on one, for it has developed one of the best adaptations for disseminating seed found in the vegetable world. A seed like that of the Magnolia has little chance of getting far from home, unless it can borrow wings by making itself attractive to birds, or legs by being sought by animals. And if all the seeds of a tree should germinate under the parent shade there would be little chance for any seedling. Hence a tree has made a long step forward in the struggle for existence when it is able to equip its seeds with wings of their own which will bear them by the aid of a favoring breeze away from the parent tree.

It is just this that the Wafer Ash has accomplished. Its fruit is a two-seeded samara, that is, a closed wooden box in which are safely stored two seeds. If that were all, although the cover might be tight and the seeds secure from harm, they could never get very far from home. At this point the life-saving appliance comes in. Upon each of the opposite sides of that oblong pointed seed-vessel there grows a thin membranous wing, which enlarges until at length each meets the other and uniting they form one continuous membrane. By this means the surface has been increased at least six fold, the weight scarcely one, and the result is a buoyant body that when freed from the anchoring stem will float upon the moving air.

One thing further bespeaks kind nature's care. The tree never lets her darlings go until early winter when winds are high, and consequently they are borne far afield. In the light of this life-story it is not surprising that the species is abundant in its native forests.

The Wafer Ash is monœcious, that is, both sterile and fertile flowers are borne in the same flower cluster. A blossom which has stamens but no pistils is called a staminate or sterile flower because it can produce no seeds. A blossom which has pistils but no stamens is called a pistillate or fertile flower because it can be fertilized by pollen from other flowers and can produce seeds. These two sorts of flowers may grow on plants produced from distinct roots ; then the plants are said to be diœcious, a word of Greek derivation which means, living in two households. Or the two kinds may occur on the same plant or in the same flower cluster ; then the flowers are said to be monœcious, that is, living in one household.

SIMAROUBÀCEÆ—AILANTHUS FAMILY

AILANTHUS

Ailánthus glandulòsa.

Ailanthus means, it is said, Tree of Heaven.

Native of China, introduced into Europe about the middle of the eighteenth century. A sturdy tree, fifty to seventy feet high, which produces an irregular and picturesque head. Grows rapidly ; roots run near the surface ; suckers freely ; short-lived. Tolerant of many soils.

Bark.—Brownish gray, with shallow fissures. Branchlets stout, clumsy, brownish green, then reddish brown, finally dark brown ; bitter.

Wood.—Pale yellow ; hard, fine-grained, satiny. Used in cabinet work.

Winter Buds.—Brown, small, flattened, obtuse.

Leaves.—Alternate, pinnately compound, one and one-half to three feet long. Leaflets twenty-one to forty-one, from three to five inches long. Ovate-lanceolate, base truncate or heart-shaped, unequal, entire, with one or two coarse blunt teeth at each side of the base, acuminate. Terminal leaflet ovate, toothed, sometimes lobed, sometimes wanting. Feather-veined, midrib and primary veins prominent. They come out of the bud a bronze reddish green, when full grown are dark green above, paler green beneath. In autumn they turn a bright clear yellow, or fall without change. Petioles, smooth, terete, swollen at base, often reddish. Stipules wanting.

Flowers.—June, when leaves are full grown. Polygamo-diœcious, small, yellowish green, borne in upright panicles. Staminate flowers ill scented. Pistillate much less so.

Calyx.—Five-lobed, lobes imbricate in bud.

Corolla.—Petals five, greenish, oblong, acute, hairy, hypogynous, imbricate in bud.

36

Ailanthus, *Ailanthus glandulosa.*

Leaves 1½° to 3° long.   Leaflets 3′ to 5′ long.

Stamens.—In pistillate flowers two or three, inserted on an hypogynous disk; in staminate flowers ten. Filaments thread-like, hairy ; anthers oblong, introrse, two-celled, opening longitudinally.

Pistil.—Ovary superior ; style erect ; stigma five-lobed.

Fruit.—One-celled, one-seeded samaras, borne in full clusters, reddish, or yellow green, slightly twisted. Abundant, beautiful. October.

When people learn for the first time that the Ailanthus which came to us from China is there known as the Tree of Heaven, they are inclined to lcok upon it as another instance of the general reversal of western standards in the Flowery Kingdom ; unless, indeed, what is meant is, that it "smells to Heaven." For the odor of the staminate blossoms in June is so far-reaching, overpowering, and sickening that the tree is very generally execrated, and all its merits fail to atone for its one demerit.

The tree has a history. Its seeds were sent to England from China in 1751 by Jesuit missionaries who believed it could be acclimated and the leaves used as the food of a certain kind of silkworm. The experiment failed, but the trees proved to be so stately, graceful, and ornamental that they were soon valued for their own sake. They were planted extensively in parks and pleasure grounds ; were soon introduced into the United States and planted first near Philadelphia, afterward in Rhode Island, and also abundantly at Flushing, New York. At first the new importations were very popular, but this popularity soon waned because of the disagreeable odor of the blossoms, and the trees were very generally cut down. Since that time, however, the tree has been slowly coming back into favor. The dealers are now able to supply their customers with pistillate plants, since the tree is diœcious, and as the unpleasant odor pertains almost wholly to the staminate flowers, that objection may be entirely eliminated. The pistillate tree in autumn loaded with its great clusters of reddish yellow samaras is both conspicuous and beautiful.

The Ailanthus really has great merits. Among these is

the one that it retains its foliage bright and fresh and green throughout the late summer when so many trees become ragged and unsightly. This characteristic especially recommends it as a city tree. Then, too, it grows rapidly, as do all trees whose roots run near the surface of the ground, and the growing stems of young plants will often make from four to six feet in a single summer. It sends forth suckers abundantly, its winged seeds are borne by the wind to many a crack and crevice, and its seedlings have a fashion of coming up close to the foundations of city houses and flourishing there. Apparently it delights in meagre and barren soils, for it often prospers where few other

Ailanthus; Cluster of Samaras.

trees will grow. No insect enemies have as yet appeared. if there are any in China they seem not to have migrated.

The branches look clumsy in winter because of the entire absence of small spray ; this is a characteristic of all trees with large compound leaves. It will be readily seen that this must be so, otherwise the twig could not sustain the accumulated weight of the leaves. All the twigs look upward, not one turns to the earth.

The beauty of the unfolding leaves is one of the sights of spring time. The tufts of young leaves with their bronze greens and madder browns and pale green tips glow in a brilliant atmosphere like the wings of a golden pheasant. Bring one into the house, put it into a proper vase, set it in the sunlight and you will have a bouquet with a color scheme rarely equalled.

The mature leaf is often three feet long, with many pairs of leaflets, and one leaflet at the end. Normally, there should be a terminal leaflet, actually, it is often wanting ; this, too, is common in pinnately compound leaves ; the Black Walnut and the Butternut are often evenly, instead of oddly, pinnate ; the terminal leaflet aborts.

The young Ailanthus and the Sumach may easily be mistaken for each other, but a moment's careful observation is sufficient to mark the difference between them. The growing shoot and last year's wood of the Sumach are velvety, while those of the Ailanthus are smooth. The margin of the Ailanthus leaflet is entire save a tooth or two at the base, the Sumach leaflet is serrate all along the margin. The under side of the Sumach leaflet is whitish, the Ailanthus pale green. But autumn tells the story unmistakably, the Ailanthus leaf either turns a lemon yellow throughout its length or drops unchanged, the Sumach glows in scarlet and orange ere it parts from the parent stem.

An Ailanthus and a Sumach Leaflet.

The Ailanthus is short-lived ; the trunk soon becomes hollow, and a tree two and a half or three feet in diameter, having every appearance of health and vigor, will go down before a strong wind only to disclose the fact that it was simply a shell.

AQUIFOLIÀCEÆ—HOLLY FAMILY

HOLLY

Ìlex opàca.

Theophrastus and other Greek authors named the Holly *Agria ;* that is, wild or of the fields ; and the Romans formed from this the word, *Agrifolium ;* and called it also *Aquifolium* from *acutum*, sharp, and *folium*, a leaf. C. Bauhin and Loureiro first named it *Ilex* on account of the resemblance of its leaves to those of the *Quercus Ilex*, the true Ilex of Virgil. Linnæus adopted the name *Ilex* for the genus, and preserved the name of *Aquifolium* for the most anciently known species. The name Holly is probably a corruption of the word holy, as Turner in his " Herbal " calls it Holy, and Holy Tree, probably from its being used to commemorate the holy time of Christmas, not only in houses but in churches. The German name Christdorn, the Danish name Christorn, and the Swedish name Christtorn, seem to justify this conjecture.   —LOUDON.

Opaca, opaque, refers to the color of the leaves of the American species, which is a duller green than that of the European.

An evergreen tree, from thirty to fifty feet in height, found sparing‧ly in New England and New York, where it is always small. Abundant on the southern coast and in the Gulf States, reaches its greatest size on the bottom lands of southern Arkansas and eastern Texas. The branches are short and slender and the head pyramidal. Roots thick and fleshy. Will grow in both dry and swampy soil, but grows slowly. Juices watery, and contain a bitter principle which possesses tonic properties.

Bark.—Light gray, roughened by excrescences. Branchlets stout, green at first and covered with rusty down, later smooth and brown.

Wood.—Brown, sapwood paler brown; light, tough, close-grained, susceptible of a brilliant polish, and is used for whip-handles, engraving blocks, and cabinet work. Sp. gr., 0.5818; weight of cu. ft., 36.26 lbs.

Winter Buds.—Brown, short, obtuse or acute.

Leaves.—Alternate, evergreen, simple, feather-veined, elliptical or oblong, two to four inches long, wedge-shaped at base, wavy toothed margin with a few spiny teeth, acute at apex; midrib prominent and depressed, primary veins conspicuous. Thick, leathery, yellow green, shining above, often pale yellow beneath. They remain on the branches for three years, finally falling in the spring when pushed off by growing buds. Petioles short, stout, grooved, thickened at base. Stipules minute.

Flowers.—May, June. Diœcious, greenish white, small, both sterile and fertile borne in short pedunculate cymes from the axils of young leaves or scattered along the base of young branches. Sterile clusters three to nine-flowered; fertile clusters one to three-flowered. Peduncles and pedicels hairy with minute bracts at base.

Calyx.—Small, four-lobed, imbricate in the bud, acute, margins ciliate, persistent.

Corolla.—Petals white, four, somewhat united at base, obtuse, spreading, hypogynous, imbricate in bud.

Stamens.—Four, inserted on the base of corolla, alternate with its lobes; filaments awl-shaped, exserted in the sterile, much shorter in the fertile flower; anthers attached at the back, oblong, introrse, two-celled, cells opening longitudinally.

Pistils.—Ovary superior, four-celled, rudimentary in staminate flowers; style wanting; stigma sessile, four-lobed; ovules one or two in each cell.

Fruit.—Drupaceous, spherical or ovoid, crowned with the remnants of the stigma, one-fourth of an inch across, red, rarely yellow, persistent all winter. Nutlets few, ribbed and veined, nearly triangular.

> On Christmas eve the bells were rung;
> On Christmas eve the mass was sung;
> That only night in all the year,
> Saw the stoled priest the chalice rear.
> The damsel donned her kirtle sheen;
> The hall was dressed with holly green;
> Forth to the wood did merry-men go
> To gather in the mistletoe.
>
> *Marmion.*—SIR WALTER SCOTT.

> The mistletoe hung in the castle hall,
> The holly branch shone on the old oak wall;
> The baron's retainers were blithe and gay
> A keeping a Christmas holiday.
>
> —THOMAS H. BAYLEY.

Fruiting Spray of Holly, *Ilex opaca.*

Leaves 2′ to 2½′ long.

HOLLY FAMILY

The custom of employing holly and other plants for decorative purposes at Christmas, is one of considerable antiquity, and has been regarded as a survival of the usages of the Roman Saturnalia, or of an old Teutonic practice of hanging the interior of dwellings with evergreens as a refuge for sylvan spirits from the inclemency of the weather. —*Encyc. Britannica.*

In English poetry and English stories the Holly is inseparably connected with the merry-making and greetings which gather around the Christmas tide. The custom is also ours, and a few days before Christmas the shops are filled with holly and mistletoe for the annual decoration of homes and churches.

The severity of our climate forbids the European Holly, with its deep green, glossy foliage and coral berries, to live here except upon a most precarious footing. But our American Holly makes an excellent second in the class where the European is first, for it very closely resembles the foreign species. The leaves are similar in outline and toothed and bristled very much in the same way, but they are a paler green, and although the surface is polished and shining it does not in brilliancy quite equal its European cousin.

The American Holly is a handsome tree and worthy of far more attention from landscape gardeners than it gets. Possibly the objection to it is its slowness of growth. The tree is low, the branches almost horizontal, and the gray bark in old trees becomes the willing host of great numbers of gray and white and bluish lichens which make the tree look venerable before its time. Its pretty white flowers appear in clusters either in the axils of the leaves or scattered along the young shoots. The berries are scarlet, contain four stony seeds and remain on the tree into the winter. The flesh of the berries is so thin and aromatic that the birds do not seem to care for it.

The Holly is usually propagated by seeds, or young plants are taken from the woods. As the seeds do not germinate until the second year, transplanting the wild young trees is the best way of obtaining them. This should be done in the spring before growth begins.

Ilex monticola, the Mountain Holly, is another species that becomes a tree, but is not very generally known. It is found in the Catskill Mountains and extends southward along the Alleghanies as far as Alabama. The leaves do not at all suggest the popular idea of a holly, as they are deciduous, light green, ovate or oblong, wedge-shaped or rounded at base, serrate, acute at apex, and utterly destitute of spines or bristles. They vary from two to six inches in length. The white flowers appear in June when the leaves are more than half grown. The fruit is spherical, nearly half an inch in diameter and bright scarlet. It is a tree of remarkably slow growth ; a specimen

Mountain Holly, *Ilex monticola.*
Leaves 2′ to 6′ long.

in the American Museum of Natural History, New York, is five inches in diameter and shows one hundred and seven layers of annual growth, of which seventy-nine are sapwood.

The genus *Ilex* is widely distributed over the world. It has no representative west of the Rocky Mountains, nor any in Australia. But South America is rich in them, the West Indies alone have ten species, eastern North America has fourteen, India twenty-four, China and Japan over thirty. Europe, strange to say, has only one, but that one has been developed into innumerable varieties. One hundred and seventy-five species have already been noted, and undoubtedly there are others not yet described.

The fossil remains which are now known give confirmation of the fact that plants are ever changing. The species of to-day are rarely the species of a former age. The rocks tell us that in the early tertiary period several forms of *Ilex* existed in the arctic regions.

Ilex spinescens, a fossil form, is believed to be the remote common ancestor of the American and European Christmas Hollies.

CELASTRÀCEÆ—STAFF-TREE FAMILY

BURNING BUSH. WAAHOO. SPINDLE-TREE

Euónymus atropurpùreus. Evónymus atropurpùreus.

Euonymus, derived from two Greek words, signifies good repute.
Atropurpureus, dark purple, refers to the flower.

Widely distributed. Usually a shrub six to ten feet high, becoming a tree only in southern Arkansas and Indian Territory. Loves the borders of woods ; prefers moist soil. Root fibrous.

Bark.—Ashen gray, furrowed, scaly. Branchlets slender, dark, purplish brown ; later become brownish gray. Bitter, drastic.

Wood.—White, tinged with orange ; heavy, hard, close-grained. Sp. gr., 0.6592 ; weight of cu. ft., 41.08 lbs.

Winter Buds.—Purple with glaucous bloom, small, acute.

Leaves.—Opposite, entire, feather-veined, elliptical or ovate, two to four inches long, one to two broad, pointed at base, finely serrate, acute ; midvein and primary veins conspicuous. In autumn they turn pale yellow. Petioles short, stout. Stipules minute, caducous.

Flowers.—May, June. Perfect, dark purple, half an inch across, borne in dichotomous, axillary, few-flowered cymes. Peduncles slender.

Calyx.—Four-lobed, lobes spreading, imbricate in bud. Disk thick, fleshy, filling the tube of the calyx, four-lobed, adherent to the ovary.

Corolla.—Petals four, inserted on calyx under margin of disk, dark purple, obovate, imbricate in bud ; margins often erose.

Stamens.—Four, alternate with the petals, inserted on the disk ; filaments very short ; anthers in pairs, two-celled ; cells opening longitudinally.

Pistil.—Ovary superior, surrounded by and adherent to the disk, four-celled ; style short ; stigma four-lobed ; ovules one or two in each cell.

46

Fruiting Spray of Burning Bush, *Euonymous atropurpureus*.
Leaves 2′ to 4′ long, 1′ to 2′ broad.

Fruit.—Fleshy capsules, borne on long drooping peduncles deeply four-lobed, angled, smooth, purple, loculicidally three to five-valved, opening to discharge the seeds which are inclosed in a scarlet aril. Ripen in October and hang upon the branch until midwinter. Cotyledons broad and coriaceous.

Burning Bush is a satisfactory name for this shrub, which retains its flame-colored fruit long after the leaves have fallen and until the winter storms beat it to the ground. Each separate seed-vessel develops a bright purple cover and opening discloses a seed clothed in scarlet. When these are borne in considerable numbers the bush is a conspicuous object upon the lawn or in the forest.

The Indians called the plant Waahoo, and used the wood in the manufacture of arrows. Spindle-tree is a name brought over seas and looks backward to a time when spinning and weaving were done at home. The wood of the European species of *Euonymus* being tough, close-grained and also reasonably easy to work, became the favorite wood for the making of spindles—whence the name.

Euonymus is the old Greek name and signifies, of good repute. Now, as a matter of fact, this particular individual is a plant of bad repute, for the leaves, bark, and fruit are acrid and poisonous. One can comprehend its name only upon the theory of opposites, the principle upon which the Greeks acted when they named the Furies, the Eumenides, the well-wishers.

The Burning Bush is not native to New England; it is a shrub in the middle and western states, and does not attain the dignity of treehood until it appears in the bottom lands of Arkansas and adjoining regions. It is interesting to note that those trees which are distinctively native to our mid-continental valley, reach their greatest development in the southwest. On the banks of the Arkansas the Tulip-tree reaches its one hundred and ninety feet, and there our little Burning Bush, a shrub in northern fields and lawns, becomes a tree twenty-five feet high with spreading branches.

RHAMNÀCEÆ—BUCKTHORN FAMILY

INDIAN CHERRY

Rhámnus caroliniàna.

Found along the borders of streams in rich bottom lands. Its northern limit is Long Island, New York, where it is a shrub ; it becomes a tree only in southern Arkansas and adjoining regions.

Bark.—Ashen gray, slightly furrowed, often marked with dark blotches. Branchlets terete, reddish brown ; later gray, shining. Bitter, acrid.

Wood.—Light brown, sapwood almost white ; light, hard, close-grained. Sp. gr., 0.5462 ; weight of cu. ft., 34.04 lbs.

Winter Buds.—Small, acute.

Leaves.—Alternate, simple, feather-veined, elliptical or oblong, two to five inches long, one to two inches broad, wedge-shaped or rounded at base, serrate or crenulate, acute or acuminate ; midrib and primary veins yellow and conspicuous. They come out of the bud conduplicate and densely coated with russet tomentum, when full grown are dark yellow green, smooth above, paler and somewhat hairy beneath. Petioles long, slender, downy. Stipules minute, caducous.

Flowers.—May, June, when leaves are half grown ; perfect or polygamo-diœcious, green, axillary, borne in few-flowered downy umbels.

Calyx —Campanulate, five-lobed, lobes triangular, valvate in bud. Disk lining the calyx tube.

Corolla.—Petals five, inserted on the disk, alternate with the calyx-lobes, minute, ovate, notched at apex, involute around the stamens in bud.

Stamens.—Five, opposite the petals, inserted on the disk ; filaments short ; anthers in pairs, introrse, two-celled, cells opening longitudinally ; rudimentary in pistillate flower.

Pistil.—Ovary superior, free, ovoid, two to four-celled ; rudimentary in staminate flower ; style long ; stigma three-lobed ; ovules one in each cell.

Fruit.—Drupaceous, globose, black, one-third of an inch in diameter, resting on the base of the calyx ; flesh thin, sweet ; nutlets two to four.

HIPPOCASTANÀCEÆ—HORSE-CHESTNUT FAMILY

OHIO BUCKEYE. FETID BUCKEYE

Æsculus glàbra.

Æsculus is derived from *esca*, nourishment. *Glabra*, smooth.

A tree varying in height from thirty to seventy feet, native only in the valley of the Mississippi. Prefers the river bottoms ; nowhere abundant, but widely distributed. Roots thick and fleshy. Reaches its greatest development in the valley of the Tennessee and in northern Alabama.

Bark.—Dark gray, densely furrowed, broken into plates. Branchlets orange brown and downy, later reddish brown and smooth, marked with many lenticular spots, finally dark brown. Fetid, medicinal.

Wood.—White, sapwood pale brown ; light, soft, close-grained. Used especially in the manufacture of wooden limbs. Sp. gr., 0.4542; weight of cu. ft., 28.31 lbs.

Winter Buds.—Pale brown, two-thirds of an inch long, acute, outer scales with glaucous bloom. Inner scales enlarge when spring growth begins, become an inch and a half to two inches long, greenish yellow tipped with red and remain until leaves are nearly half grown.

Leaves.—Opposite, digitately compound. Leaflets five, rarely seven, oval, oblong, or ovate, gradually contracted at the base, serrate, acuminate, feather-veined ; midrib and primary veins prominent. They come out of the bud a shining brownish green, downy; when full grown are yellow green above, paler beneath. In autumn they turn a rusty yellow. Petiole long, grooved, swollen at base, sometimes chaffy at the point where the leaflets diverge.

Flowers.—April, May, June. Terminal, polygamo-monœcious, yellow green, unilateral ; borne in terminal panicles five to six inches long, two to three in breadth, more or less downy ; pedicels four to six-flowered.

Flowering Spray of Ohio Buckeye, *Æsculus glabra*.
Leaflets 3′ to 6′ long.

Calyx.—Tubular, gibbous, five-lobed ; lobes unequal, imbricate in bud ; disk annular, hypogynous.

Corolla.—Petals four, pale yellow, hairy, clawed, imbricate in bud. Lateral pair oblong, superior pair oblong-spatulate, marked with red stripes.

Stamens.—Seven, inserted on the disk, exserted ; filaments long, curved, downy ; anthers dark yellow, elliptical, introrse, two-celled ; cells opening longitudinally.

Pistil.—Ovary superior, one to three-celled, downy, echinate ; style long, slender ; stigma pointed ; ovules two in each cell.

Fruit.—Coriaceous capsule, three-celled and loculicidally three-valved, the cells by abortion one-seeded. Irregularly ovate, pale brown, one to two inches long, very prickly when young, smoothish at maturity. Seeds roundish, smooth, shining, chestnut-brown with large round pale scar or hilum. October. Cotyledons thick and fleshy, remaining underground in germination.

One naturally expects to find the Buckeye in Ohio. It is called the Buckeye State, its inhabitants are called Buckeyes, and yet, strange to say, the Buckeye is not widely nor very generally known to Ohioans. The reason for this is to be sought in the character of the tree, for trees vary in social habits ; some are gregarious and live in communities, others prefer solitude. A moment's reflection will show that this is true. A maple grove is of frequent occurrence, an oak forest is common enough, the beech alone often covers vast areas of woodland, but one never hears of an elm forest ; an elm grove may be found, but even that is unusual. the elm occurs singly as do the willows and the sycamores. The Buckeye, also, is a solitary tree ; though widely distributed it is nowhere abundant and is becoming less so from a belief—well grounded it is said—on the part of farmers that its nuts are poisonous to their cattle, sheep, and horses. Consequently the trees have been very generally cut down and are now comparatively rare.

Two questions naturally arise. Why was the fetid Horse-chestnut called the Buckeye, and how did it happen that this tree gave the soubriquet to the State of Ohio ? The local and picturesque name is undoubtedly a tribute of the imagination of the early settlers. We are all familiar with the nut of the Horse-chestnut ; that of the Buckeye is similar. When the shell cracks and exposes to view the rich brown nut with the pale brown scar, the resemblance to the half-opened eye of a deer is not fancied but real. From this resemblance came the name Buckeye.

Buckeye, *Æsculus glabra*. Fruit 1′ to 2′ long.

How did it happen that Ohio was called the Buckeye State ? No direct evidence in the matter is forthcoming, but circumstantial evidence is not wanting. The younger Michaux, travelling in this country in 1810, reports in his " Sylva of North America " that he found the *Æsculus glabra* principally in Ohio, and that it was especially abundant on the banks of the Ohio River between Marietta and Pittsburg. For this reason he named the new tree Ohio Buckeye and as the Ohio Buckeye it has since been known, though its distribution is far wider than Michaux supposed. It was no doubt an easy transition from Ohio Buckeye, to Ohio the Buckeye State, but who accomplished the deed seems not to be known.

There is a great deal of confusion in the minds of many persons with regard to the Buckeye and the Horse-chestnut. Both belong to the one genus, but they are not the same tree. The Horse-chestnut is European, the Buckeye native. The Horse-chestnut is seven-fingered, the Buckeye five-fingered. The Horse-chestnut is the sturdier tree, the leaves are larger, rougher, the flowers much more profuse and more beautiful than those of the Buckeye. It is a fact well known that European plants—herbs or trees—if they flourish in America at all are very likely to produce sturdier plants than the native representatives of the same genus. We all know that our worst and most troublesome weeds are not native but introduced. The Norway maple is a sturdier tree than our native maples, the white willow is stronger than any of our willows, the white and Lombardy poplars flourish

53

where our natives would die, and the Horse-chestnut is stronger than the Buckeye. There is a certain delicacy of fibre inseparable from all American native life. Perhaps some day the biologist will read the riddle.

The Sweet Buckeye, *Æsculus octándra*, is a beautiful tree of the Alleghany Mountains, ranging from Pennsylvania to Alabama and westward to the Indian Territory. It reaches its greatest size in Tennessee and North Carolina. Its leaflets are five to seven, dark yellow green and smooth, except the midrib and veins which are sometimes downy. The flowers are borne in panicles five to seven inches long, are yellow, varying from pale to dark. The nuts are large, one and a half to two inches broad, the capsule smooth. A variety of this tree, *Æ. octandra hybrida*, characterized by its red or purple flowers, has long been a favorite in gardens, where it often makes a handsome head of pendulous branches. The name Sweet Buckeye means simply that the bark is less fetid than that of others of the genus.

HORSE-CHESTNUT

Æsculus hippocástanum.

Hippocastanum from *hippos*, a horse, and *castanea* a chestnut.

Cultivated. Introduced into Europe in the seventeenth century. Favorite tree for parks, lawns, and roadsides. Roots fleshy; prefers a strong, rich soil; reaches the height of one hundred feet.

Bark.—Dark brown, roughened with small excrescences, or divided by shallow fissures. Branchlets reddish brown, shining, at length dark brown. Abounds in tannic acid, fetid.

Wood.—White, light, soft, close-grained, not durable.

Winter Buds.—Terminal, large, an inch to an inch and a half long, covered with resinous gum, brown, axillary buds smaller. Scales in pairs, closely imbricated, within are leaves completely formed and packed in white tomentum. Scales enlarge when spring growth begins, the inner become yellow green tipped with red. One and a half to two inches long before they fall.

Leaves.—Opposite, digitately compound. Leaflets seven, obovate, five to seven inches long, wedge-shaped at base, serrate, acute or

Sweet Buckeye, *Æsculus octandra*.
Leaflets 4′ to 7′ long.

acuminate, feather-veined ; midrib and primary veins prominent. They come out of the bud conduplicate, woolly, brownish green, drooping ; when full grown are dark green, thick, rough above, paler green beneath. In autumn they turn a rusty yellow. Petioles long, grooved, swollen at the base, sometimes chaffy at the point the leaflets diverge.

Flowers.—May, June. Terminal, polygamo-monœcious, white, unilateral, borne in upright thyrsoid panicles ; pedicles jointed, four to six-flowered.

Calyx.—Campanulate, gibbous, five-lobed, lobes unequal, imbricate in bud ; disk hypogynous, annular, lobed.

Corolla.—Petals five, imbricate in bud, alternate with calyx lobes, more or less unequal, with claws, nearly hypogynous, spreading, white, spotted with yellow and red.

Stamens.—Seven, inserted within the hypogynous disk ; filaments thread-like, exserted, curved ; anthers introrse, two-celled ; cells opening longitudinally.

Pistils.—Ovary superior, three-celled ; style thread-like ; stigma pointed ; ovules two.

Fruit.—A coriaceous capsule, globular, rough, prickly, three or two or one-celled by suppression, loculicidally three-valved. Seeds or nuts solitary in each cell, brown, shining, with a large round pale scar, or hilum. October. Embryo fills the seed; cotyledons very thick and fleshy, remaining underground in germination.

The Horse-chestnut in the earlier weeks of May is a sight for gods and men. —PHILIP GILBERT HAMERTON.

No knowledge of technical terms is necessary to enable one to pull apart one of the great horse-chestnut buds, to notice the water-proof varnish on the outside, the scale armor just within, the soft downy padding which protects the minute leaves and the tip of the stem from sudden changes of temperature, to see that leaves or flower cluster are already formed in miniature ready to burst their covering when the favorable time shall come.—GEORGE D. PIERCE.

Our well-known Horse-chestnut is a native of Greece and began to be cultivated throughout Europe in the seventeenth century. Standing alone and allowed to attain its natural shape it becomes a stately tree. The trunk is erect, and the branches come out with such regularity that it develops a superb cone-like head. The branches almost invariably take the compound curve, upward from the trunk, downward as the branch lengthens, and upward at the tip.

The spray is clumsy, and in winter each twig is finished by a large terminal bud an inch or more long, which bears

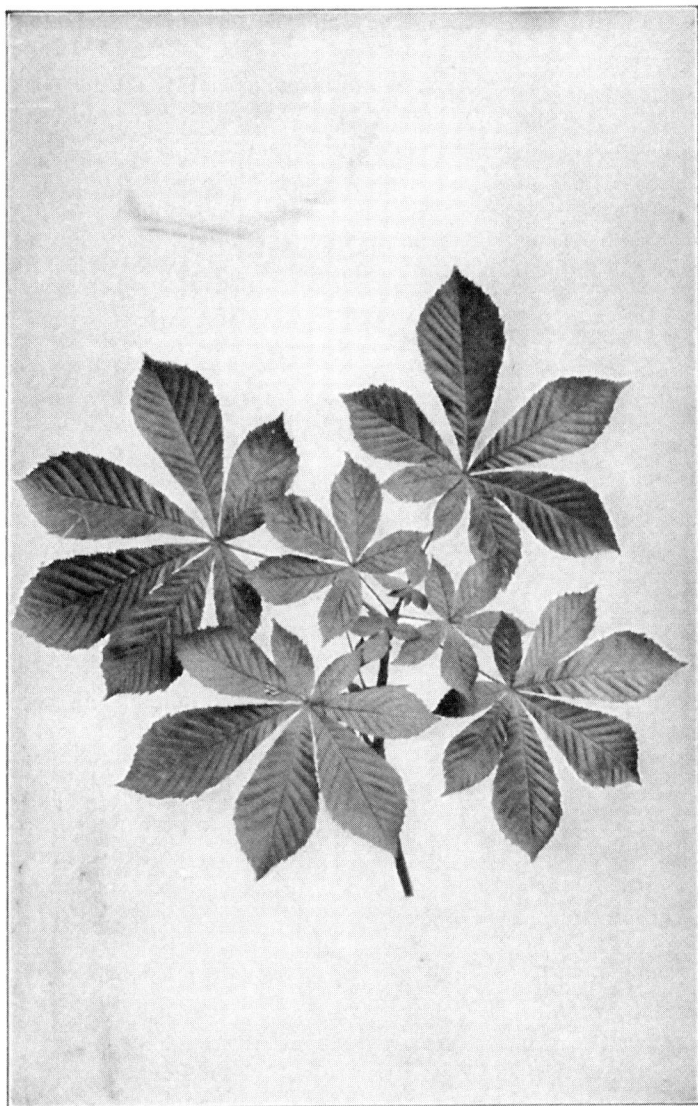

Spray of Horse-chestnut, *Æsculus hippocastanum.*
Leaflets 5′ to 7′ long.

within its scales the leaves and flowers of the coming year.

These buds are gummy and resinous all the time, but when February comes and spring is in the air, they feel its influence afar and glisten and glitter in the sunlight. When the warm days really come the resinous coats drop off and the leaves—tiny, downy, green babies, done up in woolly blankets—come out with infancy written on every line of their drooping surfaces.

> The gray hoss-chestnut's leetle hands unfold
> Softer'n a baby's be at three days old.

Not until they are full grown are they able to hold them-selves horizontal. The growth of the leaves and shoots is extremely rapid.

The flowers of the Horse-chestnut are superb, and a fine tree in full bloom is a magnificent sight. The flower clusters are what the botanists call a thyrsus. When a single flower stands upon its own stem it is said to be solitary. When this stem becomes a central axis and bears smaller stems along its length the result is a raceme. When these sec-ondary stems themselves branch, the raceme becomes a panicle, and when this panicle stiffens and holds itself erect it becomes technically a thyrsus. A well-known example is the flower cluster of the common lilac.

It is always a surprise that there should be so few nuts produced from such an abundance of bloom, for in spite of all this floral display each cluster produces but two or three fruit balls, and some of them not any. The reason is that very few of these flowers are fertile, the most of them have stamens only, with an aborted pistil which cannot produce fruit. The fertile blossoms are at the base of the cluster.

The round, prickly, fruit balls split open when autumn comes and show themselves to be lined with a strong white covering; they are partitioned in the middle and contain two nuts, which look in color, markings, and polish for all the world like a bit of well-rubbed mahogany.

This nut shares with the potato, in the minds of many people, the occult power of being able to cure rheumatism by being carried on the person of the sufferer.

The tree is subject to a serious disease, now common and widely spread throughout the northern United States, which is due to a fungus. This appears upon the leaf in early summer in the form of a yellow discoloration with a reddish margin. Later, the patches become quite brown, giving the leaves the appearance of having been scorched by fire, sometimes extending from the midrib to the margin of the leaflets. In time they shrivel and fall, leaving the tree almost leafless in midsummer. The liability to this disease is a serious objection to the tree.

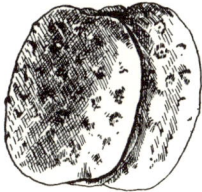

Horse-chestnut, *Æsculus hippocastanum.* Fruit 1½′ to 2′ long.

The name Horse-chestnut, which is only a literal translation of the specific Latin name *hippocastanum*, has been accounted for in many ways. The obvious fact that the scar of the leaf-stem really looks like the imprint of a horse's hoof seems the most reasonable explanation of the name : many plants have been named for less.

The finest plantation of Horse-chestnuts in the world is that of Bushey Park near Hampton Court, the ancient palace of Cardinal Wolsey. Five rows of trees stand on each side of the avenue, and when these trees are in bloom the daily papers announce the fact and all London goes out to see the sight.

The Red Horse-chestnut, *Æsculus rubicunda*, common in our gardens, is a tree of unknown origin. Professor Sargent inclines to the belief that it is a hybrid between the common Horse-chestnut, *Æs. hippocastanum* and *Æs. pavia* of the southern states. It resembles the former in its leaves and the latter in its flowers.

ACERÀCEÆ—MAPLE FAMILY

STRIPED MAPLE. MOOSEWOOD

Àcer pennsylvànicum.

A small tree, thirty or forty feet high, with short trunk, slender upright branches ; often much smaller and scrubby. Loves the shade and forms much of the undergrowth of the forests of New England and lower Canada. Roots fibrous.

Bark.—Reddish brown, marked longitudinally with broad pale stripes, and roughened with numerous, horizontal, oblong excrescences. The branchlets are pale greenish yellow; later, reddish brown and finally striped like the trunk.

Winter Buds.—Red. The terminal bud when it contains an inflorescence is half an inch long. Axillary buds much shorter. Scales enlarge when spring growth begins ; the inner scales become an inch and a half to two inches long, changing to yellow or rose before they fall.

Wood.— Pale brown, sapwood still paler ; light, soft, close-grained. Sp. gr., 0.5299; weight of cu. ft., 33.02 lbs.

Leaves.—Opposite, simple, five to six inches long, palmately three-nerved, rounded or cordate at the base, doubly serrate, three-lobed at the apex, the short lobes contracted into tapering serrate points. They come out of the bud thin, pale rose color, and downy ; when full grown are smooth, except some russet hairs at the axils of the nerves, bright green above, paler beneath. In autumn they turn a clear bright yellow. Petiole long, grooved, with enlarged base.

Flowers.—May, when leaves are nearly grown, polygamo-monœcious, yellow. Borne in slender, drooping, long-stemmed racemes ; staminate and pistillate flowers usually in different racemes. Pedicels thread-like.

Calyx.—Five-parted, lobes linear or obovate. Disk annular.

Corolla.—Petals five, inserted on the base of the disk, obovate, as long as the sepals, bright yellow, imbricate in bud.

Striped Maple, *Acer pennsylvanicum*.
Leaves 5′ to 6′ long.

Stamens.—Seven or eight in the staminate flowers, rudimentary in the pistillate. Hypogynous; filaments short; anthers introrse, two-celled; cells opening longitudinally.

Pistil.—Rudimentary in staminate flowers. In pistillate flowers, ovary superior, purplish brown, downy, two-celled, compressed contrary to the dissepiment, wing-margined; style short; stigmas two, recurved and spreading; ovules two in each cell, one of which aborts.

Fruit.—Two samaras united forming a maple key. Borne in long drooping racemes, smooth, with thin spreading wings three-fourths to an inch long; on one side of each nutlet is a small cavity. Seeds dark reddish brown. September. Cotyledons thin, irregularly plicate.

This maple is a mountain tree. It has no special economic value, but its beauty is its sufficient "excuse for being." The delicate and exquisite coloring of opening foliage is too often lost upon the heedless observer, unless something appears so striking that it cannot be ignored. But in the springtime this dryad of a tree, slender, delicate, clothed in a misty rosy sheen of buds and opening leaves, compels every passer-by to admire its beauty. Later its yellow flowers hang in long, graceful, drooping racemes and are succeeded by large showy keys with pale green, divergent wings. Its leaves are the largest of all our maples.

The New England name Moosewood refers to the fact that the bark and branchlets are the favorite food of the moose.

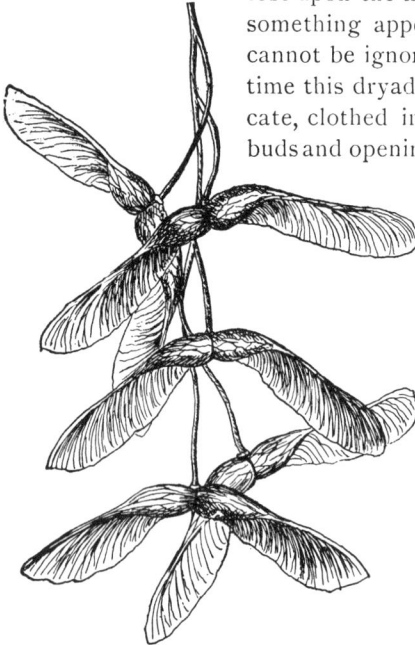

Keys of Striped Maple, *Acer pennsylvanicum.*

Emerson says that in their "winter beats" this tree is always found completely stripped. Evidently the moose

Fruiting Spray of Mountain Maple, *Acer spicatum*.
Leaves 4′ to 5′ long.   Fruit half grown.

knows a good thing when he finds it, for the young and tender shoots are filled with saccharine juice, which he fully appreciates.

It is now well known by botanists that the headquarters of the maples is not in America, but in Asia. North America has but nine species, China and Japan have over thirty. It is estimated that fully one-third of the deciduous forests of Japan is composed of different species of maples. Professor Sargent records that among these maples is one barely distinguishable from our *Acer pennsylvanicum.*

MOUNTAIN MAPLE

Àcer spicàtum.

A bushy tree sometimes thirty feet high, more often a shrub. Flourishes in the shade and forms much of the undergrowth of the forests. Ranges from lower St. Lawrence River to northern Minnesota and region of the Saskatchewan River; south through the northern states and along the Appalachian Mountains to Georgia. Roots fibrous.

Bark.—Reddish brown, slightly furrowed. Branchlets terete, at first gray and downy, then reddish, later, gray again and at last brown.

Wood.—Pale reddish brown, sapwood paler ; light, soft, close-grained. Sp. gr., 0.5330 ; weight of cu. ft., 33.22 lbs.

Winter Buds.—Terminal flower bud an eighth of an inch long, tomentose ; leaf buds smaller, acute, red ; scales enlarge when spring growth begins ; the inner scales lengthen until they are an inch or more long, become pale and papery before they fall.

Leaves.—Opposite, simple, palmately-lobed, sometimes slightly five-lobed ; conspicuously three-nerved with prominent veinlets. Four to five inches long. cordate or truncate at base, serrate ; lobes acute or acuminate. They come out of the bud pale green, very woolly on the under surface ; when full grown are smooth above and covered with whitish down beneath. In autumn they turn scarlet and orange. Petioles long, slender, with enlarged base, scarlet in midsummer.

Flowers.—June, after the leaves are full grown. Polygamo-monœcious, greenish yellow ; small, borne in upright, slightly compound, long, hairy, terminal racemes, five to six inches long ; the sterile at the end of the raceme and the fertile at the base. Pedicels thread-like.

Calyx.—Five-lobed, lobes obovate, downy, much shorter than the petals ; disk annular.

Corolla.—Petals five, linear-spatulate, greenish yellow, imbricate in bud.

Stamens.—Seven to eight, inserted on the disk, filaments thread-like, exserted in the sterile and abortive in the fertile flowers ; anthers oblong, attached at base, introrse, two-celled ; cells opening longitudinally.

Pistil.—Ovary superior, tomentose, two-lobed, two-celled, compressed contrary to the dissepiment, wing-margined ; style columnar ; stigma two-lobed. Ovules two in each cell, one of which aborts. In sterile flowers the pistil becomes a tuft of white hairs.

Fruit.—Two samaras united, forming a maple key ; bright red in July, brown in autumn ; smooth, borne in a pendulous raceme. Wings more or less divergent. Seeds dark brown. September. Cotyledons thick and fleshy.

The Mountain Maple is another example of a tree that has accepted its home in the shade of other trees. It grows on moist rocky hillsides and ranges across the continent westward to the Rocky Mountains, northward to the valley of the St. Lawrence River, and southward to Georgia. At the north it is a shrub, often seen growing by the side of a mountain road. It is our one maple that bears an upright raceme of flowers, but when the flowers have given place to fruit the raceme droops.

The fruits of all the maples are very similar. An acorn is no more the characteristic fruit of the oaks than the maple key is of the maples. This is a double samara, composed of two carpels, separable from a small persistent axis ; these carpels are compressed laterally, and each is produced into a reticulated wing. These wings are thick on the lower margin, but very thin and papery on the upper. The keys do not fly as they would were they better balanced, but they

Keys of Mountain Maple,
Acer spicatum.

ιaunch the seeds some distance from the parent tree and so perform their part in the economy of nature.

SUGAR MAPLE. ROCK MAPLE.

Àcer bárbatum. Àcer sacchárum.

Widely distributed and abundant throughout eastern North America in rich uplands and intervale. Grows rapidly with a large fibrous root which at first is near the surface but finally penetrates deep. In the forest often reaches the height of one hundred and twenty feet. Produces most of the maple sugar of commerce. A variety, the Black Maple, *A. saccharum nigrum*, is recognized.

Bark.—On young trees and large limbs light gray, smooth and slightly furrowed ; on old trees dark, with deep longitudinal furrows, shaggy. Branchlets green, later yellowish brown, shining, marked with pale lenticels, finally pale brown.

Wood.—Light brown, tinged with red ; heavy, hard, strong, tough and close-grained, capable of a fine polish. Much used in interior furnishing of buildings, manufacture of furniture, handles of tools ; has a high fuel value. Curled and bird's-eye are accidental varieties. Sp. gr., 0.6912 ; weight of c. ft., 43.08 lbs.

Winter Buds.—Purplish, quarter of an inch long, acute. Scales enlarge when spring growth begins ; the inner scales become an inch and a half long, downy and bright yellow before they fall.

Leaves.—Opposite, simple, three to five inches long and of greater breadth. Of five diverging lobes which are separated by rounded sinuses. The two lower are smaller and shorter than the others, each lobe tapers to a slender point and each contains a primary vein. Base, heart-shaped by broad or narrow sinus, or truncate, or wedge-shaped. Margin sparingly toothed. They come out of the bud tawny, coated with tomentum, when full grown are bright or dark green on upper surface, pale green on lower. In autumn they turn crimson, scarlet, orange and clear yellow. Petioles long, slender, often reddish.

Flowers.—May. Polygamo-monœcious or diœcious. Greenish yellow, appearing with the leaves in umbel-like corymbs from terminal leafy buds and lateral leafless ones. Sterile and fertile flowers are in separate clusters on the same or on different trees, fertile flowers terminal and sterile usually lateral. Pedicels hairy, thread-like, one and a half to three inches long.

Calyx.—Campanulate, five-lobed, lobes imbricate in bud, hairy. *Corolla.*—Wanting.

Sugar Maple, *Acer saccharum*.
Leaves 3′ to 5′ long.

Stamens.—Seven to eight inserted on the disk, hairy ; filaments long in the sterile flowers, short in the fertile ones. Anthers introrse, two-celled ; cells opening longitudinally.

Pistil.—Ovary superior, hairy, two-celled, compressed contrary to the dissepiments, wing-margined ; style of two long, exserted, stigmatic lobes, united at base only ; ovules two in each cell, one of which aborts.

Fruit.—Two samaras united forming a maple key. Borne in clusters on long pendulous footstalks. Wings vary from one-half to one inch long, brown, thin, divergent. One capsule of the key is usually empty. Seeds reddish brown. September. Cotyledons thick, leaf-like.

South America possesses the Milk Tree, India the Bread Tree, but it is reserved as a sort of climatic paradox for our temperate north to furnish the very top of luxury in the shape of the Sugar Tree. A man who could persuade these three staple producers to grow on his plantation could henceforth live independent of the milkman, the baker, and the grocer. It would be easy work to gather the yield of the two tropical trees, but the sweet of the maple would still have to be gained by the sweat of the brow. Besides its delicious sweetness, there is a rich, almost oleaginous quality in maple syrup which suggests what the maple nut would have been if Nature had said, " Consider the ways of the hickory, beech, and chestnut, how thrifty and hospitable ! Their bounty keeps my birds and my four-footed groundlings all winter through. Do thou ripen a kernel of thine own more toothsome than theirs." What Nature did say was briefly and practically, " Invest in sugar." More cold, more sweet, seems to be the law governing the saccharine supply, as though there were warmth and food in the sugar principle, and as though it were excited by keen weather to greater activity in order to meet the needs of the tree. The sap of all wood in early spring is perceptibly sweet. If the discharge of sap from other trees were as free as from the maple it might be profitable to tap them also, as the butternut, for example. It is plain that Nature drops a little sugar in the milk on which she rears her nursery. All young ones love sweets, even to the baby leaves on the old trees. —EDITH THOMAS.

Unquestionably, the Sugar Maple ranks among the finest of American forest trees. It is both useful and beautiful. When young its full leafy head is often a pure oval. In the forest it frequently rises seventy feet without a branch, and spreads its leaves to the sunlight one hundred and twenty feet above its base. When growing in the open it sometimes develops into a great cylindrical column, sometimes its head becomes a broad dome. The foliage is always dense. Erect in youth and maturity, in old age its trunk is often gnarled and disfigured.

The Sugar Maple makes up a great part of the native forest of New England and the middle states. In the race of life it has scored two points ; it has learned to labor and to wait. It can grow as tall as any of its forest companions and it also knows how to prosper while young, in the shade. Consequently, there is always a young maple in training ready to take the place of any dead or dying tree. This characteristic alone has enabled it to take precedence of other trees.

The leaves come out of the buds tawny and drooping, nor are they able to hold themselves out firm until they have attained nearly full size. The flowers appear with the leaves, are greenish yellow and borne in clusters on thread-like hairy pedicels, two and a half inches long. The fruit or maple key ripens in early autumn, and although it appears to be fully developed, one rarely finds perfect seed in each of the two divisions.

Key of Sugar Maple, *Acer saccharum.*

This is the tree which produces the maple sugar of commerce. The testimony of early travellers shows that the Indians, like the moose and the woodpecker, knew all about the sweetness of the maple sap, but it is doubtful if they were able to make maple sugar before the coming of the Europeans ; however, the making of maple sugar was an established industry among them during the last half of the seventeenth century. Sugar-making begins with the upward flow of the crude sap in February or March and continues until the buds begin to swell; when this occurs the sap will not run freely and thoroughly changes in character. Trees twenty or thirty years old are considered the most productive, though there are instances of trees which have yielded sugar **every year for a century and are still vigorous and fruitful.**

MAPLE FAMILY

Much of the splendor of our radiant forests in early autumn is due to the brilliant coloring of the Sugar Maple. It glows in red which deepens into crimson, it flames in yellow that darkens into orange. These wonderful leaves will show colors as pure as any on the finest porcelain ; a dark green leaf will show a single spot of crimson, a dark red bears a single lobe of rose pink. The next will have a patchwork of yellow and purple and scarlet, like a palette set for a sunset picture. Sometimes a single branch will turn bright scarlet while all the rest of the tree remains green. Individual trees vary in time and manner of change, and to some degree these peculiarities are fixed ; for example, certain trees always turn yellow, others always turn red, while there are others that vary with changing conditions.

There seems to be a very general popular impression that the colors of the leaves in autumn are dependent upon the frosts. Careful observation does not sustain this view. It is true that the brilliancy of the autumnal coloring varies ; but the changes are now referred rather to the character of the preceding summer than to the frosts of autumn. If the summer has been rainy, keeping the leaves full of sap and the cuticle thin and distended, the autumn tints are brilliant ; but if the summer has been dry the tints are dull.

Two great problems are connected with the fall of the leaves of deciduous trees. One, why do they take on such gorgeous colors ; and the other, how is it they fall leaving no open wounds behind ? What are the morphological and physiological changes which produce these results ? The following is perhaps as clear a statement of the present opinion of biologists as can be given in popular form :

The casting of the leaf is not a sudden and quick response to any single change in environmental conditions, but is brought about with a complex interplay of processes begun days or perhaps weeks before any external changes are to be seen. The leaf is rich in two classes of substances, one of which is of no further benefit to it, and another which it has constructed at great expense of energy, and which is in a form of the highest possible usefulness to the plant. To this class belong the compounds in the protoplasm, the green color bodies, and whatever surplus food may not have been previously conveyed away. The

Trunk of Sugar Maple, *Acer saccharum*.

substances which the plant must needs discard are in the form of nearly insoluable crystals, and by remaining in position in the leaf drop with it to the ground.

The plastic substances within the leaf which would be a loss to the plant if thrown away undergo quite a different series of changes. These substances are in the extremest parts of the leaf, and to pass into the plant body must penetrate many hundreds of membranes of diffusion into the long conducting cells around the ribs or nerves, and then down into the twigs or stems. The successful retreat of this great mass of valuable matter is not a simple problem. These substances contain nitrogen as a part of their compounds, and as a consequence are very readily broken down when exposed to the sunlight. In the living normal leaf the green color forms a most effective shield from the action of the sun, but when the retreat is begun, one of the first steps results in the disintegration of the chlorophyll. This would allow the fierce rays of the September sun to strike directly through the broad expanse of the leaf, destroying all within were not other means provided for protection. In the first place, when the chlorophyll breaks down, among the resulting substances formed is cyanophyll which absorbs the sun's rays in the same general manner as the chlorophyll. In addition the outer layer of cells of the leaf contains other pigments, some of which have been masked by the chlorophyll and others which are formed as decomposition products, so that the leaf exhibits outwardly a gorgeous panoply of colors in reds, yellows, and bronzes that make up the autumnal display.

At a time previous to the beginning of the withdrawal of the contents of the leaf or the formation of the autumnal colors, preparations have been steadily in progress for cutting away the leaf when the proper time should arrive. At some point near the base of the leaf-stalk the formation of a layer of special tissue had begun between the woody cylinder in the centre and the thin epidermis. When the time for the casting of the leaf arrives, this special tissue grows rapidly, pushing apart or cutting the cells which have held the leaf rigidly in position in such manner that finally the leaf stalk at this point consists of the brittle cylinder of wood surrounded by the loosely adherent cells of this newly formed layer of separation. The merest touch or breath of air will split the layer of separation, break the wood, and allow the leaf to fall to the ground.

—D. T. MacDougal.

The great leaf fall of the northern states comes some time between the fifteenth and twenty-fifth of October. As has been explained the leaves have virtually parted company with the tree some time before ; they have been falling since the first, and the ground is strewn with them, but as you look at the trees they show no perceptible diminution of foliage. But about the third week of October something happens—it may be a wind or rain storm, a heavy frost, or two or three days of excessively hot weather—and then the leaves come pouring down in showers, and though the oaks remain comparatively untouched, although the willows are green and the apple trees like summer; the sword has fallen and the end has come. Only the rear guard will linger along the line, beautiful in their isolation, pathetic in their loneliness.

SILVER MAPLE. SOFT MAPLE. WHITE MAPLE.

Àcer sacchărìnum. Àcer dasycărpum.

A large tree, ninety to one hundred feet in height with a trunk which soon divides into three or four stout, upright, secondary stems, forming a wide spreading head with drooping branches. Found abundantly throughout the valley of the Mississippi where it is one of the largest and most common of river trees; rare along the Atlantic coast. Grows rapidly. Sap produces sugar.

Bark.—Light gray, smooth until the tree is of considerable size. On old trees reddish brown, more or less furrowed, the surface separating into large loose scales. Branchlets at first pale green, later dark green, finally pale chestnut brown, smooth, shining, at last reddish gray.

Wood.—Cream, faintly tinged with brown; hard, strong, close-grained, rather brittle. Used in cabinet work. Sp. gr., 0.5269; weight of cu. ft., 32.84.

Winter Buds.—Flower buds aggregated, obtuse, red. Leaf buds one-fourth an inch long, red; inner scales enlarge when spring growth begins, become green or yellow and an inch long before they fall.

Leaves.—Opposite, simple, five to seven inches long, rather less in breadth. Palmately five-lobed with narrow acute sinuses and acute divisions. The middle lobe is often three-lobed. Base heart-shaped or truncate; margin coarsely serrate or toothed. Primary veins conspicuous. They come out of the bud pale green and downy, when full grown are bright pale green above, silvery white beneath. In autumn they turn pale yellow. Petioles long, slender, red, drooping.

Flowers. — March, April. Polygamo-monœcious or diœcious. Before the leaves, which do not appear until fruit is nearly grown. Greenish yellow, sessile on last year's wood; borne in sessile axillary fasicles.

Calyx.—Campanulate, slightly five-lobed, downy, long and narrow in the sterile, short and broad in the fertile flowers.

Corolla.—Wanting.

Stamens.—Three to seven, hypogynous ; filaments long and slender in the sterile flowers, short in the fertile. Anthers reddish, oblong, two-celled ; cells opening longitudinally.

Pistils.—In sterile flowers rudimentary ; in fertile, ovary borne on narrow disk, superior, downy, two-lobed, two-celled, compressed contrary to the dissepiment, wing-margined ; styles two, united at base only, long, exserted, red ; ovules two in each cell, one usually aborts.

Fruit.—Two samaras united forming a maple key. Borne on slender drooping pedicels an inch and a half to three inches long. Vary in length from one and one-half to three inches. Wings divergent, straight or curved, three-fourths of an inch broad, deep

Staminate and Pistillate Flowers of Silver Maple, *Acer saccharinum.*

red or pale chestnut brown. Seed reddish brown. April, May. Cotyledons thin, leaf-like. Seed germinates as soon as it falls to the ground.

The seed of *Acer* usually ripens in the autumn and germinates the following spring. The seed of the two American species with precocious flowers, *A. rubrum* and *A. Saccharinum,* however, ripens at the end of a few weeks after the trees flower, and germinates at once. This is a provision, perhaps, acquired by these species to insure their perpetuation ; they grow in low, wet land, often inundated during the winter, and the seed, if it ripened in the autumn would often lie in the water through the winter and be in danger of losing its vitality ; but it reaches the ground after the water has fallen in the swamps and before the exposed surface of the ground has become baked by the hot sun of summer, that is, when it is just in the condition to insure the germination of seed.

—CHARLES S. SARGENT.

Silver Maple, *Acer saccharinum.*
Leaves 5′ to 7′ long.

The Silver Maple, both in poise and outline, suggests the elm. Its trunk divides into secondary stems, its branches have an airy upward and outward sweep and its terminal branchlets are slender and drooping ; then, too, the bark is often shaggy on trunk and limbs, making the resemblance still greater. The finely cut leaves hang on long and slender footstalks and sway with every passing breeze, thus showing the silvery whiteness of their under surface and giving to the foliage a delicacy of texture all its own.

The tree is a rapid grower, is comparatively free from serious disease, adapts itself to a great variety of soils, and these characteristics have made it a general favorite with those who desire to secure shade trees with as little delay as possi-

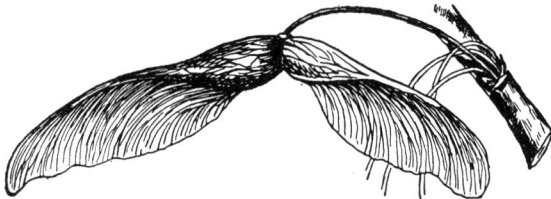

Key of Silver Maple, *Acer saccharinum.*

ble. However, it does not flourish on dry and elevated ground, and should never be planted in such locations, as it soon suffers, the branches become brittle and the tree in time unsightly. It is the first tree to blossom in early spring, coming out a week or two before either the red maple or the elm ; in fact it is ready to open its buds at the slightest provocation any time during the winter.

The fruit grows as the leaves develop and ripens in early summer. The keys are large with long stiff wings set at wide angles. If planted they will produce tiny trees before winter comes.

The autumnal tint of the Silver Maple often varies from the usual pale dull yellow to a brilliant yellow and scarlet

RED MAPLE. SWAMP MAPLE. SOFT MAPLE.

Àcer rùbrum.

Generally distributed throughout eastern North America. Loves the borders of streams and low swamp lands which it sometimes covers to the exclusion of other trees. Will grow when planted on rich, well dressed, upland soil. Roots large, and fibrous. Grows rapidly. Attains the height of eighty to one hundred feet with trunk three to four feet in diameter. Its upright branches form a narrow head. The sap will produce sugar, but not abundantly.

Bark.—Dark gray, divided by longitudinal ridges, the surface separating into large scales. Branchlets green or dark red, later bright red and shining, marked by many white lenticels, finally they become light gray tinged with red, sometimes almost white.

Wood.—Light brown tinged with red, sapwood lighter ; heavy, close-grained. Not very strong, smooth satiny surface. Presents curled and bird's eye varieties. Used for cabinet work, is sufficiently elastic to be used for oars ; fuel value is high. Sp. gr., 0.6178 ; weight of cu. ft., 38.50 lbs.

Winter Buds.—Flower buds aggregated, obtuse, red. Leaf buds obtuse, red, one-eighth of an inch long. The scales enlarge when spring growth begins, the inner become three-quarters of an inch long, narrow, and bright scarlet.

Leaves.—Opposite, simple, two to six inches long, rather longer than broad, palmately three to five-lobed, middle lobe longer than the others ; lobes irregularly doubly serrate or toothed. Base more or less heart-shaped or truncate ; principal nerves conspicuous. They come out of the bud pale green and downy, when full grown are smooth, bright green above, whitish and downy beneath. In autumn they turn scarlet or crimson. Petioles long, slender, red or green.

Flowers.—March, April, before the leaves. Polygamo-monœcious, or diœcious. Rich crimson or scarlet or dull yellowish red. Borne on the branchlets of the previous year in few-flowered fascicles, on short pedicels.

Calyx.—Sepals four to five, oblong, obtuse, red, imbricate in bud.

Petals.—Four to five, linear, red, imbricate in bud.

Stamens.—Five to six, scarlet ; filaments slender, exserted in the staminate, included in the pistillate ; anthers oblong, introrse, two-celled ; cells opening longitudinally.

Pistil.—Ovary superior, two-lobed, two-celled, compressed contrary to the dissepiments, wing-margined, smooth, borne on a narrow disk. Styles two, united for a short distance, then separated into long, exserted, stigmatic lobes. Ovules two in each cell.

MAPLE FAMILY

Fruit.—Two samaras united forming a maple key. Borne on drooping stems three to four inches long ; scarlet, dark red, sometimes brown ; wings thin, convergent at first, divergent when full grown, one-half to an inch long, one-fourth to one-half an inch broad. May, June. Seed dark red, germinates immediately after falling to the ground. Cotyledons thin.

> The scarlet maple-keys betray,
> What potent blood hath modest May.
> —RALPH WALDO EMERSON.

> The maple crimsons to a coral reef.
> —JAMES RUSSELL LOWELL.

A small Red Maple has grown, perchance, far away at the head of some retired valley, a mile from any road, unobserved. It has faithfully discharged all the duties of a maple there, all winter and summer neglected none of its economies, but added to its stature in the virtue which belongs to a maple, by a steady growth for so many months, and is nearer heaven than it was in the spring. It has faithfully husbanded its sap, and afforded a shelter to the wandering bird, has long since ripened its seeds and committed them to the winds. It deserves well of mapledom. Its leaves have been asking it from time to time in a whisper, " When shall we redden ? " and now in this month of September, this month of travelling, when men are hastening to the seaside, or the mountains, or the lakes, this modest maple, still without budging an inch, travels in its reputation—runs up its scarlet-flag on that hillside, which shows that it has finished its summer's work before all other trees, and withdrawn from the contest. At the eleventh hour of the year, the tree which no scrutiny could have detected here when it was most industrious is thus, by the tint of its maturity, by its very blushes, revealed at last to the careless and distant traveller, and leads his thoughts away from the dusty road into those brave solitudes which it inhabits ; it flashes out conspicuous with all the virtue and beauty of a maple—*Acer rubrum.* We may now read its title, or rubric, clear. Its virtues not its sins are as scarlet.
> —HENRY D. THOREAU.

Never was a tree more appropriately named than the Red Maple. Its first blossom flushes red in the April sunlight, its keys ripen scarlet in early May, all summer long its leaves swing on crimson or scarlet stems, its young twigs flame in the same colors and later, amid all the brilliancy of the autumnal forest, it stands pre-eminent and unapproachable.

The Red Maple shows a decided tendency to vary in the shape of its leaves. For this reason it has been divided into varieties, but these have been given up because the characters do not remain constant. Of two red maples standing

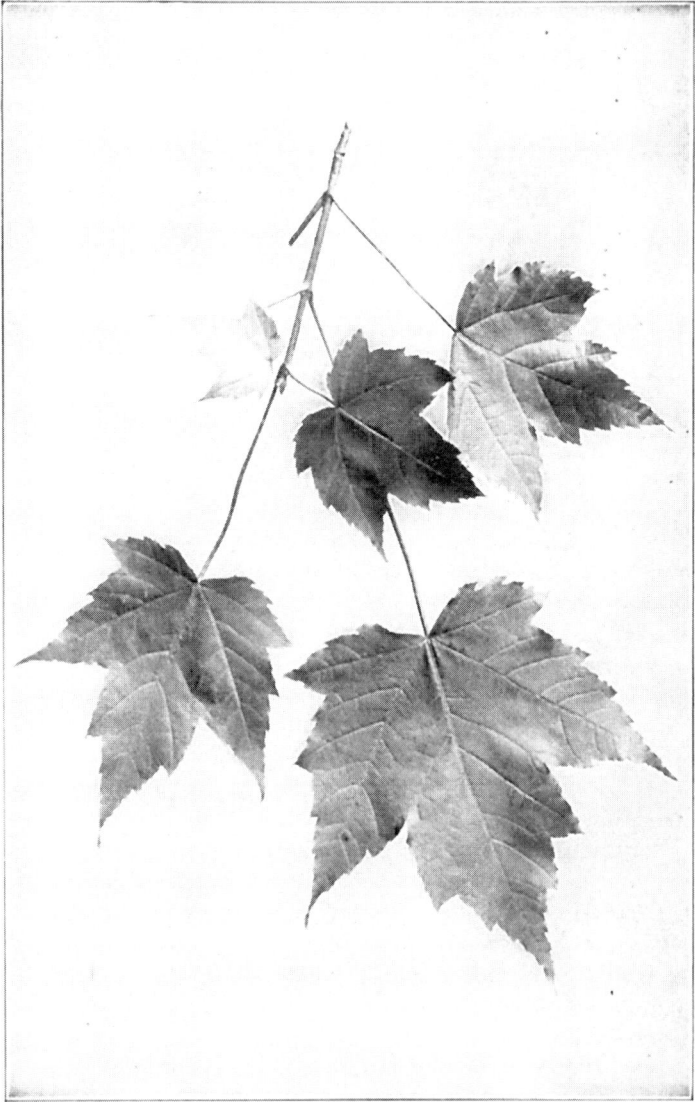

Red Maple, *Acer rubrum.*
Leaves 2′ to 6′ long.

side by side, one may have large, thin, five-lobed leaves, and the other small, thick, three-lobed leaves, or both forms may be found on different parts of the same tree, and sometimes even on the same branch.

The flowers appear very early, only those of the silver maple precede them. Perfect flowers occasionally occur, but generally the staminate and pistillate flowers are produced on separate trees, although a branch with staminate flowers can be found on a tree on which the flowers are pistillate, and individual pistillate clusters on a staminate branch. If the tree is very red, one may be certain that the flowers are pistillate, but if yellowish they are staminate.

Key of Red Maple, *Acer rubrum.*

All the maples show what is called the curled and bird's-eye varieties. These are an accidental and fortuitous arrangement of the woody fibre, and as there is no marked outward indication of these varieties, only experienced woodsmen can detect them in the living tree, which they do from some slight peculiarities of the bark. It is said that these forms are found only in old trees. Such lumber is now very valuable for the interior furnishings of rooms, railway-cars, and steamship saloons. How many such trees were destroyed in the early days through ignorance or indifference no one knows. I recall a country home where the kitchen-stove was fed one entire winter with the most beautiful curled and bird's-eye maple, carefully cut into cordwood eighteen inches in length. Of course the owner knew nothing of the existence of these trees until they confronted him in his woodpile, and his anger and dismay may be imagined as he bewailed the stupidity of his workmen.

Fruiting Spray of Norway Maple, *Acer platanoides.*
Leaves 3′ to 5′ long.

NORWAY MAPLE

Àcer platanoìdes

The beautiful Norway Maple standing by the curb-stone is a common sight in our city streets. Its roots strike deep and spread laterally, this enables it to hold its own in the struggle with city environments. It comes to us from Europe, its range there extending from Norway to Switzerland. The leaves have a marked resemblance to those of the sugar maple, in form, but are thicker in texture and darker in color. They remain upon the tree fully two weeks longer than those of our native maples and become yellow or fall with little change of color. The petioles are long and when broken exude an acrid milky sap which quickly coagulates. This peculiarity enables one to determine the tree with little difficulty. The greenish flowers appear with the leaves in a short corymbose raceme ; the fruit, also borne in short racemes, is a key with widely divergent wings.

The tree reaches the height of sixty feet, develops a broad round head, and becomes strong and sturdy. Its winter buds are large and red ; its branchlets at first are green, later they become reddish brown and shining.

SYCAMORE MAPLE

Àcer pseudo-platànus

This most beautiful of European maples is also planted as an ornamental tree, but it does not seem to take kindly to our climate, failing to become either large or long-lived in the United States. Its leaves resemble those of the sugar maple in general form, but are much darker green in color and of thicker texture.

The green flowers appear with the leaves, are about the size of a currant blossom and borne in long, drooping, com-

Fruiting Spray of Sycamore Maple, *Acer pseudo-platanus*.
Leaves 3′ to 5′ long.

pound clusters ; both rachis and pedicels are hairy. The keys likewise are borne in pendulous clusters, their wings diverge, but are not as divergent as those of the Norway Maple. Like the Norway it holds its leaves two weeks longer than our native species. This is a characteristic of all our acclimated European trees. It is native to central Europe and was brought into England in the time of Queen Elizabeth, where it has become perfectly acclimated.

The history of its common name Sycamore is most interesting. Sycamore is derived from two Greek words, one meaning fig and the other mulberry. But this sycamore bears neither figs nor mulberries, nor does its fruit in any respect resemble either. In the New Testament story it is said that Zaccheus climbed a sycamore tree in order that he might better see Jesus as he passed by. That sycamore was a fig-tree, common enough by the wayside in Palestine and Egypt, but not native in Europe. The interesting question is how did this European maple get the name of the eastern fig-tree ? Simply through word transference. In the twelfth and thirteenth centuries, when miracle plays were produced in all the churches of Europe for the instruction of the people, one of the favorite scenes for acting was the flight into Egypt of Joseph and Mary. It was easily put upon the stage. One legend says that on their way they rested under a sycamore tree. But no sycamores grew in the countries where these plays were acted and so this maple was chosen to take its place, because the leaves were somewhat like those of the true sycamore. In the play it was called sycamore, and naturally the people began to call it sycamore, and such it has remained to this day.

BOX ELDER. ASH-LEAVED MAPLE

Àcer negùndo.

Distributed across the continent, abundant throughout the Mississippi valley along banks of streams and borders of swamps. Prefers a deep rich soil and attains the height of fifty to seventy feet. The trunk often divides near the ground into a number of stout wide-spreading branches. Grows rapidly.

Bark.—Pale gray or light brown, deeply cleft into broad ridges, scaly. Branchlets pale green, later are bright green, sometimes purplish with a bloom, lenticular for several years.

Wood.—Cream-white; light, soft, close-grained, not strong; used for wooden ware and paper pulp. Sp. gr., 0.4328; weight of cu. ft., 26.97 lbs.

Winter Buds.—Terminal buds acute, an eighth of an inch long. Lateral buds obtuse. The inner scales enlarge when spring growth begins and often become an inch long before they fall.

Leaves.—Opposite, compound, of three to five leaflets. Leaflets two to four inches long, two to three inches broad, oval or ovate, rounded or wedge-shaped at base, coarsely and irregularly serrate, acute. The odd leaflet is oftener three-lobed than simple; midrib and veins conspicuous. They come out of the bud with under surface coated with tomentum, when full grown are more or less downy, bright light green above, paler beneath. In autumn they turn a pale yellow. Petioles long, slender, two or three inches long, bases enlarged and often hairy. Stipules caducous.

Flowers.—April, before the leaves, diœcious, yellow green; staminate flowers in clusters on slender hairy pedicels one and a half to two inches long. Pistillate flowers in narrow drooping racemes.

Calyx.—Yellow green; staminate flowers campanulate, five-lobed, hairy. Pistillate flowers smaller, five-parted; disk rudimentary.

Corolla.—Wanting.

Stamens.—Four to six, exserted; filaments slender, hairy; anthers linear, connective pointed.

Pistil.—Ovary hairy, borne on disk, partly enclosed by calyx, two-celled, wing-margined. Styles separate at base into two stigmatic lobes.

Fruit.—Maple keys, full size in early summer. Borne in drooping racemes, pedicels one to two inches long. Key an inch and a half to two inches long, nutlets diverging, wings straight or incurved September. Seed half an inch long. Cotyledons, thin, narrow.

MAPLE FAMILY

This is our only maple with compound leaves, and so accustomed are we to simple leaves for the maples that were it not for the keys hanging in graceful clusters from the branches we should question its right to be a maple. But just as certainly as an acorn indicates an oak, so does a maple key characterize a maple.

Keys of Box Elder, *Acer negundo.*

The Ash-leaved Maple is a handsome tree with spreading branches. Its habitat extends as far east as Cayuga Lake, New York, west to the foothills of the Rockies, north to Winnepeg and south to Florida. Compared with its companions on the river bottoms it is a small tree, and like the sugar maple it can flourish in the shade. The tree is rare east of the Appalachian range and beyond the Rockies it undergoes a mountain change and appears in California as a different variety. It grows rapidly and is now largely planted in the treeless west, and, strange to say, this lover of water accepts the climatic change and flourishes. Like the silver maple there is no touch of red in its autumnal coloring, its leaves become a pure pale yellow before they fall.

Fruiting Spray of Box Elder, *Acer negundo*.
Leaflets 2′ to 4′ long.

ANACARDIÀCEÆ—SUMACH FAMILY

VELVET SUMACH. STAGHORN SUMACH

Rhús hírta—Rhús týphina

Rhus is by some referred to a Celtic word meaning red; others derive it from the Greek word meaning run, because the roots spread underground to a considerable distance from the trunk; still others refer it to a Greek word which indicates its value medicinally. *Typhina* giant, this being the largest of the North American species. *Hirta*, hairy. Sumach is derived from Simaq the Arabic name of the plant.

A small tree with a slender and slightly leaning trunk, with stout spreading and often contorted branches which form a flat head; oftener it is a shrub spreading by suckers into thickets along fences and in neglected fields. Roots fleshy; juice milky and viscid, turning black when exposed to the air. Small branches and young stems pithy. Short-lived. Prefers calcareous soil.

Bark.—Smooth, dark brown, sometimes scaly. Branchlets stout, clumsy, coated with long, soft, pink hairs, which change to green and then brown. Branchlets do not become smooth until at least three years old; in their second year are marked with many lenticels. Bark rich in tannin.

Wood.—Orange color streaked with green; light, brittle, soft, coarse-grained, with satiny surface. Sp. gr., 0.4357; weight of cu. ft., 27.15 lbs.

Winter Buds.—Terminal bud, large, obtuse; axillary buds, smaller, globular.

Leaves.—Alternate, unequally pinnately compound, sixteen to twenty-four inches long; petiole stout, hairy, enlarged at the base, reddish, and surrounds and encloses the leaf bud in its axil. Leaflets eleven to thirty-one, two to five inches long, almost sessile, oblong, rounded or heart-shaped, slightly unequal at base, serrate, acuminate, middle pairs longer than the others; midrib prominent, and primary veins forking near the margin. They come out of the

Fruit and Leaf of Staghorn Sumach. *Rhus hirta.*

Leaves 16′ to 24′ long.   Leaflets 2′ to 5′ long.

bud yellow green, covered as are the shoot and petiole with bright red hairs. When full grown they become smooth, somewhat darker above, and pale or whitish beneath. In autumn they turn scarlet, varied by shades of crimson, yellow, and orange.

Flowers.—May, June. Diœcious, yellowish green, sometimes tinged with red. In dense panicles with downy stems and branches and large bracts which fall at the opening of the flowers. The panicle of sterile flowers is eight to twelve inches long, five to six inches broad, with spreading branches and is nearly a third larger than the more compact fertile panicle.

Calyx.—Five-lobed, lobes acute, hairy; imbricate in bud, in staminate flowers shorter than the petals; in pistillate flowers about the same length.

Corolla.—Petals five, imbricate in bud, longer than and alternate with the lobes of the calyx, inserted under the margin of the fleshy red disk surrounding the ovary. In staminate flower, yellow green tinged with red, strap-shaped; in pistillate, green, narrow and acuminate.

Stamens.—Five, inserted on the disk, alternate with the petals; in staminate flowers exserted with large, bright, orange-colored anthers; in the pistillate flower, short with rudimentary anthers. Anthers large, introrse.

Pistil.—Ovary ovoid, downy, with three short spreading styles; in the staminate flower often rudimentary.

Fruit.—Dry drupe; not poisonous. Borne in terminal thyrse-like panicles six to eight inches long, two to three inches broad, which become full grown and bright red in August but not fully mature until October and remain on the tree all winter. Depressed-globular, with a thin covering, clothed with long crimson hairs. Cotyledons flat, leaf-like.

The Velvet Sumach is well named, for its twigs and branches are really velvety to the eye and to the touch. No other of our native trees sends forth its leaves and twigs with so royal a covering. The branchlets are coated with long, soft, pink hairs when they first come forth, later these turn a bright green, then brown and finally in their second summer become short and almost black. For two years the growing wood of the Sumach is clothed in velvet.

The name Staghorn may be explained in two ways, one quite as good as the other. Some say that the early observers saw a certain likeness between the forking leafless branches and a stag's horn, others, that the soft velvety down which covers the growing shoot is the point of resemblance to a young stag's horn.

The beauty of the Sumach lies entirely in its foliage ; the leafless tree is stiff, awkward and clumsy, but after the leaves come out it is a different creature, clean-cut and beautiful all summer long. Its long, pinnately compound leaves are borne in tufts at the end of the branches, the main stem is either horizontal or slightly curved upward, while the leaflets have a decided tendency to hang down. These lift and sway with every passing breeze, and when the whole is crowned, as it so often is, with a great thyrsoid panicle of bright red fruit standing out from the centre of each leafy tuft, the effect is unique and beautiful. The little drupes which make the panicles are covered with crimson down which is charged with malic acid, sour but agreeable to the taste. They re main on the tree all winter and become the food of the birds.

In autumn all the sumachs, large and small, are wonderful for the brilliancy of their coloring. They glow in scarlet and gold which sometimes deepens to crimson and orange. The Velvet Sumach makes thickets on its own account, its smaller brother, *R. glabra*, the Smooth Sumach, follows its example, and along the fences, over deserted fields and up the rocky, gravelly, mountain-side they fling their magnificent beauty through all the October days.

> " Like glowing lava streams the sumach crawls
> Upon the mountain's granite walls."

The Velvet Sumach is dioecious. The staminate flowers have an ovary, but this aborts in process of development and only the pistillate produce fruit. The sterile trees flower fully a week or ten days earlier than the fertile ones.

The color of the wood is peculiar and striking, being a sort of greenish orange, but the tree never grows large enough to furnish wood available for anything more than sticks and boxes.

Rhus copallina, the Dwarf or Mountain Sumach, at the north is a shrub, but in the mountains of North Carolina and Tennessee it becomes a tree. The leaves are pinnate, six to twelve inches long, the rachis is wing-margined ; leaflets nine to twenty-one, ovate-lanceolate, acute, margins entire except a few serrate teeth near the apex. The fruit consists of crimson hairy drupes borne in a dense terminal panicle. The leaves and bark contain much tannin and are collected in large quantities in the southern states and used for tanning leather.

The family *Rhus* is widely distributed throughout the temperate regions of the world ; more than a hundred species have been distinguished and these are in Africa, Asia, North America, South America, Indian Archipelago, Australia and the Sandwich Islands. Its traces are also abundant in the late eocene and the miocene rocks of Europe, but rare in the arctic tertiary. Many species possess useful properties, and some are of commercial importance. The bark and leaves of all are rich in tannin, and one species, *Rhus coriaria* of southern Europe, is cultivated expressly for the tannin of its leaves, which, dried and powdered, are used in curing the best qualities of leather.

The famous lacquer of Japan which has made the cabinet work of the Japanese unequalled for centuries, is produced by a sumach tree which is cultivated expressly for its milky juice. The tree is allowed to reach the age of ten years and then incisions are made on the trunk and large branches, the sap collected, the small branches cut off and soaked in water ; the tree in short is killed for its heart's blood. The yield is surprisingly small, only two or three ounces from a single tree. It seems that the tree cannot be tapped year after year as we tap maple trees, the product of the second year is poor and that of the third year nothing whatever ; so the tree is killed outright.

Cotinus cotinoides belongs to the *Rhus* family and is the cultivated Smoke-tree of the gardens. The flowers are very small, purplish, and borne in loose panicles. After calyx and corolla drop, the pedicels lengthen, become hairy and form great feathery bunches, green or dull red, which cover the tree and transform it into a misty, cloudy, billowy mass.

Dwarf Sumach, *Rhus copallina.*
Leaves 6′ to 12′ long.   Leaflets 2′ to 4′ long.

POISON SUMACH. POISON DOGWOOD

Rhús vérnix. Rhús venenáta.

A small tree, eighteen to twenty feet high, with acrid, milky, poisonous juice which turns black on exposure. The head is round and narrow and the branches slender and rather pendulous; often it is simply a shrub. Small branches and young stems pithy.

Bark.—Smooth, light or dark gray, slightly striate. Branchlets are smooth, reddish brown, covered with small, orange colored, lenticular spots; later they become orange brown and finally light gray.

Wood.—Light yellow with brown lines; light, soft, coarse-grained, brittle. Sp. gr., 0.4382; weight of cu. ft., 27.31 lbs.

Winter Buds.—Terminal bud is much larger than the axillary buds, all are acute, dark purple.

Fruit of Poison Sumach,
Rhus vernix.

Leaves. — Alternate, pinnately compound, seven to fourteen inches long, borne on slender reddish petioles. Leaflets seven to thirteen, obovate, or oblong, three to four inches long, slightly unequal or contracted at the base, entire, acute or rounded at apex, short petiolate except the terminal one which sometimes has a stalk an inch in length. They come out of the bud orange colored and downy, when full grown are smooth, dark green and shining above, pale beneath; midrib and primary veins prominent. In autumn they turn scarlet and orange.

Flowers.—June, July. Diœcious; yellow green, borne in long, narrow, axillary panicles crowded near the ends of the branches. Bracts and bractlets are acute, downy, and fall as the flowers open.

Calyx.—Five-lobed. lobes acute, short.

Corolla.—Petals five, acute, yellow green.

Stamens.—Five, with long slender filaments and large orange colored anthers. In the fertile flowers short and rudimentary.

Pistil.—Ovary ovoid-globose, one-celled, surmounted by three thick spreading styles; ovule solitary.

Fruit.—Drupaceous, globular, white, borne in long graceful racemes, often tipped with the dark remnants of the styles. Ripens in September and frequently hangs on the tree the entire winter. Cotyledons flat, leaf-like.

Poison Sumach, *Rhus vernix.*

Leaves 7′ to 14′ long.   Leaflets 3′ to 4′ long.

The Poison Sumach is found throughout the northern states and is one of the most dangerous plants of our flora. However, it ought never to be mistaken for the other sumachs although it often is. The leaves are shorter, the leaflets fewer, margins are entire, the fruit white and about the size of a small pea. All the other sumachs have red fruit. It is found in wet soils, whereas the others like the dry. Its poisonous principle is the same as that found in *Rhus toxicodendron*, or Poison Ivy, and while it affects many people who handle it or are near to it, others are entirely immune. The poison shows itself in painful and long continued swellings and eruptions. The exact character of this poison is in dispute. It has long been considered to be a volatile acid, but recent investigations are leading to the belief that it is a fixed oil.

LEGUMINÒSÆ—PEA FAMILY

LOCUST. ACACIA, YELLOW LOCUST. BLACK LOCUST

Robínia pseudacàcia.

Robinia commemorates the botanical labors of Jean Robin, herbalist of Henry III. and director of the gardens of the Louvre under Henry IV. and Louis XIII. His son Vespasian Robin first cultivated the Locust tree in Europe. *Pseudacacia,* like the acacia.

Often cultivated as an ornamental tree throughout the north, but native from Pennsylvania to northern Georgia and westward as far as Arkansas and Indian Territory. Reaches the height of seventy feet with a trunk three or four feet in diameter, with brittle branches that form an oblong narrow head. Spreads by underground shoots.

Bark.—Dark gray brown tinged with red, deeply furrowed, surface inclined to scale. Branchlets at first coated with white silvery down. This soon disappears and they become pale green, afterward reddish brown. Prickles develop from stipules, are short, somewhat triangular, dilated at base, sharp, dark purple, adhering only to the bark, but persistent.

Wood.—Pale yellowish brown ; heavy, hard, strong, close-grained and very durable in contact with the ground. Sp. gr., 0.7333 ; weight of cv. ft., 45.70 lbs.

Winter Buds.—Minute, naked, three or four together, protected in a depression by a scale-like covering lined on the inner surface with a thick coat of tomentum and opening in early spring ; when forming are covered by the swollen base of the petiole.

Leaves.—Alternate, compound, odd-pinnate, eight to fourteen inches long, with slender hairy petioles, grooved and swollen at the base. Leaflets petiolate, seven to nine, one to two inches long, one-half to three-fourths of an inch broad, emarginate or rounded at

97

apex. They come out of the bud conduplicate, yellow green, covered with silvery down which soon disappears; when full grown are dull dark green above, paler beneath. Feather-veined, midvein prominent. In autumn they turn a clear pale yellow. Stipules linear, downy, membranous at first, ultimately developing into hard woody prickles, straight or slightly curved. Each leaflet has a minute stipel which quickly falls and a short petiole.

Flowers.—May, after the leaves. Papilionaceous. Perfect, borne in loose drooping racemes four to five inches long, cream-white, about an inch long, nectar bearing, fragrant. Pedicels slender, half an inch long, dark red or reddish green.

Calyx.—Campanulate, gibbous, hairy, five-toothed, slightly two-lipped, dark green blotched with red, especially on the upper side teeth valvate in bud.

Corolla.—Imperfectly papilionaceous, petals inserted upon a tubular disk; standard white with pale yellow blotch; wings white, oblong-falcate; keel petals incurved, obtuse, united below.

Stamens.—Ten, inserted with the petals, diadelphous, nine inferior, united into a tube which is cleft on the upper side, superior one free at the base. Anthers two-celled, cells opening longitudinally.

Pistil.—Ovary superior, linear-oblong, stipitate, one-celled; style inflexed, long, slender, bearded; stigma capitate; ovules several, two-ranked.

Fruit.—Legume two-valved, smooth, three to four inches long and half an inch broad, usually four to eight seeded. Ripens late in autumn and hangs on the branches until early spring. Seeds dark orange brown with irregular markings. Cotyledons oval, fleshy.

The value of *Robinia pseudacacia* is practically destroyed in nearly all parts of the United States beyond the mountain forests which are its home, by the borers which riddle the trunk and branches. Were it not for these insects it would be one of the most valuable timber-trees that could be planted in the northern and middle states. The character of the timber which it produces, the rapidity of its growth, its power to adapt itself to different soils and to reproduce itself rapidly by seeds which germinate readily, and by stump and root shoots, would make it a most valuable tree if it could be protected from insects. Young trees grow quickly and vigorously for a number of years, but soon become stunted and diseased, and rarely live long enough to attain any commercial value.　　　　　—CHARLES S. SARGENT.

It is an interesting question why some trees grow so much more rapidly than others, and the explanation seems to lie in the character of the roots. Any tree whose principal roots extend just beneath the surface grows rapidly because the soil there is the richest; but the cause which produces this

Locust, *Robinia pseudacacia.*
Leaves 8′ to 14′ long. Leaflets 1′ to 2′ long, ¾′ to 1′ broad.

rapidity at first may retard the growth later; for unless these spreading roots are allowed ample space on every side they soon exhaust the soil within reach. On the other hand trees whose roots penetrate deep as well as wide grow more slowly and also more steadily, and other things being equal attain the larger size.

A single Locust, given a free hand and good soil, will soon produce a thicket; for the roots creeping along the upper layers of the soil send up numerous shoots which quickly set up in life for themselves. The foliage effect of such a thicket is most beautiful. The leaves are compound with delicate, dark green leaflets. New leaves are put forth until past midsummer and these being a light yellow green stand out against the dark background of the older leaves, giving the color effect of a mass of soft velvety greens of varied values.

Raceme of Locust Blossoms,
Robinia pseudacacia.

Then, too, the leaves respond to a light breeze so quickly, the leaf surface is so smooth, the leaf texture so fine, that the tree is always clean even in dusty places.

Loudon reports that a plantation of locusts, Scotch pines, sycamores, limes, chestnuts, beeches, ashes, and oaks was made near Kensington, London, in 1812 and that the trees were measured in 1827, when it was found that the locust had grown faster than any one kind of the other trees in the proportion of 27 to 22, and faster than the average of them in the proportion of 27 to 18. But this was a case where the race was not to the swift, for at the end of forty years the locusts had been over-topped and ultimately they were destroyed by the other trees.

All the beauty of the Locust comes when it is in leaf; the

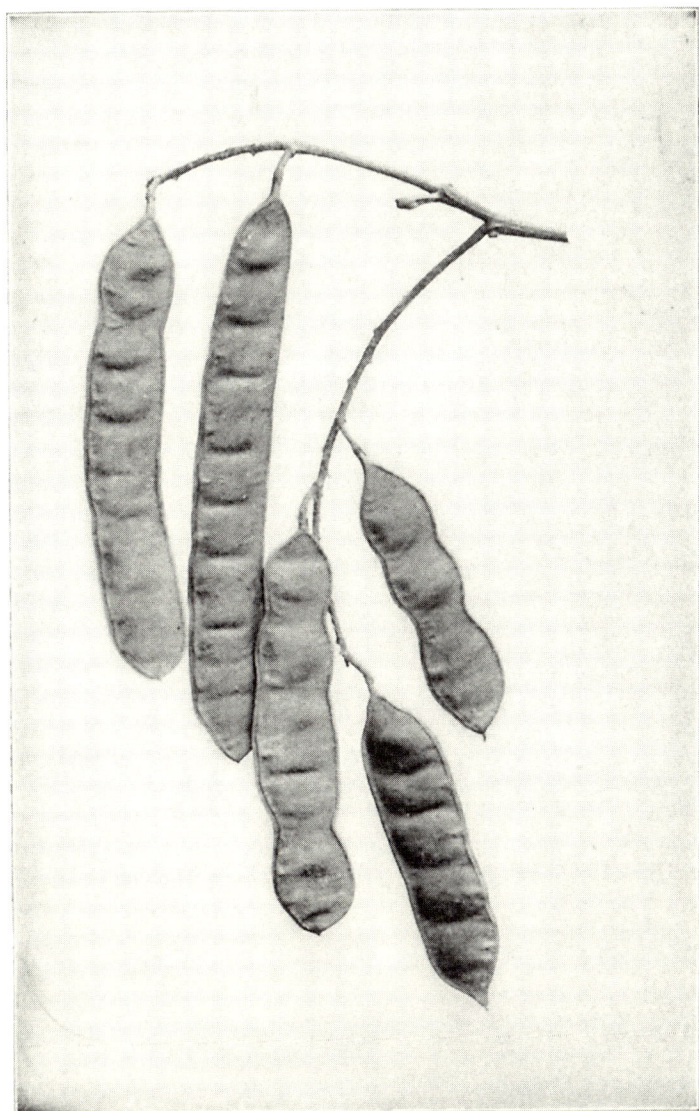

Fruit of Locust, *Robinia pseudacacia*.

Pod 3′ to 4′ long.

leafless tree is not beautiful. The trunk is often twisted, the branches are irregular and twiggy, easily broken, and so give the tree an unkempt, ragged appearance. This is an instance where the contour of the tree has nothing to do with its beauty—the beauty lies in the color and disposition of the foliage itself.

The young trees are armed with prickles, not thorns. The difference between these lies in the point of attachment. A prickle is part of the bark and will come off with it as do the prickles of the rose, while a thorn is part of the woody growth and belongs to the ligneous tissue.

The Locust begins in its third year to convert its sapwood into heartwood, which is not done by the oak, the beech, or the elm, until after the tenth or fifteenth year.

The leaflets fold together in wet weather, also at night ; some change of position at night is the habit of the entire leguminous family. This peculiarity of the tree led a child to say, " It is not bed time, the locust tree has not begun its prayer."

The name Locust is said to have been given to our *Robinia* by the Jesuit missionaries, who fancied that this was the tree that supported St. John in the wilderness. But it is native only to North America. The locust tree of Spain, which is also a native of Syria, is supposed to be the true locust of the New Testament ; the fruit of this tree may be found in the shops under the name of St. John's bread.

Robinia is now a North American genus—but traces of it are found in the eocene and miocene rocks of Europe.

CLAMMY LOCUST

Robínia viscósa

Usually a shrub five or six feet high, but known to reach the height of forty feet in the mountains of North Carolina with the habit of a tree. Commonly cultivated at the north for the beauty of its flowers.

Bark.—Smooth, dark brown tinged with red. Branchlets dark reddish brown covered with dark glandular hairs which exude a clammy sticky substance ; later, these become bright red brown, and sticky, finally they turn light brown and become dry.

Wood.—Light brown ; heavy, hard, close-grained. Sp. gr., 0.8094 ; weight of cu. ft., 50.44 lbs.

Winter Buds.—Small, naked, in groups, sunk in the scars of the fallen leaves, protected by a scale lined with tomentum ; do not appear until spring.

Leaves.—Alternate, pinnately compound, seven to twelve inches long ; petiole stout and dark, slightly enlarged at base. Leaflets thirteen to twenty-one, oblong, an inch and a half to two inches long, rounded or wedge-shaped at base, entire, rounded and mucronate at apex. Feather-veined ; midrib and primary veins as well as the secondary petioles covered with soft hairs. They come out of the bud yellow green covered with soft, silky, white down, when full grown are dark green, smooth above, pale green and downy beneath. In autumn they turn a clear pale yellow. The stipules are long, slender, sometimes fall, sometimes develop into slender spines. Each leaflet has a minute stipel which quickly falls, and a short petiole.

Flowers.—June. Perfect, pale rose colored, papilionaceous, borne in crowded, oblong, clammy, hairy racemes, slightly fragrant. Pedicels developed from the axils of dark red bracts, which extend beyond the flower buds and fall as the flowers open.

Calyx.—Campanulate, five-toothed, dark red, hairy, valvate in bud.

Corolla.—Papilionaceous, rose or flesh colored, standard narrow with a pale yellow blotch on the inner surface, wings broad. Petals inserted on a tubular disk.

Stamens.—Ten, diadelphous, nine in one group, one alone. Anthers two-celled; cells opening longitudinally.

Pistil.—Ovary superior, linear-oblong, stipitate, one-celled ; style recurved ; ovules several, two-ranked.

Fruit.—Legume, many seeded, about three inches long, narrow, winged, glandular-hispid, tipped with the remnants of the style. Seeds five to nine, dark reddish brown, mottled. Cotyledons oval, fleshy.

103

PEA FAMILY

Robinia viscosa, which appears to be one of the rarest of all our trees, was not seen growing wild in the forests of the southern Alleghany Mountains from the time of Michaux until 1882, when it was rediscovered by Mr. John Donnell Smith near Highlands, Macon County, North Carolina, covering a rocky slope known as Buzzard ridge at an elevation of four thousand five hundred feet above the sea-level, and growing as a shrub with stems only a few feet high. It has not been seen in any other locality growing wild. Bartram and Michaux speak of it as a tree forty feet high, and it often attains that height.

—Charles S. Sargent.

The Clammy Locust has always been a popular garden plant, because of its fine foliage and beautiful flowers. At least three beautiful varieties of it have been produced. A second crop of flowers often appears in August from shoots developed early in the summer, on especially vigorous young trees.

REDBUD. JUDAS-TREE

Cércis canadénsis.

Cercis is of Greek derivation and refers to a fancied resemblance in the fruit to a weaver's implement of that name.

Small tree, with a sturdy upright trunk which divides into stout branches that usually spread to form a broad flat head. Found on rich bottom lands throughout the Mississippi valley ; will grow in the shade and often becomes a dense undergrowth in the forest. Very abundant in Arkansas, Indian Territory, and eastern Texas. Hardy far north ; grows rapidly ; is a satisfactory ornamental tree.

Bark.—Red brown, with deep fissures and scaly surface. Branchlets at first lustrous brown, later become darker.

Wood.—Dark reddish brown ; heavy, hard, coarse-grained, not strong. Sp. gr., 0.6363 ; weight of cu. ft., 39.65 lbs.

Winter Buds.—Chestnut brown, obtuse, one-eighth inch long.

Leaves.—Alternate, simple, heart-shaped or broadly ovate, two to five inches long, five to seven-nerved, cordate or truncate at base, entire, acute. They come out of the bud folded along the line of the midrib, tawny green, when full grown become smooth, dark green above, paler beneath. In autumn they turn bright clear yellow. Petioles slender, terete, enlarged at the base. Stipules caducous.

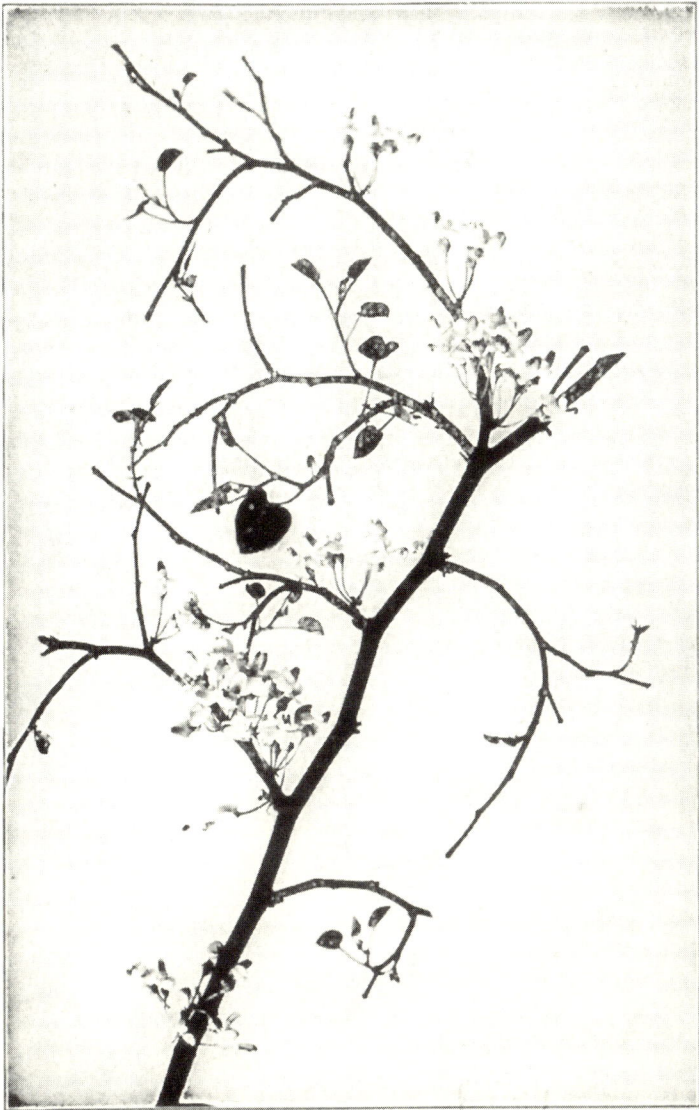

Flowering Branch of Redbud, *Cercis canadensis*.

Flowers.—April, May, before and with the leaves, papilionaceous. Perfect, rose color, borne four to eight together, in fascicles which appear at the axils of the leaves or along the branch and sometimes on the trunk itself.

Calyx.—Dark red, campanulate, oblique, five-toothed, imbricate in bud.

Corolla.—Papilionaceous, petals five, nearly equal, pink or rose color, upper petal the smallest, enclosed in the bud by the wings, and encircled by the broader keel petals.

Stamens.—Ten, inserted in two rows on a thin disk, free, the inner row rather shorter than the others.

Pistil.— Ovary superior, inserted obliquely in the bottom of the calyx tube, stipitate; style fleshy, incurved, tipped with an obtuse stigma.

Fruit.—Legume, slightly stipitate, unequally oblong, acute at each end. Compressed, tipped with the remnants of the style, straight on upper and curved on lower edge. Two and a half to three inches long, rose color, full grown by midsummer, falls in early winter. Seeds ten to twelve, chestnut brown, one-fourth of an inch long ; cotyledons oval, flat.

A tree as large as an apple tree and having something of the same habit, covered with tiny rose colored pea-like blossoms from the crown of its leafless head to its trunk, is an astonishing sight even to one accustomed to observe the wonders of vegetable life. Such is the Redbud, a low tree with a flat spreading head, growing from Canada to Virginia in the low lands, and dividing the honors of early spring with the Shad Bush and the Dogwood. These flowers which appear before the leaves, are small, borne in clusters along the branch except at the very end and sometimes on the trunk itself.

The normal place for flowers to appear is in the axils of the leaves, and when bright, beautiful, rosy blossoms break forth from the bark of old branches or from the very trunk, the fact requires explanation. Many have been offered and the one accepted is that they are produced year after year from excrescences which correspond to the axils of ancient leaves and are composed of the remnants of the axes of earlier inflorescences which have gradually united and formed a more or less prominent mass. Whatever the explanation

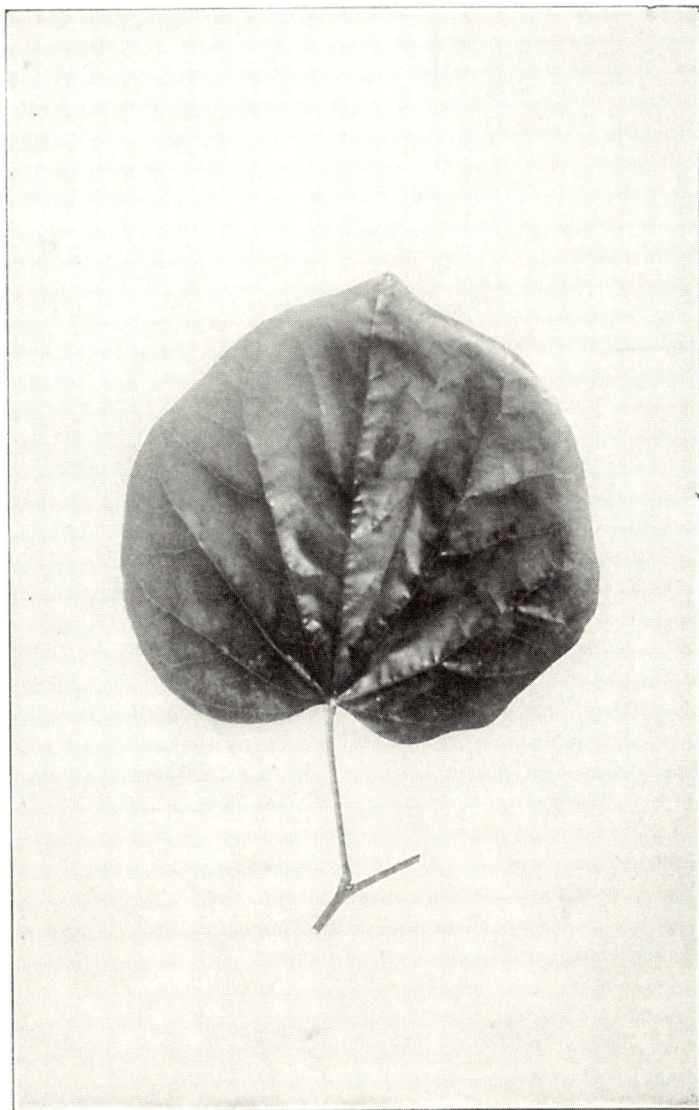

Redbud, *Cercis canadensis.*

Leaves 2′ to 5′ long.

may be, the fact remains that such blossoms may and do annually appear on this tree. These pretty blossoms have a very pleasant acid taste and are succeeded by flat, many-seeded pods that reach full size in May, when they become bright rose color, finally becoming brown ; they hang upon the tree until early winter. Many trees, however, are sterile, the blossoms falling without producing any fruit.

The leaves come out from the bud carefully doubled at the line of the midrib and bent upon the petiole. They are five to seven-nerved, that is, instead of the midrib being the principal line of the woody structure of the leaf, there come out at the base five or six ribs almost as large as the central or midrib. This kind of venation always makes a leaf broad at the base. Sometimes these primary ribs extend away from the apex, then the leaf is very likely to be lobed as are the maples, but in the Redbud the points curve toward the apex and the result is an entire, heart-shaped leaf.

Why should this beautiful creature be called Judas-tree ? Our native tree is very like the species which is common in Europe, in Japan, in Asiatic Turkey and especially in Judea. In the days when legends gathered about whatever was unusual in nature, this tree glowing red in the spring time was said to blush because Judas hanged himself upon it. The old world name has crossed the ocean and our pretty Redbud, blooming in the heart of a continent unknown to that ancient world, bears in every book the blistering name of Judas-tree.

The type is ancient and the genus has existed in Europe almost as at present from the eocene period. A white variety is recorded but has not become common.

KENTUCKY COFFEE-TREE. STUMP-TREE

Gymnócladus dióicus.

Gymnocladus is of Greek derivation and refers to the stout branches destitute of spray.

Widely distributed, but rare. Not found in New England, but ranging from New York to Arkansas and Indian Territory. Prefers bottom lands, and a rich moist soil. Varies from seventy-five to one hundred feet high with a trunk two or three feet in diameter which usually separates ten or fifteen feet from the ground into three or four divisions which spread slightly and form a narrow pyramidal head ; or when crowded by other trees, sending up one tall central branchless shaft to the height of fifty or seventy feet. Branches stout, pithy, and blunt ; roots fibrous.

Bark.—Dark gray, deeply fissured, surface scaly. Branchlets at first coated with short reddish down.

Wood.—Light brown ; heavy, strong, coarse-grained, durable in contact with the ground, takes a fine polish. Sp. gr., 0.6934 ; weight of cu. ft., 43.21 lbs.

Winter Buds.—Minute, depressed in downy cavities of the stem, two in the axil of each leaf, the smaller sterile. Bud scales two, ovate, coated with brown tomentum and growing with the shoot, become orange green, hairy and about one inch long, before they fall.

Leaves.—Alternate, bi-pinnately compound, ten to fourteen pinnate, lowest pinnæ reduced to leaflets, the others seven to thirteen foliate. One to three feet long, eighteen to twenty-four inches broad, by the greater development of the upper pairs of pinnæ. Leaf stalks and stalks of pinnæ, are terete, enlarged at base, smooth when mature, pale green, often purple on the upper side. Leaflets ovate, two to two and one-half inches long, wedge-shaped or irregularly rounded at base, with wavy margin, acute apex. They come out of the bud bright pink, but soon become bronze green, smooth and shining above. When full grown are dark yellow green above, pale green beneath. In autumn turn a bright clear yellow. Stipules leaf-life, lanceolate, serrate, deciduous.

Flowers.—June. Diœcious by abortion, terminal, greenish white. Staminate flowers in a short raceme-like corymb three to four inches long, pistillate flowers in a raceme ten to twelve inches long.

Calyx.—Tubular, hairy, ten-ribbed, five-lobed ; lobes valvate in bud, acute, nearly equal.

Corolla.—Petals five, oblong, hairy, spreading or reflexed, imbricate in bud.

Stamens.—Ten, five long and five short, free, included ; filaments thread-like ; anthers orange colored, introrse ; in the pistillate flower small and sterile.

Pistil.—Ovary superior, sessile, hairy, contracted into a short style, with two stigmatic lobes ; ovules in two rows.

Fruit.—Legume, six to ten inches long, one and one-half to two inches wide, somewhat curved, with thickened margins, dark reddish brown with slight glaucous bloom, crowned with remnant of the styles. Stalks an inch or two long. Seeds six to nine, surrounded by a thick layer of dark, sweet pulp.

When Kentucky was first settled by the adventurous pioneers from the Atlantic states who commenced their career in the primeval wilderness, almost without the necessaries of life, except as they produced them from the fertile soil, they fancied that they had discovered a substitute for coffee in the seeds of this tree; and accordingly the name of Coffee-tree was bestowed upon it. But when communication was established with the sea-ports, they gladly relinquished their Kentucky beverage for the more grateful flavor of the Indian berry ; and no use is at present made of it in that manner.   —A. J. DOWNING.

This is another of the solitary trees of our flora. It grows north as far as Montreal and south to the limits of Arkansas,

Pistillate and Staminate Flowers of Kentucky Coffee-tree.

nevertheless one may be a student of forest trees many years ere one finds the Kentucky Coffee-tree growing on its native hills. In pleasure grounds it is not uncommon, since it is often planted because of its unique appearance and interesting character. Like the Sumach it is wholly destitute of fine spray, its smaller branches are thick, blunt, clumsy and lumpish. Other trees lose their leaves but along their twigs and branchlets are borne the buds, the hope and the promise of the coming year. But the *Gymnocladus* seems so destitute of these, that the French in Canada named it Chicot, the dead tree. Even when spring comes it gives no apparent recognition of light and warmth until nearly every other tree is

Kentucky Coffee-tree, *Gymnocladus dioicus*.
Leaves 1° to 3° long.   Leaflets 2′ to 2½′ long.

in full leaf. The casual observer says it bears no winter buds, but he is mistaken, a tiny pair, so minute that they are detected only by careful searching, wrapped in down and wool, lie sleeping in the axil of every last year's leaf. One is foredoomed to die, but the other, if the fates agree, will grow and develop a tuft of great leaves which will transform the dead stump into a living tree.

The leaves of the Kentucky Coffee-tree are doubly compound and are often three feet long and two feet broad. This form of leaf is not unusual among herbs, but is rare among forest trees. In our northern flora there are but three examples, the Kentucky Coffee-tree, the Honey Locust, and the Hercules' Club. Notwithstanding the size of the leaves the tree is sparingly clothed and the foliage effect is scanty ; indeed, it has been said of it that the leaves filter the light rather than cast a shadow. The expanding leaves are conspicuous because of the varied colors of the leaflets ; the youngest are bright pink, while those which are older vary from green to bronze.

HONEY LOCUST. HONEY SHUCKS

Gledítsia triacánthos.

Gleditsia commemorates the labors of Gleditsch, a botanist contemporary with Linnæus.

A tree usually fifty to seventy-five feet high, with stout sturdy trunk, slender spreading often pendulous branches forming a broad flat top. Native to the Mississippi valley, it has become naturalized in New England. Is tolerant of many soils, but in the bottom lands of southern Indiana and Illinois attains the astonishing proportions of one hundred and forty feet in height with a trunk six feet in diameter. Roots thick and fibrous, trunk and branches spiny.

Bark.—Dark, deeply fissured, surface covered by small scales. Branchlets light reddish brown at first, later grayish brown.

Wood.—Red brown ; hard, strong, coarse-grained, durable in contact with the ground. Sp. gr., 0.6740 ; weight of cu. ft., 42.00 lbs.

Honey Locust, *Gleditsia triacanthos.*
Leaves 7′ to 8′ long.   Leaflets 1½′ to 2′ long.

Winter Buds.—Minute, three or four together, upper one larger than the others. Spine bud minute, above the axil of the leaf and embedded in the bark.

Leaves.—Alternate, pinnately or bi-pinnately compound, seven to eight inches long, main stem grooved, enlarged at the base, eighteen to twenty foliate ; sometimes bi-pinnate with four to seven pairs of pinnæ, upper pair often four or five inches long, lowest often single leaflets. Leaflets lanceolate-oblong, one and one-half to two inches long, rather unequal at base, crenulate-serrate, slightly rounded at apex. They come out of the bud reddish, when full grown are dark green and shining on upper surface, dull yellow green beneath. In autumn they turn a clear pale yellow.

Flowers.—May, June. Polygamo-diœcious, regular, small, greenish. Staminate flowers in short, many-flowered racemes, two to two and one-half inches long. Pistillate in slender, few-flowered, solitary racemes, two and one-half to three inches long.

Calyx.—Campanulate, five-lobed, hairy.

Corolla.—Petals five, greenish, imbricate in bud.

Stamens.—Five, hairy, exserted ; filaments slender, anthers green.

Pistil.—Ovary superior, stipitate, one-celled, woolly ; style short ; stigma dilated, rudimentary in the staminate flower ; ovules several.

Fruit.—Legumes, twelve to eighteen inches long, dark brown, slightly curved, borne in short racemes, walls thin and tough, inner coat papery, contain quantity of sweet pulp between the seeds. In drying they twist, fall in early winter. Seeds twelve to fourteen, oval, flattened.

The foliage of the Honey Locust is that of the common Locust etherealized. There are the same varied values in its greens, the same velvety effects in the mass, but the effect as a whole is lighter, more delicate, more beautiful, for the leaves are doubly pinnate instead of singly pinnate, the leaflets are smaller and the tree itself not being subject to attacks of insects oftener attains its normal proportions.

The most striking peculiarity of the Honey Locust is its thorns, and these thorns are of a very aggressive type. Many trees are literally covered, trunk and branches, with spines from two to six inches long, sometimes in clusters, often three pronged or compound, very sharp and rigid, making a most formidable defence against the attacks of man or beast. The origin of spines or prickles is always interesting. The thorns of *Robinia pseudacacia,* the common Locust, are developed from the most innocent-looking stipules, and always remain attached to the bark. But the spines of the Honey Locust have their origin in a spine bud which forms usually an inch above the axil of the leaf in which the normal buds are formed. These buds also form on the trunk or, formed when the stem was young, remain dormant on the trunk until stimulated into life by some means, when they push through the thick bark and develop as spines. They are in fact undeveloped branches, branches that have failed of their normal growth of leaf and bud and flower and have become simply spines, aggressive, offensive, maybe defensive spines.

All deciduous trees produce upon occasion or hold in reserve adventitious buds. The sprouts that force their way through the thick bark of stumps after the trunk has been cut down are produced by adventitious buds, long dormant but now stimulated to unusual growth. The waving twigs that feather the trunk of many an elm tree have the same genesis.

The Honey Locust frequently becomes a picturesque tree, the trunk becomes twisted and the branches extend horizontally. The leaves appear late in the spring and fall early in autumn, which is always an objection to an ornamental tree. Unlike the Locust its flowers are inconspicuous. The long, flat, pendulous pods, hang in clusters from the branches, and the sweet pulp that surrounds the seed gives the tree its common name. These pods contract in drying and so twist and curl that they are easily rolled by the wind some distance from the parent tree. Nature, like a careful mother, has many devices to aid her children, and when she does not give her seeds wings to soar with the wind, or prickles to cling to the passer-by, she sometimes provides in the seed vessel a means by which at least it may roll itself into a home of its own.

The Honey Locust has many qualities to recommend it as an ornamental tree. It grows rapidly, is tolerant of many soils, is hardy and very free from insects' attacks. It can flourish under the adverse conditions of city life and is often planted in the western states along country roads. It has also been used most successfully as a hedge plant.

The genus *Gleditsia* is found in America, Africa, and Asia but not at present in Europe, although in the tertiary period it existed there.

YELLOW-WOOD. VIRGILIA

Cladrástis lùtea

Rarest of the trees of eastern North America. Found principally on the limestone cliffs of Kentucky, Tennessee and North Carolina, but is hardy at the north and rather extensively cultivated. It likes a rich moist soil, attains the height of fifty feet, the trunk is very apt to divide into two or three stems, which with slender, wide spreading, pendulous branches form a graceful head. Roots fibrous, branches brittle.

Bark.—Smooth gray, or light brown. Branchlets at first downy, but soon become smooth, light brownish green; later red brown, finally dark brown.

Wood.—Yellow to pale brown; heavy, hard, close-grained and strong. Sp. gr., 0.6278; weight of cu. ft., 39.12 lbs.

Winter Buds.—Four in a group, making a tiny cone and inclosed in the hollow base of the petiole.

Leaves.—Alternate, pinnately compound, eight to twelve inches long, main stem stout, enlarged at base. Leaflets seven to eleven, broadly oval, three to four inches long. Wedge-shaped at base, entire, acute, terminal leaflets rhomboid-ovate. Feather-veined, midrib and primary veins prominent, grooved above, light yellow beneath. They come out of the bud pale green, downy; when full grown are dark green above, pale beneath. In autumn they turn a bright clear yellow.

Flowers.—June. Perfect, papilionaceous, white, borne in drooping terminal panicles twelve to fourteen inches long, five to six inches broad, slightly fragrant.

Calyx.—Campanulate, five-lobed, enlarged on the upper side.

Corolla.—Papilionaceous; standard broad, white, marked on the inner surface with a pale yellow blotch; wings oblong; keel petals free.

Stamens.—Ten, free; filaments thread-like.

Yellow-wood, *Cladastris lutea.*

Leaves 8' to 12' long. Leaflets 3' to 4' long.

Pistil.—Ovary superior, linear, bright red, hairy, bearing a long incurved style.

Fruit.—Legume, smooth, linear-compressed, tipped with the remnants of the styles. Seeds four to six, dark brown.

Yellow-wood is recommended as really one of the best medium sized trees for cultivation. The only objection that is mentioned is a tendency of the trunk to divide very near the ground. The autumnal coloring of the leaves is a particularly clear bright yellow.

ROSÀCEÆ—ROSE FAMILY

CANADA PLUM. RED PLUM

Prùnus nìgra

A small tree twenty feet in height, dividing five or six feet from the ground into a number of stout upright branches which form a rigid head. Prefers alluvial soil. Ranges from Newfoundland through the St. Lawrence valley to Manitoba. By cultivation is naturalized in parts of Michigan, northern New England and northern New York.

Bark.—Gray brown, outer layer comes off in thick plates. Branchlets are bright green at first, later become dark brown tinged with red.

Wood.—Bright red brown ; heavy, hard, strong and close-grained. Sp. gr., 0.6918 ; weight of cu. ft., 43.17.

Winter Buds.—Chestnut brown, acuminate, one-eighth to one-fourth of an inch long. Scales of flower buds grow with the expanding flowers and become pale green tinged with pink.

Leaves.—Alternate, simple, oblong-ovate or obovate, three to five inches long, one and a half to three inches broad, wedge-shaped or slightly heart-shaped or rounded at base, doubly crenulate-serrate, abruptly contracted to a narrow point at the apex, feather-veined, midrib conspicuous. They come out of the bud convolute, downy, slightly tinged with red, when full grown are smooth, bright green above, paler beneath. Petioles stout, bearing two large dark glands. Stipules lanceolate or three to five-lobed, early deciduous.

Flowers.—May, before the leaves. Perfect, white, slightly fragrant, borne in three to four-flowered umbels, with short thick peduncles. The pedicels of the blossoms are slender and dark red.

Calyx.—Conic, dark red, five-lobed ; lobes acute, finally reflexed, glandular, smooth on the inner surface, imbricate in bud.

Corolla.—Petals five, inserted on the calyx tube, white, turning pink in fading, margin more or less erose, ovate, rounded, with short claws, imbricate in bud.

Stamens.—Fifteen to twenty, inserted on the calyx tube ; filaments thread-like ; anthers purplish, introrse, two-celled ; cells opening longitudinally.

Pistil.—Ovary one, superior, in the bottom of calyx tube, one-celled ; ovules two.

Fruit.—Drupe, oblong-oval, an inch to an inch and a quarter long with a tough, thick, orange red skin, free from bloom, yellow flesh adherent to the stone. Stone oval, compressed. August, September. Cotyledons thick and fleshy.

The Canada Plum is a northern tree, which is distributed through the valley of the St. Lawrence and westward as far as Lake Manitoba ; its range extends southward into New England, New York, and the north-western states. It is found in the neighborhood of streams in rich alluvial soil and along the borders of the forest.

The tree is small and its branches are very stiff and rigid. They have a fashion in their second year of putting out branchlets which are spines, to all intents and purposes, though they become leafy.

Whoever played when a child under a wild plum tree will always remember the " hollow green plums " that frequently hung on the branches or were scattered over the ground in May. They were of full size, pale green, leathery to the touch and hollow, with the exception of a few fibrous bands. They were, indeed, a puzzle to childish eyes, but later we learned that they are caused by a fungus and that they are called plum pockets. This disease also attacks cultivated plums ; the young ovaries, just after the fruit sets, swell, often reach the size of full grown plums, become hollow and soon fall to the ground.

The fruit of the Canada Plum is sold in large quantities in the markets of Canada and the northern states ; it is eaten raw or cooked and is made into preserves and jellies.

The *Prunus americana*, or Wild Plum, is a southern rather than a northern tree. Beginning from middle New Jersey and central New York its range extends westward to the foot-hills of the Rockies and southward to the mountains of Mexico. It has been very generally confounded with *P.*

Fruiting Spray of Canada Plum, *Prunus nigra.*
Leaves 3′ to 5′ long, 1½′ to 3′ broad.

nigra or Canada Plum. The fruit is smaller, rounder than that of the Canada Plum and bright red in color. Many cultivated varieties have been derived from this species, as it quickly responds to the gardener's care ; it also forms an excellent stock upon which to graft the domestic plum.

Professor Sargent says of this tree, " As an ornamental plant *P. americana* has real value ; the long wand-like branches form a wide, graceful head which is handsome in winter and in spring is covered with masses of pure white flowers followed by ample bright foliage and abundant showy fruit."

Exudations of gum from the bark of plum and cherry trees are a very common sight. This is generally known as Cherry gum and is a characteristic of the *Prunus* genus. As it first appears it is liquid and colorless, but with exposure to the air it hardens and becomes dark. When dry it is brittle, with an insipid, sweet or astringent flavor.

The wild plums have been found to be the hosts of the Hop-aphis which is so destructive to the hops just at the time of their maturity and as a consequence it has been recommended that all plum trees in the vicinity of hop fields should be cut down.

WILD RED CHERRY. BIRD CHERRY

Prunus pennsylvánica.

A rapid-growing short-lived tree with bitter aromatic bark and leaves, thirty to forty feet in height, regular slender branches which form a narrow head more or less rounded at the summit ; often in the north a shrub only. Roots fibrous. Common throughout the northern states ; prefers a rich moist soil ; reaches its greatest size on the mountains of Tennessee and often occupies large areas after they have been cleared by fire of their original forests. Will grow in exposed locations.

Bark.—Dark, red brown, conspicuously marked with lenticels, smooth and polished on young stems and branches, but on older trunks separates horizontally into broad papery plates. Branchlets

Fruiting Branch of Wild Red Cherry, *Prunus pennsylvanica*.

Leaves 3' to 5' long.   Cherries ¼' in diameter.

light red and lustrous, finally red brown. They develop in their second year spur-like branchlets.

Wood.—Light brown, sapwood pale yellow; light, soft, close-grained. Sp. gr., 0.5023; weight of cu. ft., 31.30 lbs.

Winter Buds.—Brown, small, acute, often aggregated.

Leaves.—Alternate or in pairs, simple, oblong-lanceolate, three to five inches long, three-quarters of an inch to an inch broad, wedge-shaped or rounded at base, serrate, acute or acuminate. Feather veined. They come out of the bud conduplicate and bronze green; when full grown are bright lustrous green above, paler beneath. In autumn they turn a bright yellow. Petioles slender, grooved, smooth or hairy, often glandular above the middle. Stipules acuminate, serrate and early deciduous.

Flowers.—May, when leaves are half grown. Perfect, white, one-half inch across, borne on slender pedicels in four or five-flowered umbels, generally clustered, two or three together.

Calyx.—Campanulate, smooth, five-lobed; lobes obtuse, tipped with red, finally reflexed, imbricate in bud.

Corolla.—Petals five, cream-white, one-fourth of an inch long, nearly orbicular, with short claws, inserted on the calyx tube.

Stamens.—Fifteen to twenty, inserted on calyx cup; filaments thread-like, smooth; anthers introrse, two-celled; cells opening longitudinally.

Pistil.—Ovary one, superior, set in the calyx cup, smooth, one-celled; style filiform; stigma capitate; ovules two.

Fruit.—Drupe, globular, one-fourth of an inch in diameter, tipped with remnants of the style, light red with thin skin and sour flesh. July. Stone oblong; cotyledons thick and fleshy.

The ease with which the seeds of *Prunus pennsylvanica* are disseminated by birds and mountain streams, their vitality and power of germination in soil where the upper layers of humus have been destroyed by fire, and the rapid growth of the young plants, which soon form a covering for longer-lived trees, constitute the chief value and interest of this plant, which in the northern part of the country east of the mid-continental plateau, has played an important part in the reproduction and preservation of the forests.

—Garden and Forest.

The range of the Wild Red Cherry is northern, it rarely goes south and then only by way of the mountain tops. In its best estate the tree is fifty feet high, but ordinarily it is much smaller and it often constitutes the bulk of the undergrowth of a forest. It bears the reddish brown, shining bark characteristic of all the cherries, which peels off in horizontal strips which is also a characteristic of the cherries.

It loves ravines and rocky woods, will grow and flourish directly on the southern shore of Lake Erie, taking " Freedom's northern wind " all winter without the slightest detriment to its well-being.

It blooms profusely in early spring before the leaves are very much in evidence ; the tiny white blossoms are borne in clusters of five to eight-flowered umbels, and fairly cover the tree.

The shining green leaves are thickly set upon the spray making a denser foliage than that of the Black Cherry, and by the middle of July all the branches of a fruiting tree are so covered with clusters of berries as to make it as a whole look red. They do not remain long, however, for the birds love them, sour as they are, and carry them away in a few days.

When midsummer comes the leaves frequently take the poise of the peach leaf, curving in at the edges and drooping curved from the branch.

CHOKE CHERRY, WILD CHERRY

Prùnus virginiàna.

A shrub throughout the north, only becoming a tree in the south-western part of the United States.

Bark.—Dark brown, slightly fissured. Branchlets at first light brown or reddish green, later they become darker brown tinged with red, and finally dark brown ; outer layer of bark separates easily in horizontal bands from the inner. Inner bark has a disagreeable odor.

Wood.—Light brown ; heavy, hard, close-grained. Sp. gr., 0.6951 ; weight of cu. ft., 43.32 lbs.

Winter Buds.—Chestnut brown, acute or obtuse. Inner scales enlarge when spring growth begins, and often become an inch long.

Leaves.—Alternate, oval, two to four inches long, one to two inches broad, wedge-shaped, or rounded at base, serrate, acuminate. Feather-veined. They come out of the bud conduplicate, pale, hairy ; when full grown are bright green above, paler beneath. In autumn they turn yellow. Petioles grooved, slender, two glands near the apex, sometimes many-glandular. Stipules lanceolate, acute, serrate, early deciduous.

Flowers.—May, after the leaves. Perfect, white, borne in a many flowered raceme, three to six inches long, one-half to one-third of an inch in diameter.

Calyx.—Cup-shaped, five-lobed ; lobes, short, obtuse, reflexed, deciduous.

Corolla.—Petals five, white, orbicular, with short claws, inserted on the calyx tube, imbricate in bud.

Stamens.—Fifteen to twenty, inserted on calyx tube ; style short, thick ; stigma broad.

Pistil.—Ovary one, superior, at the base of the calyx tube ; ovules two.

Fruit.—Drupe, globular, dark red, or nearly black, or yellow, with shining skin, dark red flesh. In taste astringent, though there is much difference in the product of different bushes. Stone oblong-ovate ; cotyledons thick and fleshy.

> The Cherrie trees yeeld great store of cherries which grow on clusters like grapes ; they be much smaller than our English Cherrie, nothing neare so good if they be not very ripe ; they so furred the mouth that the tongue will cleave to the roofe, and the throate was horse with swallowing those red Bullies (as I may call them), being little better in taste. English ordering may bring them to be an English Cherrie, but yet they are as wilde as the Indians.
>
> —WOOD. " New England's Prospects."

Our early writer seems to have learned all there is to know about Choke Cherries, and every one whose childhood was spent in New England or the middle states has had a similar experience. Such an one would never think of the Choke Cherry as a tree. To him it is always a bush, a bush of varying height growing by creek and river side, in fence corners, at the edge of thickets, and bearing long clusters of berries of different degrees of harshness and astringency. But in that wonderful region round about Nebraska, northern Texas and Indian Territory where every vegetable creature with the slightest aspirations toward treehood seems able to gratify them, our humble Choke Cherry stretches its stem, lengthens its branches and becomes a tree. There is, however, no record that by growing larger it has grown better, the fruit is still harsh and astringent, loved, indeed, by the birds, but forsaken by the children when they can get anything better. It is recorded, that in the early days the Indians of the north and west and central part of the

Fruiting Spray of Choke Cherry, *Prunus virginiana*.
Leaves 2′ to 4′ long. 1′ to 2′ broad.

continent prized it highly, and that it was to them an important article of food.

However, the Choke Cherry has recently come into extensive cultivation on the clay flats bordering the Richelieu and St. Lawrence Rivers in the province of Quebec. It is cultivated mostly in tree form and the fruit varies greatly, not only in size and color but also in degree of astringency.

Professor Sargent says: "This is the most widely distributed North American tree. It is found within the arctic circle, ranging across the continent from the Atlantic to the Pacific, it extends southward until it reaches the Gulf states and northern Mexico."

All our wild cherries and plums carry with them a menace to the health and well-being of cultivated cherries and plums. For all are subject to a disease native to this continent, known as Black Knot. This warty excrescence was formerly supposed to be caused by insects, but it is now known to be the result of a fungus which attacks the tree and the disease easily passes from the native to the cultivated species. In many districts it is now impossible to grow cherries and plums because of it. The Choke Cherry is especially subject to its attack, and this makes the tree a dangerous neighbor to orchards of cultivated fruit.

BLACK CHERRY

Prùnus seròtina

A tree with a stout sturdy trunk, spreading branches and round head, sometimes a narrow oblong head. Usually forty to fifty feet high, but on the slopes of the southern Alleghanies reaches the height of one hundred feet. Prefers a rich moist soil, but will grow on light sandy soil, and will also endure the winds of the sea-shore. Grows rapidly. Widely distributed by the birds.

Bark.—On old trunks blackish and rough, broken into small irregular roundish plates; on young trunks and large limbs smooth and shining, red brown marked with scattered lines and sometimes separating into horizontal bands which curl at the edges. Branchlets

Fruiting Branch of Black Cherry, *Prunus serotina.*
Leaves 2′ to 5′ long. Cherries ⅓′ to ½′ in diameter.

pale green or reddish green and smooth, lenticular, later reddish brown, finally become red brown or gray brown. Inner bark has a pleasant and aromatic odor, bitter and aromatic to the taste.

Wood.—Light brown or red, darkening with exposure ; light, strong, close-grained, susceptible of a fine polish. Of great value in cabinet work and interior finish of houses, now becoming scarce. Sp. gr., 0.5822 ; weight of cu. ft., 36.28 lbs.

Winter Buds.—Chestnut brown, obtuse, one-half to two-thirds of an inch long. When spring growth begins the inner scales enlarge and become one-half to two-thirds of an inch in length.

Leaves.—Alternate, simple, oblong to lanceolate-oblong, two to five inches long, an inch to an inch and a half broad, wedge-shaped or rounded at base, serrate, edges often crinkled, gradually acuminate or rarely rounded at apex. Feather-veined, midrib grooved above, prominent beneath, primary veins slender. They come out of the bud conduplicate, reddish green ; when full grown are deep shining green above, paler beneath ; in autumn they turn a clear bright yellow. Petioles slender, terete, often marked with dark red glands. Stipules caducous.

Flowers.—May, June, when leaves are half grown. Perfect, white, about one-fourth of an inch across, borne in narrow, many-flowered racemes three to four inches long.

Calyx.—Cup-shaped tube, five-lobed, lobes obtuse, reflexed, persistent, imbricate in bud.

Corolla.—Petals five, white, obovate, inserted on the calyx tube, imbricate in bud.

Stamens.—Fifteen to twenty, inserted on the calyx tube with the petals ; filaments thread-like ; anthers introrse, two-celled ; cells opening longitudinally.

Pistil.—Ovary superior, one, set in the bottom of the calyx tube ; stigma thick, club-shaped.

Fruit.—Drupe, depressed-globular, one-third to one-half inch in diameter, shining black skin, dark purple juicy flesh. Calyx lobes persistent on the fruit. August, September. Stone oblong-ovate ; cotyledons thick and fleshy.

Wild cherry, they grow in clusters like grapes, of the same bigness, blackish red when ripe, and of a harsh taste.

—JOSSELYN. " New England Rarities."

Prunus serotina is very generally known because of its cherries. These cherries are flattened juicy globes the size of large peas, with a shining black skin and dark purple flesh ; borne in a somewhat straggling raceme. When ripe they are slightly bitter with a pleasant vinous flavor and from the standpoint of one who ate them in childhood delicious. When

Trunk of Black Cherry, *Prunus serotina.*

macerated and soaked in rum or brandy they give to the liquor a peculiar and agreeable flavor, making what is known as Cherry Bounce. This flavor is due to a principle called amygdalin, found also in laurel leaves, bitter almonds, peach and plum stones, which under the action of a ferment breaks up into grape sugar, oil of bitter almonds, and hydrocyanic or prussic acid. This active principle exists in very many of the *Rosaceæ*, notably in *Prunus caroliniana*, a southern evergreen species which is extensively used in the south as a hedge plant. It is there against the law to throw the prunings of this plant into the street or where they may be eaten by cattle. Birds in fact have been known to be overcome by a too greedy consumption of black cherries.

The bark of the Black Cherry is bitter and aromatic and held a large place among the home remedies of an earlier generation.

The flowers are small, closely set by short stems in a simple raceme. The central axis is erect or curved upward in flowering, which begins at the bottom; afterward it bends with the weight of the fruit. Only a small proportion of the flowers produce fruit.

The tree is large and sturdy with a spreading handsome head, and may be easily known by its smooth, shining, reddish brown branches, for only the trunk becomes rough, and in young trees that is smooth. The spray is slender and pendulous. The smooth shining leaves are set alternately and rather close together, and often in midsummer heat they assume the poise of the ash and at a distance when only part of the tree can be seen it may easily be mistaken for an ash.

The Black Cherry grows very rapidly, often adding an inch a year to its diameter. The wood is firm, close-grained, of a light red, darkening with age. It takes a fine polish and when perfectly seasoned will not shrink or warp, and is much used in the manufacture of furniture.

CRAB APPLE. FRAGRANT CRAB

Pýrus coronària

Pyrus is the classical name of the pear tree, which was adopted by Linnæus for this genus.

Often a bushy shrub with rigid, contorted branches but frequently becomes a small tree with a broad open head. Prefers rich moist soil ; is most abundant in the middle and western states, reaches its greatest size in the valleys of the lower Ohio basin.

Bark.—Reddish brown, longitudinally fissured, with surface separating in narrow scales. Branchlets at first coated with thick white tomentum, later they become smooth reddish brown ; they develop in their second year long, spur-like branches and sometimes absolute thorns an inch or more in length.

Wood.—Reddish brown, sapwood yellow ; heavy, close-grained, not strong. Used for the handles of tools and small domestic articles. Sp. gr., 0.7048 ; weight of cu. ft., 43.92.

Winter Buds.—Bright red, obtuse, minute. Inner scales grow with the growing shoot, become half an inch long and bright red before they fall.

Leaves.—Alternate, simple, ovate, three to four inches long, one and one-half to two inches broad, obtuse, subcordate or acute at base, incisely serrate, often three-lobed on vigorous shoots, acute at apex. Feather-veined, midrib and primary veins grooved above, prominent beneath. They come out of the bud involute, red bronze, tomentose and downy ; when full grown are bright dark green above, paler beneath. In autumn they turn yellow. Petioles slender, long, often with two dark glands near the middle. Stipules filiform, half an inch long, early deciduous.

Flowers.—May, June, when leaves are nearly grown. Perfect, rose-colored, fragrant, one and one-half inch to two inches across. Borne in five or six-flowered umbels on slender pedicels.

Calyx.—Urn-shaped, downy or tomentose, five-lobed ; lobes slender, acute, persistent, imbricate in bud.

Corolla.—Petals five, rose colored, obovate, rounded above, with long narrow claws, undulate or crenulate at margin, inserted on the calyx tube, imbricate in bud.

Stamens.—Ten to twenty, inserted on the calyx tube, shorter than the petals ; filaments by a partial twist forming a tube narrowed in the middle and enlarged above ; anthers introrse, two-celled ; cells opening longitudinally.

133

Pistil.—Of five carpels inserted in the bottom of the calyx tube and united into an inferior ovary; styles five; stigma capitate; ovules two in each cell.

Fruit.—Pome or apple ripening in October. Depressed-globular, an inch to an inch and a half in diameter, crowned with calyx lobes and remnant of filaments; yellow green, delightfully fragrant, surface sometimes waxy. Flesh white, delicate and charged with malic acid. Seeds two or, by abortion, one in each cell, chestnut brown. shining; cotyledons fleshy.

> As the apple tree among the trees of the wood,
> So is my beloved among the sons.
>
> —SONG OF SOLOMON.

Kalm, who was one of the twelve men whom Linnæus called his apostles and sent forth to explore the vegetable world, writes thus from America:

"Crab-trees are a species of wild apple-trees, which grow in the woods and glades, but especially on little hillocks, near rivers. In New Jersey the tree is rather scarce; but in Pennsylvania it is plentiful. Some people had planted a single tree of this kind near their houses on account of the fine smells which its flowers afford. It had begun to open some of its flowers about a day or two ago; however, most of them were not yet open. They are exactly like the blossoms of the common apple-trees except that the color is a little more reddish in the Crab-trees; though some kinds of the cultivated trees have flowers which are very near as red; but the smell distinguishes them plainly; for the wild trees have a very pleasant smell, somewhat like the raspberry.

"The apples, or crabs, are small, sour and unfit for anything but to make vinegar of. They lie under the trees all winter and acquire a yellow color. They seldom begin to rot before spring comes on."

When man emerges into history he has the apple in his hand and the dog by his side. We have no reason to believe that the European or Asiatic forbear from which the apple of civilization is descended was any less harsh in taste or any larger in size than our own crab. Indeed, were all the apples of civilization swept out of existence they could doubtless be regained by the cultivation of our native tree. As it is, it stands in all its wild and untrained beauty, its greatest charm lying, as Kalm clearly apprehended, in its rose-colored blossoms, exquisite in tint and delicious in fragrance. Its flowering time is ten days to two weeks later than that of the domestic apple, and its fragrant fruit clings to the branches on clustered stems long after the leaves have fallen.

Fruiting Spray of Crab Apple, *Pyrus coronaria.*
Leaves 3′ to 4′, Apple 1′ to 1½′ in diameter.

MOUNTAIN ASH

Pýrus americàna

A small tree which loves the north and climbs the high mountain ranges of Virginia and North Carolina, but does not cross the Rockies. Prefers a rich moist soil and the borders of swamps, but will flourish on rocky hillsides. Attains its largest size on the northern shores of Lakes Huron and Superior ; in the United States it is usually a shrub.

Bark.—Light gray, smooth, surface scaly. Branchlets downy at first, later become smooth, brown tinged with red, lenticular, finally they become darker and the papery outer layer becomes easily separable.

Wood.—Pale brown ; light, soft, close-grained but weak. Sp. gr., 0.5451 ; weight of cu. ft., 33.97 lbs.

Winter Buds.—Dark red, acute, one-fourth to three-quarters of an inch long. Inner scales are very tomentose and enlarge with the growing shoot.

Leaves.—Alternate, compound, unequally pinnate, six to ten inches long, with slender, grooved, dark green or red petiole. Leaflets thirteen to seventeen, lanceolate or long oval, two to three inches long, one-half to two-thirds broad, unequally wedge-shaped or rounded at base, serrate, acuminate, sessile, the terminal one sometimes borne on a stalk half an inch long, feather-veined, midrib prominent beneath, grooved above. They come out of the bud downy, conduplicate ; when full grown are smooth, dark yellow green above and paler beneath. In autumn they turn a clear yellow. Stipules leaf-like, caducous.

Flowers.—May, June, after the leaves are full grown. Perfect, white, one-eighth of an inch across, borne in flat compound cymes three or four inches across. Bracts and bractlets acute, minute, caducous.

Calyx.—Urn-shaped, hairy, five-lobed ; lobes, short, acute, imbricate in bud.

Corolla.—Petals five, creamy white, orbicular, contracted into short claws, inserted on calyx, imbricate in bud.

Stamens.—Twenty to thirty, inserted on calyx tube ; filaments thread-like ; anthers introrse, two-celled ; cells opening longitudinally.

Pistil.—Two to three carpels inserted in the bottom of the calyx tube and united into an inferior ovary. Styles two to three ; stigmas capitate ; ovules two in each cell.

Fruiting Spray of Mountain Ash, *Pyrus americana*.
Leaves 6′ to 10′ long. Leaflets 2′ to 3′ long.

Fruit.—Berry-like pome, glc ,ular, one-quarter of an inch across, bright red, borne in cymous clusters. Ripens in October and remains on the tree all winter. Flesh thin and sour, charged with malic acid ; seeds light brown, oblong, compressed ; cotyledons fleshy.

> The mountain Ash,
> Decked with autumnal berries that outshine
> Springs richest blossoms, yields a splendid show
> Amid the leafy woods.
>
> —WORDSWORTH.

Our Mountain Ash, *Pyrus americana*, so nearly resembles the European, *Pyrus aucuparia*, in general appearance of leaves and blossoms that many botanists consider it merely a variety ; but in form it differs considerably, nor does it ever become so handsome a tree.

The berries look as if they might be good to eat, but it is evident that the birds do not find them so. As a matter of fact they are sour, bitter, and of a disagreeable flavor, and go untouched by the birds so long as any other fruit is within reach ; and are finally eaten under protest.

The Mountain Ash which is usually planted in lawns and yards is the European species, and it is well worthy of cultivation on account of its foliage, its blossoms and its berries.

In Europe many curious superstitions hang about the Roan or Rowan-tree, as the Mountain Ash is there called, and a century ago it was considered by the lower classes as a sovereign charm against witches. The more uncivilized and ignorant a people, the more do they consider themselves in danger from witchcraft and evil spirits. Many plants such as St. John's-wort and clover were considered specifics against the wiles of witches, but a twig of the Rowan-tree was believed to surpass them all. For this purpose it was made into walking-sticks or branches of it were hung about the house and stables. The explanation of this is that the tree was in some way connected with the ancient Druidical worship, and the superstitions of to-day are but the far-off echoes of former religious beliefs.

Fruiting Spray of European Mountain Ash, *Pyrus aucuparia*.

A stanza of an ancient song runs thus :—

> Their spells were vain ; the hags returned
> To the queen in sorrowful mood,
> Crying that witches have no power
> Where there is roan-tree wood.

Pyrus sambucifolia is a tree of more northern range than *P. americana.* In general appearance it is not unlike it, but both blossoms and fruit are larger.

COCKSPUR THORN. NEWCASTLE THORN

Cratægus crus-gálli.

Cratægus is of Greek derivation, referring to the strength of the wood produced by the different species. *Crus-galli* refers to the character of the thorns. The name of Newcastle Thorn had its origin in the fact that this thorn was once largely used as a hedge plant by the farmers of Newcastle County, Delaware.

A small tree with stout. rigid, spreading branches and a broad flat or round head. Branches usually armed with long slender spines. Roots fibrous. Loves rich soil along the margins of swamps or near streams ; succeeds as a hedge plant.

Bark.—Light reddish brown, or ashy gray, surface separated into scales. Branchlets at first green but soon become light brown or gray tinged with brown. In their second year they become armed with spines and these continue to enlarge for many years, often becoming many branched and six or eight inches long.

Wood.—Reddish brown ; heavy, hard, close-grained with a satiny surface. Sp. gr., 0.7194 ; weight of cu. ft., 44.83 lbs.

Winter Buds.—Chestnut brown, obtuse, one-eighth of an inch long. Inner scales grow with the growing shoot and often become one-half an inch long and bright red before they fall.

Leaves.—Alternate, simple, obovate-cuneiform to broadly oval or linear-oblong, one to three inches long. tapering from the middle to the petiole, sharply serrate except toward the base, acute or rounded at apex. Feather-veined ; midrib and primary veins narrow. They come out of the bud conduplicate, when full grown are smooth, thick, dark green and shining above, paler beneath. In autumn they turn orange and scarlet. Petioles short, broad. Stipules vary in form from linear, acute to obliquely ovate, early deciduous,

Cockspur Thorn, *Cratægus crus-galli.*
Leaves 1′ to 3′ long.

Flowers.—May, June; when leaves are full grown. Perfect, white, two-thirds of an inch across. Borne in many-flowered thin-branched racemose corymbs, the lower branches from the axils of leaves. Pedicels slender, one-half to one inch in length. Bracts and bractlets acute, half an inch long.

Calyx.—Urn-shaped, narrow, five-lobed; lobes linear-lanceolate, serrate, finally reflexed, persistent, imbricate in bud.

Corolla.—Petals five, round, white, inserted on the calyx tube, imbricate in bud.

Stamens.—Ten, inserted with the petals; filaments short; anthers introrse, two-celled; cells opening longitudinally.

Pistil.—Ovary of two or three carpels inserted in the bottom of calyx tube and united with it; styles two; stigmas capitate; ovules two.

Fruit.—Drupe-like pome with bony stones, globular or pyriform, one-third to one-half an inch long, crowned with the calyx lobes, dull red; flesh thin, dry; nutlets one-fourth of an inch long, rounded at both ends, two to three-grooved on back. September; remains on the tree until spring.

When it was made certain that the Hawthorn, *C. oxyacantha,* which makes up the great body of the hedges of England, really would not flourish in this country, the attention of farmers and gardeners was turned toward our native thorns to see if any of them were available as hedge plants. The Cockspur Thorn is the only one that has at all proved itself equal to the requirements, yet since the introduction of the Osage Orange it has fallen into disuse. But cultivated as an ornamental tree it is particularly attractive. It flowers late, after its large and shining leaves are fully developed, grouping in this respect with the Horse-chestnut, the Locust, and the Catalpa. Then its fruit hangs red upon the tree all winter long; in autumn the leaves turn a bright orange and scarlet, and when the tree stands leafless the spread of its branches is very beautiful.

The leaves of the Cockspur Thorn are likely to vary considerably on different individuals and not infrequently on the same individual. Six varieties are reported to be in cultivation, each distinguished by its leaf.

WHITE THORN. SCARLET HAW. SCARLET FRUITED THORN

Cratægus coccinea.

A low tree fifteen to twenty feet high with short stout trunk, crooked spreading branches forming a broad flat head; common throughout the northern states. Roots fibrous. Found either in thickets or solitary, in upland woods, in rocky pastures or near the borders of streams.

Bark.—Light brown, or ashy gray, slightly fissured surface broken into small scales. Branchlets at first light green, lustrous, later reddish or light brown or light gray, finally become armed with slender straight or slightly curved, brown, shining, persistent spines one or two inches long.

Wood.—Brown, tinged with red; heavy, hard and close-grained. Sp. gr., 0.8618; weight of cu. ft., 53.71 lbs.

Winter Buds.—Globular, tiny, chestnut brown. Inner scales grow with the growing shoot, becoming an inch long before they fall.

Leaves.—Alternate, simple, broad-ovate, one to five inches long, wedge-shaped, rounded or truncate at base, acutely cut or slightly five to nine-lobed, sharply and finely serrate, acute. Feather-veined, midrib prominent, primary veins strongest toward the base. They come out of the bud, conduplicate, green; when full grown they are thin, smooth, shining, bright green above, paler green beneath. They turn bright yellow in autumn. Petioles long, slender, grooved, smooth or hairy. Stipules are leaf-like, serrate, acute, early deciduous.

Flowers.—May, when leaves are nearly grown. Perfect, white, borne in few-flowered corymbs, on slender pedicels; vary in size from one-half inch to one inch in diameter with strong and disagreeable odor.

Calyx.—Urn-shaped, five-lobed; lobes much shorter than the petals, finally reflexed, imbricate in bud.

Petals.—Five, inserted on the calyx tube, white, obovate, erose, imbricate in bud.

Stamens.—Ten, inserted with the petals; filaments thread-like; anthers purple, introrse, two-celled; cells opening longitudinally.

Pistil.—Ovary of two to five carpels, inserted in the bottom of the calyx tube and united with it; styles two to five; stigmas capitate; ovules two.

Fruit.—Drupe-like pome with bony stones, borne in umbels of two or three; bright scarlet, crowned with the calyx lobes; globular or slightly elongated, one-third to one-half an inch in diameter. September or October; remains all winter, somewhat edible.

Professor Sargent calls this a " bushy, intricately branched tree " and any one who has ever hunted among its branches for birds' nests will fully appreciate the felicitous characterization. This is the thorn of old pasture fields, and the race of sparrows have ever sought safety for their nests among its twisted, rigid, well-armed twigs.

The spines are not mature except on third year wood. They are undeveloped branches and appear from buds growing in the axils of former leaves. On the second year wood they reach three-eighths of an inch in length and in winter are crowned with a single globular bud, this continues the growth for another year. Then they become sharp and pointed and further growth ceases except as they enlarge with the branch.

The haws of all the thorns are alike in this, that they suggest tiny apples, but the ratio of seed to flesh is out of all reason, from the standpoint of the consumer. It is apparent that even the birds take this view of the case, for the scarlet haws are frequently left on the branches all winter long ; while their neighbors the black cherries are eagerly eaten and the sassafras berries are scarcely allowed to ripen. They are smooth, of a beautiful shining red, but they keep the promise to the eye only to break it to the hope.

SCARLET HAW. HAWTHORN

Cratægus móllis.

A small tree, with straight trunk, spreading and contorted branches, which form a round, compact head. Roots fibrous. Grows on margins of swamps, along the banks of streams, on praiies in rich soil.

Bark.—Reddish brown to ashy gray. The surface broken into small scales Branchlets when young are tomentous, then become orange brown and lustrous, finally ashy gray. Stout, zigzag, armed with stout, chestnut brown, shining spines two or three inches long, these at length become ashy gray.

Wood. — Light brown ; heavy, hard, close-grained. Sp. gr., ɔ.7953 ; weight of cu. ft., 49.56 lbs.

Fruiting Branch of White Thorn, *Cratægus coccinea.*
Leaves 1' to 5' long.   Haws ⅓' to ½' in diameter.

Winter Buds.—Obtuse, chestnut brown, one-eighth of an inch long. Inner scales grow with the growing shoot, becoming nearly an inch long before they fall.

Leaves.—Alternate, simple, broadly ovate, almost orbicular, two to four inches long, one and one-half inches to three broad, wedge-shaped, truncate or rounded at base, sharply incised with many shallow lobes, finely and unevenly serrate, acute. Feather-veined, midrib and primary veins prominent beneath and depressed above. They come out of the bud conduplicate, pale green, coated with tomentum or hairy; when full grown are then smooth or rough, light green above, paler beneath. Petioles grooved, stout, hairy, an inch to two inches in length. Stipules leaf-like, acute or linear, early deciduous.

Flowers.—May, when leaves are half grown. Perfect, white, an inch to an inch and a quarter across when expanded, borne in broad, stout, branched, hairy corymbs.

Calyx.—Urn-shaped, tomentous or hairy, five-lobed; lobes acute, serrate, finally reflexed and persistent, imbricate in bud. Calyx and peduncles glandular.

Corolla.—Petals five, white, inserted on the calyx, rounded, imbricate in bud.

Stamens.—Ten, inserted with the petals; filaments thread-like; anthers introrse, two-celled; cells opening longitudinally.

Pistil.—Ovaries inferior, two to five, inserted in the bottom of the calyx tube and united with it; styles two to five; stigmas capitate; ovules two in each cell.

Fruit.—Drupe-like pome with bony stones, globular or lengthened or pyriform, crowned with the calyx lobes, bright orange scarlet covered with glaucous bloom, one inch to one and a quarter inches in length. Ripens in September, falls at once. Flesh yellow, juicy, slightly acid and with a pleasant flavor; nutlets lunate.

This is the handsomest of the American Hawthorns and bears the only haws that by any stretch of the imagination could be considered edible. The flesh is thin for an apple, but thick for a haw and of a pleasant flavor. The fruit falls in September as soon as it ripens. For many years this Haw was confused with *C. coccinea*, but there are marked differences between them. The fruit is larger, the leaf is much larger, broader, more nearly orbicular, nor is it so deeply cut. This species is admirably adapted as an ornament to the lawn —its branches touch the ground—it will grow in a close pyramidal head—is very free from insects' attacks, it flowers and fruits profusely—and in every way is satisfactory.

Fruiting Branch of Scarlet Haw, *Cratægus mollis*.
Leaves 2′ to 4′ long. Haws 1′ to 1¼′ in length.

All our thorns are attractive in habit, foliage, flower and fruit and are worthy of cultivation. One difficulty in obtaining them lies in the slow germination of the seed, which often requires two years.

BLACK THORN. HAWTHORN

Cratægus tomentòsa.

Not very common tree, fifteen or twenty feet in height, with slender contorted branches which form a wide flat head, often a shrub with many straggling stems. Roots fibrous. Branchlets armed with sharp slender spines an inch to an inch and a half in length.

Bark.—Dark brown to ashy gray, fissured and broken into small scales. Branchlets coated at first with thick pale tomentum, later they become dark orange color, finally they become ashy gray.

Wood.—Bright reddish brown; heavy, hard, close-grained. Sp. gr., 0.7585; weight of cu. ft., 47.57 lbs.

Winter Buds.—Small, globular, chestnut brown. Inner scales grow with the growing shoot becoming nearly an inch long before they fall.

Leaves.—Alternate, simple, ovate to ovate-oblong, two to five inches long, incisely lobed and sharply and finely serrate, except at the base, gradually narrowing at the base and running into winged petioles, acute or rarely rounded at the apex. Conspicuously reticulate-veined, midrib broad and primary veins prominent. They come out of the bud conduplicate, when full grown are thin gray green, smooth above, but very downy beneath. In autumn they turn orange and scarlet. Petioles winged, grooved, sometimes glandular. Stipules linear, glandular, serrate, early deciduous.

Flowers.—May, June, later than the White Thorn. Perfect, white, half an inch across, very ill scented, borne in broad, leafy, downy, slender-branched cymes.

Calyx.—Urn-shaped, coated with pale tomentum, five-lobed; lobes lanceolate, serrate, acute, often glandular, finally reflexed, persistent, imbricate in bud.

Corolla.—Petals five, obovate, erose, inserted in the calyx tube, imbricate in bud.

Stamens.—Fifteen to twenty, inserted with the petals; filaments thread-like; anthers introrse, two-celled; cells opening longitudinally.

Pistil.—Ovary inferior, two to five carpels inserted at the bottom of the calyx tube and united with it.

Sprays of Black Thorn, *Cratægus tomentosa.*
Leaves 2′ to 5′ long.

Fruit.—Drupe-like pome with bony stones, ovoid, rarely globular, dull red, one-half inch long, crowned with calyx lobes, erect ; flesh thin and dry. Ripens in September and October and remains on branches all winter. Nutlets rounded, obscurely two-grooved on the back.

This Hawthorn is not very common in the northern states, is found most abundantly in central New York. It prefers rich alluvial soil and is found on the margin of forests. Its brilliant autumn foliage and its red winter berries recommend it as an ornamental plant. It comes into flower somewhat later than the others.

DOTTED HAW

Cratægus punctàta.

A thick wide spreading tree, forming a broad, round or flat-topped head. Branches slender, rigid, armed with straight, sharp, light brown spines, two to three inches long, sometimes unarmed. Roots fibrous. Ranges from Quebec to Ontario and southward to middle Tennessee, and along the mountains to Georgia and Alabama. Prefers rich moist soil, will grow in upland pastures where it forms thickets.

Bark.—Dark, reddish brown, broken into long scales. Branchlets at first downy, later they become light brown ; in second year are ashy gray, silvery white, or light brown.

Wood.—Bright reddish brown ; heavy, hard, close-grained. Sp. gr., 0.7681 ; weight of cu. ft., 47.87 lbs.

Winter Buds.—Pale brown, shining, obtuse.

Leaves.—Alternate, simple, wedge-obovate, two to three inches long, base wedge-shaped, tapering from above the middle of the leaf into long winged petioles, sharply and unevenly serrate above the middle, sometimes incisely cut, often entire below, apex acute or rounded. Feather-veined, midrib and primary veins depressed above, prominent beneath. They come out of the bud conduplicate, when full grown are thick and firm, pale gray green, smooth above, paler and hairy beneath. In autumn they turn bright orange or orange and scarlet. Petioles grooved, winged. Stipules lanceolate, glandular, serrated, acute, and early deciduous.

Flowers.—May, June, after the leaves. Perfect, white, one-half to three-quarters of an inch across, borne in broad, thick-branched downy or tomentous corymbs. Pedicels are stout and hairy.

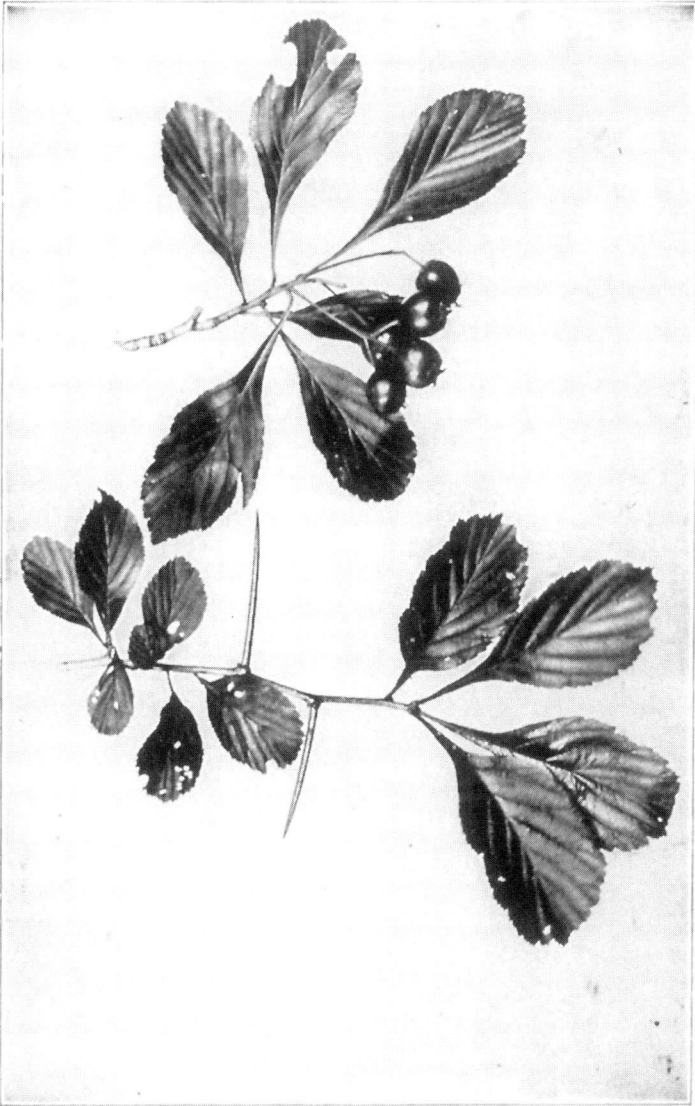

Sprays of Dotted Haw, *Cratægus punctata*.
Leaves 2′ to 3′ long.

Calyx.—Urn-shaped, more or less tomentose, five-lobed; **lobes** acute, finally reflexed, persistent, imbricate in bud.

Corolla.—Petals five, obovate, erose, inserted on the calyx, imbricate in bud.

Stamens.—Fifteen to twenty, inserted with the petals; filaments thread-like; anthers introrse, two-celled; cells opening longitudinally.

Pistils.—Ovary of two to five carpels inserted in the bottom of **the** calyx tube, united with it; styles two to five.

Fruit.—Drupe-like pome with bony seeds, globular or elongated, crowned with the calyx lobes, dull red, sometimes yellow, marked by many small white spots, three-fourths to one inch in length; flesh thin and dry; nutlets rounded and grooved on the back. Ripens in September and falls at once. Somewhat edible.

All the thorns are trees of the pasture lands. The common story of them all is that they love the moist, rich, alluvial soil, but failing that they will grow in upland fields, not solitary only but in thickets. Even the best of them in its best estate and in that most favoring region on this continent, northern Louisiana and Texas, can only reach the height of thirty feet, hence they are doomed in the forest to become of the second grade and to grow in the shade. In the forest they are outclassed by many a rapid grower, but in the pastures, not so. The seeds of ash, maple, and willow may lodge in the pasture land, they may find congenial soil and favoring climate, but they have no protection against the grazing flocks and they yield in the contest. But the thorns present so sharp a defence that in time they triumph over the hard conditions and not only live but flourish.

JUNE-BERRY. SHAD BUSH. SERVICE-BERRY.

Amelánchier canadénsis.

Amelanchier is derived from Amelancier, the popular name of the European species.

A medium sized tree with a tall slender trunk and small spreading branches which form a narrow, oblong head. It ranges throughout eastern United States, southward to Florida and westward to Minnesota. Prefers rich soil in upland woods. On the mountains of North Carolina and Tennessee it reaches its greatest size. Roots fibrous.

Bark.—Pale red brown, divided into narrow ridges the surface of which is scaly. Branchlets bright green, later become dark brown or purplish brown, smooth.

Wood.—Dark brown, sometimes tinged with red; heavy, hard, close-grained and strong. Sp. gr., 0.7838; weight of cu. ft., 48.85 lbs.

Winter Buds.—Chestnut brown, acute, one-fourth of an inch long. Inner scales enlarge with the growing shoot and are sometimes an inch long before they fall.

Leaves.—Alternate, simple, ovate to ovate-oblong, three to four inches long, one and a half to two inches broad, cordate or rounded at base, serrate, acute or acuminate. Feather-veined, midrib grooved above, prominent beneath. They come out of the bud conduplicate, reddish brown and hairy, when full grown are smooth, deep green above, paler beneath. In autumn they turn a bright yellow. Petioles slender, grooved. Stipules lanceolate, downy, early deciduous.

Flowers.—April, when leaves are about one-third grown. Perfect, white, borne in racemes from three to five inches long. Each flower has a slender pedicel, furnished with two lanceolate, purplish silky bractlets which fall as the flower opens.

Calyx.—Campanulate, five-lobed; lobes lanceolate, acute, downy, persistent, imbricate in bud.

Corolla.—Petals five, white, strap-shaped, one-half inch to an inch in length, inserted on the calyx tube, imbricate in bud.

Stamens.—Twenty, inserted on the calyx tube; filaments persistent in fruit; anthers introrse, two-celled; cells opening longitudinally.

Pistil.—Ovary two to five-celled, united to calyx tube. Styles two to five, with broad stigmas; ovules two in each cell. When mature each cell has been divided by a cartilaginous partition, giv-ing ten cells and one seed in each.

Fruit.—Berry - like pome, depressed - globulai or pyriform, open at the summit, crowned with the calyx lobes and remnants of the filaments. One-third to one-half of an inch long, rich purple with slight bloom. Ripens in June, is sweet, with delicious flavor. Seeds dark brown; cotyledons thick.

At the time when the hazy, misty cloud of bursting buds rests over the wooded hillside, a single tree suddenly detaches itself from the cloudy mist and stands forth clothed in soft, feathery, indeterminate white. This is the Juneberry, otherwise known as the Shad Bush. This homely name of Shad Bush was given it by the early inhabitants of the eastern states because it chances to bloom by the side of our tidal rivers at the time that the shad ascends them to spawn.

We know that nature's methods are gradual, that species are not cut apart by sharp divisions, but it is not often that we are permitted to trace the process of species-making, step by step. The June-berries permit us to do this. There are in America two well-defined species, the Atlantic, *A. canadensis* and the Pacific, *A. alnifolia ;* they differ in form of flower, shape of leaf, and size of fruit. Yet they are one, though two.

On one side of the continent the mist-laden atmosphere of the low lands and the cold winds from the Atlantic have developed *A. canadensis.* On the other side the subtle influence of a clearer atmosphere, together with a higher altitude and warmer winds has produced *A. alnifolia.*

On the Rocky Mountains where the two forms meet they insensibly melt into each other and it is not possible to say where one species ends and the other begins, nor of many individuals to which household they belong. Both can be referred to an earlier arctic form which, driven southward by the glaciers, returned to such different environments, that two species developed and the intermediate forms persist.

Our June-berry is little known save in its native haunts. Its leaves somewhat resemble those of the pear, but are finer and more delicate, covered with a soft, silken down as they

June-berry, *Amelanchier canadensis.*

Leaves 3′ to 4′ long, 1½′ to 2′ broad.

come from the bud but becoming smooth at maturity. The flowers are in loose racemes at the ends of the branches.

The fruit is delicious and ripens in June. The only objection to the berries is that they are so few, the largest trees rarely produce more than a quart, and the birds, knowing a good thing when they see it, get most of them. It is recorded that the Indians esteemed them highly.

The flora of Japan, which in so many respects resembles that of America, possesses a very superior June-berry which has been introduced into this country and if acclimated will be a grateful addition to our list of fruit trees.

HAMAMEIIDÀCEÆ—WITCH HAZEI FAMILY

WITCH HAZEL

Hamamèlis virginiàna.

Hamamelis is a name anciently applied to a tree which blossomed at the same time as the apple tree. Witch is a modern spelling of the Saxon *wich* or *wych*. The meaning of the word in this connection is doubtful; Loudon refers it to salt springs, moist places; other authorities think it means pendulous, drooping. Two trees are so named—the wych elm and the wych hazel.

A shrub of numerous diverging stems ten to fifteen feet high, becoming a small tree only on the mountains of North and South Carolina and Tennessee. Found in deep ravines, north shaded hillsides and at the edge of woodlands. Roots fibrous.

Bark—Light brown, smooth, scaly, inner bark reddish purple. Branchlets at first scurfy; later smooth, light orange brown, marked with occasional small white dots, finally dark or reddish brown.

Wood.—Light reddish brown, sapwood nearly white; heavy, hard, close-grained. Sp. gr., 0.6856; weight of cu. ft., 42.72 lbs.

Winter Buds.—Acute, slightly falcate, downy, light brown.

Leaves.—Alternate, simple, obovate or oval, four to six inches long, unequal at base, wavy-toothed, acute or rounded at apex. Feather-veined; midrib stout with six to seven pairs of primary veins. They come out of the bud involute, covered with stellate rusty down; when full grown are dark green above, paler beneath; midrib and veins more or less hairy. In autumn they turn yellow with rusty spots. Petioles stout, half an inch to an inch long. Stipules lanceolate, acute, infolding the buds.

Flowers.—October, November. Usually perfect, yellow, borne in three-flowered clusters on axillary, simple or rarely branched peduncles bearing two deciduous bractlets, each flower surrounded by two or three ovate bracts, slightly united at base to form an involucre. Bracts and bractlets coated with rusty hairs. The clusters of flower buds appear in August, developed from the axils of the leaves of the year.

Calyx.—Deeply four-parted, very downy, orange brown within, imbricate in bud, persistent, cohering with the base of the ovary. Two or three bractlets appear at base.

Corolla.—Petals four, inserted on the receptacle, yellow, strap-shaped, narrow, one-half to two-thirds of an inch long, alternate with the calyx lobes, involute in bud.

Stamens.—Eight, inserted in the receptacle, very short, the four which are alternate with the petals, anther-bearing, the others imperfect and scale-like. Filaments short, connective thickened and prolonged; anthers, introrse, two-celled; cells opening at the side from within by persistent valves.

Pistil.—Ovary of two carpels, free at their apex, inserted at the bottom of the cup-like receptacle, partly superior; styles two, awl-shaped, spreading, persistent, stigmatic at apex; ovules one or two in each cell.

Fruit.—A yellow brown, two-celled, woody pod, each cell containing one black shining seed. Each cell bursts open when ripe and projects the little nut from five to fifteen feet. Ripens in October when the flowers are expanding.

> Through the gray and sombre wood
> Again-t the dusk of fir and pine
> Last of their floral sisterhood
> The hazel's yellow blossoms shine.
> —JOHN G. WHITTIER.

This shrubby little tree is one of the most curious and interesting plants in our northern flora. When all other trees are making ready for winter, when its own leaves are yellow and falling, it bursts forth into abundant bloom. The clusters of tiny yellow flowers crowd upon a branch already laden with the ripe nutlets of last year's blossoms, and wave in beauty throughout the entire month of November. This peculiarity, together with the suggestive name "witch," is doubtless an explanation of the fact that those persons who profess to be able to indicate the position of hidden springs of water prefer, as divining rods, the forked twigs of Witch Hazel.

Although the flowers appear in October no growth takes place in the ovary until the following spring, the calyx lobes

Witch Hazel, *Hamamelis virginiana.*
Leaves 4′ to 6′ long.

simply surround and protect it The petals are spirally involute in æstivation, that is, each one is rolled in upon itself and when fully expanded they still look crumpled and wavy.

An interesting peculiarity of the fruit is the way the tiny nuts are discharged from their woody pod. As the pod bursts the contraction of its edges presses upon the enclosed seeds and causes them to fly to a distance of several feet. Bring home in November a fruiting spray and place it upon the table ; no sooner has the warmth of the room dried the tiny capsules than the miniature bombardment will begin and will continue until every seed is forced out of its covering.

The bark and leaves of the Witch Hazel are reputed to possess medicinal properties on account of the tradition that they were used by the Indians in the treatment of external inflammations. " Pond's Extract " is a distillation of the bark in dilute alcohol. This remedy has great popularity, but chemists so far have failed to distinguish any active medicinal properties in the plant.

SWEET GUM. LIQUIDAMBAR

Liquidámbar styraciflua.

The name is derived from *liquidus* and the Arabic word *ambar*, referring to the balsamic juices of the tree. *Styraciflua* from the name of an ancient balsam.

A tree sixty to one hundred and forty feet in height, with erect trunk two to five feet in diameter, slender branches and handsome conical head. Ranges from Connecticut to Florida on the coast and westward through Arkansas and Indian Territory. It appears on the mountain ranges in Mexico and Central America. Loves low, moist, bottom lands, but will grow in dry elevated regions. Roots fibrous ; juices balsamic.

Bark.—Light brown tinged with red, deeply fissured, ridges scaly. Branchlets pithy, many-angled, winged, at first covered with rusty hairs, finally becoming red brown. gray or dark brown.

Flowers and Fruit of Witch Hazel.

Wood.—Bright reddish brown, sapwood nearly white ; **heavy,** straight, satiny, close-grained, not strong ; will take a beautiful polish ; warps badly in drying. Has been used with good results in the interior finish of sleeping-cars and fine houses. The wood is usually cut in veneers and backed up with some other variety which shrinks and warps less. Sp. gr., 0.5910 ; weight of cu. ft., 36.83 lbs.

Winter Buds.—Yellow brown, one-fourth of an inch long, acute. The inner scales enlarge with the growing shoot, becoming half an inch long, green tipped with red.

Leaves.—Alternate, three to five inches long, three to seven inches broad, lobed, so as to make a star-shaped leaf of five to seven divisions, these divisions acutely pointed, with glandular serrate teeth. The base is truncate or slightly heart-shaped. They come out of the bud plicate, downy, pale green, when full grown are bright green, smooth, shining above, paler beneath. In autumn they vary in color from yellow through crimson to purple. They contain tannin and when bruised give a resinous fragrance. Petioles long, slender, terete. Stipules lanceolate, acute, caducous.

Flowers.—March to May, when leaves are half grown ; monœcious, greenish. Staminate flowers in terminal racemes two to three inches long, covered with rusty hairs ; the pistillate in a solitary head on a slender peduncle borne in the axil of an upper leaf. Staminate flowers destitute of calyx and corolla, but surrounded by hairy bracts. Stamens indefinite ; filaments short ; anthers introrse.

Pistillate flowers with a two-celled, two-beaked ovary, the carpels produced into a long, recurved, persistent style. The ovaries all more or less cohere and harden in fruit. Ovules many but few mature.

Fruit.—Multicapsular spherical head, an inch to an inch and a half in diameter, hangs on the branches during the winter. The woody capsules mostly filled with abortive seeds resembling sawdust.

Section of a Twig of Sweet Gum Showing the Corky Wings of the Bark.

The starry five-pointed leaves of the Liquidambar suggest the Sugar Maple, and its fruit balls as they hang upon their long stems resemble those of the Buttonwood. The distinguishing mark of the tree, however, is the peculiar appearance of its small branches and twigs. The bark attaches itself to these in plates edgewise instead of laterally, and a piece of the leafless branch with the aid of a little imagination readily

Sweet Gum, *Liquidambar styraciflua*.
Leaves 3′ to 5′ long, 3′ to 7′ broad.

takes on a reptilian form ; indeed, the tree is sometimes called Alligator-wood.

The autumnal coloring is not simply a flame, it is a conflagration ; in reds and yellows it equals the maples, and in addition it has the dark purples and smoky browns of the ash.

Liquidambar finds its most congenial home east of the Alleghanies and in the basin of the lower Mississippi. It is one of three who are the survivors of an ancient and widely distributed family. Its immediate ancestor inhabited in tertiary times Alaska, Greenland and the mid-continental plateau of North America, a similar form is also found in the miocene of Europe. The other living representatives of the genus are *L. orientalis,* found in Asia Minor, and *L. Formosana*, found in China and the Island of Formosa. The storax of commerce is a gum obtained from the inner bark of the two eastern species ; our northern tree produces very little, and that only in its most southern habitat.

Fruit of Sweet Gum.

ARALIÀCEÆ—GINSENG FAMILY

HERCULES' CLUB. ANGELICA-TREE

Aràlia spinòsa.

An aromatic spiny tree with stout wide spreading branches, twenty to thirty feet in height, trunk six to eight inches in diameter; oftener a cluster of branchless thorny stems ten to twenty feet high. Roots thick and fleshy. Prefers a deep moist soil; ranges from Pennsylvania westward to Missouri and southward to Texas. Bark of the root and the berries are used in medicine, principally in domestic practice.

Bark.—Light brown, divided into rounded broken ridges. Branchlets one-half to two-thirds of an inch in diameter, armed with stout, straight or curved, scattered prickles and nearly encircled by narrow leaf scars. At first light yellow brown, shining and dotted, later light brown.

Wood.—Brown with yellow streaks; light, soft, brittle, close-grained.

Winter Buds.—Terminal bud chestnut brown, one-half to three-fourths of an inch long, conical, blunt; axillary buds flattened, triangular, one-fourth of an inch in length.

Leaves.—Clustered at the end of the branches, compound, bi- and tri-pinnate, three to four feet long, two and a half feet broad. The pinnæ are unequally pinnate, having five or six pairs of leaflets and a long stalked terminal leaflet; these leaflets are often themselves pinnate. The last leaflets are ovate, two to three inches long, wedge-shaped or rounded at base, serrate or dentate, acute; midrib and primary veins prominent. They come out of the bud a bronze green, shining, somewhat hairy; when full grown are dark green above, pale beneath; midribs frequently furnished with prickles. In autumn they turn a beautiful bronze red touched with yellow. Petioles stout, light brown, eighteen to twenty inches in length, clasping, armed with prickles. Stipules acute, one-half inch long.

Flowers.—July, August. Perfect or polygamo-monœcious, cream white, borne in many-flowered umbels arranged in compound panicles, forming a terminal racemose cluster, three to four feet in length which rises, solitary or two or three together, above the spreading leaves. Bracts and bractlets lanceolate, acute, persistent.

Calyx. — Calyx tube coherent with the ovary, minutely five-tootued.

Corolla.—Petals five, white, inserted on margin of the disk, acute, slightly inflexed at the apex, imbricate in bud.

Stamens.—Five, inserted on margin of the disk, alternate with the petals; filaments thread-like; anthers oblong, attached on the back, introrse, two-celled; cells opening longitudinally.

Pistil.—Ovary inferior, five-celled; styles five, connivent; stigmas capitate.

Fruit.—Berry-like drupe, globular, black, one-fourth of an inch long, five-angled, crowned with the blackened styles. Flesh thin, dark.

The habit of growth and general appearance of the Hercules' Club are unique. It is usually found as a group of unbranched stems, rising to the height of twelve to twenty feet, which bear upon their summits a crowded cluster of doubly compound leaves, thus giving to each stem a certain tropical palm-like appearance. This slender, swaying, palm-like character is in the north only true of the young plants, for after a single stem has buffeted the storms of many winters it becomes a scrubby, deformed, little tree whose great leaves can scarcely cover its ugliness even in summer. In the south it is said to reach the height of fifty feet, still retaining its palm-like aspect.

The young stem is stout, thickly covered with sharp spines and for the most part branchless or slightly branching, so that when denuded of its leaves it looks very like a club, whence its common name Hercules' Club. The leaves are the largest produced by any tree of our flora, although the casual observer might not think so, as the leaflets are but two to three inches long. The leaves, however, are so compound, in this case doubly pinnate and sometimes pinnate again, that when one measures from the swollen base of the prickly petiole to the apex of the farthest leaflet the tape frequently records three feet and the spread of the pinnæ from side to side is often

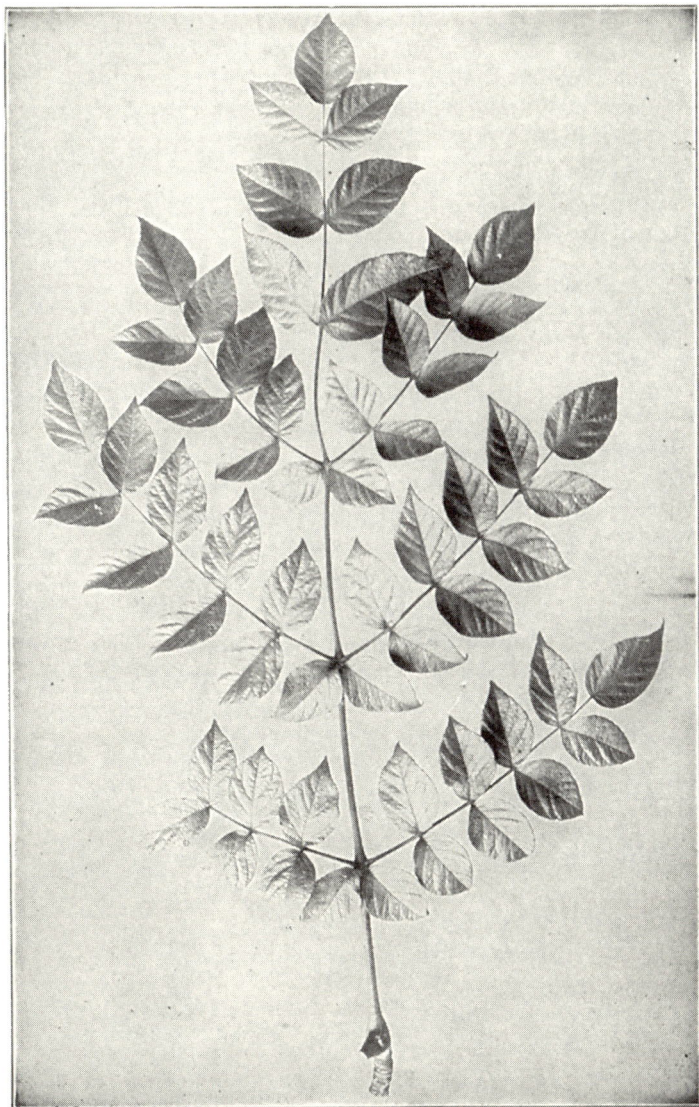

Hercules' Club, *Aralia spinosa.*
Leaves 3° to 4° long.   Leaflets 2′ to 3′ long.

two feet. In the autumn these leaves turn to a peculiar bronze red touched with yellow which makes the tree conspicuous and beautiful.

Hercules' Club, *Aralia spinosa*. Drupes ¼′ long.

The flowers are creamy white and appear in great, loose, flower clusters at the very summit of the stem. You have watched the tree all summer, June has come and gone, July is well under way, all other flowering trees are even now maturing their fruit, when, suddenly, the Hercules' Club shows signs of bloom and sometimes in July, often in August and even in September, the belated flowers come forth. The blooming spray, like the leaf, is enormous, sometimes rising three or four feet above the spreading leaves. Many of the flowers are sterile, so there is no such generous production of fruit as might be expected, but there is considerable. The little black drupes ripen quickly and hang in clusters upon the tree all winter long, for their flesh is so thin that they do not commend themselves to the birds.

CORNÀCEÆ—DOGWOOD FAMILY

FLOWERING DOGWOOD

Córnus flórida.

Cornus from *cornu* a horn, refers to the hardness of the wood.

A bushy tree, from fifteen to thirty feet high, with short trunk and spreading branches, making a flat-topped head. Roots fibrous. It prefers dry land and will grow under the shade of taller trees. Bark, leaves, and fruit, rich in tannic acid. Ranges from eastern Massachusetts to central Florida west through southern Michigan to Missouri and Texas.

Bark.—Reddish brown, divided into quadrangular plate-like scales. Bitter and tonic. Branchlets at first pale green, later they are red or yellow green, finally become light brown or reddish gray.

Winter Buds.—Formed in midsummer, terminal bud accompanied by two pairs of lateral buds making a cluster. On fertile shoots the terminal bud is replaced by the head of flower buds, which by midsummer protrudes from between the two upper lateral buds.

Wood.—Brown ; heavy, hard, strong, tough and close-grained ; will take a beautiful polish. Used for hubs of small wheels, handles of tools, mallets ; largely used in turnery. Sp. gr., 0.8153 ; weight of cu. ft., 50.81 lbs.

Leaves.—Opposite, somewhat clustered at the ends of the branches, ovate or elliptical, three to five inches long, two to three wide, wedge-shaped at base, wavy or entire, acute. Feather-veined, midrib prominent, five to six pairs of primary veins. They come out of the bud involute, at first pale green, downy ; when full grown are bright dark green above, pale and downy beneath. In autumn they turn a brilliant scarlet. Petioles short, grooved.

Flowers.—April, May. Perfect, greenish, in a close cluster, surrounded by a large, showy, four-leaved, corolla-like, white or rarely pinkish involucre, borne on a stout peduncle an inch or an inch and a half long, showy.

DOGWOOD FAMILY

Calyx.—Slightly urn-shaped, four-lobed, light green, coherent with the ovary.

Corolla.—Petals four, valvate in bud, inserted on an epigynous disk, rounded or acute at apex, slightly thickened at the margins, green, tipped with yellow. Disk orange colored.

Stamens.—Four, inserted on the disk, exserted, alternate with the petals. Filaments thread-like ; anthers oblong, introrse, versatile, two-celled ; cells opening longitudinally.

Ovary.—Inferior, two-celled ; style columnar ; stigma truncate ; ovule one in each cell.

Fruit.—Ovoid drupe, borne in clusters of three or four, crowned with the calyx lobes and remnant of the style, bright scarlet, half an inch long, smooth, shining, bitter, aromatic. October. Cotyledons foliaceous.

No other tree of our flora enables the observer so easily to study the life history of its flowers and fruit as does the Dogwood. A shrub oftener than a tree, its branches are within easy reach and it conducts its operations so openly that they invite attention. When in early spring, the great white blossoms appearing before the leaves transform the tree into one huge bouquet, it is the glory of the fields and challenges the attention and admiration of every observer. In summer, its low branching habit and dense foliage give it a peculiar and attractive appearance ; the clusters of shining red berries together with the dark red leaves mark it in the autumnal woods, and in the winter, the curious, gray, box-like, flower-buds which tip its branches are unique and striking.

In order to understand the development of those great white spring blossoms, it is necessary to study the tree in midsummer of the preceding year. By July a little group of three tiny buds has begun to form at the end of the many branchlets of a healthy, vigorous tree. If the terminal bud is to produce flowers it soon outstrips its companions and protrudes beyond them. This growth continues through the late summer and on into autumn. By the time that the clustered drupes are ripe and the leaves begin to turn scarlet, these terminal flower-buds of the next year are about the size of small peas, inclosed by four involucral scales, pointed above, rounded below, light brownish gray in color, more or

A Branch of Flowering Dogwood, *Cornus florida*, Bearing Fruit and Next
Year's Flower Buds.

Leaves 3′ to 5′ long, 2′ to 3′ broad.

less covered with pale hairs and borne on stout club-shaped peduncles a quarter of an inch or less in length. These buds stand up from the tips of the branchlets and are very conspicuous. After the leaves fall, and the red berries have been taken by the birds these gray buds remain unchanged, stiff and unyielding throughout the winter.

One of the first indications of returning activity to plant life is the gaping of these involucral scales at the apex of the flower-bud. This happens about the time that the elm-buds are beginning to swell and open, but the elm-flowers have come and gone and the samaras are well grown before our dogwood blossom is worthy of the name. But day after day the change goes on. The involucral scales begin to enlarge, unfold, grow white and at length about six weeks after the first opening of the apex they become a flat corolla-like cup, three or four inches across. Each scale is now a great white petal-like leaf, so like a petal that many consider it such ; its rounded apex blotched and darkened by the discolored remnants of the portion formed during the summer before. In color these are usually white, sometimes, however, they are pink and rarely bright red.

Within these four, white, petaloid scales is a close cluster of tiny flowers which are the real blossoms of the tree. They

Single Flower of Dogwood, *Cornus flori-da ;* enlarged.

are yellowish green, made on a plan of four, four lobes to the calyx, four petals to the corolla, and four stamens ; there is, however, but one pistil.

After our great white involucre has performed its duty, fostered and protected the tiny flowers until they have reached maturity, it falls, the blossoms fade and the tiny fruit begins to grow. Although there are from ten to thirty blossoms in each cluster rarely more than five drupes are matured in any one. Some remain in a state of arrested development, and cling to the branch small and green all summer long. The bright, shining, scarlet fruit is beautiful to look at and is finally eaten by the birds, but they exhaust other resources first, for under that shining skin is a very

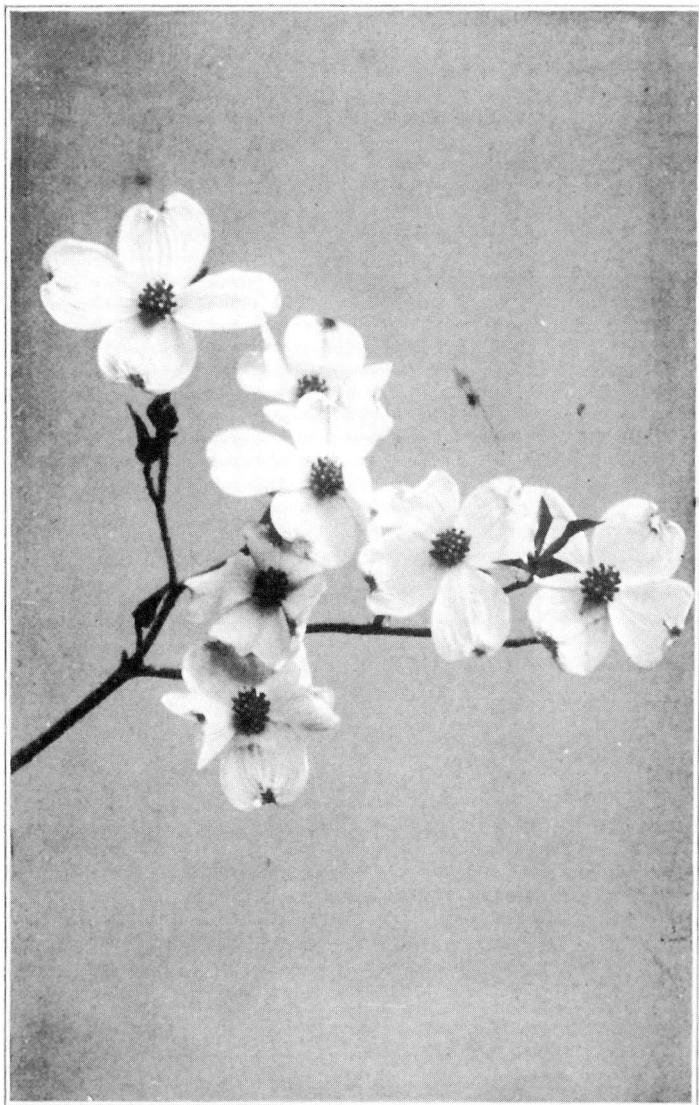

Flowering Spray of Flowering Dogwood.
Involucre 3′ to 4′ across.

bitter and aromatic flesh which no normal appetite could crave.

The generic name of this group of trees is easily explained, for *Cornus* is derived from *cornu*, a horn, and finds its justification in the well known hardness of the wood. Dogwood, however, has a different origin. Usually, the name of an animal attached to a plant means that the plant in question was believed by the early simplers, who as a rule gave the common names, to be either beneficial or baneful to that animal; for example, sheep sorrel, catnip, wolfsbane. But dog and horse in combination may and often do mean simply worthless, or coarse. The early botanists, like the biblical writers and Shakespeare, held the dog in slight repute. It is therefore questionable whether the name Dogwood was meant to convey contempt for the tree as worthless for timber, or whether it referred to the value of its astringent bark as a cure for the mange in dogs.

Dogwood, *Cornus florida*. Fruit ½′ to ¾′ long.

There are more dogwoods in North America than anywhere else in the world; sixteen species have been distinguished. Three of these are trees, two found east of the Rocky Mountains and one upon the Pacific slope. The others are mostly shrubs. One herb of the family, the Dwarf Cornel, grows in northern woods. In the early tertiary epoch *Cornus* inhabited the arctic regions and in the eocene period, forms now existing appeared in Europe.

ALTERNATE-LEAVED DOGWOOD

Córnus alternifòlia.

Usually a shrub sending up several stems from the ground; some-times a tree, flat-topped and bushy, that reaches the height of twen-ty-five feet. Found along the margins of the forest and by the bor-ders of trees and swamps; in moist, well drained soil.

Bark.—Dark reddish brown, with shallow ridges. Branchlets at first pale reddish green, later dark green.

Wood.—Reddish brown, sapwood pale; heavy, hard, close-grained. Sp. gr., 0.6696; weight of cu. ft., 41.73 lbs.

Winter Buds.—Light chestnut brown, acute. Inner scales enlarge with the growing shoot and become half an inch long before they fall.

Leaves.—Alternate, rarely opposite, often clustered at the ends of the branch, simple, three to five inches long, two to three wide, oval or ovate, wedge-shaped or rounded at base; margin is wavy toothed, slightly reflexed, apex acuminate. They come out of the bud invo-lute, reddish green above, coated with silvery white tomentum be-neath, when full grown are bright green above, pale, downy, almost white beneath. Feather-veined, midrib broad, yellowish, prominent beneath, with about six pairs of primary veins. In autumn they turn yellow, or yellow and scarlet. Petioles slender, grooved, hairy, with clasping bases.

Flowers.—April, May. Perfect, cream color, borne in many-flow-ered, broad, open cymes, at the end of short lateral branches.

Calyx.—Cup-shaped, obscurely four-toothed, woolly.

Corolla.—Petals four, valvate in bud, inserted on disk; cream col-ored, oblong, rounded at apex.

Stamens.—Four, inserted on the disk, alternate with the petals, exserted; filaments long, slender; anthers oblong, introrse, versa-tile, two-celled; cells opening longitudinally.

Pistil.—Ovary inferior, two-celled; style columnar; stigma capi-tate.

Fruit.—Drupe, globular, blue-black, one-third inch across, tipped with remnant of style which rises from a slight depression; nut obo-void, many-grooved. October.

This is the only Dogwood with alternate leaves; all the others bear their leaves opposite. The tree is very pretty because of its wide spreading shelving branches and flat-topped head, and is often found in ornamental grounds. The

Spray of Alternate-leaved Dogwood, *Cornus alternifolia*.
Leaves 3′ to 5′ long, 2′ to 3′ broad.

flower clusters have no great white involucre as have those of the Flowering Dogwood, and the fruit is dark purple instead of red and of intensely disagreeable aromatic flavor.

TUPELO. PEPPERIDGE. SOUR GUM

Nyssa sylvática.

Nyssa, the name of the nymph who reared Bacchus, was given to the genus by Linnæus. Pepperidge is meaningless.

Found in eastern North America. Loves the borders of swamps and low wet lands. Usually reaches the height of fifty feet and occasionally one hundred ; variable in form. Roots large, striking deep.

Bark.—Light reddish brown, deeply furrowed and scaly. Branchlets at first pale green to orange, sometimes smooth, often downy, later dark brown.

Wood.—Pale yellow, sapwood white ; heavy, strong, very tough, hard to split, not durable in contact with the soil. Used for turnery. Sp. gr., 0.6353 ; weight of cu. ft., 39.59.

Winter Buds.—Dark red, obtuse, one-fourth of an inch long. Inner scales enlarge with the growing shoot, becoming red before they fall.

Leaves. — Alternate, often crowded at the end of the lateral branches, simple, linear, oblong to oval, two to five inches long, one-half to three inches broad, wedge-shaped or rounded at base, entire, with margin slightly thickened, acute or acuminate. They come out of the bud conduplicate, coated beneath with rusty tomentum, when full grown are thick, dark green, very shining above, pale and often hairy beneath. Feather-veined, midrib and primary veins prominent beneath. In autumn they turn bright scarlet, or yellow and scarlet. Petioles one-quarter to one-half an inch long, slender or stout, terete or margined, often red.

Flowers.—May, June, when leaves are half grown. Polygamo-diœcious, yellowish green, borne on slender downy peduncles. Staminate in many-flowered heads ; pistillate in two to several flowered clusters.

Calyx.—Cup-shaped, five-toothed.

Corolla.—Petals five, imbricate in bud, yellow green, ovate, thick, slightly spreading, inserted on the margin of the conspicuous disk.

Stamens.—Five to twelve. In staminate flowers exserted, in pistillate short, often wanting.

Fruiting Branch of Tupelo, *Nyssa sylvatica.*
Leaves 2' to 5' long.

Pistil.—Ovary inferior, one to two-celled ; style stout, exserted, reflexed above the middle. Entirely wanting in sterile flower. Ovules, one in each cell.

Fruit.—Fleshy drupe, one to three from each flower cluster. Ovoid, two-thirds of an inch long, dark blue, acid. Stone more or less ridged. October.

The glossy beauty of the Tupelo is undoubtedly the reason why it so often is permitted to escape the levelling axe and allowed to stand in the fields with the elm, oak, and maple. In such a situation its contour is as individual as that of any of its companions.

The stem rises to the summit of the tree in one tapering unbroken shaft, the branches come out at right angles to the trunk and either extend horizontally or droop a little, making a long, narrow, cone-like head. The spray is fine and abundant and lies horizontally so that the foliage arrangement is not unlike that of the beech. The leaves are short petioled and so have little individual motion, but the branch sways as a whole.

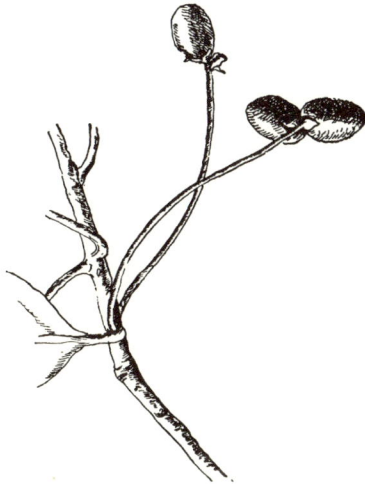

Tupelo, *Nyssa sylvatica.* Drupes ½′ to ¾′ long.

The tree rarely flourishes in exposed positions, it dies at the top and lives on in a half-hearted way until the friendly axe ends the unequal struggle. But, allowed to grow in freedom, sheltered but not crowded, it develops a full round head and lives to good old age.

The flowers are inconspicuous, but the fruit is quite marked, dark blue, in clusters of two or three, sour but eagerly sought by the birds.

Its autumnal coloring is superb ; the foliage becomes one

glowing mass of scarlet, sometimes dashed with orange. It is the most fiery and brilliant of all that brilliant group,—the maple, dogwood, sassafras, liquidambar, and tupelo.

The wood is noted for the unusual arrangement of its fibres which instead of running in parallel lines are curiously twisted and interwoven, so that it is extremely difficult to split.

The tree has different names in different parts of the country. In the south it is generally called Sour Gum, in the middle west, Pepperidge, and in New England it retains its pretty Indian name, Tupelo.

CAPRIFOLIÀCEÆ—HONEYSUCKLE FAMILY

SWEET VIBURNUM. SHEEPBERRY

Vibúrnum léntago.

Viburnum is a Latin name of unknown meaning.
Lentago, from *lentus,* an allusion to its flexible branches.

A small tree about twenty feet in height, with a short trunk, round-topped head, pendulous, flexible branches. Roots fibrous, wood ill-smelling. Loves wet soil along the borders of the forest, often found in fence corners and along roadsides. Ranges from Quebec to the Saskatchewan River, southward through the northern states to Georgia and west to Missouri and Nebraska.

Bark.—Reddish brown, divided into small thick plates, surface scaly. Branchlets at first pale green, covered with rusty down, finally become dark reddish brown, sometimes glaucous.

Wood.—Dark orange brown ; heavy, hard, close-grained. Sp. gr., 0.7303 ; weight of cu. ft., 45.51 lbs.

Winter Buds.—Light red, covered with pale scurfy down, protected by a pair of opposite scales. Flower-bearing buds are three-quarters of an inch long, obovate, long pointed. Other terminal buds are acute, one-half an inch long ; lateral buds much smaller. Bud-scales enlarge with the growing shoot and often become leaf-like.

Leaves.—Opposite, simple, ovate, two and one-half inches long, wedge-shaped, rounded or subcordate at base, serrate, acuminate. They come out of the bud involute, bronze green and shining, hairy and downy ; when full grown are bright green and shining above, pale green and marked with tiny black dots beneath. Feather veined, midrib slender, primary veins connected by conspicuous veinlets. In autumn they turn a deep red, or red and orange. Petioles broad, grooved, winged or wingless, an inch to an inch and a half in length. Stipules tiny, occasional.

HONEYSUCKLE FAMILY

Flowers.—May, June. Perfect, cream-white, borne in stout, branched, scurfy, flat, terminal cymes, from three to five inches in diameter. Bracts and bractlets, triangular, green, caducous.

Calyx.—Tubular, equally five-toothed, persistent.

Corolla.—Rotate, equally five-lobed, imbricate in the bud, cream-white, one-quarter of an inch across; lobes acute, and slightly erose.

Stamens.—Five, inserted on the base of the corolla, alternate with its lobes, exserted; filaments slender; anthers bright yellow, oblong, introrse, versatile, two-celled; cells opening longitudinally.

Pistil.—Ovary inferior, one-celled; style thick, short, light green; stigma broad; ovules one in each cell.

Fruit.—Fleshy drupe, crowned with the calyx tube, borne on slender, drooping, red stalks, in few-fruited clusters, oval, flattened, thick skinned, black or dark blue, glaucous, sweet, and rather juicy. Stone oblong oval, flattened. September.

The Sheepberry is one of the largest of the Viburnums. It is admired for its compact habit, its lustrous foliage which insects rarely disfigure, its beautiful and abundant flowers, its handsome edible fruit and its brilliant autumnal color. It readily adapts itself to cultivation, and is one of the best of the small trees of eastern America for the decoration of parks and gardens in all regions of extreme winter cold. It is easily raised from seeds which, like those of the other American species, do not germinate until the second year after they are planted.
—CHARLES S. SARGENT.

There is a softness and richness about the flowers and foliage of the Sweet Viburnum which distinguish it above all others of the same genus.
—GEORGE B. EMERSON.

The one that seems to me to bear the most resemblance to the English Wayfaring-tree is the Sweet Viburnum. Many of our shrubs produce more showy flowers, but few surpass it in the beauty of its fruit. The berries are of the size of damsons, hanging profusely from the branches like clusters of grapes. They are dark purple when ripe with a lustre that is not seen in the grape. Just before they ripen they are crimson, and berries of this color are often blended with the ripened fruit.
—WILSON FLAGG.

Sprays of Sweet Viburnum, *Viburnum lentago*.
Leaves 2′ to 2½′ long.

BLACK HAW. STAG BUSH

Vibúrnum prunifólium.

Often a shrub, sometimes a small bushy tree with short crooked trunk and stout spreading branches. Found in the undergrowth of the forest. Ranges from Connecticut to Georgia westward to Kansas and Indian Territory.

Bark.—Reddish brown, scaly. Branchlets at first red, then green, finally dark brown tinged with red.

Wood.—Brown tinged with red ; heavy, hard, close-grained. Sp. gr., 0.8332 ; weight of cu. ft., 51.92 lbs.

Winter Buds.—Coated with rusty tomentum. Flower-buds ovate, half an inch long, much larger than the axillary buds. Scales grow with the growing shoot and sometimes develop into leaf-like bodies.

Leaves.—Opposite, simple, oval, ovate or orbicular, two to three inches long, wedge-shaped or rounded at base, serrate, acute. Feather-veined, midrib and primary veins prominent beneath. They come out of the bud involute, shining, green, tinged with red, sometimes smooth, or clothed with rusty tomentum ; when full grown dark green and smooth above, pale, smooth or tomentose beneath. In autumn the leaves vary from scarlet to a vinous red. Petioles short, grooved, red, often tomentose, sometimes winged.

Single Flower of Black Haw, *Viburnum prunifolium.*

Flowers.—May. Perfect, cream-white, borne in flat-topped cymes three to four inches in diameter. The pedicels are bibracteolate ; bracts are awl-shaped, short, reddish, caducous.

Calyx.—Urn-shaped, five-toothed, persistent.

Corolla.—White, five-lobed ; lobes rounded, imbricate in bud.

Stamens.—Five, exserted, inserted on the base of the corolla, alternate with the lobes ; filaments slender ; anthers pale yellow, oblong, introrse, versatile, two-celled ; cells opening longitudinally.

Pistil.—Ovary inferior, one-celled ; style thick, pale green ; stigma flat ; ovules one in each cell.

Fruit.—Drupe, oval, half an inch long, dark blue, with glaucous bloom. Ripens in October, borne in few-fruited clusters, hangs until winter, becomes edible after being touched by the frost. Stone flat and even, broadly oval.

Sprays of Black Haw, *Viburnum prunifolium.*
Leaves 2′ to 3′ long.

ERICACEÆ—HEATH FAMILY

MOUNTAIN LAUREL. KALMIA

Kálmia latifòlia.

Kalmia commemorates the labors of Peter Kalm, a friend and pupil of Linnæus, who travelled in eastern North America in 1753.

In the north a broad dense shrub five to ten feet high with many crooked branches and a round compact head ; only becoming a tree on the mountains of North and South Carolina. Ranges from Canada to the Gulf along the highlands and mountains, and westward to Arkansas. It is tolerant of many locations, loves swamp land or dry slopes at the borders of the forest, will climb the mountain-side to an elevation of three thousand feet or more ; does not flourish in a limestone country. Roots fibrous, matted. Easily cultivated.

Bark.—Dark brown tinged with red, furrowed and scaly. Branchlets at first light reddish green, downy, later smooth, red green and shining, finally all a bright red brown.

Wood.—Brown tinged with red ; heavy, hard, rather brittle, close-grained. Sp. gr., 0.7160; weight of cu. ft., 44.62 lbs.

Winter Buds.—Leaf-buds naked, forming in midsummer in the axils of leaves just below those from which the clusters of flower-buds are produced by which they are almost covered. The tip of the branch dies when these axillary buds are formed. Inner scales enlarge with the growing shoot, becoming an inch long before falling.

Leaves.—Alternate, or in pairs, or in threes, simple, persistent, oblong, three to four inches long, one to one and a half inches wide, wedge-shaped at base, entire, acute or rounded at apex and tipped with a callous point. They come out of the bud conduplicate ; each leaf enclosed by the one directly below it, slightly tinged with pink and covered with glandular white hairs, when full grown are thick and rigid, dark shining green above, pale yellow green beneath; midrib broad, yellow, rounded above and below, veins obscure.

Fruiting Branch of Mountain Laurel, *Kalmia latifolia*.
Leaves 3′ to 4′ long, 1′ to 1½′ broad.

They remain green and fall during the second summer. Petioles short, stout, slightly flattened.

Flowers.—Flowers appear in May or June from buds which are formed in autumn in the axils of the upper leaves in the form of slender cones of downy green scales. These buds usually develop two or more lateral branches, the whole forming a compound many-flowered corymb four or five inches in diameter and overlapped at the flowering time by the leafy branches of the year. Pedicels are red or green, hairy or scurfy and furnished with two bracts at base and developed from the axils of large bracts.

Calyx.—Five-parted ; lobes imbricate in bud, narrow, acute, covered with glutinous hairs. Disk prominent, ten-lobed.

Corolla.—Saucer-shaped, rose colored, white, or pink. Tube short with ten tiny sacs just below the five-parted limb ; lobes ovate, acute, imbricate in bud. The border is marked on the inner surface with a waving rosy line and is slightly purple above the sac. The buds are ten-ribbed from the sacs to the acute apex of the bud.

Stamens.—Ten, hypogynous, shorter than the corolla, at first held in the sacs of the corolla ; filaments thread-like ; anthers oblong, adnate, two-celled ; cells opening by a short longitudinal pore.

Pistil.—Ovary superior, five-celled ; style thread-like, exserted ; stigma capitate ; ovules many in each cell.

Fruit.—Woody capsule, many seeded, depressed - globular, slightly five-lobed, five-celled, five-valved. Crowned with the persistent style, surrounded at base by the persistent calyx, covered with viscid hairs. Seeds oblong.

Flower Cluster of Mountain Laurel, *Kalmia latifolia.*

The blossoms of the Mountain Laurel are equipped with a most evident device to secure cross-fertilization. Nature has many such arrangements, but it is not often that they are so openly displayed. In this case, however, he who runs may read. Each flower has ten stamens and each corolla is provided with ten little pockets. When the flower opens each stamen is found bent back with its anther thrust into one of these tiny cavities. In the centre of the flower lies the nectar, and when the bee comes to get it, he brushes against the filaments, which fly up and scatter their pollen over his body. He leaves on the stigma of the next flower he visits the pollen he has gathered in the first, and so on he goes from flower to flower. He probably thinks that gathering honey is his business, but as a matter of fact it is a very small part of his duties in the economy of nature.

The Mountain Laurel is one of the most satisfactory shrubs for lawn or garden. When in full bloom it is of surpassing beauty, and its bright evergreen leaves make it conspicuous at any time. These leaves are believed to be poisonous to cattle, and the species, *Kalmia angustifolia*, a low shrub in pastures, is popularly called Lambkill; but the probability is that its noxious qualities have been overrated. The best observers are inclined to refer what deleterious qualities there may be to the coarse, resinous character of the leaves which make them indigestible than to any positive noxious principle contained in them.

RHODODENDRON. GREAT LAUREL. ROSE BAY

Rhododéndron máximum.

In the north a shrub with many divergent stems and contorted branches, ten or twelve feet tall. Roots fibrous. Distributed from Nova Scotia to shores of Lake Erie and southward to northern Georgia. Common on the mountains of New York, it becomes abundant in Virginia, and on the high lands of Tennessee and the Carolinas it forms dense thickets hundreds of acres in extent. Flourishes in all soils except those containing lime.

Bark.—Reddish brown, scaly. Branchlets at first green, covered with red or rusty tomentum, later become reddish brown or gray tinged with red.

Wood.—Light brown; heavy, hard, close-grained. Sp. gr., 0.6303; weight of cu. ft., 39.28 lbs.

Winter Buds.—Leaf buds clearly seen in midsummer, conical, dark green, axillary or terminal, on barren shoots covered with closely imbricated scales. Outer scales persist until shoot is half grown; inner scales enlarge with the growing shoot and are carried up with it. Flower-buds are full grown by September, terminal, cone-like, an inch and a half long, covered with many imbricated bracts which contract at the apex into long slender points.

Leaves.—Alternate, usually clustered at the ends of the branches, persistent, elliptical, oblong, four to ten inches long, wedge-shaped or rounded at base, entire, thickened slightly, revolute margin, acute apex. They come out of the bud revolute, pale green, covered with thick pale tomentum. When full grown are smooth, thick, leathery, dark green and shining above, pale beneath ; midrib broad, pale, depressed above, prominent beneath ; veinlets obscure. Petioles stout, short, terete.

Flowers.—June, after the shoots of the year from the buds below the flower-buds are well grown. Borne in umbellate clusters four or five inches in diameter, perfect, pale rose, or white. Pedicels viscid ; bracts caducous.

Calyx.—Five-lobed ; lobes rounded, imbricate in bud.

Corolla.—Campanulate, gibbous on the posterior side, hairy in the throat, pale rose, purplish, or white, five-lobed ; lobes rounded, veined ; upper lobe marked with yellow greenish spots.

Stamens.—Eight to twelve, white, inserted on a disk ; filaments, unequal, declined, bearded ; anthers attached on the back, two-celled ; each cell opening by a terminal pore.

Pistil.—Ovary superior, five-celled, hairy ; style long, white, declined ; stigma red, five-lobed ; ovules many in each cell.

Fruit.—Capsule, surrounded at base by the persistent calyx and crowned with the style.

The Rhododendron becomes a tree in the south only ; on the mountains of Pennsylvania, New York, and Virginia it remains a shrub, but one of the most attractive shrubs in our flora. Both leaf and flower are matured in midsummer and they are so large and crown the summit of the stem so perfectly that they cannot escape observation.

The Rhododendron, the Kalmia, the Holly, and the Holly-leaved Mahonia make up our northern list of broad-leaved evergreens. All other broad-leaved trees of our flora have become deciduous. Here and there individual oaks retain their leaves all winter ; so do many young beeches. These persistent leaves are brown and withered it is true, but they speak of a time when the trees were evergreen. The Oak family still retains an evergreen species, and in South America the forests of Patagonia wave green and dark with an evergreen beech.

The Rhododendron flourished in the arctic regions in tertiary times, and traces of several species are found in the miocene rocks of Europe.

Flowering Spray of the Rhododendron, *Rhododendron maximum.*
Leaves 4′ to 10′ long.

The ancestry and history of our cultivated Rhododendrons are most admirably given by Professor Sargent in "The Silva of North America." He says :

The cultivated varieties of Rhododendrons are of garden origin and mixed blood. These are chiefly of four races, Indian Azaleas, Ghent Azaleas, The Catawbiense Rhododendrons and Javanese Rhododendrons. The Indian Azaleas of the garden are improved forms of *R. Indicum*, a native of China and Japan which owes its name to the fact that it was first sent to Europe from India ; in its native countries it is a variable plant with persistent or deciduous leaves and small and usually brick-red flowers ; for centuries it has been cultivated by the Chinese and Japanese who value it as a chief ornament of their gardens, although improvement in the size, form, and coloring of its flowers is due to the skill of European gardeners, who, especially in Belgium, have devoted much attention to this plant. The race of Ghent Azaleas has been produced by crossing the yellow-flowered Oriental *R. flavum* with the North American *R. calendulaceum R. viscosum* and *R. nudiflorum*, and then by crossing their hybrid progeny with each other and with the eastern Asiatic *R. sinense* and later with the Californian *R. occidentale* and with *R. arborescens* of the Alleghany Mountains.

The product of these crosses and of years of careful selection carried on principally in Belgium and England is a race of hardy shrubs with fragrant flowers in colors passing from white through yellow and orange to pink and red.

The Catawbiense Rhododendrons have been produced by crossing *R. catawbiense*, a native of the high summits of the southern Alleghany Mountains which it sometimes covers with vast thickets, with *R. Ponticum*, the offspring being again crossed with *R. arboreum* and other Indian species with bright colored flowers or with the North American *R. maximum*. The race of Javanese Rhododendrons, conspicuous for their brilliantly colored flowers and their habit of flowering continuously, has been obtained by English gardeners by interbreeding *R. Javanicum* and other Malayan species with persistent foliage and yellow, orange, and scarlet flowers.

SOURWOOD. SORREL-TREE

Oxydéndrum arbòreum.

Oxydendrum, of Greek derivation, means sour tree.

A slender tree reaching the maximum height of sixty feet, with slender spreading branches and oblong, round-topped head. Ranges from Pennsylvania along the Alleghany Mountains to Florida and Alabama, westward through Ohio to southern Indiana and southward through Arkansas and Louisiana to the coast.

Bark.—Gray with a reddish tinge, deeply furrowed and scaly. Branchlets at first light yellow green, later reddish brown.

Sourwood, *Oxydendrum arboreum.*
Leaves 4′ to 7′ long.

Wood.—Reddish brown, sapwood paler; heavy, hard, close-grained, will take a high polish. Sp. gr., 0.7458 ; weight of cu. ft., 46.48 lbs.

Winter Buds.—Axillary, minute, dark red, partly immersed in the bark. Inner scales enlarge when spring growth begins.

Leaves.—Alternate, four to seven inches long, one and a half to two and a half inches wide, oblong to oblanceolate, wedge-shaped at base, serrate, acute or acuminate. Feather-veined, midrib conspicuous. They come out of the bud revolute, bronze green and shining, smooth, when full grown are dark green, shining above, pale and glaucous below. In autumn they turn bright scarlet. Petioles long and slender, stipules wanting. Heavily laden with acid.

Flowers.—June, July. Perfect, cream-white, borne in terminal panicles of secund racemes seven to eight inches long ; rachis and short pedicels downy.

Calyx.—Five-parted, persistent ; lobes valvate in bud.

Corolla.—Ovoid-cylindric, narrowed at the throat, cream-white, five-toothed.

Stamens.—Ten, inserted on the corolla ; filaments wider than the anthers ; anthers two-celled ; cells opening by long chinks.

Pistil.—Ovary superior, ovoid, five-celled ; style columnar ; stigma simple ; disk ten-toothed, ovules many.

Fruit.—Capsule, downy, five-valved, five-angled, tipped by the persistent style, the pedicels curving.

The Sourwood is perfectly hardy at the north and is worthy of a place in lawns and parks. Its late bloom makes it desirable and its autumnal coloring is particularly beautiful and brilliant. The leaves are heavily charged with acid, and to some extent have the poise of those of the peach.

Raceme of flowers of Sourwood, *Oxydendrum arboreum.*

EBENÀCEÆ—EBONY FAMILY

PERSIMMON

Diospyros virginiàna.

Diospyros, of Greek derivation, means the fruit of Jove. Persimmon
is the Indian name.

Small tree varying from thirty to fifty feet in height, short slender
trunk, spreading, often pendulous branches, which form sometimes a
broad and sometimes a narrow round-topped head. Prefers a light,
sandy, well-drained soil, but will grow in rich, southern, bottom lands.
Roots thick, fleshy and stoloniferous. Given to shrubby growth.

Bark.—Dark brown or dark gray, deeply divided into plates
whose surface is scaly. Branchlets slender, zigzag, with thick pith
or large pith cavity; at first light reddish brown and pubescent.
They vary in color from light brown to ashy gray and finally become
reddish brown, the bark somewhat broken by longitudinal fissures.
Astringent and bitter.

Wood.—Very dark; sapwood yellowish white; heavy, hard, strong
and very close grained. Sp. gr., 0.7908; weight of cu. ft., 49.28 lbs.

Winter Buds.—Ovate, acute, one-eighth of an inch long, covered
with thick reddish or purple scales. These scales are sometimes
persistent at the base of the branchlets.

Leaves.—Alternate, simple, four to six inches long, oval, narrowed
or rounded or cordate at base, entire, acute or acuminate. They
come out of the bud revolute, thin, pale, reddish green, downy with
ciliate margins, when full grown are thick, dark green, shining above,
pale and often pubescent beneath. In autumn they sometimes turn
orange or scarlet, sometimes fall without change of color. Midrib
broad and flat, primary veins opposite and conspicuous. Petioles
stout, pubescent, one-half to an inch in length.

Flowers.—May, June, when leaves are half-grown; diœcious or
rarely polygamous. Staminate flowers borne in two to three-flowered

cymes ; the pedicels downy and bearing two minute bracts. Pistillate flowers solitary, usually on separate trees, their pedicels short, recurved, and bearing two bractlets.

Calyx.—Usually four-lobed, accrescent under the fruit.

Corolla.—Greenish yellow or creamy white, tubular, four-lobed ; lobes imbricate in bud.

Stamens.—Sixteen, inserted on the corolla, in staminate flowers in two rows. Filaments short, slender, slightly hairy ; anthers oblong, introrse, two-celled, cells opening longitudinally. In pistillate flowers the stamens are eight with aborted anthers, rarely these stamens are perfect.

Pistil.—Ovary superior, conical, ultimately eight-celled ; styles four, slender, spreading ; stigma two-lobed.

Fruit.—A juicy berry containing one to eight seeds, crowned with the remnants of the style and seated in the enlarged calyx ; depressed-globular, pale orange color, often red-cheeked ; with slight bloom, turning yellowish brown after freezing. Flesh astringent while green, sweet and luscious when ripe.

> They have a plumb which they call pessemmins, like to a medler, in England, but of a deeper tawnie cullour ; they grow on a most high tree. When they are not fully ripe, they are harsh and choakie, and furre in a man's mouth like allam, howbeit, being taken fully ripe, yt is a reasonable pleasant fruict, somewhat lushious. I have seene our people put them into their baked and sodden puddings ; there be whose tast allows them to be as pretious as the English apricock ; I confess it is a good kind of horse plumb.
>
> —" The Historie of Travaile into Virginia Brittania."

The longest pole takes the Persimmon.—SOUTHERN PROVERB.

The Persimmon is one of the most interesting of our native trees. Its habitat is southern, it appears along the coast from New York to Florida ; west of the Alleghanies it is found in southern Ohio and along through southeastern Iowa and southern Missouri ; when it reaches Louisiana, eastern Kansas and the Indian Territory it becomes a mighty tree, one hundred and fifteen feet high. It can be grown in northern Ohio only by the greatest care, and in southern Ohio its fruit is never edible until after frost.

The peculiar characteristics of its fruit have made the tree well known. This fruit is a globular berry, from an inch to an inch and a half in diameter, varying as to seeds, sometimes with eight and sometimes without any. It bears at its apex the remnants of the styles and sits in the enlarged and

Persimmon, *Diospyros virginiana.*
Leaves 4′ to 6′ long.

persistent calyx. It ripens in late autumn, is pale orange with a red cheek, often covered with a slight glaucous bloom. One of the delights of the natives in the south is to induce strangers to taste this fruit, for its bitter astringency is something that can be known only by experience. The frost is required to make it edible, but having been subjected to this influence it becomes sweet, juicy and delicious. This peculiar astringency is due to the presence of a tannin similar to that of Cinchona. The fruit is much appreciated in the southern states and appears abundantly in the markets. It is much sought by the opossum, who is supposed to fatten upon it, and the combination of persimmon, opossum and negro was very common in the slave songs of ante-bellum days.

Fruit of the Persimmon, *Diospyros virginiana.*

The tree is greatly inclined to vary in the character and quality of its fruit, in size this varies from that of a small cherry to a small apple. Some trees in the south produce fruit which is delicious without the action of the frost, while adjoining trees produce fruit that never becomes edible.

Several varieties of the species, *Diospyros Kaki* have been cultivated in China and Japan from most ancient times. Indeed this seems to be the universally cultivated fruit tree of Japan, is there found in every garden and by every cottage. The Japanese horticulturists have developed it into almost as many varieties as our gardeners have made of the apple tree. Some of these have been introduced into California and are said to flourish there. The California persimmon often offered for sale in our northern markets is the product of this Japanese tree.

The Persimmon is very common in the southern and Gulf states, and because of its stoloniferous roots frequently makes extensive thickets in abandoned fields and along the roadsides and fences.

In respect to the power of making heartwood, the Locust and the Persimmon stand at the extreme opposite ends of the list. The Locust changes its sapwood into heartwood almost at once, while the Persimmon rarely develops any heartwood until it is nearly one hundred years old. This heartwood is extremely close-grained and almost black. Really, it is ebony, but our climate is not favorable to its production. The ebony of commerce is derived from five different tropical species of the genus, two from India, one from Africa, one from Malaya and one from Mauritius. The beautiful variegated coromandel wood is the product of a species found in Ceylon.

Although *Diospyros* is now pre-eminently a tropical tree, enduring but indifferently the cold of the temperate regions, its fossil remains are found in the miocene rocks of Greenland and Alaska and in the cretaceous formation of Nebraska.

STYRACÀCEÆ—STORAX FAMILY

SILVERBELL-TREE

Mohrodéndron carolìnum.   Halèsia tetráptera.

A tree sometimes eighty or ninety feet in height, with a tall straight trunk, short stout branches which form a narrow head ; usually much smaller, often in the north a shrub with stout spreading stems. Roots are fibrous.   Ranges from the mountains of West Virginia southward to northern Alabama and Florida, westward to southern Illinois and Arkansas and eastern Texas.

Bark.—Red brown, with broad ridges, and surface scaly. Branchlets slender, terete, at first coated with pale tomentum, later become reddish brown sometimes glaucous.   In the second year the bark darkens and begins to show pale longitudinal fissures.

Wood.—Light brown, sapwood paler brown ; light, soft, close-grained.   Sp. gr., o.5628 ; weight of cu. ft., 35.07 lbs.

Winter Buds.—Dark red, small, obtuse, hairy.   Outer scales drop when spring growth begins ; inner scales lengthen with the growing shoot, become strap-shaped, bright yellow and sometimes half an inch long.   Flower-buds ovate, obtuse.

Leaves.—Alternate, simple, exstipulate, four to six inches long, two to three wide, oval or ovate-oblong, wedge-shaped or rounded at base, obscurely serrate, abruptly contracted into long points at the apex.   Midrib slender, primary veins conspicuous.   They come out of the bud involute, bronze red, hairy above, petiole and lower surface coated with thick pale tomentum, when full grown bright green above, paler beneath.   In autumn they become pale yellow and fall late.   Petioles short, stout.

Flowers.—May, when leaves are about one-third grown.   White, perfect, about one inch long, borne on short, few-flowered racemes or fascicles developed from the axils of the previous year's leaves, subtended by bracts.   Pedicles slender, drooping, downy, one to two inches in length.   Bracts obovate, yellow green, caducous.

Fruiting Branch of Silverbell-tree, *Mohrodendron carolinum.*
Leaves 4′ to 6′ long, 2′ to 3′ broad.

Calyx.—Obconical, four-ribbed, adnate to ovary, four-toothed, tomentose.

Corolla.—Campanulate, epigynous, slightly four-lobed, white.

Stamens.—Eight to sixteen, inserted on the base of the corolla ; filaments flattened ; anthers oblong, adnate or free at base, introrse, opening longitudinally.

Pistil.—Ovary inferior, four-celled ; style long, simply stigmatic at apex.

Fruit.—Dry, crowned with the calyx limb and tipped by the persistent style ; ellipsoidal, four-winged ; one and a half to two inches long, an inch broad, ripens late and remains on branches till midwinter.

The Silverbell is a most beautiful ornament for lawn or park. A native of the mountainous regions of the south it is perfectly hardy at the north, although in New England it keeps its shrubby form and in the middle west becomes only a small tree. It reaches its greatest size on the western slopes of the mountains of North Carolina and Tennessee.

Flowers of the Silverbell-tree, *Mohrodendron carolinum.*

Its flowering time is in May. The flower buds have been upon the branches all winter and just as the leaves have fairly put forth, the blossoms appear, and clusters of drooping creamwhite bells transform the tree into one great white mass of which every branch, from highest to lowest, drips blossoms. The flowering period lasts about three weeks and the Silverbell is worthy to be grouped with the June-berry, the Dogwood and the Redbud as a flowering tree of rare elegance and beauty.

The Snowdrop-tree, *Mohrodendron dipterum,* is a closely allied species which has developed on the low lands along the southern coast. The two have nearly the same range,

Flowering Branch of Snowdrop-tree, *Mohrodendron dipterum.*
Leaves 4′ to 5′ long.

except that one prefers the mountains, the other the swamps. The Snowdrop never becomes a large tree, thirty feet is its maximum height. The leaves are ovate, when full grown are four to five inches long, three to four inches wide, with very conspicuous veins and stout petioles. The flower is cream-white, the corolla fully an inch long and divided nearly to the base into spreading divisions about as long as the stamens, which are usually eight in number. The ovary is two-celled and like the exserted stigma coated with pale tomentum. The fruit is oblong, compressed, one and one-half to two inches long, often an inch wide with two broad wings and sometimes little, narrow, supplementary wings between them. The fruit of the Silverbell has four wings, whence the early specific name *tetraptera.*

The Snowdrop-tree is perfectly hardy on the southern shore of Lake Erie where it forms a small tree with a beautiful, low, broad head. In flower and foliage and general appearance the Silverbell and the Snowdrop are twin sisters and one is not to be preferred to the other.

Fruit of Snowdrop-tree, *Mohro-dendron dipterum.*

The name of the genus has suffered vicissitudes. In the earlier botanies the generic name was *Halesia,* but that is now displaced by *Mohrodendron. Halesia* was a name given to the genus in 1759 in honor of Stephen Hales, a botanist of the eighteenth century who wrote one of the first English books upon vegetable physiology. But it happened that an explorer in Jamaica four years before had given the same name to a genus of tropical plants. So that two widely different genera appeared in the books as *Halesia.* Such duplication of names became in course of time a source of great confusion in botanic nomenclature and the American Association for the Advancement of Science decided, if possible, to bring order out of the perplexing situation. Two rules were established. One—that every plant should hereafter be known by the name under which it was first published to the world, unless that had already been given to another plant ; and the other—that no later name should stand whether the first did or did not. Now comes the result. The tropical *Halesia* was found to be no genus at all but only a species which was soon referred to its proper place. There then remained but one *Halesia*. But here the second rule came in, and so our pretty Silverbells lost their generic name. It was then suggested that they should be named *Mohrodendron* in honor of Dr. Charles Mohr, an eminent botanist of Alabama. The suggestion was accepted and so Stephen Hales was deposed and Dr. Mohr reigns in his stead.

OLEÀCEÆ—OLIVE FAMILY

WHITE ASH

Fráxinus americàna.

A graceful tree, sometimes one hundred feet in height but usually seventy or eighty, with straight trunk three feet or more in diameter at the base. When growing alone it produces a round-topped or a pyramidal head of great beauty. It is distributed from Nova Scotia and Minnesota to Florida and Texas, but attains its greatest size on the bottom lands of the lower Ohio valley. Grows rapidly, prefers rich moist soil and is recommended for city planting in the eastern states.

Bark.—Gray, deeply furrowed into narrow flattened ridges, surface scaly. Branchlets stout, terete, at first slightly hairy, dark green, later become pale orange or ashy gray.

Wood.—Brown, sapwood paler brown; heavy, tough, elastic, close-grained. Used in manufacture of furniture, carriages, agricultural implements, oars. Sp. gr., 0.6543; weight of cu. ft., 40.77 lbs.

Winter Buds.—Brown, nearly black, ovate, obtuse at apex. Terminal buds large, lateral buds smaller. Outer scales fall when spring ;rowth begins, inner scales enlarge and become green.

Leaves.—Opposite, pinnately compound, eight to twelve inches long. Leaflets five to nine; three to five inches long, one to two broad, petiolate, ovate or oblong-lanceolate, unequally wedge-shaped or rounded at base, entire, or obscurely serrate, acuminate or acute. They come out of the bud conduplicate, thin, smooth or slightly hairy; when full grown are smooth, dark green, often shining above, pale, sometimes silvery beneath, often hairy along the veins. Feather-veined, midrib compressed above, primary veins conspicuous. In autumn they turn brownish purple fading into yellow. Petioles stout, smooth, grooved, swollen at the base. Petiolules about one-fourth of an inch long.

White Ash, *Fraxinus americana.*

Leaves 8′ to 12′ long.   Leaflets 3′ to 5′ long.

Flowers.—May, before the leaves; Diœcious, borne in lengthened panicles near the end of the branches, in axils of last year's leaves. Pedicels smooth; bracts varying in size and form.

Calyx.—Campanulate; in staminate flower slightly four-lobed; in pistillate flower deeply lobed.

Corolla.—Wanting.

Stamens.—Two, rarely three; filaments, short; anthers large, oblong, reddish purple.

Pistil.—Ovary superior, two-celled, oval, contracted into a long slender style, with two spreading dark purple stigmatic lobes.

Fruit.—Samaras, borne in crowded drooping panicles six to eight inches long, these hang upon the leafless branches until midwinter. The samaras vary in length from one to two inches. Body terete, pointed, marginless below, abruptly dilated into a lanceolate or linear wing, acute or emarginate at apex. August, September. Cotyledons elliptical.

A Staminate and a Pistillate Flower of White Ash, *Fraxinus americana;* enlarged.

The White Ash is the most beautiful of all the American species. Its common name refers to the pale sometimes silvery under surface of the leaf and its specific name *americana* fully distinguishes it as the best of its type. Its fibrous roots enable it to flourish in a soil, rich but shallow, and oftentimes it may be seen clinging to rocks where with difficulty it can obtain a foothold. In the eastern and middle states it has proved itself an admirable city tree, but it has not been successfully planted in the prairie regions of the west, being unable to withstand the severe droughts to which they are subject.

Samaras of White Ash, *Fraxinus americana.*

In appearance the young tree is singularly graceful. The slender grayish trunk, the easy sweep of its branches, the slightly drooping poise of its leaves, and the soft, rich, mellow green of its foliage unite to attract our admiration. Its spray is clumsy compared with that of the beech and the maple. Although the leaves are tufted at the end of the spray, the branches are not bare ; on the contrary such is the flowing, clinging effect of its foliage that the tree may be said in a peculiar degree to be clothed with its leaves. The trunk rises more than an average height before it divides and after the division still retains a central shaft, yet this shaft disappears from sight as soon as it enters the mass of foliage, and cannot be traced through the leafy head.

The autumnal tints are most unusual and most beautiful. Wilson Flagg in "A Year Among the Trees" writes concerning them : "The colors of the ash are quite unique, and distinguish it from all other trees. Under favorable circumstances its coloring process is nearly uniform. It begins with a general impurpling of the whole mass of foliage nearly at the same time and the gradual changes remind me of those observed in sea mosses during the process of bleaching. There is an invariable succession in these tints as in the brightening beams of morn. They are first of a dark bronze, turning from this to a chocolate, then to a violet brown, and finally to a salmon color or yellow with a shade of lilac. When the leaves are faded nearly yellow, they are ready to drop from the tree. It is remarkable that with all this variety of hues neither crimson nor any shade of scarlet is ever seen in the ash. It ought to be remembered that the gradations of autumn tints in all cases are in the order of those of sunrise, from dark to lighter hues, and never the reverse. I make no reference to the browns of dead leaves which are darker than yellow or orange, from which they turn. I speak only of the changes of leaves before they are seared or dry."

Two traditions follow the ash tree. They have come to us from Europe and their origin seems lost in the mists of antiquity. One is that no serpent willingly glides beneath its branches or rests under its shade. This belief was old in Pliny's time, for he states as a fact that if a serpent be placed

Trunk of White Ash, *Fraxinus americana.*

near a fire and both surrounded by ashen twigs, the serpent will sooner run into the fire than pass over the pieces of ash; all of which is important if true. The other, refers to the peculiar liability of the ash to be struck by lightning, and this belief is embalmed in ancient folk-lore rhymes.

The rustic laborer at the approach of a thunder-storm is admonished,

> Beware the oak it draws the stroke,
> Avoid the ash it courts the flash,
> Creep under the thorn it will save you from harm.

Indeed, the oak and ash are frequently associated in country proverbs and rural lore.

> If the oak is out before the ash,
> 'Twill be a summer of wet and splash;
> But if the ash is before the oak
> 'Twill be a summer of fire and smoke.

The wood of all the ashes is singularly light, strong and elastic. Prehistoric man seeking an available weapon found it in an ashen club. Achilles fought with an ashen spear. Cupid made his arrows first of the ash. The North American Indian could find no better wood in the forest for his bow or his paddle than the ash. It is the wood most extensively used in the manufacture of agricultural implements.

The tree has many insect enemies. All the species can be easily raised from seed, which sometimes does not germinate until the second year. Varieties can be multiplied by grafting.

Fraxinus is of wide distribution and ancient type. A tree of the temperate zone it occurs in Europe, Asia and Africa and except in the extreme north is found in all parts of North America. Its fossil remains prove it to have been abundant in the tertiary period within the arctic circle.

OLIVE FAMILY

RED ASH

Fráxinus pennsylvánica. Fráxinus pubéscens.

A comparatively small tree, averaging forty feet high with stout upright branches and irregular head. Ranges from New Brunswick to Florida, westward to Dakota, Nebraska and Kansas.

Bark.—Brown or ashy gray with numerous longitudinal shallow furrows, surface scaly. Branchlets slender, terete, at first velvety-downy, finally they become ashy gray or light brown, frequently covered with bloom. Inner face of outer bark of the branches red or cinnamon color.

Wood.—Light brown with lighter sapwood. Heavy, hard, strong and coarse-grained. Sp. gr., 0.7117; weight of cu. ft., 44.35 lbs.

Winter Buds.—Leaf-buds small, acute, downy, dark rusty brown. Outer scales fall when spring growth begins. The inner scales enlarge, become green and often leaf-like.

Leaves.—Opposite, pinnately compound, ten to twelve inches long. Leaflets seven to nine, petiolate, three to five inches long, one to one and a half wide, oblong-lanceolate to ovate, unequally wedge-shaped at base, serrate, sometimes entire, acuminate or acute. They come out of the bud conduplicate, coated beneath with thick white tomentum, shining and hairy above; when full grown are firm, yellow green above, pale and velvety-downy beneath. Feather-veined, midrib and primary veins conspicuous. In autumn they turn rusty brown fading into yellow. Petioles swollen at base, grooved, hairy. Petiolules thick, grooved, downy, about one-fourth of an inch long.

Flowers.—May, with the leaves. Dioecious, borne in compact, downy, bracteate panicles, which appear from the axils of last year's leaves.

Calyx.—In staminate flowers cup-shaped, obscurely toothed. In pistillate flowers cup-shaped, deeply divided.

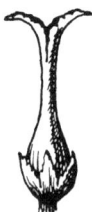

A Staminate and a Pistillate Flower of Red Ash, *Fraxinus pennsylvanica;* enlarged.

Corolla.—Wanting.

Stamens.—Two, sometimes three; anthers linear-oblong, pale greenish purple; filaments short.

Pistil.—Ovary superior, two-celled, contracted into a lengthened style, divided at apex into two green stigmatic lobes. Ovules two in each cell.

Fruit.—Samaras, borne in open panicles which remain on the branches throughout winter. One to two inches long; body slender, terete, half surrounded by a thin wing, rounded or acute at the apex.

Red Ash, *Fraxinus pennsylvanica.*
Leaves 10′ to 12′ long.   Leaflets 3′ to 5′ long.

In general appearance the Red and the White Ash strongly resemble each other. But the Red Ash is downy on branchlet and leaf and petiole while the White Ash is in the main smooth. Its specific name *pennsylvanica* emphasizes the fact that it is a tree of the North Atlantic states and grows best east of the Alleghany Mountains. It approaches the Black Ash in its preference for rich, low, moist soils, the banks of streams and the shores of lakes, but unlike it, will grow in dry localities. The wood is not so valuable as that of the White Ash, being brittle instead of elastic. The Green Ash, *F. lanceolata*, which is now considered a variety of the Red Ash, may be distinguished from it by its dark and lustrous foliage, by the smoothness of its leaves and branchlets and the bright green both of the upper and lower surface of the leaves. In New England there are marked differences, but west of the Mississippi the two are connected by intermediate forms which blend them together.

Samaras of Red Ash, *Fraxinus pennsylvanica.*

The Green Ash is recommended for parks, streets, and shelter belts in the western states, largely because of its ability to flourish in regions of small and uncertain rainfall.

BLUE ASH

Fráxinus quadrangulàta.

A tall slender tree, sometimes one hundred and twenty feet in height with a trunk two or three feet in diameter, usually much smaller. Native of the Mississippi valley, nowhere very abundant, prefers lime-stone soils.

Bark.—Light gray tinged with red, irregularly fissured: Branchlets, stout, four-angled, more or less four-winged, at first orange color with rusty pubescence, later they become light brown or ashy gray and gradually terete.

Green Ash, *Fraxinus lanceolata.*
Leaves 8′ to 12′ long.   Leaflets 3′ to 5′ long.

Wood.—Light yellow streaked with brown, sapwood a lighter yellow ; heavy, hard, close-grained. Sp. gr., o.7184 ; weight of cu. ft., 44.77 lbs.

Winter Buds.—Terminal bud one-fourth inch long ; outer scales fall when spring growth begins, inner scales enlarge and become green.

Leaves.—Opposite, compound, unequally pinnate, eight to twelve inches long ; leaflets five to nine, petiolate, three to five inches long, one to two inches broad, ovate-oblong, unequally rounded or wedge-shaped at base, serrate, acuminate. They come out of the bud conduplicate, coated with brown tomentum, when full grown are thick, dark green and shining above, pale, smooth or hairy beneath ; in autumn they turn from brown and purple to yellow. Petiolules short and grooved.

Flowers.—April, before the leaves. Perfect, borne in loose panicles developed from buds formed in the axils of leaves of the previous year.

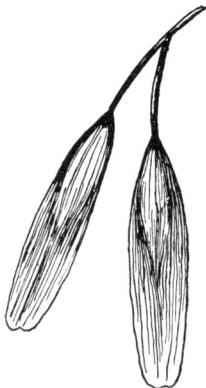

Flower of Blue Ash, *Fraxinus quadrangulata.*

Calyx.—Reduced to a ring.

Corolla.—Wanting.

Stamens.—Two, nearly sessile ; anthers dark purple, oblong, obtuse, introrse, two-celled ; cells opening longitudinally.

Samaras of Blue Ash, *Fraxinus quadrangulata.*

Pistil.—Ovary superior, two-celled ; style short with two, pale purple, stigmatic lobes. Ovules two in each cell.

Fruit.—Samaras, borne in panicles, linear-oblong, one to two inches long, one-fourth to one inch wide ; the broad wing surrounding the long flat body, emarginate, many-rayed. September, October. Cotyledons elliptical.

The Blue Ash belongs to that group of trees native to the valley of the Mississippi. Its habitat extends from southern Michigan to central Missouri and southward to eastern Tennessee and northern Alabama and through Iowa and Missouri to northeastern Arkansas. Some trees like the Rhododendron refuse to grow upon limestone ; the Blue Ash prefers it. Its chosen locations are rich limestone hills, but it will flourish in fertile bottom lands.

It may be distinguished among ashes by its peculiar stout,

Blue Ash, *Fraxinus quadrangulata*.
Leaves 8′ to 12′ long.   Leaflets 3′ to 5′ long.

tour-angled and four-winged branchiets. Its samaras resemble those of the Black Ash, in that the broad wing wholly surrounds the long flat body. Its wood has the qualities of the other ashes and probably is not distinguished commercially from them. The tree is recommended for park planting as it is hardy and grows rapidly, and its foliage is a rich, dark, shining green.

The inner bark yields a blue color to water, whence its common name.

BLACK ASH

Fráxinus nìgra. Fráxinus sambucifòlia.

A tall, slender tree, with narrow head of slender upright branches. Loves deep cold swamps and muddy banks of streams. Is distributed from Newfoundland to Manitoba, southward to Delaware and Virginia.

Bark.—Granite gray, fissured, surface scaly. Branchlets stout, terete, dark green at first, later ashy gray or yellowish, finally dark gray.

Wood.—Dark brown, sapwood light brown or white ; heavy, rather soft, tough, coarse-grained. Used for barrel hoops, baskets, cabinet work and interior of houses. Sp. gr., 0.6318 ; weight of cu. ft., 39.37 lbs.

Winter Buds.—Dark, almost black, ovate, acute at apex ; outer scales fall when spring growth begins, inner scales enlarge and become green.

Leaves.—Opposite, pinnately compound, twelve to sixteen inches long. Leaflets seven to eleven, sessile except the terminal, oblong or oblong-lanceolate, three to five inches long, one to two inches wide, unequally wedge-shaped or rounded at base, slightly serrate, acute or acuminate. They come out of the bud conduplicate, downy with rusty hairs, when full grown dark green, smooth above. paler beneath and smooth, except the midrib which is hairy. Feather-veined, midrib and primary veins conspicuous. In autumn they turn rusty brown and fall early. Petioles smooth, swollen at base, flattened or grooved.

Flowers.—May, before the leaves. Polygamous, without calyx or corolla. Borne in lengthened panicles four or five inches long which are opposite, single or in threes, in the axils of last year's leaves, many-bracted. Staminate flowers are borne on separate trees or mixed with perfect flowers on trees which produce pistillate ones.

Black Ash, *Fraxinus nigra*.
Leaves 12′ to 16′ long.   Leaflets 3′ to 5′ long.

Stamens.—Two, anthers large, oblong, dark purple, attached to the back of short filaments.

Pistil.—Ovary superior, two-celled, narrowed into a long slender style, deeply divided at the apex into two broad, purple stigmas. Ovules two in each cell.

Fruit.—Samaras, borne in panicles. Oblong-linear, an inch to an inch and a half long. Body surrounded by the wing, which is emarginate at apex. Seed solitary by abortion. September, October. Cotyledons elliptical.

The Black Ash is the slenderest of our forest trees, often reaching the height of seventy feet with a trunk whose diameter scarcely exceeds a foot. It is the most northern of American ashes flourishing on the shores of the Gulf of St. Lawrence.

A Staminate and a Pistillate Flower of Black Ash, *Fraxinus nigra ;* enlarged.

Its inflorescence is polygamous, that is, staminate, pistillate, and perfect flowers may all be found on a single tree, although usually the staminate flowers are borne on a separate tree. In this species the flower is reduced to its lowest terms. Both calyx and corolla are wanting. Many flowers consist simply of two stamens sitting on the top of the flower stem, others are only a pistil.

The Black Ash may be known among other ashes by the fact that its leaflets are sessile with the exception of the terminal one. Its samaras differ from those of the White Ash in that the wing entirely surrounds the body. The taste of the seed is aromatic.

The wood is remarkable for its toughness and elasticity. The Indians especially used it in the manufacture of baskets, preferring it to every other. The trunk is often disfigured by knobs which are sometimes taken off and made into bowls which when polished show very odd undulations of

Samaras of Black Ash, *Fraxinus nigra.*

fibre. The Black Ash does not transplant well and will flourish only in swampy places. It is considered a tree of slow growth and is short-lived.

YGGDRASIL, THE TREE OF THE UNIVERSE

It is not within the scope of this volume to enter into any extended discussion of the curious myths and traditions that among many nations gravely ascribe the descent of the human race from trees. The mystical " tree of life " was the date palm, the fig, the pine, the cedar, the oak, the elm, the ash—varying with the country and the vegetation.

Virgil in the "Æneid," Book VIII., says :

> These woods were first the seat of sylvan powers,
> Of nymphs and fauns and savage men who took
> Their birth from trunks of trees and stubborn oaks.

Juvenal in the Sixth Satire tells us :

> For when the world was new the race that broke
> Unfathered, from the soil or opening oak,
> Lived most unlike the men of later times.

In the "Odyssey," the disguised hero is asked to state his pedigree, since he must necessarily have had one. "For," says his questioner, "belike you are not come of the oak, told of in old times, nor of the rock."

The most remarkable of all these fables and the best known is that of the Tree of the Universe, in the Norse mythology, around which have clustered as many theories as legends without any definite solution of the subject.

Yggdrasil, the Tree of the Universe, is generally conceded to have been an ash tree. In the old legend it springs from the body of Ymir the earth, its trunk rises to the sky, its branches overshadow the earth and support the heavens. Three roots sustain and nourish this mighty tree. One extends into Asgard the home of the Gods ; beneath it bubbles a fountain with whose waters the tree is sprinkled. By its side is a hall where dwell three maidens, Norns—Urd the past, Verdandi the present, Skuld the future—the Scandinavian Fates who direct and sway the destinies of men.

The second root reaches Jötunheim the abode of the Giants and by its side is Mimir's spring within whose depths wit and knowledge lie hidden ; the third strikes deep into Niflheim the region of darkness and cold. The spring here feeds the serpent Nithhöggr, Darkness, which perpetually gnaws at the root.

The leaves of the tree drop honey, and upon the topmost branch sits an eagle who observes all that goes on in the world. A squirrel, Ratatöskr, runs up and down along the trunk and branches bearing messages between the eagle and the serpent and stirring up strife between them. Four stags run back and forth among the branches and bite the buds ; these are the four winds.

Such is the fantastic story of the ash tree, for which there is neither explanation nor reasonable interpretation.

FRINGE-TREE

Chionánthus virgínica.

Chionanthus is of Greek derivation and refers to the snow white flowers of the species.

A slender tree twenty or thirty feet high ; at the north a shrub of several, thick, spreading stems. Commonly planted on lawns and parks. Ornamental. Roots fibrous. Ranges from Pennsylvania to Florida, westward through the Gulf states to Texas, Arkansas and Kansas.

Bark.—Brown, tinged with red, scaly. Branchlets terete, light green, downy, at first; later they become light brown or orange color.

Wood.—Light brown, sapwood paler brown ; heavy, hard, close-grained.

Winter Buds.—Light brown, ovate, acute, one-eighth of an inch long. Outer scales fall when spring growth begins, inner scales enlarge with the growing shoot and become leaf-like, an inch or more in length.

Flowering Branch of Fringe-tree, *Chionanthus Virginica.*
Leaves 4′ to 8′ long, 1′ to 4′ broad.

Leaves.—Opposite, simple, ovate or oblong, four to eight inches long, one to four inches broad, wedge-shaped at base, entire with undulate margins, acuminate, acute or rounded at apex. Feather-veined, midrib stout, primary veins conspicuous. They come out of the bud conduplicate, yellow green and shining above, downy beneath ; when full grown are dark green above, pale below and smooth except the midrib and veins which are hairy. In autumn they turn a clear yellow and fall early. Petiole stout, hairy.

Flowers.—May, June ; when leaves are one-third grown. Perfect, white, slightly fragrant, borne in loose, downy, drooping, bracted panicles, four to six inches long, from lateral buds ; peduncles three-flowered.

Calyx.—Four-parted, small, smooth, persistent.

Fringe-tree, *Chionanthus virginica.*
Drupes ½′ to ¾′ long.

Corolla.—An inch long, white, dotted on inner surface with purple spots, deeply divided into four, varying to five and six, long and narrow lobes barely united at base ; conduplicate, valvate in bud.

Stamens.—Two, inserted on the base of the corolla, extrorse ; filaments short ; anthers pale yellow, ovate, two-celled.

Pistil.—Ovary superior, two-celled ; style short ; stigma fleshy, two-lobed.

Fruit.—Drupe, borne in loose clusters, on which the bracts have become leaf-like. Oval or oblong, dark blue, glaucous, one-half to three-fourths of an inch long, surrounded at base by the persistent calyx and tipped with remnants of the style. Skin thick ; flesh dry ; stone thin.

The Fringe-tree is one of the most beautiful of our ornamental shrubs and although a native of the south it is hardy at the north and is extensively planted. It prefers a moist soil and a sheltered situation and may be propagated by grafting on the ash.

The singular appearance of its snow white flowers which look like a fringe, give to it the common name. These flowers appear abundantly when the leaves are half grown and the foliage mass becomes a combination of soft **green** and **pure white**, which is most beautiful.

BIGNONIÀCEÆ—BIGNONIA FAMILY

CATALPA. INDIAN BEAN

Catálpa Catálpa. Catálpa bignonioìdes.

A tree with a short thick trunk, long and straggling branches which form a broad and irregular head. Loves river banks and moist shady places. Roots fibrous, branches brittle. Its juices are watery and contain a bitter principle.

Bark.—Light brown tinged with red. Branchlets forking regularly by pairs, at first green, shaded with purple and slightly hairy, later gray or yellowish brown, finally reddish brown. Contains tannin.

Wood.—Light brown, sapwood nearly white ; light, soft, coarsegrained and durable in contact with the soil.

Winter Buds.—No terminal bud, uppermost bud is axillary. Minute, globular, deep in the bark. Outer scales fall when spring growth begins, inner scales enlarge with the growing shoot, become green, hairy and sometimes two inches long.

Leaves.—Opposite, or in threes, simple, six to ten inches long, four to five broad. Broadly ovate, cordate at base, entire, sometimes wavy, acute or acuminate. Feather-veined, midrib and primary veins prominent. Clusters of dark glands, which secrete nectar are found in the axils of the primary veins. They come out of the bud involute, purplish, when full grown are bright green, smooth above, pale green, and downy beneath. When bruised they give a disagreeable odor. They turn dark and fall after the first severe frost. Petioles stout, terete, long.

Flowers.—June, July. Perfect, white, borne in many-flowered thyrsoid panicles, eight to ten inches long. Pedicels slender, downy.

Calyx.—Globular and pointed in the bud ; finally splitting into two, broadly ovate, entire lobes, green or light purple.

Corolla.—Campanulate, tube swollen, slightly oblique, two-lipped, five-lobed, the two lobes above smaller than the three below, imbricate in bud ; limb spreading, undulate, when fully expanded is an inch and a half wide and nearly two inches long, white, marked on the inner surface with two rows of yellow blotches and in the throat on the lower lobes with purple spots.

Stamens.—Two, rarely four, inserted near the base of the corolla, introrse, slightly exserted ; anthers oblong, two-celled, opening longitudinally ; filaments flattened, thread-like. Sterile filaments three, inserted near base of corolla, often rudimentary.

Pistil.—Ovary superior, two-celled ; style long, thread-like, with a two-lipped stigma. Ovules numerous.

Fruit.—Long slender capsule, nearly cylindrical, two-celled, partition at right angles to the valves, Six to twenty inches long, brown ; hangs on the tree all winter, splitting before it falls. Seeds an inch long, one-fourth of an inch wide, silvery gray, winged on each side and ends of wings fringed.

The Catalpa shares with the Horse-chestnut the distinction of bearing the most showy flowers of all our ornamental trees. Its value in this respect has long been recognized and to-day it holds an assured place in the parks and gardens of all temperate countries.

In the northern states it is a late bloomer, putting forth great panicles of white flowers the last of June or early in July when the flowers of other trees have mostly faded. These cover the tree so thickly as almost to conceal the full grown leaves. The general effect of the flower cluster is a pure white, but the individual corolla is spotted with purple and gold, and some of these spots are arranged in lines along a ridge, so as to lead directly to the honey sweets within. A single flower when fully expanded is two inches long and an inch and a half wide. It is two-lipped and the lips are lobed, two lobes above and three below, as is not uncommon with such corollas. The flower is perfect, possessing both stamens and pistils ; nevertheless, the law of elimination is at work and of the five stamens that we should expect to find, three have aborted, ceased to bear anthers and have become filaments simply. Then, too, the flowers refuse to be self-fertilized. Each flower has its own stamens and its own stigma and the natural conclusion is that the home pollen should fall upon

Flowering Spray of Catalpa.
Leaves 6' to 10' long, 4' to 6' broad.

the stigma. But this is not the case. The lobes of the stigma remain resolutely closed until after the anthers have opened and discharged their pollen ; after they have withered and become effete then the stigma opens and invites the wandering bee. There is nothing more curious in the entire field of biology than this refusal of self-fertilization on the part of so many flowers. The entire Pink family behave in this way.

The leaves appear rather late, are large, heart-shaped, bright green and as they are full grown before the flower clusters open, add much to the beauty of the blossoming tree. They secrete nectar, a most unusual proceeding for leaves, by means of groups of tiny glands in the axils of the primary veins.

The fruit is a long, slender pod packed full of light silvery seeds, each provided with a pair of pretty fringed wings to bear it afloat by wind or water in search of a home. These pods hang pendent upon the branches for the greater part of the winter, sometimes far into the spring.

The Catalpa is undoubtedly a southern tree. It seems that Europeans first observed it growing in the fields of the Cherokee Indians, by whom it was called Catalpa. But its vitality enables it to flourish at the north and the land of its nativity is somewhat in doubt. The tree is fairly free from fungal diseases and has few insect enemies. It is easily raised from seeds which germinate early in the first season. It also multiplies readily from cuttings.

Catalapa speciosa is a western species that has come into notice later than *C. catalpa ;* it is largely planted throughout the same range and is quite as satisfactory a tree for lawns and parks. The difference between them is very slight, and it may be that *C. speciosa* will some day be considered simply a variety of the other.

The genus is now found only in the United States, West Indies and China. It was common in Europe during the tertiary period and its fossil remains have been discovered in the miocene rocks of the Yellowstone.

LAURÀCEÆ—LAUREL FAMILY

SASSAFRAS

Sássafras sássafras.

Usually from thirty to fifty feet high, sometimes one hundred, with a stout trunk and flat-topped head ; often much smaller and shrubby. Thick fleshy roots penetrate deep into the ground and send out abundance of suckers, making thickets. Prefers rich sandy loam. Grows rapidly. Ranges from Massachusetts to Florida and west throughout the Mississippi valley.

Bark.—Thick, dark, red brown, deeply and irregularly divided into broad flat ridges, separating into thick appressed scales on the surface. Branchlets bright yellow green, finally reddish brown, and in two or three years begin to show shallow fissures. Aromatic and spicy. Twigs mucilaginous.

Wood.—Dull orange brown ; soft, weak, coarse-grained, brittle, though durable in contact with the soil. Used for posts and rails, small boats and ox-yokes.

Winter Buds.—Flower-buds terminal, ovate, acute ; axillary buds small. The scales enlarge with the growing shoot, the inner becoming leaf-like before falling.

Leaves.—Alternate, ovate or obovate, four to six inches long, entire or one to three-lobed, lobes broadly ovate, divided by broad sinuses ; margins entire. They come out of the bud involute, reddish green ; when full grown are smooth, dull dark green above, paler beneath. In autumn they turn to shades of yellow, tinged with red. Petioles slender, slightly grooved.

Flowers.—May, with the first unfolding of the leaves. Diœcious, rarely perfect, greenish yellow, borne in loose, drooping, few-flowered racemes ; involucre of scaly bracts.

Calyx.—Pale yellow green, six-lobed, spreading, imbricate in bud.

Corolla.—Wanting.

Stamens.—In sterile flowers nine, inserted on the base of the calyx in three rows, the inner row with a pair of conspicuous glands at the base of each; fertile flowers have six short rudimentary stamens. Anthers innate, oblong, four-celled, opening by four uplifting valves.

Pistil.—Ovary superior, nearly sessile in the tube of the calyx, simple, one-celled ; style one ; ovule one, suspended from the apex of the cell.

Fruit.—Drupe, oblong, dark blue, shining, surrounded at the base by the enlarged and thickened scarlet calyx raised on a club-shaped rather fleshy pedicel. Cotyledons thick, fleshy.

The Sassafras often grows in dense thickets. A single tree, if allowed to spread unrestrained, will soon be surrounded by a numerous and flourishing family, as its stoloniferous roots extend in every direction and send up multitudes of shoots. When full grown it is rather picturesque, as its branches are usually irregular and the head partially flattened. It has the peculiarity of looking older than it really is because of its rough, deeply furrowed, gray bark and rather warped stem. This cracking of the bark is characteristic, it begins on stems two or three years old, and continues through life.

Fruit of the Sassafras.

A peculiar foliage marks the tree in every situation, for it enjoys the distinction of bearing leaves of three different forms on the same branch ; a distinction among our common deciduous trees shared only with the Mulberry. Those leaves are oval, or oval with a lobe at one side making what are called "mittens," or regularly three-lobed. There seems to be no known law which determines the order of their appearance, but the mature tree bears more oval leaves than lobed ones.

The Sassafras will grow in any loose moist soil, and especially delights in neglected and abandoned fields.

The fruit is a beautiful, dark blue, shining berry set on a bright red, club-shaped, fleshy stem. The birds love it and

Sassafras.

Leaves 4′ to 6′ long.

so eager are they that it is often years before one succeeds in obtaining a perfectly mature specimen. Wings outclass hands when the top of a tree is in question.

The wood, bark, and roots are all aromatic. The flavor resides in an essential oil which is especially abundant in the bark of the root. At one time Sassafras enjoyed a great reputation in the *Materia medica*, but it is now valued chiefly for its power to improve the flavor of other medicines.

Sassafras is now native only to eastern North America. Its remains are found in the arctic regions and traces of it appear in the cretaceous rocks of the extreme west, it also formerly existed in Europe.

ULMÀCEÆ—ELM FAMILY

WHITE ELM. AMERICAN ELM. WATER ELM

Ûlmus americàna.

Ulmus is the ancient name of the elm tree and was adopted by
Linnæus as the name of the genus.

Abundant in moist woods, throughout the entire north, especially
in rich alluvial soil. Varies from sixty to one hundred and twenty
feet in height, the trunk sturdy and usually dividing at one-third the
height of the tree into two to five branches. Grows rapidly, is long
lived. Roots fibrous and run near the surface of the ground, often
rise above it.

Bark.—Dark gray, rough, with longitudinal and not very closely
adherent ridges. Branchlets light green, downy, later become reddish brown, smooth and finally ashy gray.

Wood.—Reddish brown, sapwood pale; heavy, hard, strong,
tough, difficult to split, rather coarse-grained; will take no polish;
used for hubs of wheels, saddletrees and cooperage. Sp. gr.,
0.6506; weight of cu. ft., 40.55 lbs.

Winter Buds.—Flower-buds larger than leaf buds, produced in
the axils of the leaves of the previous year. Leaf-buds brown, one-
eighth of an inch long, ovate, acute, slightly flattened; scales
smooth. No terminal bud is formed. When spring growth begins
the inner scales enlarge.

Leaves.—Alternate, four to six inches long, two to three inches
broad, obovate-oblong, or oval, unequal at base, doubly serrate,
acuminate. Feather-veined, midvein and primary veins conspicuous. They come out of the bud conduplicate, downy, pale green;
when full grown are dark green, rough above, pale green and downy
or smooth beneath. In autumn they turn brown or golden yellow.
Petioles short; stipules fugacious.

Flowers.—March, April, before the leaves. Perfect, small, brownish yellow or reddish, borne in loose umbel-like clusters, on slender
pedicels, on last year's wood.

Calyx.—Campanulate, four to nine-lobed, hairy, green, tinged with red, becoming brown in fading ; lobes imbricate in bud.

Corolla.—Wanting.

Stamens.—Four to nine or as many as the calyx lobes and opposite to them, exserted ; filaments long, slender ; anthers bright red, two-celled, cells opening longitudinally ; pollen shed before the stigmas mature.

Pistil.—Ovary superior, two-celled ; styles two, light green ; ovules solitary.

Fruit.—Samaras, winged all round, maturing as the leaves appear and clinging to the branch in clusters, ovate, one-seeded, one-half inch long, two-beaked, sharp points incurved and closing the notch, green, smooth on faces, densely ciliate at margins. Cotyledons flat, fleshy.

Who knows not the 'vine prop' elm, with its lofty grace and slight benedictive droop, the oriole's nest still swinging from the end of some branch?
— EDITH THOMAS.

White Elm and Silver Maple are the first trees to accept the challenge of March that spring has come, and they seal their acceptance with flowers not leaves, for the law of the wild wood is that forest trees shall produce flowers before leaves. The flower-buds are usually borne

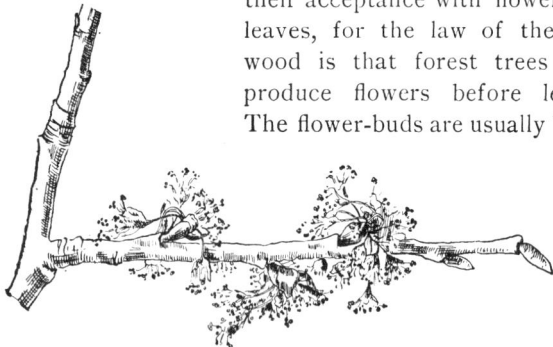

Flowering Spray of White Elm, *Ulmus americana.*

on the topmost branches of an elm tree, and even in February they respond to the kindly influence of a few warm days by becoming swollen and shining. When March stops for a day or two to take his breath and the sun shines and the warm air comes up from the south, these swollen buds shake off their brown scales and come out as little clusters of eight to

White Elm, *Ulmus americana.*
Leaves 4′ to 6′ long, 2′ to 3′ broad.

twenty, tiny, reddish brown blossoms. In cities where the elm is a common tree the sidewalks are strewn with these discarded bud scales, but the flowers are so small, so brown and so high that the world walks by, thinking, "The elm never blossoms." Six weeks later the same sidewalks are covered with little, flat, green samaras half an inch long, often as unnoticed as the blossoms which preceded them.

The typical outline form of the elm is triangular, though it is inclined to vary with location and opportunity. Probably the best description of the varied forms of the elm is found in the report of George B. Emerson upon the Trees and Shrubs of Massachusetts. He says : "From a root, which in old trees, spreads much above the surface of the ground, the trunk rises to a considerable height in a single stem. Here it usually divides into two or three principal branches, which go off by a gradual and easy curve. These stretch upward and outward with an airy sweep—become horizontal, the extreme branchlets and sometimes the extreme half of the limb, pendent, forming a light and regular arch."

"The American elm affects many different shapes, all of them beautiful. Of these, three are most striking and distinct. The tall Etruscan vase is formed by four or five limbs, separating at twenty or thirty feet from the ground, going up with a gradual divergency to sixty or seventy, and there bending rapidly outward, forming a flat top with a pendent border. The single or compound plume is represented by trees stretching up in single stem, or two or three parallel limbs to the height of seventy or even a hundred feet, and spreading out in one or two light feathery plumes. The elm often assumes a character akin to that of the oak ; that is when it has been transplanted young from an open situation and allowed always to remain by itself. It is then a broad round-headed tree."

The leaves come out of the bud a pale tender green and folded like little fans. They appear late because the flowering and fruiting is virtually over before their arrival. Cling-

White Elm, *Ulmus americana.*

ing closely to the twig as they do they have little independent motion but move with the branch. An elm leaf can be easily recognized by its unequal base, the part of the leaf on one side of the midrib is considerably larger than that upon the other. Although a favorite city shade tree the elm does not thrive where soft coal is habitually burned. The rough leaves catch the soot which sticks fast, seems to smother the trees, and in time destroys them.

Unfolding Leaves of White Elm, *Ulmus americana.*

One who recognizes it only in leaf does not really know a deciduous tree, for it is when stripped like an athlete for its contest with the winds and storms of winter, that it discloses the secret of its grace, its weakness, or its strength. No tree endures this test better than the elm and its typical form is so marked that it can be easily recognized even at night when outlined against the sky.

A peculiar characteristic of the wood is the wonderful twisting and interlacing of its fibres which give it an exceeding toughness. A characteristic immortalized by Oliver Wendell Holmes in " The Wonderful One-Hoss Shay."

> The hubs of logs from the " Settler's ellum,"
> Last of its timber,—they couldn't sell 'em,
> Never an axe had seen their chips,
> And the wedges flew from between their lips,
> Their blunt ends frizzled like celery-tips.

The Elms are an ancient race ; traces of them exist in the tertiary rocks of Greenland, and in the miocene period they flourished in Europe, western Asia and North America.

A few elm trees have become historic, either because of

Slippery Elm, *Ulmus pubescens.*
Leaves 5′ to 7′ long.

great size, or because of some great event occurring beneath their branches. For example, the Washington Elm in Cambridge, Massachusetts, is so called because beneath its shade General Washington is said to have first drawn his sword, on taking command of the American army. The famous treaty of William Penn with the Indians was made beneath the branches of an enormous elm, which remained standing in the suburbs of Philadelphia until 1810, when it was blown down. Its site is marked by a marble column and its age was estimated to be two hundred and thirty-three years.

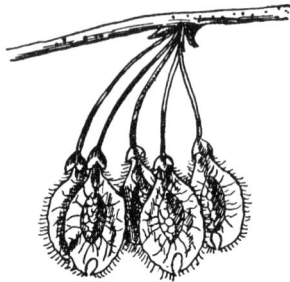

White Elm, *Ulmus americana.* Samaras ½' long.

SLIPPERY ELM. RED ELM

Úlmus pubéscens—Úlmus fúlva.

Fulva, reddish yellow, refers to the color of the wood. *Pubescens,* downy. Slippery characterizes the inner bark.

Common. Sixty to seventy feet in height, trunk sometimes two feet in diameter and spreading branches which form a broad, open, flat-topped head. Prefers banks of streams and fertile hillsides ; roots fibrous. Ranges from St. Lawrence River to Florida and throughout the entire Mississippi valley.

Bark.—Dark brown tinged with red, divided by shallow fissures, and covered with large loose plates. Branchlets stout, bright green, later light brown, finally dark gray or brown.

Wood.—Dark brown or red ; heavy, hard, close-grained, strong, tough, durable in contact with the soil, and easy to split while green. When boiled or steamed it becomes very flexible. Used for fence posts. railway ties, sills of buildings, agricultural implements. Sp. gr., 0.6956 ; weight of cu. ft., 43.35 lbs.

Winter Buds.—Leaf-buds ovate, rather obtuse, one-fourth of an inch long, covered with tawny hairs. Flower-buds larger than leaf-buds. Inner scales enlarge with the growing shoot and become green, obtuse, hairy, the innermost serve as stipules for a time.

Leaves.—Alternate, ovate-oblong, five to seven inches long, rounded at the base on one side and oblique on the other, coarsely and doubly serrate, acute or acuminate. Feather-veined, midrib very prominent beneath. They come out of the bud conduplicate, thin, light green; when full grown they are thick, firm, dark green, rough above, paler and somewhat rough beneath. In autumn they turn to a dull yellow. Petioles short, hairy; stipules caducous.

Flowers.—March, April, before the leaves. Perfect, borne in clusters on short pedicles produced from the axils of minute green bracts.

Calyx.—Campanulate, five to nine-lobed, green, hairy; lobes imbricate in bud.

Corolla.—Wanting.

Stamens.—Five to nine, exserted, light yellow; filaments slender; anthers dark red, do not shed their pollen until the stigmas have begun to wither, extrorse, two-celled; cells opening longitudinally.

Pistil.—Ovary superior, one-celled by abortion; stigmas two, reddish purple; ovules solitary.

Fruit.—Samaras, winged all round, maturing when leaves are half grown, semi-orbicular, one-half to three-fourths of an inch broad, hairy on the faces but naked at the margins; emarginate with remains of both stigmas at the apex. Wing is broad and thin and marked by the dark line of union of the two carpels.

Although the White Elm and the Slippery Elm look very much alike there are several points of difference which make it fairly easy to distinguish them. The White Elm varies greatly in the size of its leaves. There may be individual White Elms whose leaves are larger than individual Slippery Elms but upon the whole, given the same conditions, the foliage mass of a Slippery Elm is made up of larger leaves than that of the White Elm. The leaves are much rougher, they are rough whichever way you rub them, while the White Elm leaves are

Slippery Elm, *Ulmus pubescens.*
Samaras ½′ to ¾′ long.

smooth one way and rough the other. The buds are hairy, those of the White Elm smooth. In the spring the leaves of the Slippery Elm come out protected and adorned with many bud scales, there are perhaps twelve all told and the inner ones become half an inch long, a quarter of an inch wide, pale green, rounded, and tipped with rusty hairs. The enlarged bud scales of the White Elm are bright green, smooth, sometimes an inch long, narrow and acute.

The samaras are larger than those of the White Elm and more orbicular. They ripen when the leaves are half grown, those of the White Elm ripen as the leaves unfold. The seed cavity is coated with thick brown tomentum. The margins are naked, those of the White Elm ciliate. The character of the inner bark is unmistakable. It is thick, fragrant, mucilaginous, demulcent, and nutritious. The water in which the bark has been soaked is a grateful drink for one suffering from affections of the throat and lungs. The Indians of New York call the tree, Oo-hoosk-ah—"It slips."

CORK ELM. ROCK ELM

Úlmus racemòsa.

Eighty to one hundred feet in height, sometimes three feet in diameter, often free of branches for sixty feet ; with short spreading limbs at the summit which form a round-topped head. Grows on dry gravelly uplands, rocky slopes and river cliffs. Roots fibrous. Ranges from Vermont to New York, from southern Michigan and Wisconsin to northeastern Nebraska, southeastern Missouri and middle Tennessee.

Bark.—Gray tinged with red, divided by wide fissures into broad ridges, which are broken at the surface into large scales. Branchlets light brown, downy, later dark brown or ashy gray. Corky irregular ridges appear on branches two years old.

Wood.—Pale brown tinged with red ; heavy, hard, close-grained, strong and tough, takes a fine polish. Used for agricultural implements, cabinetwork, railway ties, bridge timbers, and sills of buildings. Sp. gr., 0.7263 ; weight of cu. ft., 45.26 lbs.

Winter Buds.—Leaf-buds scaly, chestnut brown, ovate, acute, hairy, one-fourth of an inch long ; flower-buds larger. Inner scales enlarge with the growing shoot. No terminal bud is formed.

Leaves.—Alternate, obovate or oblong-oval, three to four inches long, rounded or wedge-shaped at base, doubly serrate, acute.

Cork Elm, *Ulmus racemosa.*
Leaves 3′ to 4′ long.

They come out of the bud conduplicate, pale green and hairy, when full grown are thick, firm, smooth, dark green above and paler green beneath. Feather-veined. In autumn they turn a bright clear yellow. Petioles short, hairy. Stipules ovate - lanceolate, veined, green with red margins, clasping with united bases.

Flowers.—March, April, before the leaves. Perfect, greenish, borne in three-flowered clusters on long drooping pedicles.

Calyx.—Campanulate, seven to eight-lobed ; lobes oblong, rounded.

Corolla.—Wanting.

Stamens.—Seven to eight, exserted ; filaments light green ; anthers oblong, dark purple, extrorse, two-celled ; cells opening longitudinally.

Pistil.—Ovary superior, one-celled, hairy, with two styles ; ovule solitary.

Fruit.—Samaras, winged all round, mature in May when leaves are half grown, ovate, half an inch long, faces downy, margin densely ciliate ; wing narrow in proportion to the seed.

The Cork Elm is perhaps the most valuable tree of the genus, as it possesses all the good qualities of the family and none of the bad ones. It is strong, tough, easy to work, takes a fine polish, in short, is so useful that it is likely to be exterminated. Its range is quite limited, extending through northern New York and southern Michigan to Nebraska, Missouri, and middle Tennessee. It is sometimes called the Hickory Elm and often the Cliff Elm. Its leaves are about the size of those of the White Elm and have the elm shape, unequal at base, oval, doubly serrate

Cork Elm, *Ulmus racemosa.*
Samaras ½' long.

and acute. The tree may be known in the spring by the raceme of drooping blossoms and later by its samaras. But at any time, the irregular corky ridges which grow from every side of the branches and branchlets give the tree a strange shaggy appearance and mark it unmistakably.

Winged Elm, *Ulmus alata.*
Leaves 2′ to 2½′ long.

ELM FAMILY

WINGED ELM. WAHOO

Ulmus alàta.

Alata, winged, referring to the bark of the branchlets.

Small tree, forty or fifty feet high, with short spreading branches and open round-topped head, the smaller branches with corky wings. Native to the southern states, though appearing in southern Illinois and southern Indiana. Prefers dry gravelly uplands, though found in alluvial soil. Roots fibrous.

Bark.—Brown tinged with red, divided by shallow fissures into flat ridges covered with small scales. Branchlets slender, light green tinged with red, later become brown tinged with red and develop corky wings which remain for a long time.

Wood.—Light brown ; heavy, hard close-grained, not strong, but difficult to split. Has very little value. Sp. gr., 0.7491 ; weight of cu. ft., 46.68 lbs.

Winter Buds.—Leaf-buds slender, acute, one-eighth of an inch long, smooth or downy ; flower-buds longer.

Leaves.—Alternate, ovate-oblong, often slightly falcate, two to two and a half inches long, oblique or rounded at base, doubly serrate, acute or acuminate. They come out of the bud conduplicate, pale green, often tinged with red, hairy, when full grown are thick, firm, dark green and smooth above, pale green, downy below. Feather-veined, midrib and veins prominent. In autumn they turn a pale yellow. Petioles short, stout, hairy. Stipules large, caducous.

Flowers.—March, before the leaves. Perfect, greenish brown. Borne on drooping pedicels in few-flowered clusters, furnished with both bracts and bractlets.

Calyx.—Campanulate, with five ovate, rounded lobes, imbricate in bud.

Corolla.—Wanting.

Stamens.—As many as the lobes of the corolla.

Pistil.—Ovary superior, raised on a short stipe and coated with white tomentum, one-celled by abortion ; stigmas two.

Fruit.—Samaras, winged all round ; mature at the unfolding of the leaves, oblong, one-third of an inch long, borne on a drooping stem, downy on the faces, tipped with incurved downy horns, margins densely ciliate. Wing narrow compared to seed.

English Elm, *Ulmus campestris.*

Leaves 3′ to 4′ long.

ELM FAMILY

The Wahoo or Winged Elm is a native of the southern states ranging along the line of Virginia, southern Illinois, and southern Indiana, to the shores of the Gulf of Mexico.

Its leaves are smaller than those of the White Elm ; its samaras are the smallest of all the elms ; its wood has interlaced fibres which make it difficult to split; its economic value is virtually nothing. It grows rapidly, branches low to the ground, has beautiful and abundant foliage and may well claim a place in our parks and lawns.

The most remarkable thing about the tree are the corky ridges along the sides of the branches from which the name *alata* has been given to the species.

ENGLISH ELM

Úlmus campéstris.

This elm was brought over to New England at an early date in the history of the colonies and there are vigorous specimens about Boston fully one hundred and fifty years old. Although known to us as the English Elm, competent opinion inclines to the belief that it was brought into England by the Romans and is not native to the island. This is the common elm tree of Europe and has been valued there both for its timber and its beauty from very ancient times. It does not have the drooping habit of our American elms but rather takes on the appearance of the oak. The leaves are oblique, often two-shouldered, rough, feather-veined and doubly serrate. Its seedlings vary greatly.

The ancient poets frequently mention this tree which, in common with many other barren trees, was devoted by them to the infernal gods. The Greeks and Romans considered all trees which produce no fruit fit for human use as funereal trees. Homer alludes to this when he tells us that Achilles raised a monument to the father of Andromache in a grove of elms :

> Jove's sylvan daughters bade their elms bestow
> A barren shade, and in his honor grow.
>
> —Iliad, Book VI.

The elm was in Roman days and is still used in Italy as a support to the vine. It is interesting, to a stranger, to see a vineyard planted full of small elm trees and the grape vines hanging from their branches or trained from one to another. The manner of cultivation seems not to have changed from ancient times.

> " If that fair elm," he cried, "alone should stand,
> No grapes would glow with gold and tempt the hand;
> Or if that vine without her elm should grow,
> 'Twould creep, a poor neglected shrub, below."
>
> —OVID.

HACKBERRY. SUGARBERRY. NETTLE TREE

Céltis occidéntalis.

The name *Celtis* is said to refer to the tree having been known to the ancient Celts; another explanation is that it was the ancient name of a species of lotus.

A large tree with a slender trunk, rising to the height of one hundred and thirty feet, is the Hackberry in the southwest, but in the middle states it attains the height of sixty feet with a handsome round-topped head and pendulous branches. It prefers rich moist soil, but will grow on gravelly or rocky hillsides. The roots are fibrous and it grows rapidly. Native throughout the United States east of the Rocky Mountains.

Bark.—Light brown or silvery gray, broken on the surface into thick appressed scales and sometimes roughened with excrescences. Branchlets slender, light green at first, finally red brown, at length become dark brown tinged with red.

Wood.—Light yellow; heavy, soft, coarse-grained, not strong. Used for fencing and cheap furniture. Sp. gr., 0.7287; weight of cu. ft., 45.41 lbs.

Winter Buds.—Axillary, ovate, acute, somewhat flattened, one-fourth of an inch long, light brown. Scales enlarge with the growing shoot, the innermost becoming stipules. No terminal bud is formed.

Leaves.—Alternate, ovate to ovate-lanceolate, more or less falcate, two and a half to four inches long, one to two inches wide, very oblique at the base, serrate, except at the base which is mostly entire, acute. Three-nerved, midrib and primary veins prominent. They come out of the bud conduplicate with slightly involute margins, pale yellow green, downy ; when full grown are thin, bright green, rough above, paler green beneath. In autumn they turn to a light yellow. Petioles slender, slightly grooved, hairy. Stipules varying in form, caducous.

Flowers.—May, soon after the leaves. Polygamo-monœcious, greenish. Of three kinds—staminate, pistillate, perfect ; borne on slender drooping pedicels.

Calyx.—Light yellow green, five-lobed, divided nearly to the base ; lobes linear, acute, more or less cut at the apex, often tipped with hairs, imbricate in bud.

Corolla.—Wanting.

Stamens.—Five, hypogynous ; filaments white, smooth, slightly flattened and gradually narrowed from base to apex ; in the bud incurved, bringing the anthers face to face, as flower opens they abruptly straighten ; anthers extrorse, oblong, two-celled ; cells opening longitudinally.

Pistil.—Ovary superior, one-celled ; style two-lobed ; ovules solitary.

Fruit.—Fleshy drupe, oblong, one-half to three-fourths of an inch long, tipped with remnants of style, dark purple. Borne on a slender stem ; ripens in September and October. Remains on branches during winter.

When one for the first time sees an elm tree bearing berries, it gives a shock to all his former ideas. To come upon the Hackberry, " tall and stately by the river," showing its elm relationship in the poise of its trunk, in the sweep and fall of its branches, in the effect of its foliage mass ; showing this so plainly that a novice says, " of course it is an elm," and then to find that elm bearing dark purple berries is indeed a surprise. Certainly the Hackberry is not an elm, and its stunted growth in the eastern states would never permit it to be mistaken for one, but where it attains its fullest development it shows unmistakably its family relationship.

Native to the Mississippi valley, it is rare east of the Alleghanies and west of the Rockies. The wood is not very valuable, but as an ornamental tree it has much to recommend it. It is tolerant of many conditions of soil and climate, likes water but can live in dry situations. Insects rarely attack its leaves, and it is comparatively free from serious diseases. It is now extensively planted as a shade tree in the western

Fruiting Spray of Hackberry, *Celtis occidentalis*.

states. The fruit is sweet and not unpleasant, and is loved by the birds.

The type is ancient, traces of *Celtis* have been found in the miocene rocks of Europe.

The European Nettle, *Celtis australis*, is supposed to have been the Lotus of the ancients, whose fruit Herodotus, Dioscorides, and Theophrastus describe as sweet, pleasant, and wholesome. Homer makes Ulysses say :

> I sent explorers forth—two chosen men,
> A herald was the third—to learn what race
> Of mortals nourished by the fruits of earth
> Possessed the land. They went and found themselves
> Among the Lotus-eaters soon, who used
> No violence against their lives, but gave
> Into their hands the lotus plant to taste.
> Whoever tasted once of that sweet food
> Wished not to see his native country more
> Nor give his friends the knowledge of his fate ;
> And then my messengers desired to dwell
> Among the Lotus-eaters, and to feed
> Upon the lotus, never to return.
>
> —ODYSSEY, Book IX.

MORÀCEÆ—MULBERRY FAMILY

RED MULBERRY

Mòrus rùbra.

Morus is the ancient classical name.

Common. Prefers rich soil of intervale lands and low hills. Sixty to seventy feet high, with a short trunk three or four feet in diameter, stout spreading branches making a dense, broad, round-topped head. Roots fibrous, grows rapidly. Juice milky. Ranges from Massachusetts to Florida, westward to Kansas and Nebraska.

Bark.—Dark brown tinged with red, divided into irregular plates ; separating into thick scales. Branchlets at first dark green, often tinged with red ; later, red brown and finally dark brown.

Wood.—Pale orange ; light, soft, coarse-grained, not strong, very durable in contact with the soil. Used for fences and in cooperage. Sp. gr., 0.5898 ; weight of cu. ft., 36.75 lbs.

Winter Buds.—Ovate, rounded at apex, one-fourth of an inch in length, light brown. Scales grow with the growing shoot. No terminal bud is formed.

Leaves.—Alternate, variable in shape, entire, ovate or semiorbicular, three-lobed sometimes five-lobed ; three to five inches long, more or less cordate at base, serrate, acute or acuminate. Three-nerved or in the lobed leaves, palmately-veined. They come out of the bud conduplicate, yellow green with reddish tinge ; when full grown are thin, dark bluish green, shining, smooth or rough above, paler green beneath. In autumn they turn a bright yellow and fall early. Petioles stout, grooved, rather long. Stipules caducous.

Flowers.—May, June, with the leaves ; monœcious and diœcious. Staminate flowers in densely flowered spikes an inch long, on short, hairy peduncles, in the axils of later leaves. A few pistillate are often mixed with these. Pistillate flowers in narrow spikes two to two and a half inches long and borne in the axils of the first leaves. Calyx four-parted ; stamens four ; filaments elastically expanding ;

styles two, thread-like ; ovary two-celled, one cell small and finally disappearing.

Fruit.—Compound, consisting of drupes each inclosed in a thickened, fleshy calyx. Bright red at first, finally dark purple, sweet and juicy ; about an inch long. July.

The tree (the Mulberry) is found in abundance in the northwestern parts of Florida. The Choctaws put its inner bark in hot water along with a quantity of ashes and obtain filaments, with which they weave a kind of cloth not unlike a coarse hempen cloth.

—ROMANS'S "Natural History of Florida."

There are three well known mulberries, the Red, the Black, and the White ; so named because of the color of their fruit. The Red Mulberry is the American species and bears the characteristic berry of the genus which is an aggregate fruit of many drupes. It resembles a blackberry. In ripening it is first red, then dark purple. In taste it is rather insipid, but is loved by the birds.

The Red Mulberry is generally distributed, but rarely attains great size. Standing in the southern forests it reaches the height of seventy feet, but ordinarily it is a low broad branched tree with trunk proportionately thickened. Like the Sassafras it bears leaves varying in form, some heart-shaped and others lobed. But these leaves are too thick and rough even when young to make proper food for the silkworm, which in a cold climate, feeds with advantage on the leaves of the White Mulberry only.

Fruit of Red Mulberry, *Morus rubra*, about 1′ long.

Professor Sargent says of it, " Surpassing as it does in height and breadth all mulberry trees of temperate regions, the dense shade afforded by its broad compact crown of dark blue green leaves, its freedom from disease and the attacks of disfiguring insects, its prolificness, its hardiness except in its earliest years, and the rapidity of its growth in good soil, make it a most desirable ornamental tree."

The Black Mulberry, *Morus nigra*, is the tree common in Europe, introduced it is supposed from Persia, that native

Red Mulberry, *Morus rubra.*

Leaves 3′ to 5′ long.

land of so many of our fruits. Its berry is large, dark purple, almost black, very juicy and delicious. Like all the mulberries, its leaves vary apparently without law. The tree is long-lived and many individuals in England are known to be three hundred years old. In the grounds of Christ Church College at Cambridge is one planted by Milton when a student of the college and it still bears delicious fruit as the writer can testify from personal experience. In Oxford, in the Common Room Garden of Pembroke College, are two mulberry trees which are said to have been planted before the college was founded in 1624.

The Black Mulberry has been known from the earliest records of antiquity, which leads to the belief that it is one of the first trees cultivated by man. It is related in the Bible, II. Samuel, v. 23, that David came out against his enemies from behind the mulberry trees, but there is always a difficulty in identifying any tree mentioned by the ancient authors unless its characteristics are expressly noted. Ovid, however, evidently points out the Black Mulberry as the one introduced in the story of Pyramis and Thisbe, and Pliny in several ways seems to identify the tree. In addition to much else he says, " Of all cultivated trees the mulberry is the last that buds, which it never does until the cold weather is past and it is therefore called the wisest of trees."

The mulberry was very generally introduced into England about 1605 because of an edict of James I. recommending the rearing of silkworms and offering packets of mulberry seeds to all who would sow them. But the royal knowledge was imperfect and the seeds distributed were those of the Black Mulberry which the silkworm will not willingly eat, instead of the White Mulberry upon which the silkworm thrives.

Shakespeare's Mulberry is referred to this period as it was planted in 1609 in his garden at New Place, Stratford. In Drake's Shakespeare, Mr. Drake mentions a native of Stratford who remembered frequently to have eaten of the fruit of this tree in his youth, some of its branches hanging over the wall which divided that garden from his father's. Cer-

Fruiting Branch of White Mulberry, *Morus alba*.

Leaves 3' to 5' long.

tainly the flourishing plants now growing in that garden, and for the delight of tourists averred to be the scions of that classic tree, are Black Mulberries.

The mulberry was dedicated by the Greeks to Minerva, probably because it was considered the wisest of trees.

Many persons still remember a children's game played by little girls, with the refrain,—

> As we go round the mulberry bush,
> The mulberry bush, the mulberry bush,
> As we go round the mulberry bush,
> So early in the morning.

The White Mulberry, *Morus alba*, is a native of China, and although many varieties have been produced they are all alike in this, that the fruit is white. The leaves are the preferred food of the silkworm and the tree seems to have been cultivated in China from most ancient times for the purpose of rearing silkworms. It is hardy on the southern shore of Lake Erie, and doubtless throughout our temperate range, although it succumbs to excessive heat and extreme cold. The leaves are variable in form, dark green and shining.

OSAGE ORANGE

Toxylon pomiferum. Maclura aurantiaca.

Toxylon, of Greek derivation, alludes to the Indian use of the wood in the manufacture of bows. Maclura was given in honor of William Maclure, an eminent scientist.

Native to the rich bottom lands of Arkansas, Texas, and Indian Territory. Forty to sixty feet high with short trunk and handsome round-topped head. Juice milky and acrid. Roots thick, fleshy, covered with bright orange colored bark.

Bark.—Dark, deeply furrowed, scaly. Branchlets at first bright green, pubescent, during first winter they become light brown tinged with orange, later they become a paler orange brown. Branches with yellow pith, and armed with stout, straight, axillary spines.

Wood.—Bright orange yellow, sapwood paler yellow ; heavy, hard, strong, flexible, capable of receiving a fine polish, very durable

Osage Orange, *Toxylon pomiferum.*
Leaves 3′ to 5′ long, 2′ to 3′ wide.

in contact with the ground. Sp. gr., 0.7736 ; weight of cu. ft., 48.21 lbs.

Winter Buds.—All buds lateral. Depressed-globular, partly immersed in the bark, pale chestnut brown.

Leaves.—Alternate, simple, three to five inches long, two to three inches wide, ovate to oblong-lanceolate, entire, acuminate, or acute or cuspidate, rounded, wedge-shaped or subcordate at base. Feather-veined, midrib prominent. They come out of the bud involute, pale bright green, pubescent and tomentose, when full grown are thick, firm, dark green, shining above, paler green below. In autumn they turn a clear bright yellow. Petioles slender, pubescent, slightly grooved. Stipules small, caducous.

Flowers.—June, when leaves are full grown ; diœcious. Staminate flowers in racemes, borne on long, slender, drooping peduncles developed from the axils of crowded leaves on the spur-like branchlets of the previous year. Racemes are short or long. Flowers pale green, small. Calyx hairy, four-lobed. Stamens four, inserted opposite lobes of calyx, on the margin of thin disk ; filaments flattened, exserted ; anthers oblong, introrse, two-celled ; cells opening longitudinally ; ovary wanting. Pistillate flowers borne in a dense globose many-flowered head which appears on a short stout peduncle, axillary on shoots of the year. Calyx, hairy, four-lobed ; lobes thick, concave, investing the ovary, and inclosing the fruit. Ovary superior, ovate, compressed, green, crowned by a long slender style covered with white stigmatic hairs. Ovule solitary.

Fruit.—Pale green globe, four to five inches in diameter, made up of numerous small drupes, crowded and grown together. These small drupes are oblong, compressed, rounded, often notched at apex, filled with milky juice. Seed oblong, the fruit is often seedless.

The earliest account of *Toxylon pomiferum* was given by a Scotch gentleman, William Dunbar, in his narrative of a journey made in 1804 from St. Catherine's Landing on the Mississippi to the Wishita river. In 1810, Bradbury, who travelled extensively in the interior of North America in 1809, 1810 and 1811, relates that he found two trees growing in the garden of Pierre Chouteau, one of the first settlers of St. Louis. They were known as Osage Orange, the trees having been introduced from a settlement of the Osage Indians. The wood was highly prized by the Indians as material for bows and war clubs, and Bradbury relates that the price of a bow was a horse and blanket. The wood is very elastic, practically incorruptible, and extensively used wherever wood

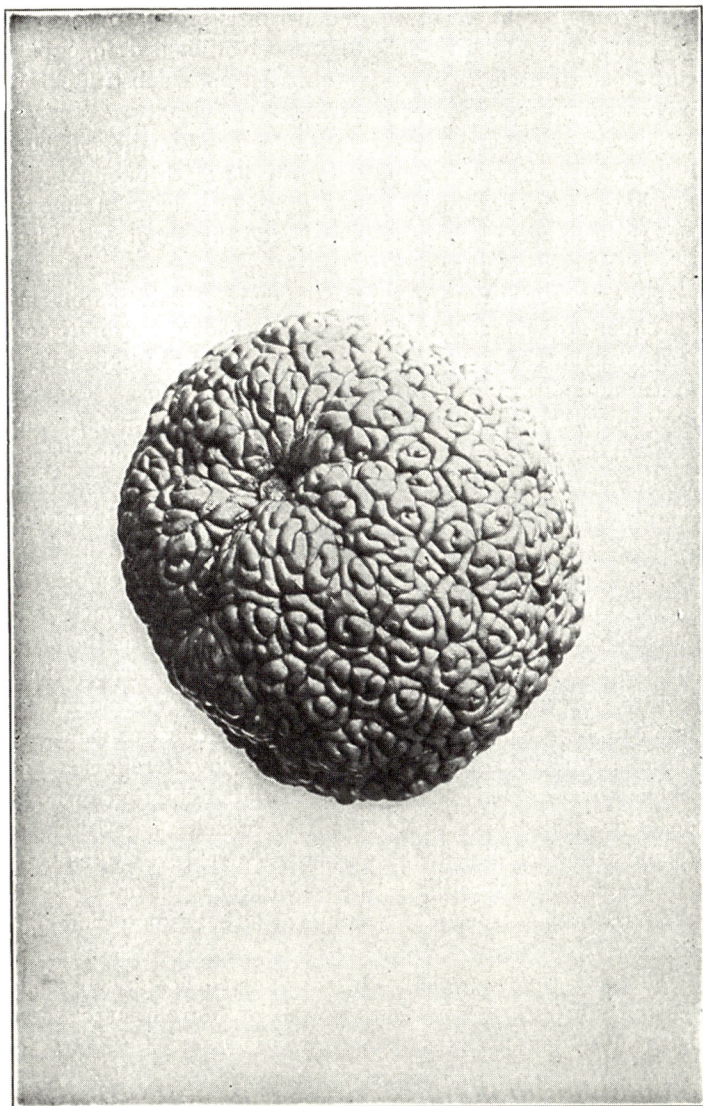

Fruit of Osage Orange.
Varies from 4′ to 5′ in diameter.

must bear alternations of wet and dry, or is brought into contact with the soil. In color it is a most brilliant orange, but this dulls with time. It is largely used as a substitute for olive wood in the manufacture of small articles.

The Osage Orange is native to a deep and fertile soil but it has great powers of adaptation and is hardy throughout the north, where it is extensively used as a hedge plant. It needs severe pruning to keep it in bounds and the shoots of a single year will grow three to six feet long.

The leaves are beautiful singly, but arranged alternately on a slender growing shoot three or four feet long, varying from dark to pale tender green, every one glistening and glittering in the sunlight, they are indeed beautiful. In form they are very simple, a long oval terminating in a slender point. In the axil of every growing leaf is found a growing spine which when mature is about an inch long, and rather formidable. The pistillate and staminate flowers are on different trees ; both are inconspicuous ; but the fruit is very much in evidence. This in size and general appearance resembles a large, yellow green orange, only its surface is roughened and tuberculated. It is, in fact, a compound fruit such as the botanists call a syncarp. Syncarp means that the carpels, that is, the ovaries have grown together and that the great orange-like ball is not one fruit but many ; in fact just as many as there are tubercles on the surface for each one represents a ripened ovary. It is heavily charged with milky juice which oozes out at the slightest wounding of the surface. Although the flowering is diœcious, the pistillate tree even when isolated will bear large oranges, perfect to the sight but lacking the seeds. The fruit is eaten by cattle but is not good for them.

The tree is very prolific and a neglected hedge will soon become fruit-bearing. It is remarkably free from insect enemies and fungal diseases.

PLATANÀCEÆ—PLANE TREE FAMILY

SYCAMORE. BUTTONWOOD

Plátanus occidéntalis.

Platanus from *platus*, broad, on account of the shape of the leaf.

Common throughout the United States. Found along the banks of streams and on rich bottom lands. Seventy to one hundred and twenty feet in height, often divided near the ground into several secondary trunks, very free from branches; spreading limbs at the top make an irregular, open head. Easily recognized by its mottled exfoliating bark. Roots fibrous. The trunks of large trees often hollow.

Bark.—Dark reddish brown, broken into oblong plate-like scales, higher on the tree smooth and light gray; separates freely into thin plates which peel off and leave the surface pale yellow, or white, or greenish. Branchlets at first pale green, coated with thick pale tomentum, later dark green and smooth, finally become light gray or light reddish brown.

Wood.—Light brown, tinged with red; heavy, weak, difficult to split. Largely used for furniture and interior finish of houses, butchers' blocks. Sp. gr., 0.5678; weight of cu. ft., 35.39 lbs.

Winter Buds.—Large, conical, three-scaled, form in summer within the petiole of the full grown leaf. The inner scales enlarge with the growing shoot. There is no terminal bud.

Leaves.—Alternate, palmately nerved, broadly-ovate or orbicular, four to nine inches long, truncate or cordate or wedge-shaped at base, decurrent on the petiole. Three to five-lobed by broad shallow sinuses rounded in the bottom; lobes acuminate, toothed, or entire, or undulate. They come out of the bud plicate, pale green coated with pale tomentum; when full grown are bright yellow green above, paler beneath. In autumn they turn brown and wither before falling. Petioles long, abruptly enlarged at base and inclosing the buds. Stipules with spreading, toothed borders, conspicuous on young shoots, caducous.

Trunk of the Sycamore, *Platanus occidentalis.*

Flowers.—May, with the leaves; monœcious, borne in dense heads. Staminate and pistillate heads on separate peduncles. Staminate heads dark red, on axillary peduncles; pistillate heads light green tinged with red, on longer terminal peduncles. Calyx of staminate flowers three to six tiny scale-like sepals, slightly united at the base, half as long as the pointed petals. Of pistillate flowers three to six, usually four, rounded sepals, much shorter than the acute petals. Corolla of three to six thin scale-like petals.

Stamens.—In staminate flowers as many as the divisions of the calyx and opposite to them; filaments short; anthers elongated, two-celled; cells opening by lateral slits; connectives hairy.

Pistil.—Ovary superior, one-celled, sessile, ovate-oblong, surrounded at base by long, jointed, pale hairs; styles long, incurved, red, stigmatic; ovules one or two.

Fruit.—Brown heads, solitary or rarely clustered, an inch in diameter, hanging on slender stems three to six inches long; persistent through the winter. These heads are composed of akenes about two-thirds of an inch in length. October.

> Clear are the depths where its eddies play,
> And dimples deepen and whirl away;
> And the plane tree's speckled arms o'ershoot
> The swifter current that mines its root.
>
> —WILLIAM CULLEN BRYANT.

The distinguishing peculiarity of the Sycamore is that it "casts its bark as well as its leaves." All trees do this more or less, it is a necessity of life that the bark should yield to the pressure of the growing stem; and the outer layers becoming dead fall off in scales or plates of varying size. In the case of the Silver Maple and the Shagbark Hickory the process is not hidden, but the Sycamore proclaims the fact more openly than any other tree of the forest. The bark of the trunk and larger limbs flakes off in great irregular masses leaving the surface mottled, greenish white and gray and brown, sometimes the smaller limbs look as if whitewashed. In winter it can be recognized from afar by this characteristic alone; and as it likes to grow upon river banks the course of the stream may often be traced for a long distance by the white branches of this tree. The explanation of this is found in the rigid texture of the bark tissue, which entirely lacks the expansive power common to the bark of other trees, so that it is incapable of stretching to accommodate the growth of the wood underneath and the tree is therefore obliged to slough it off.

A second peculiarity is the way the leaves protect the growing buds. Examine a branch of almost any tree in early August and nestled in the axils of the leaves you will find the tiny forming buds which will produce the leaves of the coming year. The Sycamore branch apparently has no such buds. Are there then to be no more leaves on Sycamores in coming years? The conclusion is hasty. Observe the sudden enlargement of the petiole, pull it from the branch, and there inclosed in a little tight-fitting case made of the base of the petiole is the bud.

The great merit of the Sycamore is its vigor and luxuriance of growth; although at present the trees are greatly threatened by a fungus which attacks and destroys the first leaves and growing shoots. This fungus was first discovered in Germany more than twenty years ago, but its occurrence in the United States was only recently recognized by botanists. The disease makes its appearance soon after the leaves have expanded, appearing in the form of small black spots which lie close to the veins. As a result the half grown leaves turn brown, shrivel, and fall. It is very common in early June to see tnese trees putting forth their second crop of leaves while the first hang brown, dead, and unsightly on the ends of the branches. No efficient remedy has as yet been applied and if none develops the Sycamore is practically out of the race, for a tree which does not really get its leaves until July

Fruit of the Sycamore, *Platanus occidentalis.*

Sycamore, *Platanus occidentalis.*
Leaves 4' to 9' long.

is too severely handicapped to compete successfully in the struggle for life.

In old age the tree is picturesque rather than beautiful. The stiff branches strike out from the huge trunk irregularly and wander away without law or order. The branchlets likewise are arranged on a plan of hit or miss. But, when the leaves are out, this scrambling lawless arrangement is seen to have its good points, no leaf unduly shades another and the foliage effect is light and airy.

The Sycamore is able to triumph over the hard conditions of city life and is extensively planted as a shade tree. It bears transplanting well and grows rapidly.

A Sycamore, probably our present Sycamore, made up a large part of the forests of Greenland and arctic America during the cretaceous and tertiary periods. It once grew abundantly in central Europe whence it has now disappeared. Evidently there is something in present conditions inimical to its development.

JUGLANDÀCEÆ—WALNUT FAMILY

BLACK WALNUT

Jùglans nìgra

Juglans is contracted from *Jovis, Jove's,* and *glans* a mast, or acorn; and was applied by the Roman writers to this tree on account of the excellence of its fruit as food, compared with other masts or acorns; the only species that was known to the Romans having been the *Juglans regia,* the tree bearing the walnut of commerce.

Generally distributed, least common in the Atlantic states, abundant in the middle Mississippi valley. Prefers rich bottom lands and fertile hillsides. Deep perpendicular roots; grows slowly; reaches the height of one hundred feet with a trunk four to six feet in diameter. Bark and husk contain tannic acid.

Bark.—Dark brown, slightly tinged with red, deeply divided into broad rounded ridges, broken on the surface into thick scales. Branchlets hairy, dull orange brown, later becoming darker brown.

Winter Buds.—Terminal buds ovate, slightly flattened, one-third of an inch long, covered with silky tomentum. Axillary buds obtuse, one-eighth of an inch long, covered with silky tomentum; two to four together.

Wood.—Dark purplish brown; heavy, hard, close-grained, strong. Very durable in contact with the soil; used for furniture, interior finishing of houses, gunstocks. Sp. gr., 0.6115; weight of cu. ft., 38.11 lbs.

Leaves.—Alternate, compound, unequally pinnate, often equally pinnate, one to two feet long. Fifteen to twenty-three leaflets. Leaflets ovate-lanceolate, three to three and a half inches in length, often unequal at base, serrate, long-pointed, and sessile on the central stem. They come out of the bud shining, yellow green, smooth above, tomentose beneath, when full grown are thin, bright yellow green, smooth. In autumn they turn bright yellow and fall early. Petioles minutely downy.

Flowers.—May, when leaves are half grown ; monœcious. The catkins of staminate flowers appear in the autumn as short cone-like buds, slightly hairy, solitary or in pairs ; when mature are three to five inches long. The perianth, subtended by an acute triangular bract, coated with tomentum, is six-lobed; lobes imbricate, nearly orbicular. Stamens twenty to thirty, arranged in several rows, with purple anthers surmounted by slightly lobed connectives. Pistillate flowers are borne in a two to five-flowered spike, ovate, pointed, maturing later than the staminate. The bract and bractlets which form the outer covering of the flower are green and hairy above, covered with pale hairs beneath, sometimes cut into a laciniate border, sometimes undivided, sometimes greatly reduced. Calyx four-lobed ; lobes imbricate, acute, light green, hairy. Styles two ; stigmas recurved, yellow green, tinged with red. Ovary inferior, ovule solitary.

Fruit.—Nut inclosed in an indehiscent involucre, making a kind of dry drupe, solitary or in pairs, globose or slightly pyriform, yellow green, roughly dotted, one and a half to two inches in diameter. The nut is oval or oblong, slightly flattened, without sutural ridges, one and a quarter to one and a half inches in length, dark brown, four-celled at top and bottom. Kernel sweet and edible. Cotyledons deeply lobed.

The Black Walnut growing alone is one of the grandest and most massive trees of our flora. Given a rich soil and ample space, "it equals in the boldness of its ramifications and the amplitude of its head the best specimens of the oak or chestnut." Its lower branches often sweep the ground, while its upper tower sixty or seventy feet into the air. Then, too, its plumy yellow green foliage, tufted at the end of the spray, long-petioled and narrow-leaved, catches and throws the sunlight and makes of its very shade a golden glow.

This is the free creature protected by man. In the forest living under the law of competition it becomes entirely different. There, the trunk rises straight as a column forty, fifty, or sixty feet, without the suggestion of a branch, and finally puts forth a narrow round-topped somewhat rigid head,

> So much a long communion tends
> To make us what we are.

A single Black Walnut will lighten a dense foliage mass wonderfully and has great value in a landscape for that rea-

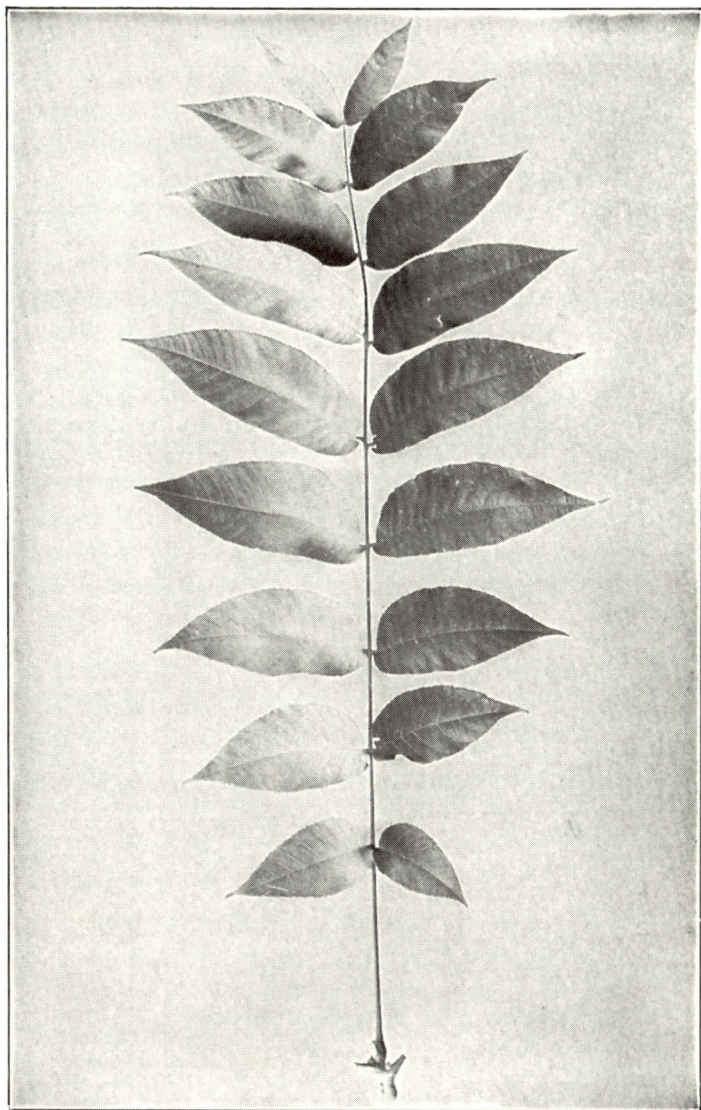

Black Walnut, *Juglans nigra.*

Leaves 12′ to 24′ long.   Leaflets 3′ to 3½′ long.

son. The objection to the tree is that the leaves are late in coming out in the spring and fall early in the autumn so that it often stands naked when its neighbors are apparently in full leaf ; moreover, it is the host of many caterpillars.

The bark of the trunk is very dark and the branches seen in contrast with the light foliage look positively black. The walnut grows more rapidly than is generally supposed, and had there been reasonable care in cutting only the large trees and protecting the small ones, it need never have become as rare as it now is. The nut cannot compare in flavor and sweetness with that of the European species, but the wood is far superior.

During the tertiary period many species of walnut were abundant in Europe ; now the genus is native only in America and Asia.

The European Walnut, *Juglans regia*, is a native of Persia, the home of the peach and the apricot. It was known to the Greeks whose names for it were Persicon and Basilicon, the Persian and royal nut. Curiously enough, it was the fruit of the walnut and not of the oak that the Romans called the acorn. When Ovid tells us that the people of the golden age lived upon

> Acorns that had fallen
> From the towering tree of Jove,

he had in mind not *Quercus*, the oak, but *Juglans*, the walnut.

Cowley, in his poem on Plants, says :

> The walnut then approached, more large and tall
> Her fruit which we a nut, the gods an acorn call ;
> Jove's acorn, which does no small praise confess,
> To have called it man's ambrosia had been less.

By the Greeks it was highly esteemed and dedicated to Diana whose festivals were held beneath its shade. The Greeks and Romans strewed walnuts at their weddings, and Horace, Virgil, and Catullus allude to the custom. Spenser mentions walnuts as employed in Christmas games.

Trunk of Black Walnut, *Juglans nigra.*

For some reason the ancients thought the shade of the walnut unwholesome to men and plants. It is certain that neither grass, field, nor garden crops thrive well under the walnut. The explanation given is that the injury comes from the decaying of the fallen leaves and the washing into the soil of their astringent properties; if such is the case the evil may be averted by raking them up and carrying them away as soon as they fall.

BUTTERNUT. WHITE WALNUT

Jùglans cinèrea.

Common. Prefers rich moist lowlands, and fertile hills. Usually fifty to seventy feet high, with broad, spreading, horizontal branches forming a low symmetrical head. Deep perpendicular roots, with a few, thick, fibrous rootlets.

Bark.—Light grayish brown, deeply divided into broad ridges which separate on the surface into small plate-like scales. Young trunks and branches, smooth and light gray. Branchlets at first orange brown or bright green, coated with rusty clammy hairs, becoming later light gray. Contains tannic acid.

Wood.—Light brown; light, soft, coarse-grained and not strong. Will take a beautiful polish; used for furniture and interior of houses. Sp. gr., 0.4086; weight of cu. ft., 25.46 lbs.

Winter Buds.—Terminal buds hairy, somewhat flattened, one-half to three-fourths of an inch in length. Axillary buds hairy, ovate, flattened, rounded at the apex, one-eighth of an inch long, in groups of three or four, almost naked. Inner scales enlarge when spring growth begins.

Leaves.—Alternate, compound, unequally pinnate, often equally pinnate, fifteen to thirty inches long, hairy, with eleven to seventeen leaflets. Leaflets oblong-lanceolate, three to five inches long, one and a half to two inches wide, unequally rounded at base, serrate, acute or acuminate, sessile or short petioled, the terminal leaflet often borne on a stalk two inches in length. They come out oi the bud yellow green and sticky, shining and scurfy above, hairy below; when full grown thin, yellow green, pale; midribs rounded above, primary veins conspicuous. In autumn they turn yellow. Stipules wanting. Petioles downy with clammy hairs.

Flowers.—May, when the leaves are half grown; monœcious. The catkins of staminate flowers appear in the autumn as short cone-like buds covered with pale tomentum; when mature they are from three to five inches long. The perianth, subtended by an acute

Fruit of the Black Walnut and of the Butternut.

hairy bract, is one-fourth inch long, bright yellow green, slightly hairy, usually six-lobed, the side lobes bearing tufts of brown hairs. Stamens from eight to twelve, with nearly sessile dark brown anthers, surmounted by darker connectives. Pistillate flowers are borne in six to eight-flowered spikes ; one-third of an inch long, maturing later than the staminate. The bract and bractlets which form the outer covering of the flowers are coated with white or pink glandular hairs ; bract linear and acute ; bractlets ovate, acute or laciniate ; calyx four-lobed ; lobes imbricate, linear, hairy ; styles two ; stigmas two, fringed, spreading, bright red, half an inch long. Ovary inferior, ovule solitary.

Fruit.—Nut closed in an indehiscent involucre, making a kind of dry drupe. Three or five often ripen on one branch. Cylindrical, obscurely two to four-ridged, ovate-oblong, pointed, coated with rusty clammy hairs, one-half to two and one-half inches long. Nut is brown, ovate, acute at apex, deeply sculptured and rough with ragged ridges, two-celled at base. Kernel sweet and pleasant but very oily and soon becomes rancid. Cotyledons ovate-oblong.

The Butternut when young much resembles the Black Walnut. It is, perhaps, more generally distributed. The form of the fruit differs greatly from that of the Black Walnut, being oblong, oval, and narrowed to a point at the end. The husk is covered with a sticky gum and when green is used domestically to dye a dull yellow. The surface of the nut is much rougher than that of any other of the walnut genus. The bark is lighter gray than that of the Black Walnut, and the ridges are very much broader. The leaves are very similar in general appearance, but the petiole of the Butternut leaf is covered with clammy hairs as are the young branchlets.

HICKORY

Hicôria. Cârya.

The name *Carya* was applied by the Greeks to the common walnut, in honor of Carya, daughter of Dion, King of Laconia, who was changed by Bacchus into that tree. Diana had the surname of Caryata from the town of Carya in Laconia where her rites were always celebrated in the open air under the shade of a walnut tree. Plutarch says the name of Carya was applied to the walnut tree from the effect of the smell of the leaves on the head.

—LOUDON.

Hickory is derived from the Indian name of the liquor obtained by pounding the kernels. These the Indians beat into pieces with stones and putting them,

Butternut, *Juglans cinerea.*

Leaves 15' to 30' long.   Leaflets 3' to 5' long.

shells and all, into mortars, mingling water with them, with long wooden pestells pound them so long together untill they make a kind of mylke, or oylie liquor. which they call powcohicora.

—Historie of Travaile into Virginia Britannia.

The Hickories, of which there are nine species on this continent, are strictly American trees, no representatives of the genus having been found elsewhere. They are closely allied to the walnuts; the chief botanic distinction between them lies in the husk which in the Hickories separates into four pieces and discharges the nut, instead of adhering in an unbroken coat upon it as is the case with the Black Walnut and the Butternut.

All the Hickories have alternate, exstipulate, compound leaves of five, seven, nine or eleven leaflets, and although the leaves vary considerably they have a common typical form well expressed by *Hicoria ovata*, the Shellbark. All have stout perpendicular taproots and thick fibrous rootlets as well. Like the oaks they take strong hold of the earth. The noticeable quality of the wood is its strength and elasticity as well as its fuel value, but it decays when subjected to alternations of wet and dry.

The flowers are monœcious and apetalous, appearing after the leaves are well grown. The staminate flowers appear in aments which are borne in threes on a common peduncle which is produced either from the terminal bud or from the lateral buds in the axils of last year's leaves. The staminate flowers consist of a two, sometimes three-lobed calyx, subtended by an elongated bract which is free nearly to the base, usually much longer than the ovate, rounded calyx-lobes. The corolla is wanting

Staminate Aments of Shellbark Hickory, *Hicoria ovata*; 4' to 5' long.

278

The stamens vary from three to ten, are inserted on the slightly thickened inner and lower face of the calyx. Filaments short, free ; anthers oblong, two-celled ; cells opening longitudinally. The ovary is wanting.

The pistillate flowers appear in a two to ten-flowered cluster, borne on a peduncle which is terminal on a leafy branch of the year. The calyx consists of a single lobe. The stamens are wanting. The ovary is inferior, one-celled, inclosed in a slightly four-ridged involucre formed by the union of the chief bract and two smaller bracts ; the bract much larger than the calyx-lobe and the bractlets. The ovule is solitary.

The fruit is a nut inclosed in a four-valved involucre. This nut varies in size and shape but when once known is readily recognized under all its protean forms. That of the Shellbark is typical of them all.

The autumn color of the leaves is a clear bright yellow ; the leaflets frequently separate from the petiole in falling.

The Hickories range from the valley of the St. Lawrence to the mountains of Mexico and traces of the genus are found in the tertiary rocks of Greenland, also in the upper tertiary formations of Europe. There is a prevailing opinion that they are difficult to rear and, to a degree, this is true, for the seedlings need protection against the wind and the sun. But when this is given they flourish, and a well grown hickory is a tree of great dignity and beauty.

BITTERNUT. SWAMP HICKORY

Hicòria mínima. Càrya amàra.

Widely distributed, but absent from the mountains of New York and New England, abundant throughout the Mississippi valley. Prefers low wet woods, borders of streams and swamps, but is often found on high uplands remote from streams. Reaches the height of one hundred feet, has a tall straight trunk, stout spreading limbs and forms a broad handsome head. Grows most rapidly of all the hickories.

Bark.—Light grayish brown tinged with red, broken into thin plate-like scales. In old trees very rugged. Branchlets slender, marked with pale lenticels, at first bright green, downy, later become reddish brown, during the first winter reddish or orange brown, shining, with small, elevated, obscurely three-lobed leaf-scars, in the second year dark or light gray.

Wood.—Dark or light brown, sapwood much paler ; heavy, hard, close-grained, tough and strong. Used for cooperage and for fuel. Sp. gr., 0.7552 ; weight of cu. ft., 47.06 lbs.

Winter Buds.—Terminal buds one-third to three-fourths of an inch long, compressed, narrow oval, oblique at apex. Lateral buds much smaller. Inner scales enlarge when spring growth begins, the innermost becoming an inch and a half long and half an inch broad, strap-shaped, pinnate at the apex, one and a half inch long, one-half inch broad, yellow green, downy.

Leaves.—Alternate, compound, six to ten inches long. Leaflets seven to eleven, lanceolate, ovate-lanceolate, or oblong, often unequally wedge-shaped or partly cordate at base, sessile with the exception of the terminal leaflet, serrate, acute or acuminate. Leaflet vernation involute. They come out of the bud bright yellow green or bronze red, shining, hairy and tomentose ; when full grown are thick, firm, dark yellow green above, paler beneath ; midribs prominent. In autumn they turn clear or rusty yellow. Petioles slender, hairy, slightly grooved.

Flowers.—May, June, when leaves are half grown ; monœcious. Staminate flowers, green, borne in triple catkins, three or four inches long. Common peduncle about an inch long ; stamens four; anthers yellow ; bract longer than calyx lobes. Pistillate flowers one-half inch long, slightly angled, covered with yellow tomentum. Bract lanceolate, hairy ; bractlets broadly ovate, shorter than the calyx lobes ; stigmas pale green, mature and wither before the staminate flowers open.

Fruit.—Obovate or globular, three-fourths to one and one-half inches long, with four wings or ridges from the apex to the middle which mark the valves, apex shows the remnants of the stigmas, surface more or less thickly covered with golden scurfy pubescence, and marked on inner surface with dark veins. Nut ovate or oblong, compressed, marked at base with dark lines, gray with reddish tinge. Kernel very bitter. October.

Distinguishing Characters.—Winter buds bright yellow, bud scales valvate. Leaflets seven to eleven, lanceolate to oblong-lanceolate. Fruit four-winged from apex nearly to the middle : nut often broader than long, thin-shelled, slightly four-angled. Kernel bitter.

The Swamp Hickory or Bitternut has the smallest leaflets of any of the hickories ; they are narrow, almost slender, and suggest willow leaves in their contour. They are a distin-

Bitternut, *Hicoria minima.*

Leaves 6′ to 10′ long.   Leaflets 2′ to 4′ long.

guishing character and differ in general aspect from those of the other hickories. The fruit also is individual, four

Bitternut, *Hicoria minima.* Fruit
¾' to 1½' long.

ridges or wings reach from the apex half way to the base ; sometimes two of these reach the base, all of them never. The kernel is extremely bitter.

This species loves the water and in Ohio should be sought at the margins of streams, but in the south it changes its nature and crowds upon the poor, dry, gravelly soil of Alabama and Mississippi. It grows rapidly for a hickory, but the entire family are slow of growth.

The nuts should be planted where they are to grow, as the trees are difficult to transplant.

SHELLBARK HICKORY. SHAGBARK

Hicòria ovàta. Càrya álba.

Shagbark refers to the loose shaggy appearance of the bark, and as this peels off easily the tree is also known as Shellbark.

Not abundant in New England, reaches its largest size in the valley of the Ohio. In the forest attains the height of one hundred feet with a straight columnar trunk. Prefers a deep, rich, rather moist soil. Its tap root is very large and vigorous, and the tree is best reared directly from the nut.

Bark.—Dark gray, separates into strips often three feet or more long, three to eight inches wide, which cling to the trunk usually by the middle giving it a rough shaggy appearance. On young stems and branches smooth and light green. Branchlets stout, at first green, slightly angled, downy and covered with brown scurf, during first year reddish or light gray, smooth and shining, later becoming dark gray, finally light gray. Leaf-scars are ovate to semi-orbicular or very obscurely three-lobed, pale.

Wood.—Light brown, sapwood nearly white; heavy, tough, close-grained and extremely elastic. Used in manufacture of agricultural implements, carriages, axe-handles, hoops. Best fuel of American woods. Sp. gr., 0.8372 ; weight of cu. ft., 52.17 lbs.

Winter Buds.—Terminal buds are broadly ovate, obtuse, one-half to three-fourths inch long, one-third to one-half inch broad, three to four outer scales are broadly ovate, dark brown and usually fall in late autumn or early winter. The inner scales enlarge as spring growth begins, the innermost becoming two and one-half to three inches long, an inch to one and one-half inches broad, oblong-obovate, yellow green tinged with red, downy, and persist until leaves are half grown.

Leaves.—Alternate, eight to fourteen inches long, compound, of five, rarely seven, leaflets. Leaflets vary in size. The terminal one is decurrent upon a short stalk, the others are sessile. Terminal one is obovate, wedge-shaped at base, serrate, acute, the lower pair of leaflets are much smaller than the second pair. The leaflets of the second pair are obovate and often equal the terminal leaflet in size. Leaflet vernation is involute. They come out of the bud thin, shining, light yellow green, woolly coated ; when full grown are dark yellow green, smooth above, paler yellow green sometimes downy below ; midrib prominent, primary veins conspicuous. In autumn they turn a rusty yellow. Petiole stout, smooth or hairy, obscurely grooved and enlarged at the base.

Flowers.—May, when the leaves are well grown. Monœcious. Staminate catkins three in a group, slender, light green, hairy, four to five inches long ; common peduncle often an inch long ; bracts linear-lanceolate, caducous. Staminate flowers are hairy, borne on short pedicels ; bracts long, acute, ovate-lanceolate, much longer than the calyx. Stamens four ; anthers nearly sessile, yellow tinged with red. Pistillate flowers in two or five-flowered spikes, brownish, tomentose ; bract and bractlets green and hairy. Stigmatic lobes green, do not mature until the anthers have withered.

Fruit.—Solitary or in pairs, globular, longer than broad, or slightly obovate, depressed at the apex, crowned with the remnants of the stigmas, dark reddish brown or black, one inch to two and a half inches long ; husk four-valved, splits freely, usually one-half inch thick, hard, woody and pale within. Nut varies from oblong to a form broader than long, compressed, clearly or obscurely four-ridged which corresponds to the valve of the husk, acute or rounded at apex, tipped with a point, pale or brownish white. Kernel sweet with aromatic flavor. October.

Distinguishing Characters.—Bud scales imbricate ; leaflets five to seven, obovate to oblong-lanceolate. Catkins of staminate flowers borne on branches of the year only. Fruit spherical, depressed at apex, without wings ; nut ovate, more or less flattened, four-angled, pale or nearly white, kernel sweet. Bark hanging in long, loose plates.

> The squirrel on the shingly shagbark's bough
> Now saws, now lists with downward eye and ear
> Then drops his nut.
>
> —JAMES RUSSELL LOWELL.

The Shellbark Hickory has three typical forms. When it grows in the forest it rises a tall shaft straight as a column, free from branches until the very top where it sends out a few limbs and makes a small flat head ; again, when a young tree has been permitted to remain after its companions were removed its stout limbs rise and spread, droop a little and make a cone-like head ; the third form, however, seems the really characteristic one, where the central shaft rises in the main intact, but sends out many short, small, lateral branches almost at right angles to the trunk, and forms a long cylindrical body of foliage, round-topped at the summit and drooping a little at the base. This cylindrical body is often broken.

Other trees hold their bark loosely, the Silver Maple often looks as if she would be glad to be rid of hers, the Sycamore frankly and absolutely casts hers and is done with it, but the Shellbark, letting " I dare not wait upon I would," holds hers in long unsightly pieces, loose at the edges yet clinging at the centre until the trunk becomes simply shaggy, hence the name Shagbark.

A Shellbark just about to put forth its leaves presents a unique and striking appearance, as if covered with brilliant flowers. Early in the spring the outer bud scales fall off and the inner scales enlarge to an astonishing size, frequently becoming five inches long and two inches broad. They are then of a soft leathery texture, very downy, beautifully fringed and take on a gorgeous red or salmon yellow color. In the midst of these petal-like scales appear the leaves, woolly and downy and shining, late indeed but not belated, for they grow rapidly and by the end of June are of full size. Out of this terminal bud come the pistillate flowers always, and the staminate flowers very frequently.

The wood is light, tough, strong and elastic. "Tough as hickory" became a stock phrase among the early settlers of this country. The well-known sobriquet given to President Jackson was " Old Hickory," and this name was no less an expression of personal affection than of appreciation of his

Fruiting Spray of Shellbark Hickory, *Hicoria ovata*.

Leaves 8′ to 14′ long.

character. The excellence of the American axe is believed to be due quite as much to the handle of hickory as to the quality of its steel.

Hickory nuts were highly appreciated by the Indians. Bertram, in his "Travels in North America," relates that he had seen above one hundred bushels of these nuts belonging to a single family. The Indian name of the nut appears in English as Kiskitomas, Kiskytom, and, according to Michaux, Kiskythomas. All are believed to be corruptions of an Indian word Kwaskadamenné which means that it "must be cracked with the teeth." Since this fruit is so excellent in its natural state one cannot help thinking what it might become were it improved by systematic cultivation.

The Big Shellbark, *Hicoria laciniòsa*, is a tree reaching the height of sixty or seventy feet. The bark is loose, leaflets seven to nine, fruit four-ribbed above the middle, husk very thick, nut large. It may be known by the orange color of the young branchlets. Ranges from Pennsylvania through central and western New York to Indiana and Illinois and southward to the Indian Territory.

MOCKERNUT. BIG BUD HICKORY

Hicòria álba.   Càrya tomentòsa.

Rare in New England, abundant in the middle west and southwest. Prefers rich uplands, but will grow in sandy soil; is the only hickory found in the maritime Pine-belt of the southern states. Rises high in the forest as do all the hickories, but when growing alone becomes a broad round-topped tree. Leaves, buds, and husks have a strong resinous odor.

Bark.—Light or dark gray, with shallow fissures and closely appressed scales. In old trees it becomes very rugged. Branchlets stout, terete, at first slightly angled, tomentose, during first year bright red brown marked with conspicuous lenticels, in winter with large pale leaf-scars, which are equally lobed or with middle lobe two or three times as long as the others; in the second year the branches become light or dark gray.

Trunk of Shellbark Hickory, *Hicoria ovata.*

WALNUT FAMILY

Wood.—Dark brown, sapwood nearly white ; heavy, hard, strong, close-grained, tough, elastic. Confounded commercially with that of the Shellbark hickories. Sp. gr., 0.8218 ; weight of cu. ft., 51.21 lbs.

Winter Buds.—Terminal buds one-half to three-fourth of an inch long, broadly ovate, acute or obtuse, two or three times as large as the axillary bud. The three or four outer scales are ovate, acute, often keeled, dark reddish brown and often fall late in autumn or early winter. The innermost scales enlarge when spring growth begins becoming one and a half inches long and half an inch wide, ovate, pale green without and bright red within, downy, persist until the leaf is half grown.

Leaves.—Alternate, compound, eight to twelve inches long. Leaflets seven to nine, oblong-lanceolate or obovate-lanceolate, equally or unequally rounded or wedge-shaped at base, serrate, acute or acuminate. Usually sessile except the terminal leaflet which is decurrent on a short stalk. Upper leaflets five to eight inches long. Leaflet vernation involute. They come out of the bud thin, pale yellow green, downy ; when full grown are dark yellow green, shining above, pale green or orange or brown and downy beneath ; midrib stout, prominent. In autumn they turn a clear or rusty yellow.

Flowers.—May, when leaves are half grown. Monœcious. Staminate flowers are borne in triple catkins, four to five inches in length, slender, green, hairy. Bracts ovate-lanceolate, hairy, longer than the yellow green calyx. Stamens four ; anthers bright red. Pistillate flowers in two to five-flowered tomentose spikes. Anterior bract longer than the bractlets and calyx-lobe. Stigmas dark red ; begin to wither before the anthers shed their pollen.

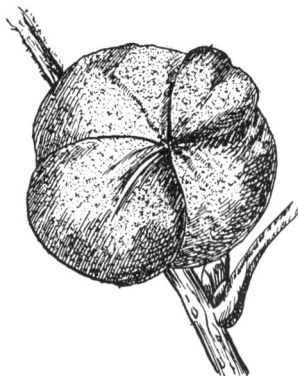

Mockernut, *Hicoria alba.* Fruit 1½' to 2' long.

Fruit.—Spherical, oblong or obovate, dark reddish brown, one and one-half to two inches long ; husk splitting to middle or nearly to base. Nut spherical or oblong, often long-pointed, four-ridged toward the apex, pale reddish brown, with very thick hard shell and very small sweet kernel. October.

Distinguishing Characters — Buds large, bud scales imbricate. Staminate catkins borne on branches of the year. Leaflets seven to nine, oblong-lanceolate or obovate-lanceolate, more or less tomentose on under surface, fragrant. Fruit without or with obscure sutural ridges ; nut globose, or oblong often long-pointed. Four-ridged toward apex, thick-shelled, reddish brown ; kernel sweet.

Mockernut, *Hicoria alba*.

Leaves 8′ to 12′ long.

Hicoria alba evidently gained the common name Mocker-nut because of the disappointing character of its nuts. These are usually of large size and look like Shellbark nuts, but they keep their promise to the sight only to break it to the hope, for the kernel is very small and very difficult to extract.

The Mockernut varies toward the Shellbark on one side and the Pignut on the other. In its foliage it resembles the Shellbark, in its bark it resembles the Pignut. Its distinguishing characters are its nuts, its large leaves of seven to nine leaflets, its large terminal bud and the pleasant resinous fragrance of its leaves.

PIGNUT

Hicòria glàbra. Cárya porcìna. Cárya microcárpa.

Common throughout the northern states, ranges south as far as Florida and southwest to Texas. Prefers dry ridges and hillsides, but tolerates many different conditions. Rises to a hundred feet in the forest, but in the open is shorter, with a narrow head of slender, sometimes pendulous branches. Has the stout tap roots of all the hickories.

Bark.—Light gray with shallow fissures and close appressed scales, rarely exfoliate. Branchlets slender, marked with pale lenticels, at first slightly angled, pale green, scurfy or downy ; later they become light red brown, smooth, and finally turn dark gray. The leaf-scars are comparatively small, semiorbicular to oblong, obscurely lobed, slightly emarginate at apex.

Wood.—Either dark or light brown, sapwood nearly white ; heavy, hard, close-grained, tough and elastic. Largely used in the manufacture of agricultural implements. Sp. gr., 0.8217 ; weight of cu. ft., 51.21 lbs.

Winter Buds.—Terminal buds one-fourth to one-half of an inch long, narrow-oval, acute, or obtuse, two or three times as large as the axillary buds. The outer scales are acute, often slightly keeled, frequently long pointed at apex, reddish brown, beginning to unfold early in autumn, frequently fall before winter or early in spring. The inner scales increase in size when spring growth begins, frequently becoming two and a half inches long, and one and one-fourth inch wide, lanceolate to obovate, yellow green, more or less tinged with red, downy and persistent until the leaf is half grown.

Leaves.—Alternate, compound, eight to twelve inches long. Leaflets five to seven, rarely nine. Variety *microcarpa* habitually five.

Fruiting Spray of Pignut, *Hicoria glabra* (*Carya porcina*).
Leaves 8′ to 12′ long.

Terminal leaflet larger than the others, often decurrent on slender stalk. Other leaflets are oblong to obovate-lanceolate, rounded equally or unequally at base, sharply serrate with incurved teeth, acute or acuminate. Leaflet vernation involute. Upper leaflets six to eight inches long, two to two and one-half broad, the lowest pair much smaller. They come out of the bud bright bronze green, hairy; when full grown are thick, firm, smooth, dark yellow green above, paler beneath. In autumn they turn clear or rusty yellow. Petioles slender, usually smooth, grooved slightly, enlarged at base.

Flowers.—May, June, when leaves are half grown. Monœcious. Staminate flowers borne in slender catkins, three to seven inches long, usually three catkins on one stout peduncle. The flowers are on short pedicels, yellow green, tomentose; bract lanceolate, acute, hairy; calyx-lobes rounded, ovate; stamens four, anthers nearly sessile, dark yellow. Pistillate flowers in a two to five-flowered spike; bract is lanceolate, acute; bractlets and calyx dark green, hairy; stigmas yellow, and wither before the anthers shed their pollen.

Fruit.—Variable, fig-form, ellipsoidal, subglobose, rounded or depressed at apex, abruptly or gradually narrowed at the base, often obscurely winged to the middle or entirely to the base. In some forms the four valves open and discharge the nut, in others they partly open and retain it. Nut is oblong, oval, or subglobose, with smooth hard shell, thick or thin. Kernel small, sweet or slightly bitter.

Distinguishing Characters.—Bud scales imbricate; staminate catkins borne on branches of the year. Leaflets five, seven or nine, oblong or obovate-lanceolate. Fruit pyriform or globose; husk thin, slightly ridged at the sutures, not splitting freely to the base; nut varying in form, thick-shelled, kernel sweet; bark closely furrowed, rarely hanging in loose plates.

Hicoria glabra is a beautiful tree and certainly worthy of a pleasanter name than that of Pignut. But the early settlers of this country judged trees by the standard of use rather than beauty; and as the fruit of this tree did not compare favorably with that of the Shellbark, both tree and fruit were given over to the pigs without question. However, another explanation of the name is given. The typical shape of the fruit is pyriform, it looks not unlike a small fig and it has been suggested that pignut is a corruption of fignut. But there seem to be no facts upon which to base this theory as there is no record that the tree was ever called fignut, and the earliest records mention it as pignut.

Fruiting Spray of Pignut, *Hicoria glabra* (*Carya microcarpa*).
Leaves 4′ to 7′ long.

WALNUT FAMILY

Hicoria glabra now includes *Carya microcarpa* and *Carya porcina* of Gray. In the species as now constituted the fruit varies greatly in form, being oval or globular as well as pyriform. The husk is always thin, smooth, often obscurely winged, and divided into four unequal valves. The kernel at first is sweet to the taste, but finally bitter.

The number of leaflets varies from five to seven. In the variety *C. microcarpa* the leaflets are five and the leaf as a whole is a small but faithful copy of that of the Shellbark. But other trees are found whose leaflets are oftener seven than five.

The bark is firm, close, usually divided by small fissures; it rarely exfoliates, but when it does the plates are not more than five or six inches long.

BETULÀCEÆ—BIRCH FAMILY

BIRCH

Bétula.

Betula is derived by Pliny from bitumen. Birch by some is
derived from *Betu* its Celtic name; by others from the Latin
batuere, to beat, because the fasces of the Roman lictors, which
were always made of birch rods, were used to drive back the
people.

There are in North America nine birches of which six are
trees, and five of these flourish east of the Rocky Mountains.
All are trees of singular grace and beauty and possess a certain distinction of character which fits them for an honored
place in parks and pleasure grounds. The roots are fibrous
and the trees can be readily transplanted. All grow rapidly.

The bark of all the birches is characteristically marked
with long horizontal lenticels, and often separates into thin
papery plates, especially upon the Paper Birch. It is practically imperishable, due to the resinous oil it contains. Its
decided color gives the common names Red, White, Black,
and Yellow to the different species. The buds form early
and are full grown by midsummer, all are lateral, no terminal
bud is formed ; the branch is prolonged by the upper lateral
bud. The wood of all the species is close-grained with satiny
texture and capable of taking a fine polish ; its fuel value is
fair.

The leaves of the different species vary but little. All
are alternate, doubly serrate, feather-veined, petiolate, and

stipulate. Apparently they often appear in pairs, but these pairs are really borne on spur-like two-leaved lateral branchlets.

The flowers are monœcious, opening with or before the leaves and borne in three-flowered clusters in the axils of the scales of drooping or erect aments. Staminate aments are pendulous, clustered or solitary in the axils of the last leaves of the branch of the year or near the ends of the short lateral branchlets of the year. They form in early autumn and remain rigid during the winter. The scales of the staminate aments when mature are broadly ovate, rounded, yellow or orange color below the middle, dark chestnut brown at apex. Each scale bears two bractlets and three

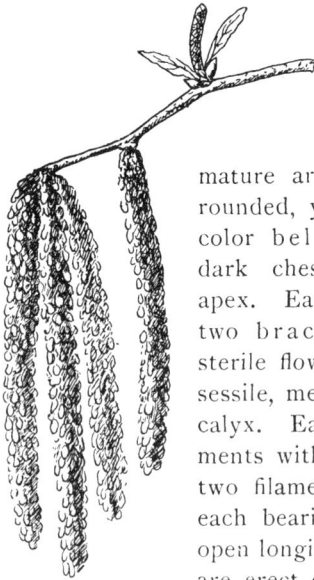

Branch of Red Birch, *Betula nigra*, Showing the Staminate Aments as they Appear in Winter.

Four Staminate and One Pistillate Ament of Sweet Birch, *Betula lenta*. Staminate Aments 3′ to 4′ long.

sterile flowers, each flower consisting of a sessile, membranaceous, usually two-lobed, calyx. Each calyx bears four short filaments with one-celled anthers or strictly, two filaments divided into two branches, each bearing a half-anther. Anther cells open longitudinally. The pistillate aments are erect or pendulous, solitary ; terminal on the two-leaved lateral spur-like branchlets of the year. The pistillate scales are oblong-ovate, three-lobed, pale yellow green often tinged with red, becoming brown at maturity. These scales bear two or three fertile flowers, each flower consisting of a naked ovary. The ovary is compressed, two-celled, crowned with two slender styles ; the ovule is solitary.

The ripened pistillate ament is called a strobile and bears tiny winged nuts, packed in the protecting curve of each brown and woody scale. These nuts are pale chestnut brown, compressed, crowned by the persistent stigmas. The seed fills the cavity of the nut. The cotyledons are flat and fleshy. All the species are easily grown from seed.

Michaux arranged the birches into two groups — one, including trees whose pistillate aments are sessile and erect : the Black, the Yellow and the Red ; the other,

Rear View of a Staminate Scale and Front View of a Pistillate Scale of Yellow Birch, *Betula Lutea* ; Enlarged.

those whose pistillate aments are stalked and pendulous : the Canoe, the White and the common *Betula alba* of Europe.

Remains of the group appear in the cretaceous rocks of Dakota, and during the tertiary period the genus existed throughout the northern central plateau of North America and at the same time abounded in Europe.

WHITE BIRCH. GRAY BIRCH. ASPEN-LEAVED BIRCH

Bétula populifòlia.

Least common of the birches ; found on dry, gravelly, barren margins of swamps and ponds. Short-lived, twenty to thirty feet high. Grows very rapidly. Ranges from Nova Scotia and lower St. Lawrence River southward mostly in the coast region to Delaware, and westward through northern New England and New York to southern shore of Lake Ontario. Leaves tremulous.

Bark.—Chalky white or gray white, usually firm but easily seperable into thin plates ; dark triangular markings scattered over the trunk and especially below the branches. At the base of large trees nearly black and broken irregularly by shallow fissures. Branchlets at first reddish brown, closely dotted with round lenticels, then dark brown, and finally white near the trunk. Practically incorruptible.

Wood.—Light brown, sapwood paler; light, soft, close-grained, not strong, checks badly in drying, not durable in contact with the ground, takes a fine polish. Used for spools, shoe pegs, wood pulp and barrel hoops. Fuel value not high, but burns with bright flame. Sp. gr., 0.5760; weight of cu. ft., 35.90 lbs.

Winter Buds.—Slender, brown, one-fourth of an inch long.

Leaves.—Alternate, simple, triangular, two and a half to three inches long, one and one-half to two inches wide, truncate or slightly wedge-shaped at base, doubly serrate, with spreading glandular teeth, acute or acuminate. They come out of the bud bright yellow green, glutinous. When full grown are dark shining green above, paler shining green beneath; midribs yellow, raised, rounded, often marked with minute black glands, primary veins conspicuous. In autumn they turn a pale yellow. Petioles long, slender, slightly twisted, often reddish. Stipules ovate, pale green, tinged with red, caducous.

Flowers.—April, before the leaves. Staminate flowers borne on terminal catkins which are solitary or in pairs; when mature are from three to four inches long. These form in the late summer, and during the winter they vary from one and one-quarter to one and one-half inches long, bright pale green, and very rigid. Scales ovate, acute, apiculate. Pistillate aments slender, one-half inch long; scales ovate, acute pale green, glandular; peduncles furnished with conspicuous bractlets.

Fruit. — Strobiles cylindrical, an inch long, obtuse at base and apex; peduncles slender, drooping; scales pubescent, wedge-shaped at base, three-lobed, lateral lobes larger than the middle, spreading. Nut oval, acute or rounded at base, winged; the wings rather broader than the seed.

White Birch, *Betula populifolia.* Strobiles pendulous, 1′ long.

> Most beautiful
> Of forest trees—The Lady of the woods.
>
> —COLERIDGE.

> The silvery stems
> Of delicate birch trees.
>
> —KEATS.

Sometimes trees ascend vertically and having arrived at a certain height, in an air perfectly unobstructed, fork off in various tiers, and send out their branches horizontally like an apple tree; or incline them towards the earth like a fir; or hollow them in the form of a cup, like the sassafras; or round them into the shape of a mushroom like the pine; or straighten them into a pyramid like the poplar; or roll them as wool upon the distaff like the cypress; or suffer them to float at the discretion of the winds like the birch.

> —ST. PIERRE.

Fruiting Branch of White Birch, *Betula populifolia.*
Leaves 2½′ to 3′ long, 1½′ to 2′ wide.

This description, " to float at the discretion of the winds," admirably characterizes the attitude of the White Birch. The white stem rises unbroken to the summit of the tree, the branches come out at a large angle, go out horizontally, or perhaps dip a little and divide into branchlets so long, slender, and delicate that they have no rigidity but yield to every impulse of the passing breeze. The leaves flutter as freely as those of the Aspen for the petioles though not laterally compressed are long, slender, and slightly twisted, which puts the leaf into such unstable equilibrium that it responds to the lightest motion of the air.

The outer layer of the bark is thin and white, both on the stem and larger limbs, but neither it nor the inner layer will separate from the wood as easily as will that of the Canoe or Paper Birch. A marked characteristic is the triangular black spots appearing on the trunk beneath every limb as well as in other places.

Although the wood quickly decays in contact with the earth, the bark under similar conditions remains unchanged. This is due to a peculiar resin found in the bark which renders it impervious to water.

The tree loves rocky barren woods, old fields and abandoned farms, and in New England has the familiar name of Old Field Birch. It is the least common of all the birches and is rarely found growing in groups. It is plainly unable to hold its own in competition with other trees, and is found largely on exhausted sandy soils where other trees are unable to grow. When planted, however, it does not disdain moist, fertile land and acts as an excellent nurse for other trees, but under no conditions is it long-lived.

The Gray Birch so closely resembles the common European birch, *Betula alba*, that it has by some botanists been classed as a variety of that species. However, it grows with less vigor and does not attain so large a size.

The European Birch appears in American lawns and parks principally in its cultivated varieties. The most common of these is *Betula alba* var. *laciniata*, the cut-leaved Birch.

Trunk of White Birch, *Betula populifolia.*

BIRCH FAMILY

Others are var. *pendula,* weeping ; var. *fastigiata,* pyramidal ; var. *pubescens,* leaf covered with white down. All are beautiful.

PAPER BIRCH. CANOE BIRCH. WHITE BIRCH

Bétula papyrifera.

Widely distributed over a northern range. Sixty to seventy feet high. When young forming a compact pyramidal head, in old age becoming a branchless trunk, supporting a round-topped open head of pendulous branches. Prefers rich moist hillsides, borders of streams, lakes, and swamps. Sap flows freely in spring and by boiling can be made into syrup.

Bark.—On old trees, near the ground, dark brown or nearly black, sharply and irregularly furrowed. At the base of young trees, brown tinged with red, separating irregularly into large plates. Higher on the trunks of old trees, on young stems and large limbs, creamy white, shining on the outer surface, bright orange on the inner, marked with horizontal lenticels and separating freely into thin papery layers. Branchlets slender, light green, then orange and finally through red and brown in the course of years they become white. Bark contains not only an astringent principle but a resinous balsamic oil.

Wood.—Light brown tinged with red ; light, hard, tough, close-grained and strong. Used for spools, shoe-lasts, wood pulp, fuel. Sp. gr., 0.5955 ; weight of cu. ft., 37.11 lbs.

Winter Buds. — Ovate, acute, dark brown, resinous, a quarter of an inch long.

Leaves.—Alternate, simple, two to three inches long, one-half to two inches wide, ovate, heart-shaped or rounded or wedge-shaped at base, coarsely, doubly, or irregularly serrate with spreading teeth, abruptly acuminate ; midrib slender, yellow, raised and rounded, and marked with minute black glands. They come out of the bud bright green, pubescent, resinous ; when full grown are thick, firm, dull dark green above, pale yellow green beneath, covered with minute black glands. In autumn they turn clear pale yellow.

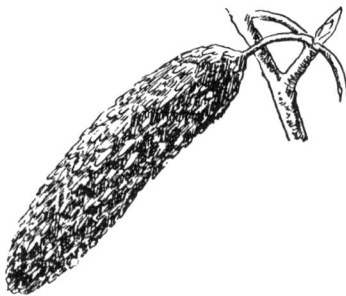

Paper Birch, *Betula papyrifera.* Strobiles pendulous, 1½′ to 2′ long.

302

Fruiting Sprays of Paper Birch, *Betula papyrifera*.
Leaves 2′ to 3′ long. ½′ to 2′ broad.

Petioles stout, yellow, covered with black glands, enlarged at base, slightly grooved.   Stipules ovate, acute, light green, caducous.

Flowers.—April, monœcious, before the leaves.   Staminate catkins clustered or in pairs, when mature become three to four inches long.   Pistillate catkins one inch to one and a half inches long, peduncles bibracteolate, three-fourths to one inch in length.   Scales lanceolate, pale green ;   styles bright red.

Fruit.—Strobiles, cylindrical, elongated, pendulous, long-stalked. Scales glabrous, wedge-shaped at base, rather longer than broad, with short, wide-spreading, rounded lobes.   Nut oval, small, narrower than its wings.

> Give me of your bark, O Birch-tree !
> Of your yellow bark, O Birch-tree !
> Growing by the rushing river
> Tall and stately in the valley !
> I a light canoe will build me,
> Build a swift Cheemaun for sailing,
> That shall float upon the river,
> Like a yellow leaf in Autumn,
> Like a yellow water-lily !
>
> —HENRY W. LONGFELLOW.

The great triumph of the birch is the bark canoe.   The design of a savage, it yet looks like the thought of a poet and its grace and fitness haunt the imagination.   I suppose its production was the inevitable result of the Indians' wants and surroundings, but that does not detract from its beauty.   It is, indeed, one of the fairest flowers the thorny plant of necessity ever bore.

—JOHN BURROUGHS.

The Paper Birch possesses the most wonderful bark of any of our native trees.   In outward color it is a lustrous creamy white, so brilliant that its gleam can be seen in the forest as far as the eye can reach.   Beneath the smooth white skin are the paper-like layers which readily separate into thin sheets and vary in color from cream to light tan. This bark is the joy and pride of every woodsman whether he be tourist, guide, or hunter.   It makes his canoe, it roofs his cabin, it becomes for the time his dinner-service, it is a cup, a pail, a cloak, an umbrella.   The thin papery layers into which the bark separates are of so firm a texture that it is possible both to write and paint upon them.   Curious traditions gather about this natural paper.   Pliny and Plutarch agree that the famous books of Numa Pompilius, written

Trunk of Paper Birch, *Betula papyrifera.*

seven hundred years before Christ, were of birch bark ; and the sibylline leaves purchased by Tarquin are by some believed to have been of the same material.

The inner bark contains starch so abundantly that it is a valuable resource to the people of the extreme north who bruise and mix it with their food.

RED BIRCH. RIVER BIRCH

Bétula nìgra.

Eighty to ninety feet in height, trunk often dividing into two or three slightly diverging limbs and forming a round-topped picturesque head. Branches slender and pendulous. Loves the banks of streams and ponds and swamps, where the water overflows. Ranges from Massachusetts to Florida and reaches its largest size in the low lands of the south.

Bark.—Dark red brown, deeply furrowed, scaly. On branches and young stems bright red or reddish brown, or silver white, marked with horizontal lenticels. Separates into thin papery plates, which curl back and show the pinkish inner layer. Branchlets at first coated with tomentum, later become dark red and shining and marked with pale lenticels ; finally they become dull red brown and after a time the bark begins to separate into thin flakes.

Wood.—Light brown, sapwood pale ; light, strong, close-grained, used in manufacture of furniture and wooden ware. Sp. gr., 0.5762 ; weight of cu. ft., 35.91 lbs.

Winter Buds.—Bright chestnut brown, shining, ovate, acute, one-fourth inch long, inner scales enlarge when spring growth begins and become three-fourths of an inch long, strap-shaped, pale brown tinged with red, hairy.

Leaves.—Alternate, one and one-half to three inches long, one to two inches broad, broadly ovate, wedge-shaped at base, doubly serrate, often almost lobed, acute. They come out of the bud, pale yellow green, hairy and tomentose ; when full grown are thin, tough, deep shining green above, pale yellow green ; midrib stout, conspicuous, hairy beneath. In autumn they turn a pale dull yellow. Petioles short, slender, flattened, tomentose. Stipules ovate, pale green, caducous.

Flowers.—March, April, before the leaves. Staminate catkins clustered in threes, form in late summer, during winter are three-fourths of an inch long, rigid. Scales dull chestnut brown. When flowers open the catkins are two to three inches long, scales light yellow and bright chestnut brown. Pistillate catkins are about one-

Red Birch, *Betula nigra.*

Leaves 1½' to 3' long, 1' to 2' broad.

third of an inch long ; scales bright green, ovate, downy ; peduncles tomentose, bibracteolate.

Strobiles.—Ripen in May and June ; cylindrical, oblong, erect, an inch to an inch and a half long, half an inch thick. Scales oblong-obovate, hairy, three-lobed, lateral lobes shorter than the central. Nut oval, downy ; wing as broad or broader than the seed.

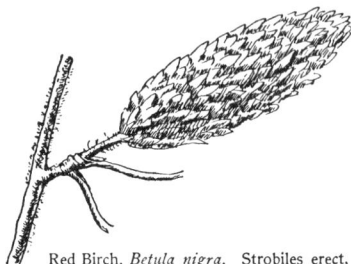

Red Birch, *Betula nigra.* Strobiles erect, 1′ to 1½′ long.

Nearly every genus of trees contains one species that loves the water. Among the maples it is the Red, among the ashes it is the Black, among the oaks it is the Swamp White and among the birches it is the Red. Like other trees that grow from choice upon lands subject to inundation, it ripens its fruit early and casts it broadcast in June when streams are low. Germination takes place at once ; and each little seedling becomes several inches high and well established in life before the autumn rains inundate its birthplace and threaten its existence.

Other birches love the north, climb to the mountain tops and make their way well into the arctic regions ; but the Red Birch seeks warmth not cold, crowds to the water's very edge and dips its pendulous branches into the quiet or running stream. It is the water nymph of the birches ; and reaches its greatest size in the damp misty lowlands of Texas or among the bayous of Louisiana or in the swamps of Florida. And yet it possesses all the family ability of harmonizing with its environment and will grow rapidly in good soil quite remote from water.

The Red Birch is a beautiful tree ; the bark of a full grown trunk is dark, but small stems and branchlets are really red and in the sunlight are positively brilliant. This red bark easily sloughs loose and shows the paler bark beneath. The spray is particularly delicate, the twigs and branchlets long, flexible, and pendulous.

Yellow Birch, *Betula lutea*.
Leaves 3' to 4' long, 1' to 2' broad.

YELLOW BIRCH. GRAY BIRCH

Bétula lútea.

Usually thirty to forty feet in height, occasionally one hundred; reaches its largest size in Canada, northern New England and New York. Ranges as far south as Tennessee and North Carolina. Prefers rich moist uplands. Forms a broad round-topped head with pendulous branches.

Bark.—Aromatic and slightly bitter. On old trunks, silvery yellow gray, divided by irregular fissures into large thin plates; on young trunks silvery gray or dull yellow or shining golden, either close and firm or somewhat divided, the edges of the irregular fissures breaking into thin layers, more or less rolled at border. The branchlets at first are green, afterward lustrous brown, finally dull brown.

Wood.—Light brown tinged with red; heavy, strong, hard, close-grained with satiny surface, susceptible of a fine polish. Used in the manufacture of furniture, hubs of wheels, small boxes, butter moulds and for fuel. Sp. gr., 0.6553; weight of cu. ft., 40.84 lbs.

Winter Buds.—Acute, light chestnut brown, a quarter of an inch long.

Leaves.—Alternate, often in pairs, three to four inches long, an inch to two inches wide, ovate or oblong-ovate, wedge-shaped or slightly heart-shaped at the slightly oblique base, doubly serrate, acute or acuminate, slightly aromatic. They come out of the bud plicate, bronze green or red, hairy; when full grown are dull dark green above, yellow green below; midrib stout, primary veins conspicuous, impressed above, hairy below. In autumn they turn a clear pale yellow. Petioles short, slender, grooved, hairy; stipules ovate, pale pinkish green, caducous.

Flowers.—April, before the leaves; monœcious. Staminate catkins form in late summer, usually in groups, three-fourths to one inch long. Scales pale chestnut brown, ovate. When the flowers open the catkins are three to three and one-half inches long; scales pale yellow green below the middle, dark brown above. Pistillate catkins about two-thirds of an inch long; scales acute, pale green below, light red, hairy above.

Yellow Birch, *Be-tula lutea.* Strobiles erect, 1′ to 1½′ long.

Fruit.—Strobiles erect, sessile or short-stalked, oblong-ovoid, an inch to an inch and a half in length, three-quarters of an inch thick. Scales wedge-shaped, broad or narrow, three-lobed, lobes variable. Nut oval or obovate, one-eighth inch long; wing rather narrower than the seed.

This birch is named from its golden bark. On an old trunk, the bark simply suggests the color, it is rather a silver gray with a yellow flush ; and in extreme old age the surface is shaggy with light gray plates the size of a hand. On young trees, when the yellow inner bark is covered by an unbroken, thin, brown, outer layer the result is a dull yellowish brown. But, now and then, in the leafless woods one comes upon a young tree six or eight inches in diameter upon whose trunk the thin outer bark has been loosened and frayed by the wind until it clings a mass of silvery shreds and patches, revealing in the March and April sunshine an inner bark of the most exquisite golden yellow. This disheveled wood-nymph of the forest is rare, but once found its beauty is never forgotten.

SWEET BIRCH, BLACK BIRCH, MAHOGANY BIRCH

Bétula lénta.

Generally distributed, most abundant northward, but reaches its greatest size on the mountains of Tennessee. Usually seventy to eighty feet high with a round-topped, open head. Prefers moist situations, mountain slopes and borders of streams.

Bark.—Spicy aromatic. Dark brown with a reddish tinge. On old trunks deeply furrowed and broken into thick irregular plates ; on young stems and on branches close, smooth, lustrous and marked with pale horizontal lenticels. Does not separate into thin layers as the paper birch. Branchlets at first pale green, slightly viscid, later they change from dark orange brown to bright red brown and finally to dark reddish brown.

Wood.—Dark brown tinged with red, sapwood light brown or yellow ; heavy, very strong, hard, close-grained, satiny and capable of receiving a fine polish. Used largely in the manufacture of furniture, hubs of wheels, small articles and fuel. Sp. gr., 0.7617 ; weight of cu. ft., 47.47 lbs.

Winter Buds.—Pale chestnut brown, slender, acute, one-fourth of an inch long.

Leaves.—Alternate, two and one-half to six inches long, one and a half to three inches wide, ovate or oblong-ovate, heart-shaped or rounded, often unequal at base, doubly serrate, acute or acuminate. They come out of the bud plicate, pale green, downy ; when full grown are dull dark green above, pale yellow green below ; midrib yellow, primary veins indistinct above but conspicuous and hairy below. In autumn they turn a clear bright yellow. Petioles stout, hairy, deeply grooved above. Stipules ovate, pale green or nearly white, caducous.

Sweet Birch, *Betula lenta*. Strobiles erect, 1' to 1½' long.

Flowers.—April, before the leaves. Staminate catkins form in late summer, during winter are three-fourths of an inch long. When the flowers open the catkins become three to four inches long, and in general appearance become bright yellow due to the abundant anthers. Scales ovate, bright red brown above the middle, pale brown below. Pistillate catkins from one-half to three-fourths of an inch long, scales ovate, pale green ; styles exserted, slender, pale pink.

Fruit.—Strobiles oblong-ovoid, smooth, sessile, erect, one to one and one-half inches long, one-half an inch thick. Scales smooth, with rounded or acute lateral lobes. Nut obovate, pointed at base, about as broad as its wing.

The Black Birch which is a handsome tree with its tall dark stem, graceful fragrant branches and dark green foliage, is especially beautiful in early spring when its long staminate catkins hang from the leafless branches changing them for a few days into fountains of golden spray and making it the most conspicuous of the American birches.

—CHARLES S. SARGENT.

The names White, Black, and Yellow are often given to trees with very little justification, but in the case of the birches they express differences which are apparent to the most casual observer. The trunk of the White Birch is really white, the bark of the Yellow Birch is indeed yellow and that of the Black Birch is so dark that it may easily be considered black. The bark resembles in general appearance that of the common cherry tree, whence the name Cherry Birch, and like that of the other birches, it divides in lines running horizontally around the tree. On old trees it becomes very rough and clings in horizontal plates, loosened and often curled at one end. The inner bark is very fragrant and has a pleasant spicy taste. For this reason it is called Sweet Birch. The bark of the Yellow Birch is also aromatic but not to the same degree. This flavor is due to an essen-

Sweet Birch, *Betula lenta.*
Leaves 2½′ to 6′ long, 1½′ to 3′ broad.

tial oil identical with that obtained from *Gaultheria procumbens,* and which under the name of Wintergreen Oil is employed as a remedy for rheumatism. The remedial agent is salicylic acid, of which it contains a large percentage.

The wood when first cut has a beautiful rosy tinge which deepens with age and exposure. The difference between the annual circles gives it a general clouded appearance and this is especially marked in a section taken from the point of union of a large limb with the body of the tree. When such a piece is skilfully stained and polished, it closely resembles mahogany. As a matter of fact, all good imitations of mahogany are birch. However, the wood is beautiful enough to have a value of its own.

ALDER

Alnus glutinósa.

The northern native alders east of the Rocky Mountains are shrubs, following the water-courses and nowhere attaining the arborescent form. They are aquatic, enjoying situations too wet for either willow or poplar.

The only alder tree which is commonly found in the northern states is *Alnus glutinosa,* a European species which is fairly naturalized. It is native to the entire continent of Europe and although naturally aquatic will grow in good soil, somewhat removed from water.

The leaves are orbicular, obtuse, wedge-shaped at base and serrated at margin. When young the leaves and stems are somewhat glutinous, whence the specific name. The bark is dark and furrowed, and the wood is valuable for but one purpose. It will not endure alternate wet and dry, but if constantly submerged it becomes extremely hard and virtually incorruptible.

The flowers are monœcious, the staminate blossoms are long drooping catkins which form in the late summer and hang

Fruiting Spray of Alder, *Almus glutinosa.*

Leaves 1½′ to 2′ long.

upon the tree stiff and rigid all winter long, but respond to the first warmth of returning spring.

The pistillate blossoms are little cone-like catkins produced in the spring. When these mature they open to let the seeds fall but themselves remain upon the tree all winter and frequently through the second summer.

HOP HORNBEAM. IRONWOOD

Óstrya virginiàna.

Small, slender tree. Usually found on dry gravelly slopes and ridges, often in the shade of oaks, maples, and other larger trees. In Arkansas and Texas it reaches the height of fifty feet; ranges throughout the United States east of the Rocky Mountains.

Bark.—Grayish brown, furrowed and broken into narrow oblong scales. Branchlets slender, tough, at first pale green, later dark red brown. Rich in tannic acid.

Wood.—Light brown tinged with red, sapwood nearly white; heavy, tough, exceedingly close-grained, very strong and hard. Durable in contact with the soil and will take a fine polish. Used for small articles like levers, handles of tools, mallets. Sp. gr., 0.8284; weight of cu. ft., 51.62 lbs.

Leaf Buds.—Ovate, acute, light chestnut brown, one-fourth of an inch long. Inner scales enlarge when spring growth begins. No terminal bud is formed.

Leaves.—Alternate, oblong-ovate, three to five inches long, rounded, cordate, or wedge-shape, or sometimes unequal at the base, sharply and doubly serrate, acute or acuminate; feather-veined, midrib and veins prominent on the under side. They come from the bud light bronze green, smooth above and hairy beneath; when full grown are thin,

Branch of Hop Hornbeam, *Ostrya virginiana,* Showing the Staminate Aments as they Appear in Winter.

extremely tough, dull dark yellow green above, pale yellow green beneath. In autumn they turn a clear yellow. Petiole short, slender, hairy; stipules caducous.

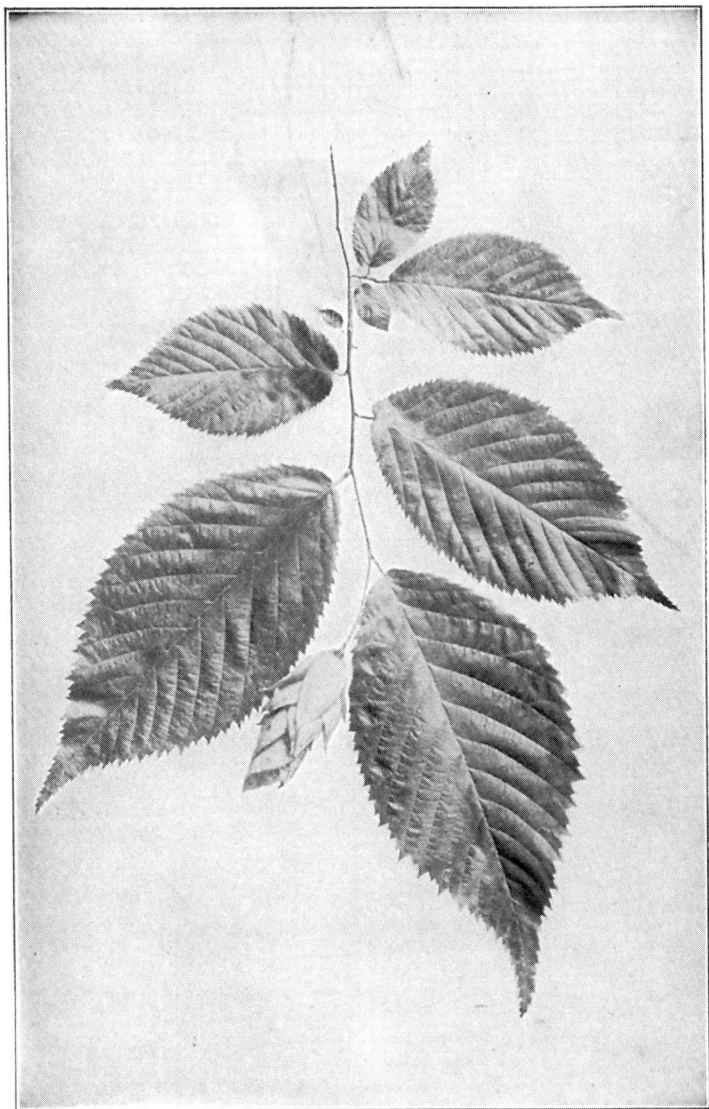

Fruiting Spray of Hop Hornbeam, *Ostrya virginiana*.

Leaves 3′ to 5′ long.

Flowers.—April, May, with the leaves. Monœcious, apetalous; the staminate naked in long pendulous aments. These aments appear in midsummer about one-half an inch long, stiff, tomentose, with light red brown scales ; they develop from lateral buds and are conspicuous during the winter. In the spring they become about two inches long, loose and drooping. The staminate flower is composed of from three to fourteen stamens crowded on a hairy torus, adnate to the base of a broadly ovate concave scale, which is contracted at the apex into a sharp point, ciliate at margin, longer than the stamens. The pistillate flowers are borne in erect lax aments, each flower enclosed in a hairy sac-like body formed by the union of a bract and two bractlets. Ovary, two-celled ; style short, two-lobed ; ovule solitary.

Fruit.—Strobile, consisting of a number of fruiting sac-like involucres, each inclosing a small flat nut. The fruit cluster is from one to two inches long, borne on a hairy stem and resembles a hop.

To find in the forest a hop-bearing tree is to the uninitiated an experience, and the fruit of this Hornbeam so closely resembles that of the common hop-vine that it has given the name to the tree. Indeed, the tree seems to have very little that it can really call its own, for it resembles the birch in its leaf and the beech in its spray. One thing, however, is individual, it excels all the other trees of the forest in strength. When woodmen need a lever they seek at once for a Hop Hornbeam, whence its wild-wood name of Leverwood.

Pistillate and Staminate Aments of Hop Hornbeam,
Ostrya virginiana.

This is one of the solitary trees ; never found in masses, it stands here and there in the forest and chooses only cool, fertile, shaded situations. The wood being exceedingly close-grained, the growth of the tree is correspondingly slow. It can be easily raised from the seeds which do not usually germinate until the second year after they are planted. Traces of leaves and fruit are found in the eocene and miocene rocks of Europe and in tertiary times it ranged to Greenland.

HORNBEAM. BLUE BEECH

Carpinus caroliniàna.

Some derive *Carpinus* from the Celtic words *car*, wood and *pix*, the head, because of the use of the wood in making yokes for oxen; others refer it to *carpentum*, a sort of chariot which the Romans made of this wood. Hornbeam alludes to the horny texture of the wood.

—LOUDON.

Common along the borders of streams and swamps, loves a deep moist soil. Varies from shrub to small tree, and ranges throughout the United States east of the Rocky Mountains.

Bark.—On old trees near the base, furrowed. Young trees and branches smooth, dark bluish gray, sometimes furrowed, light and dark gray. Branchlets at first pale green, changing to reddish brown, ultimately dull gray.

Wood.—Light brown, sapwood nearly white; heavy, hard, close-grained, very strong. Used for levers, handles of tools. Sp. gr., 0.7286; weight of cu. ft., 45.41 lbs.

Winter Buds.—Ovate, acute, chestnut brown, one-eighth of an inch long. Inner scales enlarge when spring growth begins. No terminal bud is formed.

Leaves.—Alternate, two to four inches long, ovate-oblong, rounded, wedge-shaped, or rarely subcordate and often unequal at base, sharply and doubly serrate, acute or acuminate. They come out of the bud pale bronze green and hairy; when full grown they are dull deep green above, paler beneath; feather-veined, midrib and veins very prominent on under side. In autumn bright red, deep scarlet and orange. Petioles short, slender, hairy. Stipules caducous.

Flowers.—April. Monœcious, apetalous, the staminate naked in pendulous aments. The staminate ament buds are axillary and form in the autumn and during the winter resemble leaf-buds, only twice as large; these aments begin to lengthen very early in the spring, when full grown are about one and one-half inches long.

The staminate flower is composed of three to twenty stamens crowded on a hairy torus, adnate to the base of a broadly ovate, acute, boat-shaped scale, green below the middle. bright red at apex. The pistillate aments are one-half to three-fourths of an inch long with ovate, acute, hairy, green scales and bright scarlet styles.

Fruit.—Clusters of involucres, hanging from the ends of leafy branches. Each involucre slightly incloses a small oval nut. The involucres are short stalked, usually three-lobed, though one lobe is often wanting ; halberd-shaped, coarsely serrate on one margin, or entire.

In time it waxeth so hard that the toughness and hardness of it may be rather compared to horn than unto wood ; and therefore it was called hornebeam or hard-beam. The leaves of it are like the elme, saving that they be tenderer ; among these hang certain triangular things, upon which are found knaps or little buds in which is contained the fruit or seed.

—GERALD.

The Horne bound tree is a tough kind of wood that requires so much paines in riving as is almost incredible, being the best for to make bolles and dishes, not being subject to cracke or leake.

—NEW ENGLAND'S PROSPECT.

A Pistillate and a Staminate Ament of Hornbeam, *Carpinus caroliniana.*

This is a tree of temperate climates enjoying neither extreme heat nor extreme cold. In texture, its bark resembles that of the beech, is dark bluish gray instead of light gray and for this reason is called Blue Beech. It is credited in the books with forty feet of height but rarely attains more than twenty. A peculiarity of its growth is the manner in which the sinews of the branches seem to run down the trunk as if the tree construction were Gothic. The beech often shows the same peculiarity but rarely so marked as the hornbeam.

The branches are long, irregular, crooked and often pendulous. Sometimes a broad flat-topped head of foliage is formed, sometimes only a shapeless mass. The branches are so tough and the tree so tolerant of the

Fruiting Spray of Hornbeam, *Carpinus caroliniana*.
Leaves 2′ to 4′ long.

knife that it has become the favorite tree for arbor-walks in parks.

The flowers are monœcious ; the staminate flowers appear in long, loose, pendulous catkins from axillary buds. The pistillate, in loose half-erect catkins at the end of the spray. Each pistillate flower is subtended by a bract which expands with the growth of the fruit into a sort of leaf which gathers around and protects a small oval nut. These fruit clusters often remain on the trees long after the leaves have fallen.

The tree can be easily raised from the seed which does not germinate until the second year. Traces of *Carpinus* have been found in the tertiary rocks of Alaska and in the upper miocene of Colorado and Nevada, regions from which the genus has entirely disappeared.

CUPULÌFERÆ—OAK FAMILY

OAK

Quercus.

Quercus by some authorities is derived from two Celtic words *quer,* fine, and *cuex,* a tree.

> Jove's own tree
> That holds the woods in awful sovereignty ;
> For length of ages lasts his happy reign,
> And lives of mortal men contend in vain.
> Full in the midst of his own strength he stands,
> Stretching his brawny arms and leafy hands,
> His shade protects the plains, his head the hills commands.
>
> —VIRGIL.

The oak is the most majestic of forest trees. It has been represented as holding the same rank among the plants of the temperate hemispheres that the lion does among the quadrupeds, and the eagle among birds ; that is to say it is the emblem of grandeur, strength and duration ; of force that resists as a lion is of force that acts.

—LOUDON.

The acorn is the only seed I can think of which is left by nature to take care of itself. It matures without protection, falls heavily and helplessly to the ground to be eaten and trodden on by animals, yet the few which escape and those which are trodden under are well able to compete in the race for life. While the elm and maple seeds are drying up on the surface, the hickories and walnuts waiting to be cracked, the acorn is at work with its coat off. It drives its tap root into the earth in spite of grass and brush and litter. No matter if it is so shaded by forest trees that the sun cannot penetrate ; it will manage to make a short stem and a few leaves the first season, enough to keep life in the root which will drill deeper and deeper. When age or accident removes the tree which has overshadowed it, then it will assert itself. Fires may run over the land destroying almost everything else ; the oak will be killed to the ground but it will throw up a new shoot the next spring, the root will keep enlarging and when the opportunity comes will make a vigorous growth and throw out strong

side roots and often care no more for its tap root which has been its only support than the frog cares for the tail of the tadpole after it has got on its own legs."
—ROBERT DOUGLAS in *Garden and Forest.*

This genus is one of close family ties and marked resemblances. The bark of every species is heavily charged with tannic acid. The roots take hold of the earth in two ways; a strong tap root goes down deep into the ground and at the same time wide spreading horizontal roots keep near the surface. The very poise of the tree denotes strength and this quality is present in the humblest member of the family.

Sprouting Acorn.

The leaves vary in form. In those groups which contain the representative species of the genus the leaves are of a shape unlike those of any other trees.

The character of the inflorescence is the same in every species. It is monœcious; that is, the stamens and pistils are separated, borne in different flowers, but both kinds of flowers are produced on the same branch. These appear together, just when the leaves are half grown. The staminate flowers are found in the axils of quick falling bracts which are borne on the rachis of slender drooping aments produced from separate or leafy buds in the axils of last year's leaves, or from the axils of the inner scales of the terminal bud, or from the axils of the leaves

Staminate Aments of Scarlet Oak, *Quercus coccinea.* Ovaries of Preceding Year.

of the year. There is no corolla. The calyx is bell-shaped and divided into four to six divisions. The stamens, usually four to six, with exserted filaments and oblong two-celled anthers, are borne on the torus. The ovary has aborted.

The pistillate flowers are subtended by a quick falling bract and are borne in few-flowered spikes, or on solitary peduncles produced from the axils of the leaves of the year. The calyx is urn-shaped and grows fast to the ovary. The stamens have aborted.

The ovary is inferior, incompletely three-celled and inclosed more or less by a growing scaly involucre which in time develops into the acorn cup. Styles are usually three, short or long, erect or curved, generally persistent on the fruit. There are two ovules in each cell, but all save one fail to be nourished. The nut is a fruit formed by the adhesion of an ovary to the calyx and matures either the first or second year; it is always surrounded at the base, or more or less inclosed, by a woody involucre called the cup. The acorn cup is of woody texture made up of a large number of tiny scales which have grown together, sometimes entirely, sometimes with free tips. The seed fills the nut. The cotyledons are thick and fleshy, the radicle minute. An acorn should never be allowed to become dry if it is desired that it should germinate, for the vital principle is fleeting.

A Staminate and a Pistillate Flower of Scarlet Oak, *Quercus coccinea* ; enlarged.

American oaks in the popular mind have the reputation of being slow growers, but this is based upon the habit of two or three species rather than upon the habit of the family. The White and the Bur Oaks grow slowly. The Scarlet Oak is moderately slow. But the Black, the Swamp White, the Pin, and the Red, under favorable conditions, will all grow rapidly in their youth. Probably most oaks require a century to reach maturity ; they rarely bear acorns under twenty years of age

and increase in productiveness as they grow older. The entire family is especially subject to attacks of the gall-fly.

Quercus belongs to the long-lived trees ; the life of some species is believed to reach one thousand years. There are of course no records of long life in America, but there are oaks in England which are believed to have been old trees in the time of William the Conqueror. Pliny mentions a *Quercus Ilex* which was an old tree when Rome was founded and which was still living in his time. In the United States the largest specimens of the genus are found in the Mississippi valley.

Remains of oak trees are found far north of their present home in the miocene and eocene rocks of North America.

American oaks naturally divide themselves into groups which are characterized by the shape of their leaves and the time required to bring their fruit to maturity.

The first division comprises those species whose leaves have either rounded lobes or are sinuate toothed, or entire, but are destitute of bristles. These bloom in the spring and mature their acorns the same season. They are called the White Oak Group, or the Annuals. The White, Post, Bur, Swamp White, Chestnut, Yellow, and Chinquapin are Annuals.

The second division comprises those species whose leaves have pointed lobes which terminate in bristles. These bloom in the spring, but the acorn does not mature until the autumn of the following year. They are called the Red Oak Group, or the Biennials. The Red, Scarlet, Black, Spanish, Pin, Bear, Black Jack, Shingle and Willow are Biennials. The leaves of the Shingle and the Willow oak are destitute of bristles, but the acorns mature the second year.

White Oak, *Quercus alba.*
Leaves 5′ to 9′ long, 3′ to 4′ broad.

WHITE OAK

Quércus álba.

Alba, white, referring to the pale tint of the bark.

Common ; grows to the height of eighty or one hundred feet with a trunk three or four feet in diameter. Is tolerant of many soils, often forms the principal tree of large tracts. Reaches its greatest size in the valley of the lower Ohio. Is difficult to transplant and is best grown from seed planted where the tree is to remain. Grows rapidly.

Bark.—Light gray, varying to dark gray and to white ; shallow fissured and scaly. Branchlets at first bright green, later reddish-green and finally light gray.

Wood.—Light brown with paler sapwood ; strong, tough, heavy, fine-grained, durable and beautiful. Used for construction, ship-building, cooperage, agricultural implements, cabinet-making, interior finish of houses. Sp. gr., 0.7470 ; weight of cu. ft., 46.35 lbs.

Winter Buds.—Reddish brown, obtuse, one-eighth of an inch long.

Leaves.—Alternate, five to nine inches long, three to four inches wide. Obovate or oblong, seven to nine-lobed, usually seven-lobed with rounded lobes and rounded sinuses ; lobes destitute of bristles ; sinuses sometimes deep, sometimes shallow. On young trees the leaves are often repand. They come out of the bud conduplicate, bright red above, pale below and covered with white tomentum ; the red fades quickly and they become silvery greenish white and shining ; when full grown are thin, bright yellow green, shining or dull above, pale, glaucous or smooth below ; midrib stout, yellow, primary veins conspicuous. In late autumn they turn a deep red and drop, or on young trees remain on the branches throughout the winter. Petioles short, stout, grooved, and flattened. Stipules linear, caducous.

Flowers.—May, when leaves are one-third grown. Staminate flowers borne in hairy aments two and a half to three inches long ; calyx bright yellow, hairy, six to eight-lobed, lobes shorter than the stamens ; anthers yellow. Pistillate flowers borne on short peduncles ; involucral scales hairy, reddish ; calyx lobes acute ; stigmas bright red.

Acorns.—Annual, sessile or stalked ; nut ovoid or oblong, round at the apex, light brown, shining, three-quarters to an inch long ; cup cup-shaped, encloses about one-fourth of the nut, tomentose on the outside, tuberculate at base, scales with short obtuse tips becoming smaller and thinner toward the rim.

Trunk of White Oak, *Quercus alba.*

OAK FAMILY

It seems idolatry with some excuse
When our forefather Druids in their oaks
Imagined sanctity.

—COWPER.

The White of all American oaks is most akin to the common and familiar
tree of European countries, the oak of myths and of poetry, of Dodona and
Hercynia, the tree which Celt and Briton worshipped, which shaded the Druid's
sacred fire and has at all times been the emblem of strength and longevity.

—*Garden and Forest.*

Although called the White Oak it is very unusual to find an
individual with an absolutely white bark, the usual color is an
ashen gray. All in all, this is the most valuable as well as
the most stately and beautiful of our oaks. In the forest it
reaches a magnificent height, in the open it develops into a
massive broad-topped tree with great limbs striking out at
wide angles and carrying the idea of rugged strength to the
very tips of their branches.

In spring the young leaves are exquisite in their delicate
silvery pink, covered with soft down as with a blanket. The
petioles are short, and the leaves which cluster close to the
ends of the shoots are pale green and downy with the result
that the entire tree has a misty, frosty look which is very
beautiful. This lovely vision continues for several days passing through the opalescent changes of soft pink, silvery white
and finally yellow green.

The autumnal tints of the White Oak are also beautiful ; its
rich purplish red glows in the forest and gives a splendor to
November days long after the maples and sumachs have shed
their leaves.

The leaves unfold late ; although they vary in form somewhat they keep fairly true to the type and need never be mistaken. The most divergent form approaches a skeleton leaf.
Oblong or obovate, they are usually seven-lobed with both
lobe and sinus rounded and the lobe destitute of a bristle at
its apex. The acorn is the product of the blossom of the
year and the kernel is sweet ; not sweet like that of the
chestnut or hickory but sweet compared to other acorns.

The White Oak lives long. The famous Charter Oak of

White Oak, *Quercus alba.*
Leaves 5′ to 9′ long, 3′ to 4′ broad.   Acorns ¾′ to 1′ long.

Hartford was believed to be several hundred years old. " When the first settlers were clearing their land the Indians begged that it might be spared. 'It has been the guide of our ancestors for centuries,' said they, 'as to the time of planting our corn ; when the leaves are the size of a mouse's ears, then is the time to put the seed into the ground.' The Indians' request was granted and the tree, afterward becoming the custodian of the lost charter, became famous for all time. It fell in a windstorm, August 21, 1856, and so deeply was it venerated that, at sunset on the day of its fall, the bells of the city were tolled and a band of music played funeral dirges over its ruins."

The White Oak like the Black Walnut is passing and unless replanted will ere long disappear. Two causes are at work to bring this about. First, its valuable timber which marks it for the axe ; and second, the sweetness of its nuts which causes them to be eaten by the wild creatures, while the bitter nuts of other oaks are allowed to germinate undisturbed.

The White Oak hybridizes freely with the Bur, the Post, and the Chestnut Oaks.

POST OAK

Quércus minor.

A tree reaching the height of fifty or sixty feet, often a shrub. Grows on dry sandy soil, or gravelly uplands. Ranges from Massachusetts to southern New York and Michigan, southward to Florida, and is the most abundant oak of central Texas.

Bark.—Grayish brown, deeply fissured into broad scaly ridges. Branchlets at first covered with thick yellow brown tomentum, soon they become light orange or reddish brown, still downy, finally they are dark or gray brown.

Wood.—Brown, sapwood paler brown ; heavy, hard, close-grained, durable in contact with soil. Used for fuel, fencing, and railway ties. Sp. gr., 0.8367 ; weight of cu. ft., 52.14 lbs.

Winter Buds.—Chestnut brown, ovate, downy, about one-eighth of an inch long.

Post Oak, *Quercus minor.*
Leaves 5′ to 8′ long, 3′ to 6′ broad.

Leaves.—Alternate, five to eight inches long, three to six inches wide, oblong-obovate, base wedge-shaped or rounded, five-lobed ; lowest pair of lobes small, middle pair broad and undulate or lobed, terminal lobe itself three-lobed ; midrib broad, yellow, downy, primary veins conspicuous. They come out of the bud convolute, dark red above, densely covered with thick orange brown tomentum ; when full grown are thick, leathery, deep dark green, with stellate tufts of hairs scattered over the upper surface, the under surface covered with pale pubescence. In autumn they turn dull yellow or brown. Petiole stout, flattened, downy. Stipules brown, caducous.

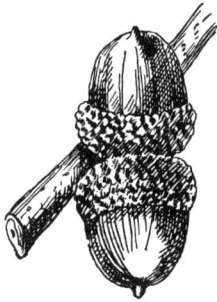

Flowers.—May, when leaves are one-third grown. Staminate flowers borne on aments three to four inches long, hairy. Calyx hairy, yellow ; segments five, ovate, acute, laciniate ; anthers yellow, hairy. Pistillate flowers sessile or on peduncles ; stigmas bright red.

Post Oak, *Quercus minor.*
Acorns ½′ to 1′ long.

Acorns.—Annual, sessile or stalked. Nuts one-half to one inch long, oval or ovoid, reddish brown, sometimes striped with darker brown, sometimes pubescent at apex. Cup cup-shaped or turbinate, rarely saucer-shaped, usually enclosing one-third to one-half the nut, reddish brown, tomentose, covered with close free scales.

The Post Oak loves to grow at the edge of the timber-land, sheltered but not crowded by other trees. The bark is nearly the color, but appears thicker than that of a White Oak of the same age. It has a fine-checked, " alligator-skin " appearance but is even more regular, the vertical furrows being so continuous as to suggest an up and down corrugation ; this feature is a conspicuous characteristic of the trunk.

The tree has a straggling ungraceful habit of growth compensated by the pleasing arrangement of the leaves ; the branches do not subdivide freely but put out new shoots all along their length, which gives them a close-wreathed appearance ; and so the foliage is distributed evenly through the tree instead of forming a canopy. The leaves are coarse and rough on both sides. As to their shape, there seem to be two varieties of tree ; on one tree the leaves have uniformly the characteristic cross-shape, while on a Post Oak just beside it the leaves are irregular and varied in shape, with here and there one of typical form.

BUR OAK. MOSSY-CUP OAK

Quércus macrocárpa.

Macrocarpa refers to the large size of the acorn.

The average height is eighty feet, but in the valley of the lower Ohio it has been known to reach one hundred and sixty. Is tolerant of many soils and grows rapidly. Ranges from Nova Scotia to Manitoba, south to Massachusetts, Pennsylvania, Kansas and Texas. Forms the " Oak Openings " of Minnesota.

Bark.—Light gray brown, deeply furrowed, scaly. Branches with corky ridges. Branchlets stout, at first greenish, very pubescent, afterwards light orange yellow, later ashy gray or light brown, finally dark brown.

Wood.—Brown with paler sapwood, heavy, strong, close-grained, durable in contact with the ground, valuable. Used in ship and boat building, all sorts of construction, interior finish of houses, cabinet-making, cooperage, carriages, agricultural implements, railway ties, fencing. Sp. gr., 0 7453 ; weight of cu. ft., 46.45 lbs.

Winter Buds.—Light reddish brown, broadly ovate or acute or obtuse, pubescent, one-eighth to one-fourth of an inch long.

Leaves.—Alternate, six to twelve inches long, three to six inches wide, obovate or oblong, lyrately pinnatifid or deeply sinuately-lobed or divided. Base usually long wedge-shaped, sinuses round, sometimes deep, sometimes shallow, lobes five to seven ; the terminal lobe is largest, oval or obovate in outline, and crenately lobed ; or smaller and three-lobed ; the lateral lobes are larger than the basal lobes. A second form is broadly ovate and deeply or slightly crenately-lobed. A third form is pinnatifidly cut into five or seven pairs of lateral lobes with a three-lobed terminal. They come out of the bud convolute, downy, yellow green above and silvery white below. When full grown are thick, leathery, bright green, shining above, pale green or silvery and coated with pale or rusty pubescence below ; midrib stout, pale, often pubescent below, primary veins conspicuous. In autumn they turn dull yellow or yellowish brown. Petioles short, stout, flattened and grooved, enlarged at the base. Stipules varying in form, usually an inch in length, sometimes persistent.

Flowers.—May, when leaves are one-third grown. Staminate flowers borne in slender hairy aments from four to six inches long ; calyx yellow green, four to six-lobed, downy ; stamens four to six ; filaments short; anthers yellow. Pistillate flowers are sessile or borne on short peduncles, involucral scales reddish, tomentose ; stigmas bright red.

Acorns.—Annual, sessile or stalked, solitary, variable in size and shape. Nut oval or ovate, pubescent, from one-half to two inches in length ; cup cup-shaped, rarely shallow but usually deep, enclosing from one-third to nearly the entire nut, light brown, downy inside, outside dark brown, tomentose, covered with large imbricated scales which near the rim become half free and form a fringe-like border. Kernel white.

The Bur Oak ranges from Manitoba to Texas and from the foot-hills of the Rocky Mountains to the Atlantic coast. It goes farther to the northwest than any other of our eastern oaks, it varies in size from a shrub in Manitoba, to a magnificent tree one hundred and sixty feet high in southern Illinois. It is the most abundant oak of Kansas and of Nebraska, it forms the scattered forests known as " The Oak Openings " of Minnesota.

Three marked characters distinguish the Bur Oak. Its leaves have a peculiar though variable outline which is unmistakable, rarely if ever are two alike, yet all bear so marked a resemblance that there is no difficulty in distinguishing them. Every Bur Oak leaf is somewhere, usually about the middle, cut by two opposite sinuses nearly to the midrib.

Bur Oak, *Quercus macrocarpa.*
Acorns ½' to 2' long.

The terminal lobe so formed may itself be lobed or toothed or repand, the lower division may be lobed or entire, but with all these variations the leaves retain a general similarity.

In the spring they are yellow green as they burst from the bud and do not like so many others take on a stain of red. At first they are downy and woolly but soon become smooth and shining. The leaves spread out horizontally from the new shoots and the aments hang down in thick clusters. Their autumn col

Bur Oak, *Quercus macrocarpa.*
Leaves 6′ to 12′ long. 3′ to 6′ broad.

oring, like their spring coloring, is without red, being bright yellow or yellowish brown. The acorns are peculiar, but the cup is the most noticeable thing about them. The scales are so large and free that they make the cup look mossy. The rim is beautifully fringed. Then, too, this mossy cup fairly embraces the nut, covers two-thirds to three-fourths of its surface. This is the normal fruit ; at the north where the tree changes to a shrub the acorn is small and the cup loses its furbelows.

The corky wings which are frequently found on the young branches form a third distinguishing character. These ridges begin to form usually the third or fourth season and remain for several years, finally disappearing as the branches become old. When it is remembered that the cork of commerce is the outer bark of an oak tree native to southern Europe, it is interesting to see a northern species showing a tendency to produce the same thing.

CHESTNUT OAK. ROCK CHESTNUT OAK

Quércus prìnus.

A mountain tree though found in the low lands, usually sixty to seventy feet high, sometimes one hundred ; the trunk dividing into large limbs not very far from the ground. Ranges from Maine to Georgia and Alabama, westward through Ohio and southward to Kentucky and Tennessee.

Bark.—Dark, fissured into broad ridges, scaly. Branchlets stout, at first bronze green, later they become reddish brown, finally dark gray or brown. Heavily charged with tannic acid.

Wood.—Dark brown, sapwood lighter ; heavy, hard, strong, tough, close-grained, durable in contact with the soil. Used for fencing, fuel, and railway ties. Sp. gr., 0.7499 ; weight of cu. ft., 46.73 lbs.

Winter Buds.—Light chestnut brown, ovate, acute, one-fourth to one-half of an inch long.

Leaves.—Alternate, five to nine inches long, three to four and a half wide, obovate to oblong-lanceolate, wedge-shaped or rounded at base, coarsely crenately toothed, teeth rounded or acute, apex

Chestnut Oak, *Quercus prinus.*
Leaves 5′ to 9′ long, 3′ to 4′ broad.

rounded or acute. They come out of the bud convolute, yellow green or bronze, shining above, very pubescent below. When full grown are thick, firm, dark yellow green, somewhat shining above, pale green and pubescent below ; midribs stout, yellow, primary veins conspicuous. In autumn they turn a dull yellow soon changing into a yellow brown. Petioles stout or slender, short. Stipules linear to lanceolate, caducous.

Flowers.—May, when leaves are one-third grown. Staminate flowers are borne in hairy aments two to three inches long ; calyx pale yellow, hairy, deeply seven to nine-lobed ; stamens seven to nine ; anthers bright yellow. Pistillate flowers on short spikes ; peduncles green, stout, hairy ; involucral scales hairy ; stigmas short, bright red.

Acorns.—Annual, singly or in pairs ; nut oval, rounded or acute at apex, bright chestnut brown, shining, one and a quarter to one and one-half inches in length ; cup, cup-shaped or turbinate, usually inclosing one-half or one-third of the nut, thin, light brown and downy within, reddish brown and rough outside, tuberculate near the base. Scales small, much crowded toward the rim sometimes making a fringe. Kernel white, sweetish.

The Chestnut Oak, *Q. prinus,* and the Yellow Oak, *Q. acuminata,* have many characters in common. The extreme typical forms of each differ, but they vary toward each other

until the dividing line is difficult to draw ; at their widest they are no farther apart than the different forms of the black oaks. The Chestnut Oak is accredited in the books to dry soil and sandy ridges but it loves wet situations as well. The little streams of northern Ohio which make their way into Lake Erie cut for themselves deep channels through the yielding shale and form ravines from fifty to two hundred feet deep. Down the sides of these ravines and into the narrow intervale crowd the chestnut oaks,

Chestnut Oak, *Quercus prinus.* Acorns 1¼' to 1½' long.

until the lowest stands at the water's edge, its pendulous branches bending over the stream.

The leaves are obovate to oblong, with rounded teeth and

Trunk of Chestnut Oak, *Quercus prinus.*

eleven to thirteen pairs of primary veins. The foliage mass is a light yellow green, the tree in the open becomes round-topped. The acorns are large, long-oval, usually in pairs and borne in deep cups which are rough outside and very downy within. They are endowed with the power of quick germination and scarcely reach the ground before the shell breaks and the radicle protrudes. The kernel is sweetish and eagerly eaten by the squirrels. The fruit is never abundant.

YELLOW OAK. CHESTNUT OAK. CHINQUAPIN

Quércus acumináta.

A tree varying from thirty to one hundred or one hundred and sixty feet high, head small, narrow, round-topped. Prefers a limestone soil, ranges from New York westward through southern Ontario to southeastern Nebraska and eastern Kansas, southward in the Atlantic region to the District of Columbia, and west of the Alleghanies southward to the Gulf of Mexico.

Bark.—Light silvery gray, sometimes white, scaly. Branchlets reddish green at first, then dark brown, finally gray or brown.

Wood.—Dark brown, sapwood pale brown ; heavy, hard, strong, close-grained, durable in contact with the soil. Used for fencing, cooperage, manufacture of wheels and railway ties. Sp. gr., 0.8605 ; weight of cu. ft., 53.63 lbs.

Winter Buds.—Pale chestnut brown, ovate, acute, one-fourth of an inch long.

Leaves.—Alternate, four to seven inches long and two to five inches broad, oblong or lanceolate, wedge-shaped or rounded at base, sinuately toothed, teeth acute or rounded, each tipped with a small glandular point, apex acute or acuminate. They come out of the bud convolute, bronze green, hairy above, tomentose below, when full grown are thick, light yellow green above, pale often silvery white, downy below ; midribs stout, yellow ; primary veins conspicuous. In autumn they turn deep yellow and scarlet. Petioles slender, slightly flattened. Stipules linear or lanceolate, brown, caducous.

Flowers.—May, when leaves are one-third grown. Staminate flowers borne in hairy aments, three or four inches long ; calyx light yellow, hairy, deeply six to eight-parted ; filaments short ; anthers yellow. Pistillate flowers sessile or borne in short spikes, tomentose : stigmas bright red.

Yellow Oak, *Quercus acuminata.*
Leaves 4′ to 7′ long. 2′ to 5′ broad.

Acorns.—Annual, sessile or stalked, solitary or in pairs; nut oval, rounded at apex, pubescent at apex, from one-half to one inch in length, light chestnut brown ; cup cup-shaped inclosing one half of the nut, thin light brown and downy inside, red brown outside, tomentose, scales thickened at the base, tips free toward the edge and forming a fringe at the rim. Kernel sweet.

The Yellow Oak is one of the mid-continental trees, abundant throughout the Mississippi valley and reaching the greatest size in southern Indiana and Illinois. Like *Quercus alba* it frequently occurs with a white bark. The three chestnut oaks, *Quercus prinus*, *Quercus acuminata*, and *Quercus prinoides* run into each other by insensible gradations, and specimens will always be found on the border line that will puzzle the observer. Often when the leaves vary, the acorns will fix the species. Those of the Yellow Oak are small compared with those of the others. All are to a certain degree edible.

Yellow Oak, *Quercus acuminata.*
Acorn ½′ to 1′ long.

The foliage mass of the Yellow Oak is a light yellow green. The leaves unfold a bronze green, the newest sometimes with a purple tinge, and are so crowded at the end of the branchlets that the foliage has a tufted look. The autumnal tint is yellow, sometimes flushed with scarlet.

DWARF CHINQUAPIN OAK. SCRUB CHESTNUT OAK

Quércus prinoìdes.

A shrub growing in clumps, varying in height from two to twelve feet. Ranges from Massachusetts to North Carolina, westward to Missouri, Nebraska, central Kansas, Indian Territory and eastern Texas. In Missouri and Kansas becoming tree-like. Prefers dry sandy or rocky soil.

Chinquapin Oak, *Quercus prinoides.*
Leaves 3' to 6' long, 1' to 3' broad.

OAK FAMILY

Bark.- Light brown ; branchlets at first dark green and scurfy, finally reddish brown or ashen gray ; charged with tannic acid.

Winter Buds.—Light brown, ovate or globose, obtuse, one-eighth of an inch long.

Leaves.—Alternate, obovate or oblong, three to six inches long, one to three inches wide, wedge-shaped at base, coarsely undulate-toothed with rounded or acute teeth, acute or acuminate apex ; midrib and primary veins conspicuous. They come out of the bud convolute, reddish yellow, hairy above, coated with silver tomentum below, with dark glands at the points of the teeth, when full grown dark yellow green, rather shining above, pale green or silvery white, covered with soft fine pubescence below. In autumn they turn bright orange and scarlet. Petioles stout, short, flattened, grooved ; stipules caducous.

Flowers.—Appear when leaves are one-third grown. Staminate aments one and one-half to two and one-half inches long, hairy. Calyx is pale yellow green, hairy, five to nine-lobed. Stamens five to nine ; filaments slender ; anthers yellow. Pistillate flowers on short peduncles ; involucral scales covered with silvery white tomentum ; stigmas bright red.

Chinquapin Oak, *Quercus prinoides.*
Acorns ½' to ¾' long.

Acorns.—Abundant, annual, sessile or stalked ; nut oval, rounded or obtuse at apex which is covered with white down, pale chestnut brown, shining, one-half to three-fourths of an inch long ; seed sweet ; cup covers one-half to two-thirds of the nut, thin, deeply cup-shaped, light brown and downy inside, hoary with tomentum outside. Scales loosely imbricated, red-tipped, acute, thickened toward the base of the cup. The acorns are not only eaten by swine and cattle but the wild creatures like them as well.

SWAMP WHITE OAK

Quércus platanoìdes.   Quércus bìcolor.

Ordinarily sixty to seventy feet high maximum height, one hundred and ten, with narrow round-topped head and pendulous branches. Ranges from Quebec to Georgia and westward to Arkansas. Never abundant. Loves the borders of swamps.

Bark.—Gray brown, deeply fissured into flat ridges, scaly. Branches greenish gray, smooth. On young stems smooth, flaky. Branchlets at first stout, green, shining, later reddish brown, finally gray brown or dark brown.

346

Swamp White Oak, *Quercus platanoides*.
Leaves 5' to 6' long, 3' to 4' broad.

Wood.—Pale **brown, sapwood the same** ; heavy, hard, strong, tough, coarse-grained, checks in drying. Used in construction, interior finish of houses, carriage and boat building, agricultural implements, railway ties, fuel and fencing. Sp. gr., 0.7662 ; weight of cu. ft., 47.75 lbs.

Winter Buds.—Pale chestnut brown, hairy, ovate, one-fourth of an inch long.

Leaves.—Alternate, five to six inches long, two to four inches broad, obovate or oblong-obovate, gradually narrowed and wedge-shaped at base, margin coarsely sinuate-dentate or sometimes almost pinnately lobed, apex rounded, sometimes acute ; midrib stout, pale, rounded above ; primary veins conspicuous. They come out of the bud convolute, pale bronze green, hairy above, coated below with silvery tomentum ; when full grown are thick, bright yellow green above, pale green, downy, often silvery white, below. In autumn they turn dull yellow bronze. Petioles short, stout, grooved and flattened. Stipules linear, brown, caducous.

Flowers.—May, when leaves are half grown. Staminate flowers are borne in hairy aments three to four inches long ; calyx yellowish-green, hairy, five to nine-lobed ; lobes narrow, acute, shorter than the stamens ; filaments slender, anthers yellow. Pistillate flowers are borne on tomentose or long peduncles, in few-flowered spikes ; involucral scales covered with thick rusty tomentum ; stigmas bright red.

Acorns.—Annual, on long peduncles, often in pairs. Nut pale chestnut brown, oval, broad at base, pubescent at apex, an inch to an inch and a half long ; cup, cup-shaped, light brown and downy within, chestnut brown without, roughened toward the base by the thickened tips of the acute scales, higher on the cup these are small, crowded, often free, and sometimes form a fringe about the rim. Kernel, white, sweet.

Swamp White Oak, *Quercus platanoides.* Acorns 1′ to 1½′ long.

Unlike the White Oak whose leaves unfold a beautiful red, those of the Swamp White come out a bronze green ; their autumnal tint is a dull yellow without a gleam of red ; this quickly changes to a pale yellow brown.

The famous Wadsworth oak, so named from the estate on which it grew, was a Swamp White Oak. It stood for many years on the bank of the Genesee River about a mile from the village of Geneseo, New York. Its circumference of twenty-seven feet has kept its memory green although the tree has long since been destroyed by the washing away of the river-bank.

RED OAK

Quércus rùbra.

Usually seventy to eighty feet high, maximum height one hundred and forty, with stout branches growing at right angles to the stem; forming a narrow round-topped head; grows rapidly; is tolerant of many soils and varied situations, but prefers the glacial drift and well-drained borders of streams. Ranges from Maine to Georgia and Tennessee, westward to Minnesota and Kansas.

Bark.—Dark gray brown tinged with red, with broad, thin, rounded ridges, scaly. On young trees and large stems, smooth and light gray. Rich in tannic acid. Branchlets slender, at first bright green, shining, then dark red, finally dark brown.

Wood.—Pale reddish brown, sapwood darker; heavy, hard, strong, coarse-grained. Checks in drying, but when carefully treated may be successfully used for furniture. Also used in construction and for interior finish of houses. Sp. gr., 0.6621; weight of cu. ft., 41.25 lbs.

Winter Buds.—Light chestnut brown, ovate, acute, one-fourth of an inch long.

Leaves.—Alternate, seven to nine-lobed, oblong-ovate to oblong, five to nine inches long, four to six inches broad; lobes tapering gradually from broad bases, acute, and usually repandly-dentate and terminating with long bristle-pointed teeth; the second pair of lobes from apex are largest; midrib and primary veins conspicuous. They come out of the bud convolute, pink, covered with soft silky down above, coated with thick white tomentum below. When full grown are dark green and smooth, sometimes shining above, yellow green, smooth or hairy on the axils of the veins below. In autumn they turn a rich red, sometimes brown. Petioles stout, one to two inches long, often red; stipules caducous.

Flowers.—May, when leaves are half grown. Staminate aments four to five inches long, hairy. Calyx four to five-lobed, greenish; stamens four to five; filaments slender; anthers yellow. Pistillate flowers borne on short peduncles; involucral scales broadly ovate; dark reddish-brown; stigmas elongated, bright green.

Red Oak, *Quercus rubra.*
Leaves of broad type, 7′ to 9′ long.

Red Oak, *Quercus rubra.*
Leaves of narrow type, 5′ to 7′ long.

OAK FAMILY

Acorns.—Ripen in the autumn of the second year ; solitary or in pairs, sessile or stalked ; nut oblong-ovoid with broad base, full, sometimes narrowed at apex, three-fourths to one and one-fourth of an inch long ; cup, saucer-shaped, usually covers only the base, sometimes one-fourth of the nut, thick, shallow, reddish brown, somewhat downy within, covered with thin imbricated reddish brown scales. Kernel white and very bitter.

> What gnarled stretch, what depth of shade is his !
> There needs no crown to mark the forest's king.
> How in his leaves outshines full summer's bliss !
> Sun, storm, rain, dew, to him their tribute bring.
>
> How towers he, too, amid the billowed snows,
> An unquelled exile from the summer's throne,
> Whose plain, uncinctured front more kingly shows,
> Now that the obscuring courtier leaves are flown.
> —JAMES RUSSELL LOWELL.

What delicate fans are the great Red Oak leaves now just developed, so thin and of so tender a green ! They hang loosely flaccidly down at the mercy of the wind, like a new-born butterfly or dragon fly. A strong cold wind would blacken and tear them. They have not yet been hardened by exposure, these raw and tender lungs of the tree. —HENRY D. THOREAU.

The Red Oak finds its finest development in the states lying north of the Ohio river ; on the southern shore of Lake Erie it becomes a beautiful tree with a massive trunk, a magnificent rounded head and smooth clean-cut limbs which strike out from the trunk at large angles. The bark is smooth ; even in old age the trunk never becomes extremely rough and the limbs are always smooth. In color it is a brownish gray until the tree is old, when it becomes dark brown.

The leaves vary from oblong to obovate and are of two typical forms. The full leaf with the shallow sinuses is the youthful form although old trees are often found bearing it. That with the deeper sinuses is perhaps the more common form. Often the petiole and midvein are a rich red color in midsummer and early autumn, though this is not true of all red oaks. The leaves come out of the bud a lovely pink and white, in midsummer they become a deep shining green and in autumn they turn a rich, dark, purplish red. The en-

Trunk of Red Oak, *Quercus rubra.*

tire subject of spring and autumn tints is becoming more and more interesting as it is more carefully studied. It is now well understood that the frost is not a factor in the problem and that both spring and autumn tints arise from changes in the character of the chlorophyll; the one when the chlorophyll is not yet mature and the other when it is dying.

The acorns are characteristic, and need never be mistaken. They are the largest borne by any oak of the Biennial group, and sit in flat shallow cups with prominent rims and close scales. The kernel is white and extremely bitter. Wildwood creatures care little for them and they remain under the trees all winter unless eaten by swine. The Red Oak ranges farther north than any other of the Biennials; it has been found on the banks of the Saskatchewan. Climatic conditions so affect it that there it ceases to be a tree, nor is it even a shrub, but it transforms itself by stress of circumstances into burls and knobs and low knotted heads only a foot or two high.

Red Oak, *Quercus rubra.*
Acorns ¾′ to 1¼′ long.

SCARLET OAK

Quércus coccínea.

Usually seventy or eighty feet high, maximum height one hundred and sixty, with slender trunk, rather small branches, open narrow head. Prefers a dry, sandy soil. Ranges from Maine through central New York to southern Ontario, west through Michigan and Minnesota to Nebraska, south on the Alleghanies to North Carolina and Tennessee.

Bark.—Dark brown, with shallow fissures, scaly. Young stems and branches smooth and light brown. Inner side of bark reddish or gray. Branchlets at first scurfy, later pale green and shining, finally reddish, at last light brown.

Scarlet Oak, *Quercus coccinea.*
Leaves 3′ to 6′ long, 2½′ to 5′ broad.

OAK FAMILY

Wood.—Light reddish brown, sapwood darker; heavy, hard, coarse-grained, strong. Sp. gr., 0.7095; weight of cu. ft., 42.20 lbs.

Winter Buds.—Dark reddish brown, hairy, acute, one-eighth to one-fourth of an inch long.

Leaves.—Alternate, three to six inches long, two and one-half to five broad, oblong or obovate or oval in outline, truncate or wedge-shaped at base, deeply divided by wide sinuses into seven or nine lobes, which are repandly dentate, terminating with bristle-pointed teeth. Terminal lobe is three-toothed, the middle division being much longer than the other furnished with two small teeth near its apex. Lateral lobes are obovate, oblique or spreading or falcate, the middle ones usually the largest of all; midrib and primary veins conspicuous. They come out of the bud convolute, bright red, coated beneath with silvery white tomentum, finally become green though still silvery; when full grown are bright green, smooth and very shining above, paler and less shining beneath. In autumn they turn a brilliant scarlet color. Petioles slender, terete, one and one-half to two inches long. Stipules caducous.

Flowers.—May, when leaves are half grown. Staminate aments slender, three to four inches long. Calyx is hairy, red in bud, four to five lobed. Stamens usually four; filaments slender; anthers yellow. Pistillate flowers borne on downy peduncles; involucral scales ovate, downy; stigmas bright red.

Acorns.—Ripen in the autumn of second year. Sessile or stalked, solitary or in pairs. Nut oval, or oblong-ovate or hemispherical, truncate or rounded at base, rounded at apex, one-half to one inch long, light reddish brown, occasionally striate; cup cup-shaped or turbinate, incloses one-third to one-half of nut; light reddish brown on inner surface, covered with closely imbricated, light reddish brown scales. Kernel whitish.

Stand under this tree and see how finely its leaves are cut against the sky, as it were only a few sharp points extending from a midrib. They look like double, treble or quadruple crosses. They are far more ethereal than the less deeply scalloped oak leaves. They have so little leafy *terra-firma* that they appear melting away in the light and scarcely obstruct our view. The leaves of very young plants are like those of full-grown oaks of other species, more entire, simple, and lumpish in their outlines, but these raised high on old trees have solved the leafy problem. Lifted higher and higher and sublimated more and more, putting off some earthiness and cultivating more intimacy with the light each year, they have at length the least possible amount of earthy matter, and the greatest spread and grasp of sky influences. There they dance arm in arm with the light,—tripping it on fantastic points, fit partners in those aërial halls. So intimately mingled are they with it, that what with their slenderness and their glossy surfaces, you can hardly tell at last what in the dance is leaf and what is light.

I am again struck with their beauty, when, a month later, they thickly strew the ground in the woods piled one upon another under my feet. They are then brown above, but purple beneath, with their narrow lobes and their bold deep scallops reaching almost to the midrib. They suggest that material must be cheap or else there has been lavish expense in their creation, if so much has been cut out.

—HENRY D. THOREAU.

A Scarlet Oak growing in the open forms a round dome-like head whose lower branches frequently sweep the ground. Its leaves are a bright shining green, borne on slender petioles so that they respond to every zephyr's breath. Their spring-time tint is bright pink and silvery white, but by the time the flowers come the leaves are pale green, growing darker as they grow older, but never even in midsummer do they become dark green. The especial glory of the species lies in the brilliant color which the leaves assume late in autumn. The autumnal tints of other oaks are beautiful, but they pale their fires before the ruddy gleam of the Scarlet.

Scarlet Oak, *Quercus coccinea.* Acorns ½' to 1' long.

The acorns greatly resemble those of the Black Oak, but the kernel is white instead of yellow. This difference is characteristic and persistent and may often decide the question of species for a doubtful tree.

BLACK OAK. YELLOW OAK

Quércus velutìna.   Quércus tinctòria.

A tree ordinarily seventy to eighty feet high ; in the lower Ohio valley reaching one hundred and fifty feet with slender branches and narrow open head. Prefers the glacial drift, but is found on the mountain side ; ranges farther south than any other of the Red Oak group.

Bark.—Dark brown or black on old trees, deeply furrowed, scaly; on young trees, stems and branches, smooth. Inner bark is deep orange yellow, heavily charged with tannic acid and largely used in tanning. Branchlets stout, covered with rusty tomentum at first, later they become reddish brown, finally dark brown.

357

Wood.—Bright brown tinged with red, sapwood paler ; heavy, hard, strong, coarse-grained, checks in drying. Sp. gr., 0.7045 ; weight of cu. ft., 43.90 lbs.

Winter Buds.—Brown, ovate, angled, obtuse, covered with tomentum, one-fourth to one-half inch long.

Leaves.—Alternate, five to six inches long, three to four inches wide, ovate or obovate, usually seven-lobed and sometimes divided nearly to the middle by wide, rounded sinuses into narrow, obovate, dentate lobes with stout bristle-pointed teeth ; or sometimes the lobes are nearly entire, tapering gradually from a broad base, each tipped with a bristle ; or the sinuses are shallow, the heavy part of the leaf toward the apex, the lobes broad-dentate or sinuate-dentate, but always tipped with a bristle. The terminal lobe is oblong, elongated, acute, with large or small teeth ; or, it is broad and coarsely repandly-dentate. They come out of the bud convolute, bright crimson, covered with white hairs above, and coated below with silvery-white tomentum. The lobes are tipped with long white hairs. When full grown the leaves are thick, leathery, dark shining green above and yellow green, brownish, or tawny, more or less pubescent below ; midribs stout, primary veins conspicuous. In autumn they turn brown, or dull red, or yellow and brown and fall late, sometimes remaining until spring. Petioles long, yellow, generally flattened on upper side. Stipules linear, hairy, caducous.

Flowers.—May, when leaves are half grown. Staminate flowers borne in the axils of brown, hairy, fugacious bracts, in hairy or tomentose aments four to six inches long. Calyx of staminate flower, hairy, reddish ; lobes ovate, shorter than the four stamens ; anthers acute, yellow. Pistillate flowers borne on short tomentose peduncles, reddish ; involucral scales ovate, shorter than the acute, hairy calyx-lobes ; stigmas reflexed, bright red.

Acorns.—Ripen in autumn of second year, sessile, or stalked, solitary or in pairs ; nut ovate-oblong, obovate, oval, or hemispherical, broad and rounded at base, rounded at apex, light reddish brown often striate, frequently pubescent, from one-half to one inch long ; cup cup-shaped or turbinate, embraces one-third to one-half the nut, covered with chestnut brown scales which at base are closely appressed but above are looser, and at the rim form a fringe-like border. Kernel yellow and bitter.

The name Black Oak refers evidently to the color of the bark of the trunk which is almost or quite black. The inner bark is deep yellow and this characteristic is persistent and unchanging. Before the era of modern dyes this inner bark was highly prized because of a yellow dye which was obtained from it called quercitron.

The tree is protean in the form of its leaves. Besides its

Black Oak, *Quercus velutina.*
Leaves 4′ to 6′ long.

own well distinguished types it varies toward the red oaks on the one side and the scarlet oaks on the other. But whatever the individual leaf the foliage mass is always beautiful. In early spring the unfolding leaves are red, the freshest of them nearly scarlet. The long, white, silky hairs are dense on the upper velvety surface and the under surface is white with tomentum. As the red fades out and before the green darkens there is a time when the tree mass takes on a silvery greenish white through which the sunlight plays with magical effect. The deeply divided leaves are borne on rather long petioles which are bent down at first but soon spread out from the branches. The new shoots are yellowish green, sometimes stained dark red but covered with rusty down. The divided leaves give the foliage a feathery appearance and the long yellow aments respond to the slightest impulse, so that a light wind transforms the tree into a misty, shimmering mass. The exquisite effects of spring-time coloring must be caught at the supreme moment, they do not remain unchanged for a day, scarcely for an hour.

The mature leaf is dark green, in texture always thick, firm and almost leathery. The surface is always shining, sometimes showing a " wet gloss." The petioles are usually long and somewhat slender so that these shining leaves move freely, apart from the motion of the branch, and toss the sunlight from a thousand glittering points as they wave in the summer breeze. In autumn their tint is usually brownish yellow, rarely running into dark red, but even then the brown leaves shine as in midsummer and dance in the November sunlight as if it were May.

These leaves often remain upon the tree all winter long, successfully resisting the rough buffeting of storm and wind and falling only when pushed off by the growing buds of spring. I once knew a pair of robins who selected an oak bough thickly covered with these winter leaves for their nesting place. The nest was built, the eggs were laid, and all went well in the sheltered nook. But, by the time the mother bird was sitting, the bursting buds pushed off the

Black Oak, *Quercus velutina.*
Leaves of obovate type, 5′ to 7′ long.

dry brown leaves and day after day the poor bird sat in her nest at the end of a leafless bough, in full sight of every jay and crow in the neighborhood. In fact, they gathered about and assured her of their deep interest in her enterprise.

Black Oak, *Quercus velutina.*
Acorns ½′ to 1′ long.

The robins stood out bravely for awhile but one day we found the nest deserted and the eggs gone.

The acorn is much smaller than that of the Red Oak and varies in shape. In color it is reddish brown which is often striped with a darker brown. It sits in a deep cup which embraces nearly one-half the nut. The kernel is yellow and very bitter.

The Black Oak hybridizes, sports, and generally conducts itself so as to make it the despair of the amateur who wishes to know his trees " on sight." For unless tried by careful tests there are many trees which will deceive the most elect botanist.

SPANISH OAK

Quércus digitàta.

A tree usually seventy to eighty feet high, with spreading branches which form a round topped open head. Rare in the north Atlantic states, abundant in the south. Tolerant of many soils, it flourishes in dry sandy barrens and on wet low lands.

Bark.—Dark brown with shallow fissures, scaly, rich in tannic acid. Branchlets stout, covered with rusty tomentum at first, becoming later reddish brown or ashy gray.

Wood.—Light reddish brown, sapwood much lighter ; strong, coarse-grained, checks badly in drying. Has high fuel value, sometimes used in construction. Sp. gr., 0.6928 ; weight of cu. ft., 43.17 lbs.

Winter Buds.—Chestnut brown, ovoid, acute, one-eighth of an inch long.

Spanish Oak, *Quercus digitata*.
Leaves 6' to 7' long, 4' to 5' broad.

The Variant Leaves of Spanish Oak.
Quercus digitata.

Leaves.—Alternate, six to seven inches long, four to five inches wide. Of two forms; first form oblong or obovate, usually wedge-shaped at base, five to seven-lobed, lobes often falcate, bristle-tipped, sinuses broad; second form is obovate with a broad apex which is three-lobed, otherwise entire. Both forms are found on the same branch, but sometimes character-ize different trees. They come out of the bud convolute, when full grown are dark shining green above, pale green covered with rusty pubescence below; midribs stout, tomentose; primary veins prominent. In autumn they turn a bright clear yellow or dull yellow brown. Petioles short, flattened. Stipules oblong, caducous.

Flowers.—May, appearing with the leaves. Staminate flowers borne in hairy aments three to five inches long. Calyx four to five-lobed, pubescent; lobes ovate, rounded, shorter than the stamens. Stamens four to five with oblong yellow anthers. Pis-tillate flowers borne on stout pe-duncles. Involucral scales tomen-tose, as long as the calyx lobes; stigmas long, dark red.

Acorns.—Ripen in the summer of second year. Sessile or stalked. Nut is globular to oblong, one-half inch long, pale orange brown; cup thin and saucer-shaped, sometimes deep, often em-braces one-half the nut, covered with reddish brown, pubescent scales.

The Spanish Oak is really a southern tree although it appears in New Jersey, southern Illinois and Indiana. Its leaves vary greatly in

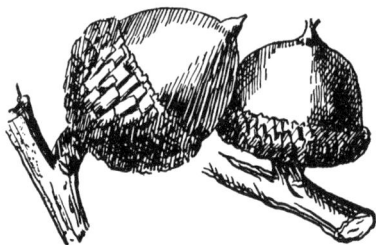

Spanish Oak, *Quercus digitata.* Acorns ½′ long.

form but as they do not resemble those or any other oak, the tree may be readily recognized. It is recommended as a shade tree for cities in the south Atlantic and Gulf states.

PIN OAK. SWAMP SPANISH OAK

Quércus palústris.

Usually fifty to seventy feet high, maximum height one hundred and twenty, with pyramidal head and somewhat pendulous branches. Loves a moist rich soil and is found on the borders of swamps and in river bottoms ; attains its greatest size in the valley of the Ohio. Ranges from Massachusetts to Kentucky and westward to Arkansas and Indian Territory. Roots deep and also spreading. Bark filled with tannic acid.

Bark.—Pale, steel brown, generally smooth, sometimes scaly ; young stems and branches smooth, pale brown, shining. Branchlets slender, tough, dark red at first, tomentose, later becoming reddish brown and finally gray brown.

Wood.—Pale brown with dark colored sapwood ; heavy, hard, strong, coarse-grained. Sometimes used in construction. Sp. gr., 0.6938 ; weight of cu. ft., 43.24 lbs.

Winter Buds.—Chestnut brown, ovate, acute, one-eighth of an inch long.

Leaves.—Alternate, four to six inches long, two to four inches wide, obovate or broadly oval in outline, base wedge-shaped, five to seven-lobed, sinuses wide and deep, rounded at bottom ; terminal lobe three-toothed toward apex, or entire lateral lobes spreading or oblique or falcate, tapering and acute at apex or obovate and broad at apex. The middle pairs are longer than the others, dentate-lobed ; lobes and teeth ending in long slender bristles. They come out of the bud, convolute, pale reddish green, shining and hairy above, covered with whitish scurfy down below ; when full grown are dark, shining green above, pale green below, bearing tufts of pale hairs in the axils of the primary veins ; midribs stout, rounded above, primary veins conspicuous. They turn a deep scarlet in autumn and fall late. Petioles yellowish, one-half to two inches long. Stipules red, one-half of an inch long, become brown before falling.

Flowers.—May, when leaves are half grown. Staminate flowers are borne in hairy catkins from two to three inches long ; pistillate flowers on short tomentose peduncles. Calyx of staminate flower is hairy, divided into four or five oblong rounded segments, cut at the margins, shorter than the four or five stamens ; anthers oblong, yellow. The involucral scales of the pistillate flower are ovate, tomentose, shorter than the calyx-lobes ; stigmas bright red, re-curved.

Acorns.—Ripen in the autumn of the second season ; sessile or short-stalked, solitary or clustered ; nut nearly hemispherical, about one-half an inch long, less in breadth, light brown, usually striate ; cup thin, shallow, saucer-shaped, dark red brown and hairy within and covered by closely appressed ovate, light reddish brown scales, darkest along the margin. Kernel bitter.

The Pin Oak when young is a most graceful tree. The stem rises an unbroken shaft ; the branches at the top are short, the middle branches are long and drooping and rather overbear the lower ones which sometimes sweep the ground, thus form-ing the beautiful pyramidal head character-istic of the species. The leaves are small, deeply lobed, borne on long petioles which allow them to toss in the wind. These leaves are the especial prey of a gall-fly and are frequently covered with small brown galls.

Pin Oak, *Quercus palustris.* Acorns ¼′ long.

The acorns are small, light brown, striped. The name Pin Oak seems to refer to the great number of tiny branches which are intermingled with the large ones. Of this tree Mi-chaux says, " Its secondary branches are much more slender and numerous than is common on so large a tree and are so intermingled as to give it at a distance the appearance of being full of pins. This singular disposition renders it dis-tinguishable at first sight in winter and is perhaps the cause of its being called Pin Oak."

BEAR OAK. SCRUB OAK

Quercus ilicifolia. Quercus pumila.

A shrub, with numerous intertwined and contorted branches, oc-casionally becoming a small round-topped tree. Found in New England and along the Alleghanies, on rocky hillsides and on sandy plains.

Bark.—Dark brown, smooth, scaly. Branchlets slender, at first dark green, tinged with red, tomentose, later red brown and finally dark brown.

Pin Oak, *Quercus palustris*.
Leaves 4′ to 6′ long, 2′ to 4′ broad.

Wood.—Light brown ; hard, strong.

Winter Buds.—Dark chestnut brown, ovate, obtuse, one-eighth of an inch long.

Leaves.—Alternate, two to five inches long, one and one-half to two and one-half inches wide, wedge-shaped at base, usually five-lobed, sometimes three, sometimes seven-lobed ; every lobe bristle-tipped ; sinuses wide and shallow ; form of lobes variable. They come out of the bud convolute, dull red and coated with tomentum, when half grown are pale green ; when full grown thick, dark green and shining above, covered with pale or silvery pubescence below ; midribs stout, yellow, primary veins conspicuous. In autumn they turn dull red or yellow. Petioles slender, terete, downy, one to one and one-half of an inch long. Stipules linear, caducous.

Flowers.—May, when leaves are half grown. Staminate flowers are borne in reddish, hairy aments four to five inches long which often remain until midsummer. Calyx is red or reddish green, hairy, three to five rounded lobes, shorter than the stamens. Stamens three to five ; filaments short ; anthers bright red, becoming yellow. Bracts linear, red, hairy. Pistillate flowers borne on stout tomentose peduncles. Involucral scales red, as long as the calyx lobes, tomentose ; stigmas dark red.

Acorns.—Abundant, ripen in autumn of second year, sessile or stalked, in pairs or solitary. Nut somewhat variable in form, ovoid, broad, acute or rounded at apex, one-half inch long, light brown, shining, sometimes striate ; cup cup-shaped, embracing half the nut, thick, light reddish brown, the free tips of upper scales forming a fringe-like border. Kernel deep yellow.

This little, straggling, shrubby oak loves rocky hillsides and dry sandy barrens. Wherever it grows it indicates the sterility of the soil. The name Scrub Oak follows it everywhere, but the early settlers of New England called it Bear Oak as well, because the bears loved its bitter little acorns. It produces these in great numbers ; a fruiting branch is often very picturesque because of them. It rarely rises more than six or eight feet and its stem is usually one or two inches in diameter. Both leaves and acorns are variable in form.

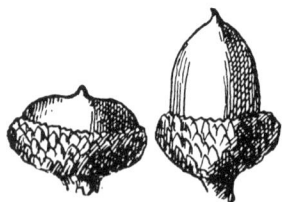

Bear Oak, *Quercus ilicifolia.*
Acorns ½' long.

This is one of the gregarious trees, it is never found as a

Bear Oak, *Quercus ilicifolia.*
Leaves 2′ to 5′ long, 1½′ to 2½′ broad.

single specimen or mingled with other trees but always in tracts which it covers almost exclusively. Evidently it can flourish where other species cannot.

BLACK JACK. BARREN OAK

Quércus marilándica. Quércus nìgra.

A small shrubby tree, with small trunk, spreading and contorted branches. Grows on sandy barrens, and ranges from southern New York westward to Kansas and Nebraska and southward to the Florida coast. Rare in the north, but abundant in the south where it is often found on heavy clays. Hybridizes freely.

Bark.—Dark brown almost black, divided into rectangular plates which are covered with small scales. Branchlets stout, at first light red and scurfy, later reddish brown, finally dark brown.

Wood.—Dark brown, sapwood lighter; heavy, hard, strong, used for fuel and in manufacture of charcoal. Sp. gr., 0.7324; weight of cu. ft., 45.64 lbs.

Winter Buds.—Light reddish brown, angled, acute, hairy, one-fourth of an inch long.

Leaves.—Alternate, five to seven inches long, broadly obovate, rounded or cordate at the narrow base, usually three-lobed at the broad apex. Form of lobes extremely variable, sometimes rounded sometimes acute, each lobe bristle-tipped. They come out of the bud pale pink, coated with tomentum, when half grown they are still coated with the pale hairs. When full grown they are thick and leathery, dark yellow green, shining above, and yellow, orange or brown and scurfy below; midrib broad, dark yellow, raised and rounded above, primary veins stout. In autumn they turn brown or yellow. Petioles stout, yellow, grooved above, one-half to three-fourths of an inch long. Stipules three-fourths of an inch long, caducous.

Flowers.—May, when leaves are half grown. Staminate flowers borne in hairy catkins two to four inches long. Calyx of staminate flowers thin, scarious, tinged with red, covered with pale hairs and divided into four to five rounded lobes. Stamens usually four; anthers dark red. Pistillate flowers borne on short peduncles covered with thick rusty tomentum. Involucral scales are coated with tomentum and about as long as the calyx lobes; stigmas reflexed, short, broad, dark red.

Acorns.—Ripen in autumn of second year, solitary or in pairs, short stalked; nut three-fourths of an inch in length, oblong, full and rounded at both ends, a trifle broader below than above the middle, light yellow brown, often striate. Shell thin, lined with coat

Black Jack, *Quercus marilandica*.
Leaves 3′ to 8′ long. 2′ to 5′ broad.

of dense tawny tomentum. Cup turbinate, deep, covers one-third to two-thirds of nut, is thick, pale brown and downy within, without it is covered by large, reddish brown, loosely imbricated scales, coated with tomentum. On top of cup are rows of smaller scales which form a thick rim around the inner surface.

Black Jack is such a peculiar name for a tree that on hearing it for the first time, one immediately asks for an explanation. The authorities are silent on the subject so one can develop his own theory without fear or favor. This oak varies from shrub to small tree. Its very presence marks the sterility of the soil. Its wood is worthless compared with that of other oaks. It is the pariah of its kind. Since very early times Jack has, in certain ways, been used as a word of opprobrium. A worthless fellow was a Jack. What more likely, than that the first settlers of this country finding this worthless oak upon worthless land should name it in opprobrium the Jack Oak. As the bark was dark, almost black, it became Black Jack Oak and oak soon dropping out, it became as we know it to-day—Black Jack.

Black Jack, *Quercus marilandica.* Acorn ¾′ long.

The leaves of this oak are extremely variable, always obovate or pear-shaped they vary from a form having no lobes at all to one of three lobes and one of five lobes.

SHINGLE OAK. LAUREL OAK

Quèrcus imbricària.

A tree usually fifty to sixty feet high, maximum height one hundred, with broad pyramidal head when young, becoming in old age broad-topped and open. A tree of the mid-continent ; rare in the east, abundant in the lower Ohio valley. Reaches its largest size in southern Illinois and Indiana.

Bark.—Light brown, scaly ; on young stems light brown, smooth. Branchlets slender, dark green and shining at first, later become light brown, finally dark brown.

Shingle Oak, *Quercus imbricaria.*
Leaves 4′ to 6′ long, 1′ to 2′ broad.

OAK FAMILY

Wood.—Pale reddish brown, sapwood lighter; heavy, hard, coarse-grained, checks badly in drying; used for shingles and sometimes in construction. Sp. gr., 0.7529; weight of cu. ft., 46.92 lbs.

Winter Buds.—Light brown, ovate, acute, one-eighth inch long.

Leaves.—Alternate, oblong or obovate, four to six inches long, one to two inches wide, wedge-shaped or rounded at base, acute or rounded at apex, sometimes entire or with undulated margins, sometimes more or less three-lobed. They come out of the bud involute, bright red, covered with rusty down above and white tomentum below. When full grown are dark green, smooth and shining above, pale green or pale brown, downy below; midribs stout yellow, grooved above, primary veins slender. In autumn they become dark red above, pale beneath, midribs darken, then the leaf. Petioles stout, hairy, flattened, grooved. Stipules about one-half inch long, caducous.

Flowers.—May, when leaves are half grown. Staminate flowers borne on tomentose aments two to three inches long. Bracts linear-lanceolate. Calyx pale yellow, downy, four-lobed; stamens four to five; anthers yellow. Pistillate flowers borne on slender tomentose peduncles. Involucral scales are downy, about as long as the calyx lobes; stigmas short, reflexed, greenish-yellow.

Shingle Oak, *Quercus imbricaria.* Acorns ½' to ⅔'.

Acorns.—Ripen in autumn of second year; stalked, solitary or in pairs; nut almost spherical, one-half to two-thirds inch long; cup embraces one-half to one-third nut, is cup-shaped covered with light red brown, downy scales, rounded or acute at apex. Kernel very bitter.

The Shingle Oak has a smooth bark and for three-fourths of its height is laden with branches. It has an uncouth form when bare in winter, but is beautiful in summer when clad in its thick tufted foliage. The leaves are long, lanceolate, entire, and of a shining green.   —MICHAUX.

The leaves of Laurel Oak or Shingle Oak are very narrow, almost linear at first with their edges so straightly revolute that they almost touch each other. They are slightly hairy, the ground color yellowish green with a purple tinge. The fresh twigs are flushed with red on the upper side where most exposed to the light. The young leaves stand out stiffly from the ends of the branchlets, studding them with sharply outlined stellate clusters. Being so narrow the foliage is very open and one can see through the tree top in almost any direction so that the tree has an appearance quite distinct from other oaks.

—Garden and Forest.

WILLOW OAK

Quércus phéllos.

A tree seventy to eighty feet high, ranging from southern New York along the inland plain to Florida, is also found in the south-western states. Hybridizes easily.

Bark.—Pale reddish brown, stem of young tree smooth, that of old trees covered with shallow fissures and scaly. Branchlets slender, smooth, reddish brown, later dark brown or grayish brown

Wood.—Pale reddish brown, sapwood paler; heavy, strong, coarse-grained. Occasionally used in construction. Sp. gr., 0.7472 ; weight of cu. ft., 46.56 lbs.

Winter Buds.—Brown, ovate, acute, one-eighth of an inch long.

Leaves.—Alternate, linear, oblong, narrowed at both ends, some-times falcate, two to five inches long, one-half to one inch wide, wedge-shaped at base, entire or slightly undulate at margin, sharply acute at apex. They come out of the bud involute, pale yellow green, shining above, coated with pale down beneath ; when full grown are light green, smooth and shining above, paler green below ; midribs yellow, rounded above, primary veins obscure. In autumn they turn pale yellow and fall late. Petioles stout, and grooved. Stipules caducous.

Flowers.—May, when leaves are small. Staminate flowers borne in hairy slender aments two to three inches long. Calyx yellow, hairy, divided into four to five acute lobes. Stamens four to five ; anthers oblong, yellow. Pistillate flowers are borne on short, smooth peduncles. Involucral scales are brown, hairy, as long as the calyx lobes; stigmas bright red, reflexed.

Willow Oak, *Quercus phellos.* Acorns ½' in diameter.

Acorns.—Not abundant. Ripen in autumn of second year, short stalked, solitary or in pairs. Nut half-sphere, half an inch in diameter, pale yellow brown, downy, sometimes striate ; cup saucer-shaped, covers the base of nut only ; scales dark reddish brown, thin, ovate, hairy. Kernel orange yellow and very bitter.

The Willow Oak is a most interesting tree. In the first place its leaf is an anomaly among northern oaks for it has the shape, poise, and general appearance of that of the willow. Then, too, the shoots are straight and slender, so in its spray it resembles the willow. Like its namesake it loves to keep its feet in water, seeks the low wet borders of swamps

Willow Oak, *Quercus phellos*.
Leaves 2′ to 5′ long, ½′ to 1′ broad.

and but rarely climbs even a hillside ; and yet it avoids the sea-coast.

The Willow Oak hybridizes most freely ; all oaks do more or less, but this species seems especially inclined to stray out of bounds.

The acorns are tiny, not abundant, the kernel yellow and exceedingly bitter. The tree is recommended as a shade tree for southern cities.

FAGÀCEÆ—BEECH FAMILY

BEECH

Fàgus atropuníceq.   Fàgus ferrugínea.

Fagus from *phago,* to eat, because the nuts were used as food in
the early ages.

Widely distributed, growing on uplands and mountain slopes, also
on alluvial bottom lands and borders of streams.   Usually seventy
to eighty feet high.   In the crowded forest, tall,
slender, with narrow head; in open situations,
short stemmed, forming a round-topped head of
slender, slightly drooping branches beset with
short lateral branchlets.   But one species is
native to North America.   Grows well on limestone.

Bark.—Compact, smooth, ashy gray.   Branchlets at first pale green, then olive green, finally
changing through brown to ashy gray.

Wood.—Light red, varying in color in different localities; hard, strong, tough, very close
straight-grained and susceptible of a fine polish.
Used in manufacture of chairs, agricultural
implements and handles of tools.   Sp. gr.,
0.6883; weight of cu. ft., 42.89 lbs.

Leaf-Buds.—Cylindrical, long-pointed, light
chestnut brown, three-fourths to one inch long.

Leaves.—Alternate, oblong-ovate, rounded or
cordate at base, coarsely serrate with spreading
or incurved teeth, acute or acuminate.   Feather-
veined.   They come out of the bud plicate, pale
green and silky, when full grown become dark green above, pale
green beneath.   In autumn they turn a clear golden yellow, and

Unfolding Leaves of the
Beech.

Fruiting Spray of the Beech, *Fagus atropunicea*.

Leaves 3' to 4' long.

becoming brown on young trees often cling to the branches all **win-ter.** When the leaves first appear in the spring they are heavily charged with acid juice. Petioles short, slightly grooved, hairy. Stipules caducous.

A Staminate and a Pistillate Flower of the Beech ; enlarged.

Flowers.—April, when leaves are one-third grown. Staminate borne in globose heads an inch in diameter on slender hairy peduncles, the staminate flowers are yellowish green and consist of a bell-shaped four to seven-lobed calyx, corolla wanting, stamens eight to ten, inserted on the calyx ; filaments white, slender, exserted ; anthers green, oblong, introrse, two-celled ; cells opening longitudinally ; o v a r y wanting Pistillate flowers are borne in two-flowered clusters from the axils of the upper leaves surrounded by numerous awl-shaped bractlets. They consist of an urn-shaped calyx, tube three-angled, adnate to ovary ; limb four to five-lobed, corolla wanting, stamens wanting ; ovary inferior, three-celled, styles three, slender, exserted ; ovules two in each cell. The inner bracts in time become the fruiting involucre. When full grown this is dark green covered with prickles ; in autumn it becomes light brown, the prickles strongly recurved ; it is opened by the first severe frosts and remains on the branch after the nuts have fallen.

Fruit.—Nut, triangular, pale chestnut brown, three-fourths of an inch long. Seed is sweet. It is believed that a beech must be fully forty years old before it fruits.

We sometimes think that the birds are the first heralds of the spring, but it is not so. Vegetation sleeps like a dog, with one eye open, and no sooner has the sun turned from his southern course than nature in all her myriad buds

Staminate and Pistillate Flower Cluster of the Beech.

watches for his coming. There are signs of spring to the wise before a blue wing has beat toward the north or a robin

A Beech Tree.

redbreast alighted on our lawn. Willows glow in green and yellow long before any other indication of quickening life appears, the last year's wood of the Lombardy Poplars becomes tawny and shining, and the Beech tree fairly challenges the snow on its limbs by the frosty white of its smaller branches and twigs.

It is surprising since our trees are leafless one-half of the year, that so little attention is paid to planting for winter beauty. A great success is awaiting the artist who can achieve this planting, and in the mean time a small but ever increasing number of persons are appreciating the grace and beauty of the leafless trees. The winter beauty of the Beech is only equalled not surpassed by that of the elm. Then the sinewy strength of its trunk is most evident, the white of its bark is the clearest, the structure of its noble head is most apparent, and the fine spray of its delicate branches stands clear cut in exquisite tracery against the sky.

It is no less charming in early spring, when the half-opened leaves clinging to the branches make a shimmering mist of soft green and pearly white. In midsummer, because of the lateral arrangement of the branches, the foliage lies in great shelving masses and as the leaves are short petioled they have little independent motion but sway with the branch. In autumn, the head becomes a glowing sphere of golden yellow touched with russet, and as the last leaf flutters to the ground it marks the close of a cycle of unequalled beauty.

Lumbermen have always insisted upon two species of Beech, the Red and the White, distinguished by the color of their wood. There are no botanical characters by which such trees can be distinguished, and the reason for the difference is unknown.

The Beech is gregarious and often forms pure forests of considerable extent. In the first place, it is a tree that suckers ; in the second, it makes a shade so dense that it is difficult for the young of other trees to flourish near. Furthermore, it readily adapts itself to environment, flourishes on the bottom lands and climbs the mountain slopes.

The genus has several evergreen species. These are all found in the southern hemisphere,—in Terra-del-Fuego, New Zealand, and Australia. Traces of *Fagus* have been discovered in the cretaceous rocks of the Dakota group, in the miocene of Alaska and in the gold-bearing gravels of California ; existing once over a broad territory from which it has now entirely disappeared.

There was so firm a belief among the Indians that a beech tree was proof against lightning, that on the approach of a thunder-storm they took refuge under its branches with full assurance of safety. This belief seems to have been adopted by the early settlers of this country and it is very common to hear a farmer say, " A beech is never struck by lightning." This popular belief has recently had scientific verification. As a result of careful experiments it has been found that the beech really does resist the electric current much more vigorously than the oak, poplar or willow. The general conclusion from a series of experiments is that trees "poor in fat" like the oak, willow, poplar, maple, elm and ash oppose much less resistance to the electric current than trees " rich in fat " like the beech, chestnut, linden and birch. Of course varying conditions modify the practical working of these facts, but the Indians' conclusion was well founded.

Of cultivated beeches the most popular is the well-known Purple or Copper Beech. Individual trees of this variety have appeared at different times in the forests of Europe. In a natural history published in 1680, three beech trees with red leaves were recorded as growing in a wood near Zurich. Twenty-five years later a popular legend had grown up that these red-leaved beeches marked a place where five brothers had murdered each other. Most of the Purple Beeches now cultivated are believed to be derived from a tree discovered in the last century in a forest at Thuringia, which is supposed to be about two hundred years old, and is still alive.

The beech tree figures in ancient literature because of its shade ; the ancient writers from Virgil down were continually sending their heroes, seeking rest and recreation, to recline under wide-spreading beeches. For example :—

> Beneath the shade which beechen boughs diffuse,
> You, Tityrus, entertain your sylvan muse.
>
> —VIRGIL.

> I ran to meet you as a traveller
> Gets from the sun under a shady beech.
>
> —THEOCRITUS.

> Under the branches of the beech we flung
> Our limbs at ease and our bent bows unstrung.
>
> —From the Spanish.

> There at the foot of yonder nodding beech
> That wreathes its old fantastic roots so high,
> His listless length at noontide he would stretch
> And pore upon the brook that bubbled by.
>
> —GRAY.

The following curious story is told by Pliny in his Natural History. " There was a little hill called Corne, in the territory of Tusculum, not far from the city of Rome, that was clad and beautified with a grove and tufts of beech trees, which were as even and round in the head as if they had been curiously trimmed with garden shears. This grove was, in old times consecrated to Diana, by the common consent of all the inhabitants of Latium who paid their devotions to that goddess there. One of these trees was of such surpassing beauty, that Passenius Crispus a celebrated orator who was twice consul, and who afterwards married the Empress Agrippina was so fond of it, that he not only delighted to repose beneath its shade, but frequently poured wine on the roots, and used often to embrace it."

The ancients also knew that beech wood absorbed very little water and for that reason made excellent bowls.

> No wars did men molest
> When only beechen bowls were in request.
>
> —VIRGIL.

> In beechen goblets let their beverage shine,
> Cool from the crystal spring their sober wine.
>
> —MILTON.

Trunk of the Beech, *Fagus atropun....*

The beech tree has evidently been the shining mark of lovers from earliest days.

> Or shall I rather the sad verse repeat
> Which on the beech's bark I lately writ?
>
> —VIRGIL.

> On the smooth beechen rind the pensive dame
> Carves in a thousand forms her Tancred's name.
>
> —TASSO.

It is perhaps scarcely necessary to say that the beech tre of ancient literature is not the American beech but *Fagu sylvatica*, the common beech of Europe. Our beech differs from the European species in its paler bark and the lighter green of its leaves.

CHESTNUT

Castànea dentàta. Castànea vésca.

From Castanea a town in Thessaly, or from another town of that name in Pontus. New York Indians call the chestnut, O-heh-yah-tah, Prickly Bur.

Occasionally one hundred feet high ; grows rapidly and lives to great age. Very common on glacial drift of northern states, rarely found on limestone soils. Has stout tap root and thick rootlets. Juices are astringent. Attains its greatest size in western North Carolina and eastern Tennessee.

Bark.—Grayish brown divided by shallow irregular fissures into broad flat ridges. Branchlets at first light yellow green, finally olive green and ultimately dark brown.

Wood.—Reddish brown, sapwood lighter ; light, soft, coarse-grained, not strong, easily split and very durable in contact with the soil ; largely used in manufacture of cheap furniture, interior of houses, railway ties, fence posts and rails. Sp. gr., 0.4504 ; weight of cu. ft., 28.07 lbs.

Winter Buds.—Dark chestnut brown, ovate, acute, one-fourth an inch long ; all lateral.

Leaves.—Alternate, oblong-lanceolate, six to eight inches long, acute or wedge-shaped base, coarsely serrate, acute or acuminate. Feather-veined ; midrib and veins prominent on the under side. Convolute in the bud, late in unfolding ; when full grown are a dark shining green above, a paler green beneath. In autumn they turn a

Chestnut, *Castanea dentata.*

Leaves 6′ to 8′ long.

bright clear yellow.   Petioles short, stout, slightly angled.   Stipules caducous.

Flowers.—June, July.   Monœcious, fragrant.   Staminate catkins six to eight inches in length, with stout, green, hairy stems covered with flower clusters.   The androgynous catkins are slender, hairy, from two and a half to five inches in length, near their base are two or three clusters of pistillate flowers ; above these pistillate flowers are scattered clusters of staminate flowers ; these are smaller than those on the staminate catkins and fall from the persistent rachis ; which continues to rise above the short raceme of fruit.   The staminate flowers appear in three to seven-flowered cymes in the axils of minute bracts which are borne on the rachis of the ament.   Calyx bell-shaped, pale straw color, six-lobed, lobes imbricate in bud, corolla wanting.   Stamens ten to twenty inserted on the torus ; filaments exserted, white ; anthers pale yellow, introrse, two-celled, cells opening longitudinally.   Ovary has aborted.   Pistillate flowers appear solitary or two or three together within a short stemmed involucre of closely imbricated green scales, at the base of a bract borne on the rachis of the pistillate aments.   Calyx bell-shaped, six-lobed.   Stamens rudimentary.   Ovary inferior, six-celled, styles six, white, hairy, exserted ; ovules two in each cell.   The involucres or burs grow rapidly, are full size by the middle of August, begin to open with the first frost and shedding their nuts fall late in autumn.

Fruit.—Nuts much compressed, two or three in a bur, coated at the apex with thick pale tomentum.   The shell is lined with thick rufous tomentum and the seed is sweet.

> Defenseless in the common road she stands
> Exposed to restless war of vulgar hands,
> By neighboring clowns and passing rabble torn
> Battered with stones by boys and left forlorn.
>
> —COWLEY.

The amber buds of the chestnut are unfolding into long green fans, though it will be long ere the trees decked with their drooping tassels hum like great hives with the music of the bees.

—EDITH THOMAS.

in some places we fynd chestnutts, whose wild fruict I maie well saie equalize the best in France, Spaine, Germany, Italy or those so commended in the Black Sea by Constantinople, all of which I have eaten.

—HISTORIE OF TRAVAILE INTO VIRGINIA BRITANNIA.

The Chestnut stands unnoticed in the forest until midsummer when, all at once, after the other trees have blossomed and some of them fruited, after the elm has scattered her samaras, the red maple dropped her keys, when cherries are ripe and apples half grown, the Chestnut flings out her

Chestnut Burs.

creamy tinted catkins in a wealth of bloom and proclaims that she, too, belongs to the fruit-bearing race and though late she is not belated. Though she blooms in midsummer, her nuts are ripe in early autumn, and the first frosts open the prickly burs and scatter the shining contents at the feet of any passer-by.

Wilson Flagg speaking of the Chestnut says : " On this continent it is a majestic tree remarkable for the breadth and depth of its shade. It displays many of the superficial characters of the red oak so that in winter we cannot readily distinguish them. The foliage bears some resemblance to that of the beech but displays more variety. The leaves are long, lengthened to a tapering point and of a bright and nearly pure green. Though arranged alternately like those of the beech on the recent branches, they are clustered in stars, containing from five to seven leaves, on the fruitful branches that grow out from the perfected wood. When the tree is viewed from a moderate distance the whole mass seems to consist of tufts, each containing several long, pointed leaves, drooping divergently from a common centre."

The relation between the American Chestnut and the Sweet Chestnut of Europe has long puzzled botanists. Loudon considers ours but a variety of the European ; Professor Sargent prefers to consider it a distinct species. The difference between them in any case is slight and ours has the sweeter nut.

Chestnut trees attain enormous size and great age. Loudon says that the Tortworth Chestnut tree in Gloucestershire, England, which is still in a healthy condition, was remarkable for its great size in the reign of King Stephen, 1135 A.D., and is probably more than a thousand years old. The species has the peculiarity of sending forth vigorous shoots from a stump and these, growing in a sort of brotherhood, finally unite into a single tree. The famous Chestnut of a Hundred Horsemen on Mt. Etna in Sicily is believed to have been formed in this way by a group of five. A hundred years ago it had the circumference of two hundred feet at

Trunk of Chestnut, *Castanea dentata*.

the surface of the ground. Two sections of the trunk have disappeared and a road now runs through what is left.

The wood is valuable chiefly because of the tannic acid it contains, which makes it very durable in contact with the soil.

During the tertiary period *Castanea* ranged to Greenland and Alaska and traces of it are found in the miocene rocks of Oregon and Colorado.

The Chinquapin, *Castanea pumila*, is a southern tree often a shrub, which bears an abundance of small sweet chestnuts. The leaf resembles that of *C. dentata* but is smaller and very downy on the under surface. This tree is reported as hardy in the Arnold Arboretum.

SALICÀCEÆ—WILLOW FAMILY

WILLOW

Sàlix.

The Willows are a family of trees and shrubs which differ greatly in size and habit of growth but are very much alike in other respects. All have abundant watery juice, furrowed scaly bark which is heavily charged with salicylic acid, soft, pliant, tough wood, slender branches and large fibrous often stoloniferous roots. These roots are remarkable for their toughness, size, and tenacity of life. Willows are often planted on the border of streams in order that their inter-lacing roots may protect the bank against the action of the water. They make the first growth on the changing, shifting banks of western rivers, and after the soil has been made sufficiently stable, the poplar comes. Frequently the roots are much larger than the stem which grows from them. All the buds are lateral, no absolutely terminal bud is ever formed. These are covered by a single scale, inclosing at its base two minute opposite buds, alternate with two, small, scale-like, fugacious, opposite leaves.

The leaves are alternate except the first pair which fall when about an inch long. They are simple, feather-veined, and typically linear-lanceolate. Usually they are serrate, rounded at base, acute or acuminate. In color they show a great variety of greens, ranging from yellow to blue. The petioles are short, the stipules often very conspicuous, look-ing like tiny round leaves and sometimes remaining for half the summer. On some species, however, they are small, inconspicuous, and fugacious.

The character of the inflorescence is the same in every species. It is diœcious, that is, the stamens and pistils are separate and borne on different trees. This makes the family difficult to classify, for it is necessary to study two trees in order to determine one species, and the two trees are not always at hand. Furthermore, the species readily hybridize, and also quickly respond to environment, so that only an expert is competent to decide a question with regard to species among willows.

The staminate flowers are without either calyx or corolla ; they consist simply of stamens, in number varying from two to ten, accompanied by a nectariferous gland and inserted on the base of a scale which is itself borne on the rachis of a drooping raceme called a catkin, or ament. This scale is oval and entire and very hairy. The anthers are rose colored in the bud but orange or purple after the flower opens, they are two-celled and the cells open longitudinally. The filaments are thread-like, usually pale yellow, often hairy.

A Staminate and a Pistillate Flower of a Willow.

The pistillate flowers are also without calyx or corolla ; and consist of a single ovary accompanied by a small flat gland and inserted on the base of a scale which is likewise borne on the rachis of a catkin. This ovary is one-celled, the style two-lobed, and the ovules numerous. The fruit is a one-celled, two-valved, cylindrical, beaked capsule, containing many minute seeds which are furnished with long, silky, white hairs. The catkins appear before or with the leaves. Although catkin and ament are interchangeable words, catkin seems most appropriate for the flowers of the willow because of their furry appearance when half developed.

The genus *Salix* is admirably fitted to go forth and inhabit the earth, for it is tolerant of all soils and asks only water. It creeps nearer to the North Pole than any other woody plant except its companion the birch. It trails upon the ground or rises one hundred feet into the air. In North America it follows the water-courses to the limit of the temperate zone, enters the tropics, crosses the equator and appears in the mountains of Peru and Chili. In the old world its range is quite as extensive as in the new. It creeps or runs or stands, looks like a weasel or is backed like a camel according to its surroundings. The books record one hundred and sixty species in the world and these sport and hybridize to their own content and to the despair of botanists. Then, too, it comes of an ancient line. Impressions of leaves in the cretaceous rocks show that it is probably one of the oldest forms of dicotyledonous plants.

BLACK WILLOW

Sàlix nìgra.

Banks of streams and lakes ; the common native willow that becomes a tree. Twenty to forty feet high. Ranges from New Brunswick to Florida, westward to the foot-hills of the Rocky Mountains and south into Mexico ; also appears in California.

Bark.—Dark brown or nearly black, sometimes lighter brown, deeply divided into broad, flat, connected ridges. Branchlets slender, very brittle at the base, rather bright reddish brown.

Wood.—Light reddish brown, sapwood nearly white ; light, soft, close-grained and weak. Sp. gr., .4456 ; weight of cu. ft., 27.77 lbs.

Winter Buds.—Acute, small, reddish brown.

Leaves.—Alternate, lanceolate, three to six inches long, often curved at tip, and frequently conspicuously scythe-shaped (var. *falcata*), round or wedge-shaped base, serrate, and the entire leaf above the middle gradually narrowed to a tapering tip. Feather-veined. Involute in bud, silky when unfolding, when full grown are a bright pale, shining green above, pale green beneath. In autumn light yellow, or fall without changing. Petioles short, slender. Stipules semi-cordate or crescent-shaped, leaf-like, persistent, or small and deciduous.

Flowers.—March, April ; before the leaves. Catkins borne on short leafy branches, narrowly cylindrical, one to three inches long ; stamens vary from three to six; ovary is ovate, smooth, apex stigmatic. The fruiting catkins vary from an inch and a half to three inches in length.

WILLOW FAMILY

Fruit.—Capsule, ovate, conical, smooth, and reddish brown. Seed minute, surrounded by a tuft of long, white, soft hairs.

> Then saffern swarms swing off from all the willers
> So plump they look like yaller caterpillars.
> JAMES RUSSELL LOWELL.

There is now but little black willow down left on the trees. I think I see how this tree is propagated by its seeds. Its countless minute brown seeds, just perceptible to the naked eye in the midst of their cotton are wafted with the cotton to the water, most abundantly about a fortnight ago ; and then they drift and form a thick white scum together with other matter, especially against some alder or other fallen or drooping shrub where there is less current than usual. There within two or three days a great many germinate and show their two little roundish leaves, more or less tingeing with green the surface of the scum, somewhat like grass-seed in a tumbler of cotton. Many of these are drifted in amid the button bushes, willows and other shrubs, and the sedge along the river side, and the water falling just at this time when they have put forth little fibres, they are deposited on the mud just left bare in the shade, and thus probably a great many of them have a chance to become perfect plants. But if they do not get into sufficiently shallow water, and are not left on the mud just at the right time probably they perish. The mud in many such places is now green with them, though perhaps the seed has often blown thither directly through the air. —HENRY D. THOREAU.

This is the native willow which oftenest attains tree-like proportions in eastern North America. It is usually found leaning over the water of streams and lakes, and may be recognized by its long, narrow, yellow green, shining leaves, which taper gradually to a long point and give the effect of delicate foliage. These leaves usually curve in growth, so that they take a sickle shape ; this peculiarity is frequent though not invariable, but the tip is often curved, when the body of the leaf is not. Moreover, each leaf bears small green stipules, crescent-shaped, finely toothed, and persistent as long as the leaf is growing. The bark is rather rough and blackish, although individuals are found with bark fairly light brown.

Staminate Flower of Black Willow, *Salix nigra.*

Pistillate Flower of Black Willow, *Salix nigra.*

Black Willow, *Salix nigra*.
Leaves 3' to 6' long.

SHINING WILLOW

Sàlix lùcida.

A bushy tree sometimes twenty feet in height, found on banks ot streams and swamps, with short trunk and erect branches which form a round-topped symmetrical head. Ranges from Newfoundland westward across the continent to the Rocky Mountains, southward as far as Pennsylvania and Nebraska.

Bark.—Smooth, dark brown. Branchlets smooth at first, orange color and shining, later dark brown.

Winter Buds.—Ovate, acute, light brown, one-fourth of an inch long.

Leaves.—Alternate, oblong-lanceolate, three to five inches long, narrowed or wedge-shaped, or rounded at base, finely serrate, acute with long tapering often falcate points. Involute in bud, they come out green, when full grown are leathery, smooth, shining, dark green above, paler beneath, midrib conspicuously prominent beneath. Petioles short, stout, yellow, grooved, glandular. Stipules semicircular, serrate, membranous and often persistent.

Flowers.—April, before the leaves. Staminate catkins oblong-cylindrical, densely flowered, an inch to an inch and a half long, terminal, on short leafy branches ; stamens five. Pistillate catkins slender, an inch and a half to two inches long, becoming three or four inches long when the fruit ripens, often persisting until late.

Fruit.—Capsule, cylindrical, one-third of an inch long, shining.

PEACH WILLOW—ALMONDLEAF WILLOW

Sàlix amygdaloìdes.

Sometimes sixty to seventy feet high, with straight trunk and straight ascending branches, usually much smaller. Follows the water-courses and ranges across the continent ; less abundant in New England than elsewhere. In the west it becomes the common willow along the banks of streams.

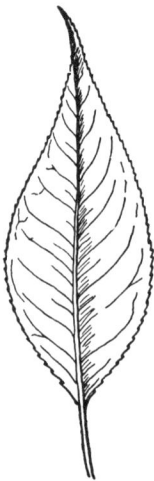

Almondleaf Willow,
Saltx amygdaloides.
Leaves 2′ to 3′ long.

Shining Willow, *Salix lucida.*

Leaves 3′ to 5′ long.

Leaves.—Lanceolate, frequently falcate, wedge-shaped or rounded often unequal at base, finely serrate, narrowed into long slender points at the apex. When full grown they are light green and shining above, pale and glaucous beneath. The midrib is stout, yellow or orange ; the petioles are slender, one-half to three-quarters of an inch long ; the stipules reniform, serrate, frequently half an inch broad and usually caducous.

Flowers.—The catkins are two to three inches long, the scales are yellow, very hairy, the stamens from five to nine.

Fruit.—Capsule, globose-conical, pale reddish yellow, and about a quarter of an inch long.

SANDBAR WILLOW—LONG LEAF WILLOW

Sàlix fluviátilis.

This willow is usually about twenty feet in height, with a trunk only a few inches in diameter, and short erect branches, spreading

by stoloniferous roots into broad thickets. Rarely it becomes a tree sixty feet high ; frequently a shrub five or six feet high.

Bark.—Smooth, dark brown, slightly tinged with red and scaly. Branchlets are slender, smooth, light or dark orange color or purplish red.

Leaves.—Come out of the bud involute, are linear-lanceolate, often falcate, gradually narrowed at both ends, finely dentate-serrate, acute or acuminate. When they first appear they are exceedingly silky, when mature they are thin, smooth, yellow green above, paler green below. They vary from two to six inches long, one-eighth to one-half an inch wide. Midribs raised and prominent ; petioles grooved ; stipules leafy, deciduous.

Flowers.—Aments are very silky, on the staminate plant they are about an inch long, terminal and axillary, the terminal flowers opening first. The pistillate aments are two to three inches long and terminal on leafy branches. Stamens are two with free filaments, ovary is very silky and crowned with deeply lobed stigmas.

Fruit.—Capsule, light brown, one-fourth an inch long.

Longleaf Willow,
Salix fluviatilis.
Leaves 2′ to 6′ long, ⅛′ to ½′ broad.

The range of Sandbar Willow covers the continent from the arctic circle to northern

Mexico. It grows on the river banks and is the first tree or shrub in all the northern interior region to spring up on newly formed sand-bars and banks of rivers, holding the soft mud in place with its long rigid roots. It is the herald of the poplars and prepares the river banks for their growth. It is an exceedingly valuable tree throughout the entire mid-continental region.

BEBB WILLOW

Sàlix bebbiàna. Sàlix rostràta.

A bushy tree sometimes twenty feet high usually much smaller, frequently a shrub. The bark is reddish or olive green or gray tinged with red. Branchlets slender, reddish purple, orange brown or reddish brown.

Leaves.—Come out of the bud conduplicate, are oblong-obovate, wedge-shaped or rounded at base, remotely serrate or entire, acute or acuminate. When full grown they are thick dull green and smooth above, pale blue, or silvery white, downy below; one to three inches long, half an inch to an inch wide. Petioles are often reddish ; stipules leaf-like, semicordate, acute, sometimes one-half an inch long, deciduous.

Flowers.—Catkins appear with the unfolding leaves, erect and terminal on short leafy branches. The staminate catkins are silvery white before flowering and pale yellow after, about an inch long and half an inch broad. Pistillate catkins are about an inch long. Stamens two, filaments free. Ovary very silky, crowned with spreading yellow stigmas.

Fruit.—Capsule, elongated, narrowed into a long slender beak, borne on a slender stalk which is longer than the persistent scale.

The Bebb Willow will grow in moist and in dry soil, on the borders of streams and on dry hillsides. It is more abundant in British America than in the United States where it ranges southwest to Pennsylvania and westward to Minnesota. It has appeared, heretofore, in the books as *S. rostrata*, but the name has been changed to *S. bebbiana*, to commemorate the labors of Mr. Michael S. Bebb who was an authority upon the willows of this country.

Bebb Willow, *Salix bebbiana.*
Leaves 1′ to 3′ long.

GLAUCOUS WILLOW. PUSSY WILLOW

Sàlix dìscolor.

A small tree rarely more than twenty feet in height, more often a shrub.

Bark.—Light greenish brown sometimes tinged with red, scaly. Branchlets at first are stout, dark reddish purple, coated with pale pubescence, later dull green. Buds are dark reddish purple, flattened, acute, three-eighths of an inch long.

Leaves.—Come out of the bud convolute, are oblong or oblong-ovate or lanceolate, gradually narrowed at both ends, wedge-shaped or rounded at base, crenately-serrate, acute. When full grown are thick and firm, smooth, bright green above, glaucous or silvery white below, from three to five inches long, from an inch to an inch and a half wide. Midribs are broad, yellow ; petioles slender ; stipules leaflike, semilunate, acute, dentate, about one-fourth of an inch long, deciduous.

Flowers.—Catkins appear in very early spring, before the leaves, over an inch long, two-thirds of an inch thick, white and silky before the flowers open. Stamens two with long slender filaments. Ovary is elongated, downy, long-stalked and crowned with a short style and broad spreading stigmas.

Fruit.—Capsule, cylindrical, long pointed, pale brown and downy.

This willow is common along the banks of streams and ranges from Nova Scotia to Manitoba and south to Delaware ; west to Indiana and Illinois and northwestern Missouri.

The leaves and twigs of many willows are subject to gall growths caused by the stings of insects. The great cone-like buds, an inch or more long and three-fourths of an inch in diameter which are found at the tips of the branches of *Salix discolor* especially, are an interesting example of these. One often sees a Pussy Willow, growing by or fairly in the bed of a small stream, virtually covered with these monstrous buds. But open one of them with a sharp knife and within will be found the sleeping larva of a gall-fly. This bud is formed of many overlapping scales which are crowded and modified leaves, all diverted from their normal purpose and compelled to serve as the covering of an enemy.

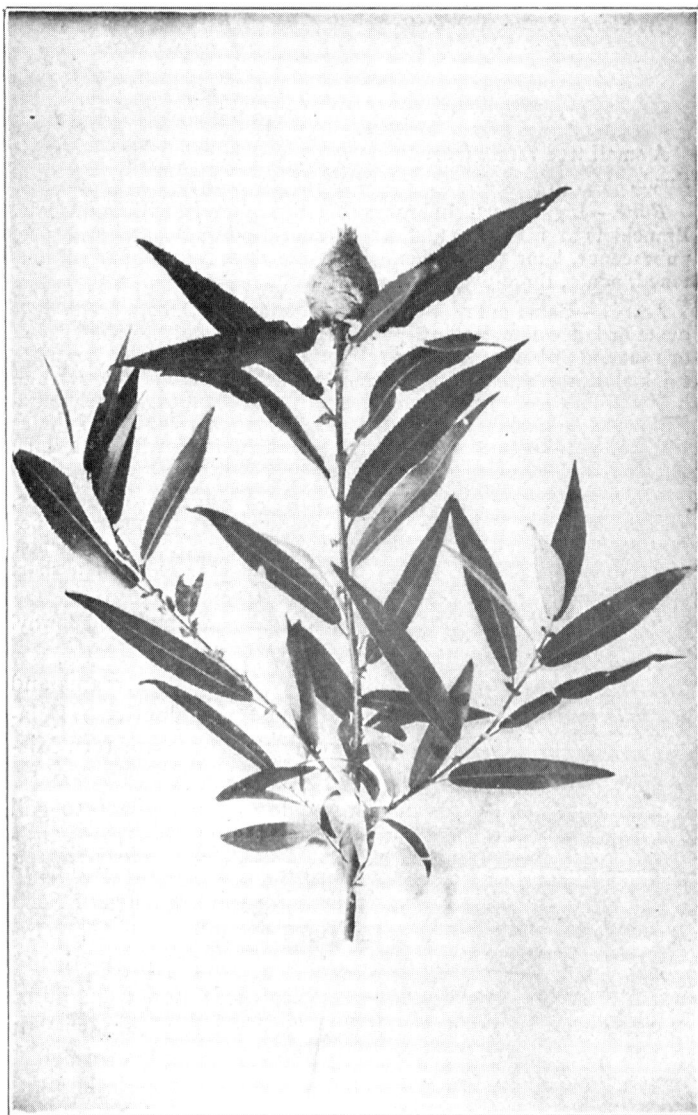

Glaucous Willow, *Salix discolor.*
Leaves 3′ to 5′ long.   Showing a Gall-bud.

WHITE WILLOW. YELLOW WILLOW. BLUE WILLOW

Sàlix álba var. *vitellìna ;* var. *cærùlea.*

The magnificent willow tree which waves its narrow pointed leaves above our heads in cultivated grounds is in all probability a direct descendant, or a variety, or a hybrid, of the White Willow of Europe which was very early introduced into this country and has become very generally naturalized. It is one of the few foreign trees which finds no equal among American trees of the same genus.

Gray says that the original form of *Salix alba* is now rarely found in this country. The common form is *Salix vitellina* or Yellow Willow, so named because of the color of the branchlets. A less common form, *Salix cærulea*, is often seen having green branchlets and dull, bluish green leaves.

The best characteristic of this willow is its wonderful tenacity of life. Push a White Willow wand ten inches into the ground at the edge of a stream where it may always have water and it will grow, and grow rapidly.

Loudon says that a plant of *Salix alba* can be made to turn a summersault, that is, the branches of a young plant may be buried in the soil and the roots left above ground, and that the roots will become branches and the branches will change into roots.

CRACK WILLOW

Sàlix frágilis.

This is one of our largest willows, often making a magnificent tree. A native of Europe, it was introduced into this country that its twigs might be used in basket-making ; it has also been cultivated to produce charcoal for gunpowder. Now thoroughly naturalized it is common along the banks of streams and will flourish in any moist situation.

Ordinarily, it grows fifty or sixty feet high with a full round head, spreading limbs and green branchlets. The

White Willow, *Salix alba*, var. *vitellina*.
Leaves 3½′ to 4′ long.

Crack Willow, *Salix fragilis.*
Leaves 4′ to 7′ long.

leaves are four to seven inches long, one to one and one-half inches wide, narrow—oblong with wedge-shaped base, long, tapering, pointed apex, and serrate margin with thickened teeth. The midrib is very prominent on the under side and shows greenish white above. In color the leaves are a dark shining green above, and smooth, whitish, and glaucous beneath. The twigs are very brittle at the base, and after a high wind the ground under the tree is often strewn with them. At these times Crack Willow seems an appropriate name. The tree, however, is particularly beautiful in a light wind for the leaves are so poised that they readily turn and show the white of their under surfaces. The species may be identified by the leaf which in addition to the characteristics already given has two tiny excrescences at the base just at the junction of the leaf with the petiole. The tree is worthy of more attention than it has yet received.

Prehistoric man knew the uses of the willow. The strong, yielding, flexible withes made natural ropes and their use as such has come down to recent times. The modern world has to-day no material better for baskets than the willow, and the Romans used it precisely as we do.

> From Britain's painted sons I came,
> And Basket is my barbarous name;
> But now I am so modish grown
> That Rome would claim me for her own.
>
> —MARTIAL.

Herodotus is the first of ancient writers to mention the willow and he speaks of the divining rods of the ancient Scythians.

Exactly why this tree should be considered the emblem of despairing love is not clear but that it has been so considered from early times is evident. Shakespeare represents Dido lamenting the loss of Æneas :

> In such a night
> Stood Dido, with a willow in her hand,
> Upon the wild sea banks, and waved her love
> To come again to Carthage.

WEEPING WILLOW

Sàlix babylônica.

By the waters of Babylon we sat down and wept, when we remembered thee, O Zion! As for our harps we hanged them up upon the willow trees that are therein. —PSALM 137.

The native land of the Weeping Willow is Asia. On the banks of the Euphrates, near Babylon, it is abundant. It is also found in China, in Egypt and elsewhere in Africa. Some authorities say it was brought into England about 1730 ; others give the date of its introduction as 1692.

A pretty story is told of Pope in connection with this tree. It seems that he was present when Lady Suffolk received a package from Turkey and, observing that some of the withes bound around it appeared alive, said taking them up, " Perhaps these may produce something that we have not in England." Whereupon, the story adds, he planted one of them in his garden at Twickenham which became the Weeping Willow, afterwards so celebrated. Years after, this willow was cut down by the owner of the villa for the same reason that Haskell cut down Shakespeare's mulberry tree, because he was annoyed by persons asking to see it.

That this willow is a favorite tree in China is clear from the prominence given it in all Chinese pictures of landscape. The famous landscape on the old Canton plates shows Weeping Willows bordering the stream and surrounding the home of the irate father. The Chinese also plant it in their cemeteries. It must, likewise, at one time in this country have been considered a tree fitted to express elegant sorrow, for funeral prints of a tombstone, shaded by a Weeping Willow under which a mourner stands in the abandonment of grief, are among the venerable treasures of many a New England household.

Perhaps, the most famous tree of the species is that growing upon the site of Napoleon's grave at St. Helena. Among the trees that had been introduced into the island was a Weeping Willow which attracted Napoleon's notice and under which he used frequently to sit. About the time of his death a storm shattered it and after the interment of the Emperor, Madame Bertrand planted several cuttings of the tree outside the railing which surrounded the grave. After various vicissitudes one of the willows was found to be in a flourishing condition and from this one have been obtained the cuttings which have enabled so many to possess a plant of the true Napoleon's Willow.

Landscape gardeners plant the Weeping Willow by streams or waterfalls in conjunction with the Weeping Birch or in contrast with the Lombardy Poplar. To treat it artistically is oftentimes a problem, as it is difficult to make it harmonize with other trees.

It roots freely by cuttings and grows with great rapidity in a rich soil, near water. Its shoots are brittle and neither they nor the wood seem ever to have served any economic purpose.

POPLAR

Pôpulus

The word *Populus* is derived by some from *pallo*, to vibrate or shake ; others suppose that the tree obtained its name from being used in ancient times to decorate the public places in Rome, where it was called *arbor populi*, or tree of the people.

The Poplars are a group of rapid growing trees closely allied to the willows. Their range includes both temperate and arctic regions and in the extreme north they produce extended forests. Nine species occur in the United States of which five are native to the eastern part of the continent, the others are Rocky Mountain or western trees. In addition to these, three European species are naturalized here ; the White Poplar, *P. alba*, the Lombardy Poplar, *P. nigra* var. *italica*, and the Black Poplar, *P. nigra*.

The wood has become valuable of late for paper making. The bark is heavily charged with tannic acid and in Europe is used for tanning leather.

Weeping Willow, *Salix babylonica.*
Leaves 3′ to 5′ long.

The flowers are diœcious and appear in early spring before the leaves. They are borne in long, drooping, sessile or pedunculate aments which are produced from buds formed in the axils of the leaves of the previous year. The pistillate aments lengthen very considerably before maturity. The flowers are solitary, each one seated in a cupshaped disk which is borne on the base of a scale which is itself attached to the rachis of the ament. The scales are obovate, lobed and fringed, membranous, hairy or smooth, usually caducous. The staminate flowers are without calyx or corolla and consist simply of a group of stamens, four to twelve, or twelve to sixty, inserted on a disk ; filaments short, pale yellow; anthers oblong, purple or red, introrse, two-celled ; cells opening longitudinally.

Cottonwood, *Populus deltoides.* Staminate Aments, 3′ to 4′ long.

The pistillate flower is equally destitute of calyx and corolla and consists of a one-celled ovary seated in a cup-shaped disk. The style is short, stigmas two to four, variously lobed ; ovules numerous. The fruit is a two to fourvalved capsule, ripening before the full development of the leaf ; greenish or reddish-brown. The seed is light brown and surrounded by a tuft of long, soft, white hairs.

Cottonwood, *Populus deltoides.* Pistillate Aments, 3′ to 4′ long.

Populus is the oldest type of dicotyledonous plants yet identified. When Sequoias, Pines and Cycads made up the bulk of the cretaceous forests of Greenland, the Poplar alone of deciduous trees waved its fluttering leaves among their dark branches.

ASPEN. QUAKING ASP

Pópulus tremuloìdes.

Tremuloides refers to the fluttering habit of the leaves.

Most widely distributed tree of North America. Prefers a rather moist sandy soil and gravelly hillsides. Small, slender, rarely reaching the height of fifty feet, but credited with one hundred feet in northern Arizona at an elevation of 8,000 feet above the sea. Grows rapidly and forms a narrow round-topped head. Roots large, vigorous and stoloniferous.

Bark.—On old trees near the base almost black ; higher on the trunk and on young stems, pale greenish brown or yellow brown or nearly white, often roughened with horizontal bands or wart-like excrescences and marked below the branches with large, dark, lunate scars. Branchlets at first red brown, and shining. turning finally to a light gray, afterward becoming dark gray, for two or three years much roughened by leaf-scars. The sweet inner bark in early spring is used as food by the Indians of the north.

Wood.—Light brown, sapwood nearly white, soft, close-grained, neither strong nor durable. Largely used in the manufacture of paper ; and in the west for flooring and turnery. Burns freely when green. Sp. gr., 0.4032 ; weight of cu. ft., 25.13 lbs.

Winter Buds.—Leaf-buds slightly resinous, reddish brown, conical acute, somewhat incurved, one-fourth of an inch long ; narrower than the obtuse flower-buds.

Leaves.—Alternate, simple, one and a half to two inches long, ovate or nearly round, slightly cordate or truncate at base, finely serrate with glandular-tipped teeth, acute. Feather-veined, midrib and primary veins conspicuous. They come out of the bud involute, smooth, light green, shining, ciliate on margins, when full grown are thin, dark green, shining above, pale, dull, yellow green beneath. In autumn they turn a clear bright yellow. Tremulous. Petioles long, slender, and laterally compressed. Stipules caducous.

Flowers.—April, borne in pendulous aments one and a half to two and a half inches long, from buds formed the season before. The one-flowered scales are deeply divided into three to five linear, acute lobes fringed with long, soft, gray

A Staminate and a Pistillate Flower of Aspen, *Populus tremuloides ;* enlarged.

hairs. Stamens from six to twelve, inserted on a disk which is oblique, with entire margin. Ovary is conical; style short, thick ; stigmas two, divided into lobes. Ovary surrounded by broad oblique disk, which is persistent.

Fruit.—Oblong-conical capsules, two-valved, thin-walled, light green and nearly one-fourth an inch long, borne in drooping aments about four inches long. Seeds obovate, light brown and surrounded with long, soft, snowy white hairs. May and June.

Nature chooses wisely her place for *Aspen tremuloides* at the edge of a wood, with darker, higher trees behind as a background.

—EDITH THOMAS.

The entire Poplar family are a restless folk and the Aspen the most so of the group. The reason lies in a personal peculiarity. The character of the petiole or leaf stem has much to do with the movement of the foliage of every tree. In the beech and elm, for example, the petiole is short and stiff and as a consequence the leaves have little independent motion but sway with the branch. The Poplars, on the other hand, have long slender petioles to begin with, and these are laterally compressed—pinched sidewise, not flattened—and this compression being vertical to the plane of the leaf, counteracts the ordinary waving motion which a leaf has in the wind and causes it to quiver with the slightest breeze, whence the proverbial comparison, "Trembling like an aspen leaf." From Homer to Tennyson the race of poets have noted this peculiarity of all aspens.

> Some wove the web,
> Or twirled the spindle, sitting, with a quick
> Light motion like the aspen's glancing leaves.
>
> —ODYSSEY.

> His hand did quake
> And tremble like a leaf of aspen green.
>
> —SPENSER.

> A perfect calm, that not a breath
> Is heard to quiver through the closing woods,
> Or rustling turn the many twinkling leaves
> Of aspen tall.
>
> —THOMSON.

> Willows whiten, aspens quiver.
>
> —TENNYSON.

The small Aspen is a very common tree, little prized and rarely planted. Often an undergrowth in an oak wood, it is

Aspen, *Populus tremuloides.*
Leaves 1½′ to 2′ long.

perhaps better known when, forming a little thicket, it makes a mass of trembling leaves on a gravelly bank by the roadside, or skirts the border of a swamp, or forms the first growth on dry upland which has been swept by fire. Under favorable conditions it becomes a tree fifty feet in height and in the mountains of Arizona will reach one hundred feet. Small and quivering leaves necessarily make a tree look fragile and it is doubtful if any size could take from it the appearance of weakness which is its marked characteristic.

The trunk is slender, the head round-topped, the bark pale green becoming whitish and blotched and marred with age. The leaf is almost round, with a slightly heart-shaped base, serrate margin and acute apex. It comes out of the bud involute, pale green, shining and downy, but finally becomes smooth and firm in texture, dark green above and dull yellow green beneath. The seeds ripen in May and by means of the long white hairs which surround them are borne by the winds to a considerable distance from the parent tree.

It ranges from Hudson's Bay to Mexico. It grows farther north than the spruce and the larch, and flourishes on the mountain ranges of Chihuahua.

Professor Sargent says : " The great value of the Aspen lies in the power of its small seeds, supported by their long hairs and wafted far and near by the wind, to germinate quickly in soil which fire has rendered infertile ; and in the ability of the seedling plants to grow rapidly in exposed situations. Preventing the washing away of the soil from steep mountain slopes and affording shelter for the young of longer-lived trees, it has played a chief part in determining the composition and distribution of the subalpine forests of western America and in recent years it has spread over vast areas of the slopes of the Rocky Mountains from which fire had swept the coniferous trees." Loudon considers our American Aspen to be but a variety of the Aspen of Europe, *Populus tremula*.

There lingers in Scotland, it is said, the belief that the

Large-toothed Aspen, *Populus grandidentata.*
Leaves 3′ to 4′ long.

Aspen is the tree of whose wood the cross of our Saviour was made and that it still shivers in remembrance of that fact.

> Far off in highland wilds 'tis said,
> But truth now laughs at fancy's lore,
> That of this tree the cross was made
> Which erst the Lord of Glory bore;
> And of that deed its leaves confess
> E'er since a troubled consciousness.
>
> *—Spirit of the Woods.*

LARGE-TOOTHED ASPEN

Pópulus grandidentàta.

Common in the forest, preferring rich, moist, sandy soil, near the borders of swamps and streams. Reaches the height of sixty feet, with a trunk two feet in diameter and slender spreading branches which form a narrow round-topped head. Ranges from Nova Scotia through Ontario to Minnesota; southward to Delaware, along the Alleghanies to North Carolina, Kentucky and Tennessee.

Bark.—On old trees near the base, dark brown, fissured and divided into broad flat ridges; on younger stems and on the branches smooth and light gray tinged with green. Branchlets stout, coated at first with pale tomentum, later they become redbrown or dark orange, finally become dark gray, much roughened by the leaf scars.

Wood.—Light brown, sapwood nearly white; light, soft, close-grained but not strong. Largely manufactured into wood pulp, occasionally used for wooden-ware. Sp. gr., 0.4632; weight of cu. ft., 28.87 lbs.

Leaf Buds.—Spread from the branch at a wide angle, broadly ovate, acute, one-eighth of an inch long; about half the size of the flower-buds which otherwise resemble them.

Large-Toothed Aspen, *Populus grandidentata.* Fruiting Ament, 4′ to 5′ long.

Leaves.—Alternate, simple, three to four inches long two to three inches broad, broadly-ovate, three-nerved, wedge-shaped, truncate or rounded at base, coarsely and irregularly crenate with incurved teeth, acute or acuminate; midrib and veins conspicuous. They come out of the bud involute, coated with hoary tomentum, when full grown are dark green above, pale green beneath. In

418

autumn they turn a clear bright yellow. Petiole slender, laterally compressed, one and a half to two and one-half inches long. Stipules caducous.

Flowers.—April, borne in pendulous aments, one and a half to two and a half inches long, from buds formed the season before. The one-flowered scales are deeply divided into five or six acute lobes, with soft light gray hairs which also cover the disk. Stamens from six to twelve, inserted on a shallow oblique disk with entire margin ; filaments short, slender ; anthers light red. Ovary oblong-conical, light green, hairy ; style short ; stigmas spreading, divided into filiform lobes. The ovary enclosed in the persistent disk.

Fruit.—Oblong, curved capsule, light green, thin-walled, hairy, two-valved, one-eighth inch long, borne on a drooping ament four to five inches long. Seed minute, dark brown, surrounded by rather short, snowy white hairs. May.

The Large-toothed Aspen is gregarious, loves to grow in thickets ; its leaves twinkle on the gravelly hill-side or along the river-bottom ; it ripens its long, drooping, necklace-like aments in May as its leaves unfold and in every particular proves itself a poplar.

The high-sounding name, *P. grandidentata*, means simply that the teeth of the leaf margin are a little larger than those of *P. tremuloides*.

SWAMP COTTONWOOD. BLACK COTTONWOOD. DOWNY POPLAR

Pópulus heterophýlla.

Rare in New England, common in the south Atlantic states, abundant in the lower Mississippi valley. Loves low wet land. In the north is a tree forty feet high, with a rather round-topped head, its maximum height is ninety feet.

Bark.—On old trees, light brown tinged with red, often broken into long narrow plates attached only at the middle ; on young trees divided by narrow shallow fissures into flat ridges. Branchlets contain an orange-colored pith, at first are dark red brown or ashy gray, later much darker and roughened by leaf scars.

Wood.—Dull brown, sapwood lighter brown ; light, soft and close-grained. Is now often manufactured into lumber in the west and south and used in interior finish of buildings. Sp. gr., 0.4089 ; weight of cu. ft., 25.48 lbs.

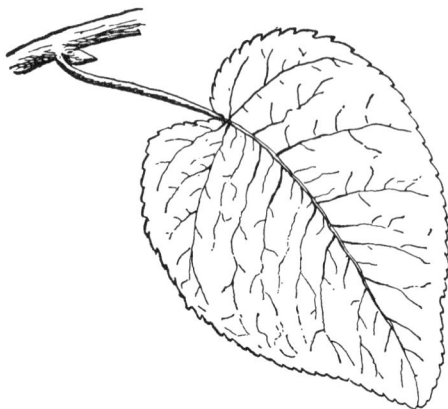

Swamp Cottonwood, *Populus heterophylla.* Leaves 4′ to 7′ long.

Leaf Buds.— Slightly resinous, ovate, acute, covered with bright red brown scales, one-fourth an inch long and half the size of the flower-buds.

Leaves.—Alternate, four to seven inches long, two to three inches broad, broadly ovate, cordate or truncate or rounded with a small sinus at base, finely or coarsely crenately-serrate with incurved glandular teeth, acute, or short pointed or rounded at apex; midrib and veins conspicuous, and sometimes downy. They come out of the bud involute, covered with thick white tomentum, when full grown are dark green above pale and smooth beneath. In autumn they turn dull yellow or brown. Petioles terete, slender, tomentose or smooth, two and one-half inches long; stipules caducous.

Flowers.—March, April. Staminate aments are broad, densely flowered, erect at first but finally pendulous, two to two and one-half inches long with stout, brittle, hairy stems. Their scales are narrowly oblong-ovate, brown, divided into many narrow light red brown lobes and falling as the aments lengthen. Stamens, twelve to twenty, with slender filaments and large dark red anthers, are inserted on an oblique, slightly concave disk, with spreading border. Pistillate aments few-flowered, one to two inches long; ovary ovoid, terete or three-angled; style short, stout with two or three dilated, two or three-lobed stigmas.

Fruit.—In maturing the fruiting aments become four to six inches long, pedicels half an inch long; capsules ripen in May, are ovate, acute, red brown, two to three-valved, one-half an inch long; seed small, dark brown, surrounded by many short, silvery white hairs which are often tinged with orange.

Part of the Fruiting Ament of Swamp Cottonwood. *Populus heterophylla.*

Balsam, *Populus balsamifera.*
Leaves 3′ to 5′ long, 1½′ to 3′ broad.

WILLOW FAMILY

Though heart of oak be e'er so stout
Keep me dry, and I'll see him out.
—*Old inscription on a poplar plank.*

The wood of this tree under the name of Black Poplar is much used in the west in the interior finish of buildings.

This is the one poplar whose petioles are not laterally compressed—therefore the leaves do not flutter as do those of other species. It is called the Downy Poplar because the leaves retain the down on their veins more abundantly than other poplars.

BALSAM. TACMAHAC. BALM OF GILEAD

Pópulus balsamífera.

In New England and middle States about sixty feet high, but in the Valley of the Mackenzie River in Canada it reaches one hundred feet, with a trunk six or seven feet in diameter. Prefers the bottom-lands of rivers and borders of swamps

Bark.—On old trees dark brownish gray, divided into broad rounded ridges covered with small closely appressed scales. On younger stems and branches light brown tinged with green, and smoothed or roughened by dark excrescences. Branchlets stout, dark red brown, shining or downy at first, later they become dark orange, finally gray tinged with yellow green.

Wood.—Light brown, sapwood nearly white ; light, soft close-grained, not strong. Used extensively in the manufacture of paper. Sp. gr., 0.3635 ; weight of cu. ft., 22.65 lbs.

Winter Buds.—Leaf-buds ovate, long pointed, brownish yellow, the terminal bud nearly an inch long. The axillary three-quarters of an inch long. Saturated with a yellow balsamic sticky exudation, shining, beginning to open soon after midwinter, they are covered with five oblong, closely imbricated, thick scales. Flower-buds similar to terminal leaf-buds.

Leaves.—Alternate, three to five inches long, one and one-half to three inches wide, ovate-lanceolate, rounded or cordate at base, crenate-serrate with slightly thickened margins. acute or acuminate ; midrib and primary veins conspicuous. They come out of the bud involute, light yellow green coated with the gummy secretions of the bud and slightly hairy, when full grown are deep dark green, shining above, pale green often ferruginous below. In autumn they turn a bright yellow. Petioles long, slender, compressed later-

Balm of Gilead, *Populus balsamifera candicans.*
Leaves 4' to 6' long.

ally, enlarged at the base. Stipules vary in shape and remain until the leaf is half grown.

Flowers.—March, April, before the leaves. Pistillate aments are two and one-half to four inches long, one-third of an inch thick ; scales are broadly ovate, light brown, scarious, often irregularly three-lobed or parted at the apex which is fringed with short thread-like lobes. Stamens twenty to thirty, with short filaments and large light red anthers, inserted on an oblique, slightly concave, short-stalked disk. Ovary ovate, slightly two-lobed, sessile in a deep cup-shaped disk. Stigmas two, sessile, dilated.

Fruit.—Fruiting aments four to six inches long ; capsules open May or June, are ovate-oblong, often curved, two-valved, light brown. Seeds oblong-ovate, light brown surrounded by slender hairs which surround the aments with masses of snow-white cotton which is wafted with the seed great distances from the tree.

A Staminate and a Pistillate Flower of Balsam, *Populus balsamifera;* enlarged.

The greatest part of the drift timber that we observed on the shores of the Arctic Sea was Balsam Poplar. Its Cree name is Matheh-metoos, which means ugly poplar.

—SIR JOHN FRANKLIN'S Report of Last Journey.

The Balsam or Tacmahac is the largest tree of northwestern America. In the valley of the Mackenzie and upper Yukon it attains magnificent proportions, reaching the height of one hundred feet with a diameter of six or seven, and forms dense forests thousands of square miles in extent. It possesses all the poplar characteristics ; of drooping catkins, whitish trunk, fluttering shimmering leaves, and cottony seeds.

Populus balsamifera candicans is the tree in northeastern United States and Canada known as the Balm of Gilead. It is more and more frequently cultivated as a shade-tree, especially in cities where bituminous coal is habitually used. Three varieties are distinguished in cultivation.

Balsam, *Populus balsamifera.* Fruiting Aments 4′ to 6′ long.

It differs from the specific form in its more spreading branches, in its broader heart-shaped leaves which are more

Trunk of Cottonwood, *Populus deltoides*.

coarsely serrate, and in the pubescence which when young is found on both leaves and petioles. The buds and apex of the growing shoots are heavily laden with a fragrant gummy secretion.

COTTONWOOD

Pópulus deltòides.   Pópulus monilífera.   Pópulus angulàta.

Deltoides, like the Greek letter delta, refers to the shape of the leaf; *monilifera* refers to the necklace-like pistillate ament; *angulata* refers to the angled stem of the shoots.

Comparatively rare and of small size in the eastern states, the Cottonwood is the largest and most abundant tree along the streams between the Appalachian and the Rocky Mountains, reaching the height of a hundred feet.

Winter Branch of Cotton-wood, *Populus deltoides.*

Bark.—On old trees ashy gray and deeply divided into broad rounded ridges broken into scales which cover the light yellow inner bark. On young stems and branchlets smooth light yellow green tinged with red. Young shoots become angular in their second year.

Wood.—Dark brown, sapwood nearly white; light, soft, close-grained, not strong. Warps badly in drying; is now used only in the manufacture of paper-pulp, cheap packing cases and fuel. Sp. gr., 0.3889; weight of cu. ft., 24.24 lbs.

Leaf Buds.—Resinous, shining, acute, chestnut brown, half an inch long. Flower-buds ovate, obtuse, half an inch long.

Leaves —Alternate, three to five inches in length, deltoid or broadly ovate, truncate, slightly cordate or wedge-shaped at base, crenately-serrate with coarse, incurved, glandular teeth. They come from the bud involute, gummy, fragrant with balsamic odor, pale green or tawny, drooping, but at maturity they are thick, bright shining green above, paler green beneath. In autumn they turn a clear bright yellow. Petioles slender, two to three inches long, compressed laterally, yellow or red. Stipules vary in size, caducous.

Flowers.—March, April, before the leaves. Staminate trees densely flowered, aments three to four inches long, one-half inch thick. Scales are scarious,

426

Cottonwood, *Populus deltoides.*

Leaves 3′ to 5′ long.

light brown, smooth, dilated and irregularly divided, caducous. Stamens sixty or more, with short filaments and large dark red anthers, inserted on a broad oblique disk. Pistillate tree sparsely flowered. Ovary subglobose, surrounded at base by a cup-shaped disk. Stigmas three to four, dilated or lobed.

Fruit.—Mature aments eight to twelve inches long. Capsule oblong-ovate, acute at apex, dark green, three to four-valved. Seed oblong-ovate, rounded at apex, surrounded by a tuft of long white or slightly rusty hairs which make up the mass of delicate cotton that has given this tree its common name.

With its massive pale stem, its great spreading limbs and broad head of pendulous branches covered with fluttering leaves of the most brilliant green, *Populus deltoides* is one of the stateliest and most beautiful inhabitants of the forests of eastern America.

—CHARLES S. SARGENT.

This is the tree that under the name of Carolina Poplar is extensively planted in cities. It is proving itself an admirable shade-tree for the cities of the middle west where soft coal is burned. Its smooth glossy leaves have just enough natural varnish about them to keep the soot from clinging, and so they are bright and clean and healthy when those of the elm and the maple are soiled and choked and dying.

WHITE POPLAR. ABELE-TREE

Pópulus álba.

The poplar that with silver lines his leaf.

—COWPER.

The green wood moved and the light poplar shook
Its silver pyramid of leaves.

—BARRY CORNWALL.

The ancients consecrated the White Poplar to time because the leaves are in continual agitation ; and being of a blackish green on one side, with a thick white cotton on the other they were supposed to indicate the alternation of day and night.

—*Sentiment of Flowers.*

The English name of this tree is derived from the Dutch name, Abeel ; it is believed to have come into England by way of Holland.

White Poplar, *Populus alba.*
Leaves 2′ to 3′ long.

The foliage effect of a tree is often compounded of the different colors shown by the two sides of its leaves, of which the White Poplar gives a marked example ; or by new leaves coming out and showing themselves upon the dark background of older leaves as is the case with the locusts and the conifers. This mingling of green and white makes the White Poplar a most effective ornamental tree, but it is never safe to allow it a free hand, for the root is creeping and produces suckers indefinitely, so that in a brief period a parent tree will be surrounded by a numerous and well-grown family that will soon convert the place into a thicket.

The White Poplar is native of both Europe and Asia and was brought to this country very early. In favorable situations it rises to the height of eighty or one hundred feet, with a sturdy trunk and spreading head. The bark of the lower part of the trunk is dark and furrowed and that of the upper part and larger branches is greenish gray with dark markings and blotches. The young shoots are covered with a white down and continue to come out far into midsummer, thus increasing the white appearance of the tree. The leaves are either lobed or coarsely and sparingly toothed, very dark green and smooth above, covered with a thick snowy down beneath, and tremulous like all their kind. With the elm and the early maples it responds to the first warm days of spring and when in full bloom may be said fairly to drip catkins, so covered is every branch with the pendulous aments, three inches long and as large as one's finger.

According to ancient mythology the White Poplar was consecrated to Hercules because he destroyed Cacus in a cavern adjoining Mt. Aventinus, which was covered with these trees ; and in the moment of his triumph he bound his brows with a branch of White Poplar as a token of his victory. Persons offering sacrifices to Hercules were always crowned with branches of this tree ; and all who had gloriously conquered their enemies in battle wore garlands of it, in imitation of Hercules. Homer in the " Iliad " compares

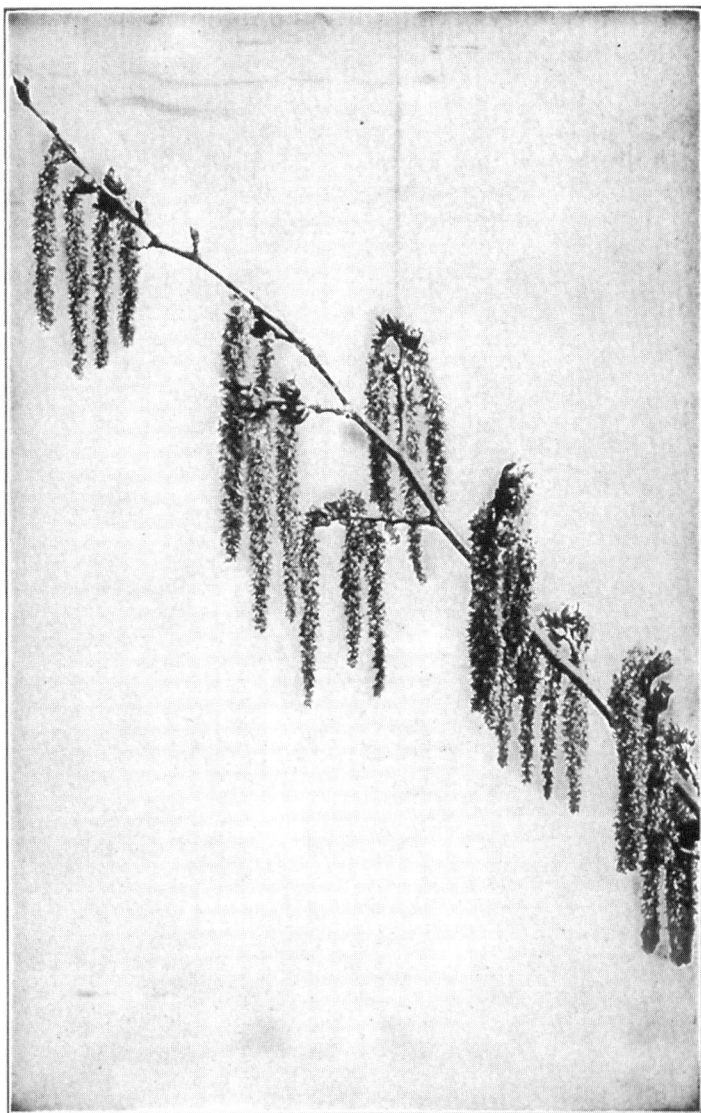

Staminate Aments of White Poplar, *Populus alba*.

the fall of Simoisius when killed by Ajax to that of a poplar.

> So falls a poplar that on watery ground
> Raised high its head with stately branches crowned.

Ovid mentions that Paris had carved the name of Ænone on a poplar, as Shakespeare makes Orlando carve the name of Rosalind upon the trees of the forest of Arden.

Virgil gives directions for the culture of this tree and Horace speaks of the White Poplar as delighting to grow on the banks of rivers.

LOMBARDY POPLAR

Pópulus nìgra itálica.

> The poplar there
> Shoots up its spire, and shakes its leaves i' the sun.
> —BARRY CORNWALL.

The Lombardy Poplar was the first ornamental tree introduced into the United States. A century ago it was extremely fashionable, and although it has fallen from its high estate, nevertheless, it is by no means to be despised. Two things it can do. It can make a narrow leafy wall sooner and more satisfactorily than any other tree, and it can grow by the roadside and not shade the street. It is the only deciduous tree whose branches hug the stem and resulting from that is its peculiar spiry shape, which is individual. When the wind blows, unlike other trees that wave in parts, it waves in one simple sweep from top to bottom.

> The poplar shoot
> Which like a feather waves from head to foot.
> —LEIGH HUNT.

The native home of the Lombardy Poplar has been a subject of much discussion, but good opinion now is that it originated in Afghanistan. It is said to grow wild in a forest near Cabul at an elevation of 7,500 feet above the level of the sea. In early times it was cultivated in western Asia,

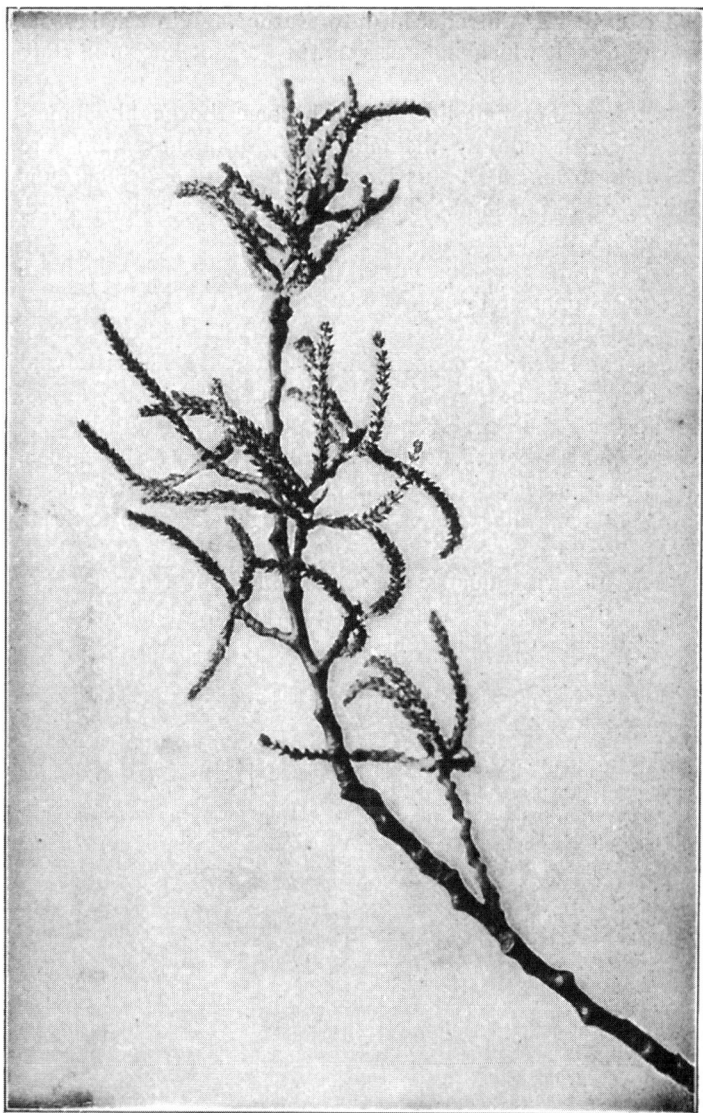

Pistillate Aments of White Poplar, *Populus alba.*

whence it was introduced into Europe. Pliny makes no mention of it which indicates that it was not known in Italy in his time.

Although not long-lived it has become thoroughly domesticated with us. By the middle of April the catkins are drooping from all our native poplars and the Lombardy is not to be left behind. The Abele or White Poplar, indeed, hung out its plumes first of all, but now the Lombardy appears bearing hers—or rather his for they are all staminate —on the topmost branches of the tree. So high are they that it is difficult to get them ere they fall. They appear on the second year's wood and come out stiff and curved and reddish brown but, by and by, like all their kind they droop, and casting their useless pollen to the wind they pass away.

The leaves come out from the bud a lovely yellow green, become firm and darker as the days go by and flutter on appressed stems all summer long, turning in autumn to a rich golden yellow.

The following quotation given by Loudon from the *Gentleman's Magazine* shows the estimation in which the Lombardy Poplar was held in his day:

The Lombardy Poplar, considered as a tall conical mass of foliage, becomes of great importance in scenery when contrasted with round-headed trees. It is a known rule, in the composition of landscape that all horizontal lines should be balanced and supported by perpendicular ones; hence a bridge displaying a long and conspicuous horizontal line, has its effect greatly increased by poplars planted on each end of it. Lombardy Poplars may be advantageously planted whenever there is a continuance of horizontal lines, but they should be so arranged as to form part of those lines and to seem to grow out of them, rather than to break or oppose them in too abrupt a manner. In the case of a stable or other agricultural building where the principal mass extends in length rather than in height it would be wrong to plant Lombardy Poplars or other tall fastigiate trees immediately before the building, but they will have a good effect when placed at the sides or behind it.

This poplar or some equally fastigiate tree should appear in all plantations and belts that are made with a view to picturesque effect. Masses of round-headed trees, though they might be seen to advantage in some situations, when grouped with other objects, yet, when contemplated by themselves are quite uninteresting, from their dull and monotonous appearance, but add poplars and you immediately create an interest and give a certain character to the group which it did not before possess.

Lombardy Poplar, *Populus nigra italica.*
Leaves 1½′ to 3′ long.

GYMNOSPERMAE

PINACEÆ—PINE FAMILY

PINES. CONIFERS

Pinàceæ. Coniferæ.

The Cone Bearers form an extremely interesting natural group of trees. They were so named originally, because of their fruit of which the pine cone is a typical example. They are commonly known as Evergreens because with the exception of the Larch and the Bald Cypress their leaves remain upon the branches over the winter. These, however, are but outward and visible signs of an inward and structural difference which removes the Pines far away from their companions in the forests of to-day. Without going into technical details, two general principles may be noted. In the first place, every plant is rated in the natural system according to the simplicity or complexity of its floral organs, and by its antiquity as indicated in the geological record.

Now the Pines are a survival from the devonian age. They were contemporaries of the Lycopods, the Sigillards and the Cycads, whose remains constitute our coal measures to-day. They are the oldest living representatives of the forests of the ancient world, and they retain the simplicity of floral structure which marked the vegetation of those early times. In the flower of a conifer there is no ovary; the ovule lies naked upon the surface of a scale. There are no stigmas, no insect is needed to aid in the fertilization, the fate of the Pines depends upon the wind. The scientists calmly assign the *Coniferæ* to a place, with the Club-mosses on one side and the Cat-tails on the other. This arrangement fairly takes the breath of a layman or an amateur but it is unassailable, they belong there.

PINE FAMILY

The *Pinaceæ* as now constituted comprises the Pine, Larch, Spruce, Hemlock, Fir, Cypress, Sequoia, Cedar, Arborvitæ, and Juniper. The Yew and the Gingko, a naturalized Chinese tree, belong to the *Taxaceæ* or Yew family.

THE PINE

Pìnus.

There occur within the limits of the United States thirty-nine species of Pine ; seven are found in New England and middle Atlantic states, seven flourish principally in the lowlands of the south and twenty-five are recognized in the west. The central basin of the Mississippi has none. They are tolerant of many conditions of soil and climate ; they flourish on the lowlands at the water's edge ; they climb the mountains to the timber line ; they inhabit the drifting sands upon the shore and keep back the waves of the sea. The method of growth is peculiar and characteristic. The branches are disposed in regular order, circularly in imperfect whorls around the central trunk. One of these whorls is formed each year from the row of branch buds which encircle the main stem and these whorls furnish an easy way to tell the age of young trees. But in the forest these branches die and even the marks of them disappear so that the trunk rises a smooth unbroken shaft for sixty or one hundred feet.

The roots of the Pine never descend deep and they are practically imperishable by the action of the elements alone. When pine lands are cleared, the stumps are often made into fences, by placing them in rows, with their roots interlacing. Such fences are both picturesque and enduring.

The wood may be hard or soft but it is usually resinous. The other products are turpentine, rosin and tar. Turpentine is the resinous exudation of the tree, obtained in this country by cutting a pocket through the bark into the wood and allowing the resinous juices to collect there. This crude turpentine when distilled gives pure spirits of turpentine and rosin. Tar is obtained by the destructive distillation of the wood, which in the southern states is done in a very crude and wasteful manner.

The leaves are of two kinds, primary and secondary. The primary leaves are usually simple scales but sometimes they appear green and linear. The secondary are the evergreen needles which make up the ordinary foliage of the tree. These arise from the axils of the primary leaves in clusters of two to five, surrounded by a sheath which is formed by the union of several bud scales.

In the two-leaved clusters the needles are flat above, convex below ; in those clusters containing three or more, the needles are triangular, more or less keeled. The margins are serrulate, the tips usually callous.

The flowers are naked, monœcious and appear in early spring. The staminate flowers are clustered at the base of the leafy shoots of the year in the axils of bracts ; are yellow, orange, or scarlet ; oval, cylindrical, or oblong. They are composed of many, sessile, two-celled anthers, imbricated in many ranks, upon a central axis, each anther surmounted by a crest-like, semiorbicular connective. Each flower is surrounded at base by an involucre of scale-like bracts, usually definite in number in each species, the two external bracts strongly keeled at the back. The pollen of the pine is very abundant. The pistillate or ovule-bearing flowers are subterminal or lateral, solitary, in pairs, or in clusters, erect or recurved, sessile or pedunculate, borne near the apex of the axils of bud-scales. They are composed of many carpel-like scales, each in the axil of a small bract, and spirally arranged about a central axis. Each bract is rounded, obtuse, and bears on the inner surface near the base two, naked, inverted ovules.

The fruit is a woody strobile called a cone, which matures the second or third year after flowering. The seeds are in pairs, attached at the base in shallow depressions on the inner surface of the scales. As they fall away they take with them portions of the membranaceous lining of the scale which form wing-like attachments. The cotyledons vary from three to eighteen. Pines may be easily raised from seeds which, however, must not be permitted to become dry as they soon lose their vitality.

The world finds many of its most important timber trees among the Pines, and the wood is used in such enormous quantities that the destruction of the forests is inevitable. Even if left to itself it, undoubtedly, would in course of time have succumbed under the hard conditions of the modern world ; but now that man has come into the field with axe and torch, there is no escape, the Pine is doomed ; and must live hereafter, if it lives at all, as a domestic tree, the object of man's care and protection.

As Darwin states the situation, "The Oaks have driven the Pines to the sands." The Pine is handicapped in the race of life because of its inability to reproduce itself with the vigor of other trees. As soon as it is cut down the root dies, there exists no power of sending forth shoots from the stump and forcing new growth. There are exceptions to this rule but this is the general law. The pine seed is light, its vitality fleeting, and it must find favorable conditions at once or its chance is gone. The acorn can wait, and so the Pines have been steadily driven backward by the nut-bearing trees and especially the oaks, foot by foot, from the deep rich soil until the proper characterization of their habitat is not, "Centres of Distribution," but "Areas of Preservation."

The following table will assist in the determination of species.

Leaves 5 in a sheath; 3′ to 4′ long ; cone-scales slightly thickened at the tip.
　　　　　　　　　　　　　　　P. strobus.　White Pine.
Leaves 2 or 3, in a sheath ; cone-scales much thickened at the tip.

　I—*Cones Terminal or Subterminal :*
　　Leaves 2 in a long sheath ; 4′ to 6′ long ; cone ovate-conical, 1½′ to
　　　2¼′ long ; scales without prickles.　*P. resinosa.*　Red Pine.

Leaves 3 in a long sheath; 10′ to 16′ long; cones 6′ to 10′ long; scales prickle-tipped. *P. palustris.* Long-leaved Pine.

I—*Cones Lateral:*

Leaves 3 in a sheath (rarely 2 or 4); 6′ to 10′ long; cones ovate-oblong, 3′ to 5′ long; scales with stout recurved prickles.
P. taeda. Loblolly Pine.

Leaves 3 in a sheath; 3′ to 5′ long; cones ovoid-conical or ovoid, 1′ to 3½′ long, often clustered; scales with short, stout, recurved prickles. *P. rigida.* Pitch Pine.

Leaves 2 in a sheath; ¾′ to 2½′ long; cones oblong-conical, incurved, 1½′ to 2′ long; scales with minute often deciduous prickles.
P. divaricata. Gray Pine.

Leaves 2 in a sheath (rarely 3); 3′ to 5′ long; cones oblong-conical or ovate, 1½′ to 2½′ long; scales with slender prickles.
P. echinata. Yellow Pine.

Leaves 2 in a sheath; 1½′ to 3′ long; cones oblong-conical often curved, 1½′ to 3′ long; scales with slender, straight or incurved prickles. *P. virginiana.* Jersey Pine.

Leaves 2 in a sheath; 4′ to 6′ long; cones ovate, 2′ to 3′ long; scales spineless; cultivated.
P. laricio. var. *austriaca.* Austrian Pine.

Leaves 2 in a sheath; 2′ to 4′ long, twisted, bluish green; cones ovoid-conic, 2′ to 3′ long; scales spineless; cultivated.
P. sylvestris. Scotch Pine. Scotch Fir.

WHITE PINE. WEYMOUTH PINE

Pìnus stròbus.

Strobus, the name of a Persian tree now unknown. Weymouth is the name common in England because this pine was first cultivated by Lord Weymouth.

When growing under favorable conditions reaches the height of one hundred and twenty feet with a diameter of three to four feet, rarely, it becomes much higher. Flourishes on sandy soil especially that formed by disintegration of granite rock. Roots stout, horizontal, practically imperishable. Branches horizontal and in whorls. Grows rapidly and forms dense forests. Ranges from Newfoundland to Manitoba, south along the Alleghanies to Georgia and southwest to the valley of the Iowa. Ascends 4,300 feet in North Carolina and 2,300 feet in the Adirondacks.

PINE FAMILY

Bark.—On old trees dark gray, divided by shallow fissures into broad scaly ridges. On young stems and branches, thin, smooth, lustrous, brownish green. Branchlets slender at first covered with rusty tomentum, later they become dark yellow brown, smooth, becoming darker as the branch becomes older. Charged with tannic acid.

Wood.—Light brown, sapwood nearly white; light, soft, compact, straight-grained, very resinous, easily worked, takes a fine polish. Pumpkin pine is the close-grained valuable wood of large trees that have grown to a great age on rich well-drained soil. Used for lumber, shingles, cabinet-making, interior of houses, masts and spars of vessels. Sp. gr., 0.3854; weight of cu. ft., 24.02 lbs.

Buds.—The branch buds are ovate-oblong, acuminate, covered by ovate-lanceolate, light brown scales; terminal bud usually about one-half an inch long, sometimes as short as the lateral ones that surround it.

Leaves.—In clusters of fives; they come out of the buds which are enclosed under the scales of the branch bud. The buds of leaf clusters are covered by eight scales which lengthen with the growing leaves. The leaves when full grown are soft, slender, bluish green, glaucous, three to five inches long, sharply serrate, mucronate with pale tip; usually turn yellow and fall in September of second year. Fibro-vascular bundle one; sheath loose, deciduous.

White Pine, *Pinus strobus.* Leaves 3′ to 4′ long.

Flowers.—June. Staminate flowers oval, light brown, about one-third of an inch long, surrounded by six to eight involucral bracts; anthers with short crests; involucral bracts six to eight. Pistillate flowers cylindrical, subterminal, about one-fourth an inch long; scales pinkish purple on the margins; peduncles stout, clothed with bracts. Pollen very abundant.

Cones.—Subterminal, drooping, cylindrical, often slightly curved, four to six inches long, one inch in diameter. Mature in autumn of second year; open and discharge seeds during September and fall gradually during the winter and early spring. Scales one and one-fourth to one and one-half inches long. Seven-eighths of an inch wide, oblong-ovate, slightly thickened at apex, obtuse or nearly truncate, without spine or prickle; seeds red brown, mottled; wing nearly an inch long; cotyledons eight to ten.

> Its cloudy boughs singing as suiteth the pine,
> To snow bearded sea kings, old songs of the brine.
> —James Russell Lowell.

444

White Pine, *Pinus strobus*.
Leaves 5 in a sheath, 3′ to 4′ long.

PINE FAMILY

The murmuring pines and the hemlocks
Bearded with moss and in garments green, indistinct in the twilight
Stand like Druids of eld with voices sad and prophetic,
Stand like harpers hoar with beards that rest on their bosoms.
—HENRY W. LONGFELLOW.

Many voices there are in Nature's choir, and none but were good to hear
Had we mastered the laws of their music well, and could read their meaning
clear ;
But we who can feel at Nature's touch, cannot think as yet with her thought ;
And I only know that the sough of the pines with a spell of its own is fraught.
—FRASER'S MAGAZINE.

The White Pine is the tallest, the most stately and beautiful of all our eastern conifers, it is the most ornamental for parks and lawns, as well as by far the most valuable economically. In the forest it grows straight as an arrow, towering branchless until it gains the forest roof where it spreads out a more or less open head ; in the open it takes on the form of all free growing trees, the lower branches live and lengthen, the trunk gets fat and sturdy. But no one pine is ever so beautiful as a grove of pines. The great shafts towering upward like corinthian columns—the ceaseless murmur of the wind in the tree-tops—the soft brown carpet of fallen needles —the subdued light—the stillness—the absence of joyous life —all unite to induce feelings of reverence and awe.

The White Pine bears the smoothest bark of all the pines, on old trunks it does indeed fissure and separate into small plates but they are simply loose at the edges and do not scale off. On young stems the bark is very smooth, a reddish green or reddish brown and covered in summer with a very striking ashy or pearly gloss. The primary leaves are simply thin and chaff-like bud-scales, from their axils proceed the secondary needle-shaped evergreen leaves in clusters of five. A cross section of these needle-shaped leaves is triangular. The edges are serrate. The massed foliage is beautiful ; the needles are bright bluish green, soft, slender, delicate, and disposed in pretty tassels upon the branch. Although, apparently, to an evergreen all seasons are the same, yet the White Pine has a fashion of folding its needles

Trunk of White Pine, *Pinus strobus*.
A Cultivated Tree.

together when cold weather comes as if it were preparing for a long winter's sleep.

The cones are long, slender, loose, and terminal, without spine or prickle, and fall in the winter of their second year. The seeds should be sown in the spring and covered lightly, if at all. The seedlings are delicate and should always be protected from both wind and sun.

The expression, " Bearded with moss," is more than a poet's fancy. Tufts of gray moss are found abundantly on the trunks of all pines that grow in damp, close, northern woods, the thread is round and fine like a hair, and a bunch of the moss constantly suggests the gray beard of an old man. This moss plays an important part in the domestic life of the northern Indians, it is in this warm, soft substance that the Indian babies are packed for transportation on their cradle boards. A good Indian mother gathers it by the bushel, it is like linen for the tender flesh, it is soft, resinous, aseptic, porous, healthful; and the small brown baby swathed in moss may be quite as well off physically as his civilized neighbor clothed in flannel and linen.

The economic value of the White Pine gives to its life history an interest which under other circumstances it might not have. It is clear that the commercial supply will soon be exhausted. The best pines of the northern states have already been cut, a few forest tracts still remain but they are in process of extinction.

The White Pine has considerable vitality and has shown itself capable of taking possession of the abandoned lands of New England, where vigorous young forests are springing up on land worthless for any other crop. But it cannot come again on a tract that has been devastated by fire.

White Pine, *Pinus strobus.*
Cones 4′ to 6′ long.

RED PINE. NORWAY PINE. CANADIAN PINE

Pìnus resinòsa.

Usual'y seventy to eighty feet high, with straight trunk two to three feet diameter ; in old age forming an open picturesque head. Range is northward from Newfoundland to Manitoba, in United States is most abundant in Michigan, Wisconsin, and Minnesota. Found on dry gravelly or light sandy soils, or dry rocky ridges. Grows rapidly in cultivation.

Bark.—Bright reddish brown, divided by shallow fissures into shallow scaly ridges. Branchlets stout, smooth, pale orange at first, then darker orange and finally reddish brown. Charged with tannic acid.

Wood.—Pale red, sapwood yellow or white ; light, hard, close-grained. Contains broad, dark-colored, very resinous bands of small summer cells. Used for buildings, bridges, piles, masts and spars ; largely exported from Canada. Sp. gr., 0.4854 ; weight of cu. ft., 30.25 lbs.

Buds.—Branch-buds ovate, acute, one to three-fourths of an inch long, covered with loosely imbricated, pale brown scales ; bases of scales persistent for several years.

Leaves.—In clusters of two ; four to six inches long, slender, flexible, dark green, shining, serrulate, acute with callous tips ; fibro-vascular bundles two ; sheaths firm, persistent, half an inch to an inch long.

Flowers.—Staminate flowers borne in a dense cluster on the recent shoots, occupying the place of the leaves for an inch or more, linear-oblong, one-fourth to three-fourths of an inch long ; anthers dark reddish purple with orbicular toothed crests ; scales six, deciduous by articulation above the base. Pistillate flowers terminal, almost globular ; scales scarlet, ovate, borne on stout peduncles covered with pale brown bracts.

Red Pine, *Pinus resinosa.*
Leaves 4′ to 6′ long.

Cones.—Subterminal, solitary or clustered, mature the second year, ovate-conical, two to two and one-half inches long, smooth, scales slightly thickened at the apex, rounded, devoid of spine or prickle.   Seeds oval, compressed, one-eighth of an inch long, chest-nut brown, mottled ; wings three-quarters of an inch long one-quarter wide, broadest below the middle.

The Red Pine is a northern tree and finds its most con-genial home in Newfoundland and westward along the north-ern shore of the St. Lawrence, through Ontario and Mani-toba, coming but sparingly into the United States. It does not make close forests, hence it is not a timber tree. It grows when possible in the open ; in the forest one looks for it at the edge of a lake where, at least, it may have light and air and freedom on one side. It is usually found alone on dry, sandy, gravelly or rocky places, never on flat lands with cold clay bottoms. It is a very beautiful tree. The branches are in distinct whorls, the branchlets are stout and covered with a thick false bark, composed of the bases of the leaf scales which run down along the stem. The leaves are four to six inches long, in clusters of two, and form very conspicu-ous tufts at the end of the branchlets. The sheaths are long and it is a common amusement among children to pull out one leaf, put the point of the remaining one into the vacant place, and so make a link of a leafy chain.

The glory of the Red Pine is its staminate blossoms. Imagine a tree, eighteen inches in diameter and fifty feet high, branching near the ground as regularly as an oak and stand-ing in an open space on the bank of a northern lake. The dark green leaves covered with pale bloom give a shim-mering effect as they respond to the slightest movements of the wind. From top to bottom, on the tip of every branch may be seen in early spring the dark red tassels of staminate blossoms, short and thick and crowded forming a cluster that so far as effect goes is a deep red rose. The supreme mo-ment is brief, the flowers wither very soon, cast their pollen to the wind and are gone. Well developed Red Pine trees are so rare in northern Minnesota that they are landmarks ; the finest are found on the Indian reservations where they have escaped the axe and the torch. The cones are short, unarmed, ovate-conical, a bright cinnamon brown like the bark, and fairly clear of resin. They are scattered along the branches and are not very numerous. They hold their seeds fairly well. In the spring as the snow begins to go and the birds come back, the little red-breasted cross-bill stops on its way north to feed on these seeds. The birds come in flocks and take possession of a tree ; and it is interesting to see their little hooked bills jerk out the seeds from the cones. The Red Pine should find a place in every park.

LOBLOLLY PINE. OLD FIELD PINE

Pìnus taèda.

Taeda, the torch, was the classical name of a resinous pine tree.

Varying from eighty to one hundred feet with a tall straight trunk. A southern tree but ranging as far north as New Jersey. Inhabits the low lands adjacent to tide-water : rarely makes pure forests. Loves the swamps, but is found in the sandy borders of Pine-barrens. In the southwest it becomes an important timber tree. Grows rapidly; tap root large and strong. Fragrant.

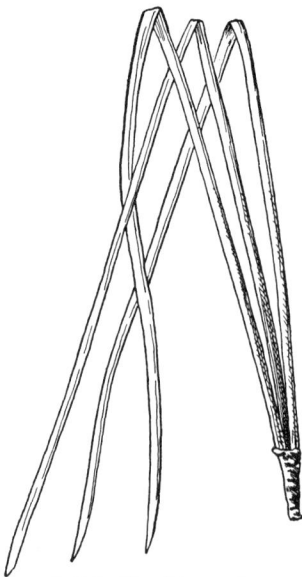

Loblolly Pine, *Pinus taeda.*
Leaves 6′ to 10′ long.

Bark.—Reddish brown with shallow fissures and broad, flat, scaly ridges. B r a n c h l e t s glaucous, smooth, yellow brown and covered with the brown, reflexed, inner scales of the branch-buds which persist for several years.

Wood.—Variable in value, light brown, sapwood pale. The more northern tree produces lumber which is weak, brittle, coarse-grained, not durable ; the southern tree produces a better quality ; resinous.

Buds.—Branch - buds, obovate-oblong, acute or acuminate at apex, with brown scales which terminate in long, slender, dark tips. Terminal buds much larger than the lateral buds.

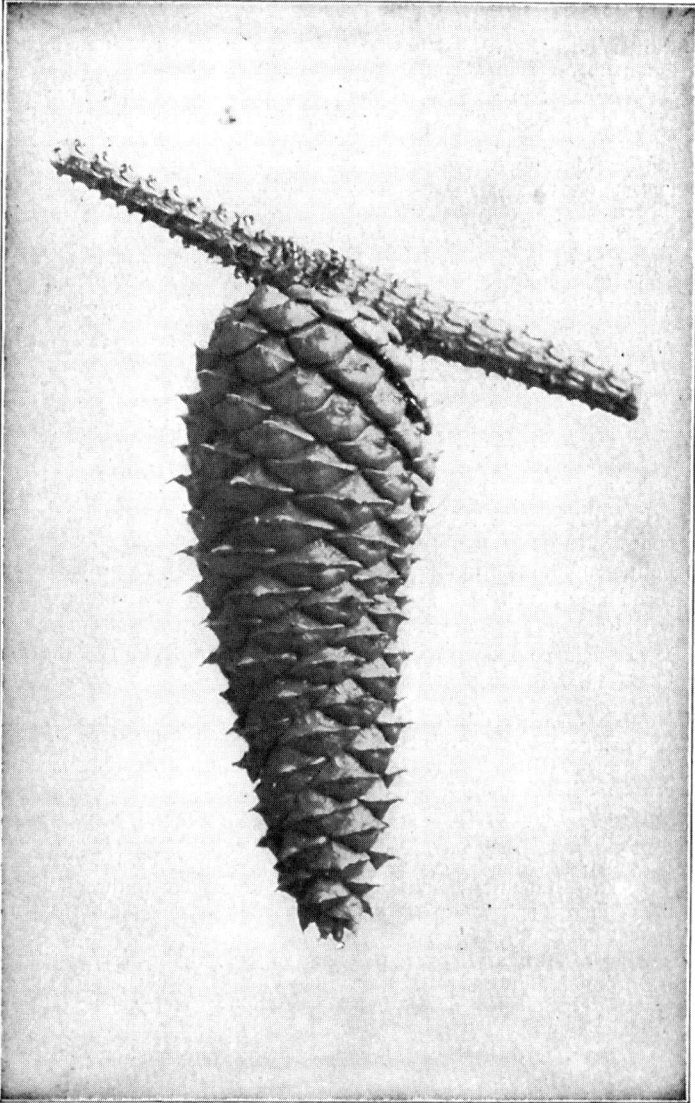

Loblolly Pine, *Pinus taeda.*
Cones 3′ to 5′ long.

PINE FAMILY

Leaves.—In clusters of three, slender, stiff, slightly twisted, acute with callous tips, serrulate, pale green, glaucous, six to ten inches long; fibro-vascular bundles two. Sheaths close, thin.

Flowers.—April, May. Staminate flowers clustered, cylindrical, three-fourths of an inch long; anthers yellow with rounded denticulate crests; involucral bracts eight to ten. Pistillate flowers lateral, not far from the apex of the growing shoot which is several inches long before they appear; solitary or in pairs, sometimes in clusters of three. Scales yellow; peduncles short, covered by brown acuminate bracts.

Cones.—Lateral, ovate-oblong, three to five inches long. Scales armed with stout recurved prickles, slightly concave, rounded at the apex. Seeds dark brown blotched with black, rhomboidal; wings thin, fragile, three-fourths of an inch long.

Scales thickened at apex, transverse ridge prominent, armed with stout recurved prickles, slightly concave, rounded.

PITCH PINE. TORCH PINE

Pinus rígida.

Usually fifty or sixty feet in height, with short trunk; bears cones when quite small; capable of producing vigorous shoots from both stem and stump after injury by fire. Bears both primary and secondary leaves. Ranges from New Brunswick to Georgia, westward to Kentucky and Tennessee. Found in dry sands or rocky soil and in cold deep swamps. Ascends 3,000 feet above the sea in Virginia.

Bark.—Dark reddish brown, with deep fissures and broad, flat, scaly ridges. On young stems thin and broken into plate-like, dark, red brown strips. Branchlets smooth, bright green at first, become orange yellow, finally a dark gray brown.

Wood.—Light brown or red, sapwood yellow or white; light, soft, not strong, coarse-grained, durable, very resinous. Used for lumber, fuel, and charcoal. Sp. gr., 0.5151; weight of cu. ft., 32.10 lbs.

Buds.—Branch-buds obovate-oblong, acute, one to three-fourths of an inch long; scales dark brown, shining, fringed; bases persistent for years.

Leaves.—Primary leaves are often borne on vigorous shoots starting from an injured trunk. Secondary leaves in clusters of three, stout, rigid, dark yellow green, three to five inches long; fibro-vascular bundles two; sheaths one-half to one inch long.

Flowers.—April, May. Staminate flowers clustered on the stem, cylindrical, three-fourths of an inch long; anthers yellow with nearly orbicular entire crests; involucral bracts six to eight. Pistillate flowers lateral, clustered; scales pale green tinged with rose, acute, with slender tips; peduncles covered with dark brown bracts.

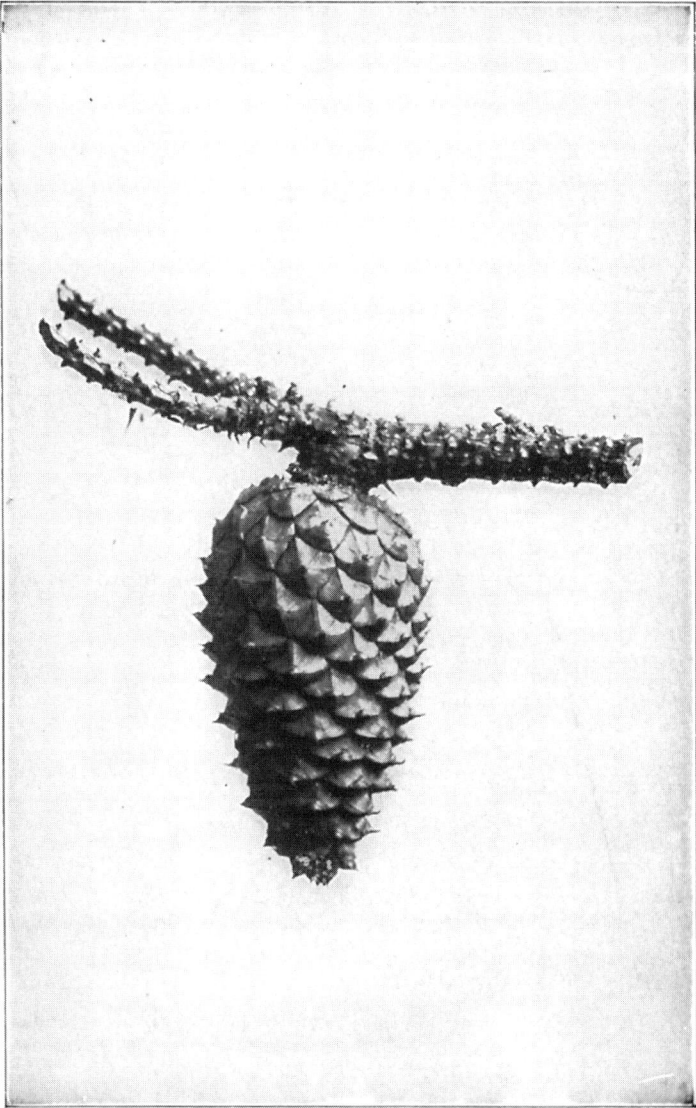

Pitch Pine, *Pinus rigida.*
Cones 1′ to 3′ long.

Cones.—Ovoid-conical or ovate, one to three inches long, often clustered ; scales thickened at apex, the transverse ridge acute, armed with short recurved prickles, flat. Often persist on the branches for several years. Seeds nearly triangular, dark brown mottled with black ; wings three-fourths of an inch long, broadest below the middle.

The Pitch Pine is, perhaps, the most virile of the genus ; it certainly flourishes under most adverse conditions, for it will "cling like a limpet to the rocks," or it will go down to the barren sands of the sea-shore and cover vast tracts so densely that the moving dunes can move no more. It is even tolerant of a salt sea bath. It is the only pine that can send forth shoots after injury by fire.

Its economic value is not great, the wood is too thoroughly saturated with resin to be valuable as lumber. Its value is chiefly as fuel. Tar and turpentine can be obtained from it but much more easily and of better quality from the southern pines. In dense woods the trunk grows erect but in the open it becomes tortuous, angled and often picturesque.

Pitch Pine, *Pinus rigida.* Leaves 3′ to 5′ long.

JERSEY PINE. SCRUB PINE

Pìnus virginiàna. Pìnus inóps.

Usually thirty or forty feet high with a short trunk, long horizontal branches in remote whorls forming a broad pyramidal head. Found on light sandy soil and especially in Virginia and Maryland on exhausted lands. In Indiana it is found one hundred feet high. In Virginia it ascends 3,300 feet above the sea.

Bark.—Dark brown with reddish tinge, divided by shallow fissures into flat scaly plates. Branchlets are pale green and glaucous at first, sometimes with purple tinge, finally becoming pale gray brown.

Wood.—Pale orange, sapwood nearly white ; light, soft, brittle, slightly resinous. Sp. gr., 0.5309 : weight of cu. ft., 33.09 lbs.

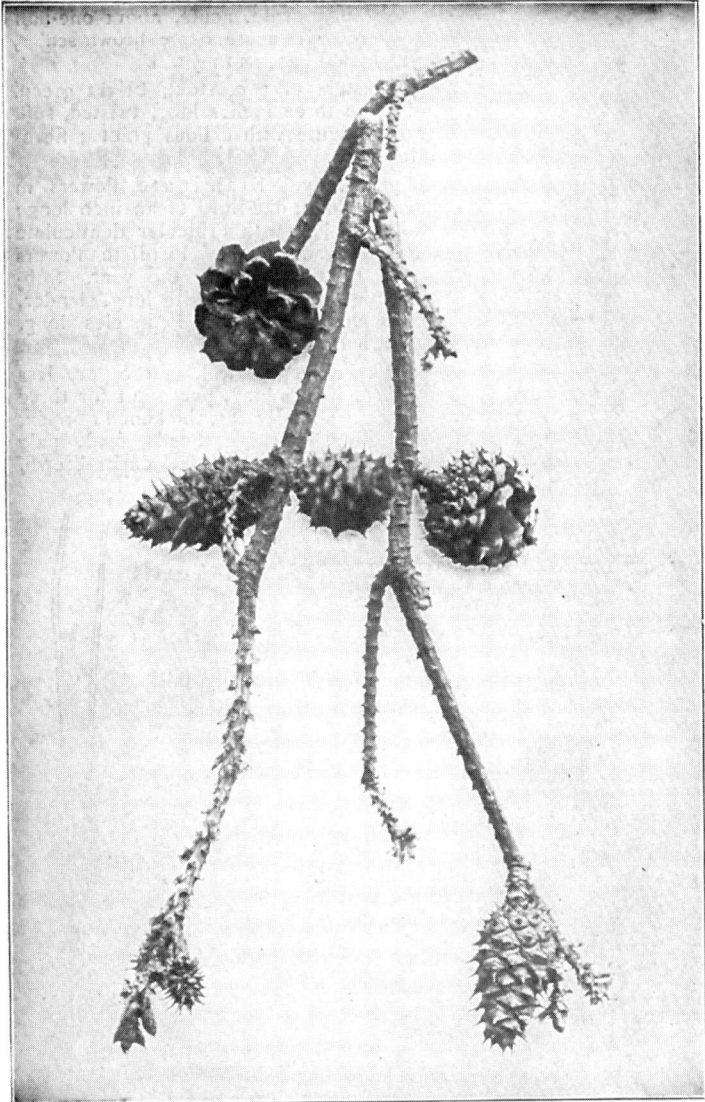

Jersey Pine, *Pinus virginiana.*
Leaves 1′ to 3′ long.   Cones of one, two, and three years' growth.

Buds.—Branch-buds ovate, acute, about one-half an inch long, covered with acute, ovate, brown scales, leaving their thickened base as they fall.

Leaves.—In clusters of two, stout, bright green, one and one-half to three inches long, twisted, soft, fragrant, serrulate, acute with callous points ; fibro-vascular bundles two.

Flowers.—April, May. S t a m i n a t e flowers in crowded clusters, oblong, one-third of an inch long ; anthers brownish yellow with orbicular denticulate crests ; involucral bracts eight. Pistillate flowers near the middle of the shoot of the year. Sub-globose, scales pale green, ovate with long, slender, reddish tips ; scales orbicular. Peduncles long, covered with brown bracts.

Cones.—Lateral, oblong-conical, more or less curved, one to three inches long, persistent for three or four years. Scales nearly flat, thickened at apex, armed with persistent prickles. Seeds oval, pale brown ; wings broadest at middle, dark brown, thin, smooth, one-third of an inch long.

Jersey Pine, *Pinus virginiana.* Leaves 1½′ to 3′ long.

YELLOW PINE. SHORTLEAF PINE. SPRUCE PINE

Pìnus echinàta.

Usually eighty or one hundred feet high, with a tall tapering stem and a short pyramidal head of slender branches. Trunks injured by fire will often produce shoots which are covered with lanceolate, long-pointed, gray green primary leaves. Ranges in sandy soil from southern New York to Florida and west to Illinois, Kansas and Texas. Often forms pure forests. A valuable timber tree, sometimes worked for turpentine. Fruits when very young.

Bark.—Pale reddish brown, irregularly fissured, covered with small appressed scales. Branchlets stout, pale green or purple, glaucous, later become red brown, finally dark brown.

Wood.—Orange or yellow brown, sapwood nearly white ; varies in quality, the best is heavy, hard, strong, coarse-grained, very resinous. Sp. gr., 0. 6104 ; weight of cu. ft., 38.04 lbs.

Leaves.—Borne in clusters of two, or of three,

Yellow Pine, *Pinus echinata.* Leaves 3′ to 5′ long.

458

Yellow Pine, *Pinus echinata*.
Cones 1½′ to 2′ long.

rarely of four, slender, dark blue green, serrulate, acute, with callous tips, soft, three to five inches long ; fibro-vascular bundles two. Sheaths thin, silvery white at first, later become dark grayish brown. Persist from two to five years.

Flowers.—Staminate flowers in short crowded clusters, near the tip of the growing shoots, oblong-cylindrical, three-quarters of an inch long ; anthers pale purple with orbicular, slightly denticulate crests ; involucral bracts eight to ten. Pistillate flowers in clusters of two, three or four, subterminal, oblong or subglobose, one-third of an inch long ; scales ovate, rose pink, with slender tips ; bracts nearly orbicular.

Cones.—Lateral, very abundant, ovate or oblong-conical, one and a half to two and a half inches long, persist several years. Scales nearly flat, obtuse, thickened at apex, marked with a prominent transverse ridge, armed with small, slender, nearly straight, deciduous prickles. Seeds triangular, brown, mottled with black ; wings broadest at the middle, thin, pale brown, one-half an inch long.

GRAY PINE. JACK PINE. SCRUB PINE

Pinus divaricàta.

Frequently seventy feet high with straight branchless trunk, long spreading branches forming an open symmetrical head ; often much shorter and sometimes shrubby. Fruits when very young. A northern tree, ranging from Nova Scotia southward to Maine, New Hampshire, and Vermont, westward to northern Indiana and Illinois, and in the northwest to the valley of the Mackenzie River, where it is the only pine tree. In sandy soil, sometimes forming exclusive forests.

Gray Pine, *Pinus divaricata.* Leaves 1′ to 2½′ long.

Bark.—Dark brown with reddish tinge, with shallow rounded ridges separating into small appressed scales. Branchlets slender, tough, flexible, pale yellow green, becoming dark reddish purple and later dark purplish brown.

Wood.—Pale brown, rarely yellow, sapwood nearly white ; light, soft, not strong, close-grained. Used for fuel, railway ties, and posts. Indians prefer it for frames of canoes.

Buds.—Branch-buds ovate with rounded apex, terminal bud one-fourth of an inch long, as long again as the lateral buds. Covered with ovate-lanceolate pale brown scales with spreading tips, whose bases persist after the body of the scale has fallen and roughen the branch.

Gray Pine, *Pinus divaricata*.
Cones 1½′ to 2′ long.

Leaves.—In clusters of two, three-fourths to two and one-half inches long, stout, curved, divergent, dark grayish green, serrulate, acute with short callous point, persistent until second or third year ; fibro-vascular bundles two. Sheaths short, loose, pale brown and silvery white.

Flowers.—April, May. Staminate flowers in crowded clusters, about an inch and a half in length ; oblong, one-half inch long ; anthers yellow ; crests orbicular, slightly denticulate ; involucral bracts six to eight. Pistillate flowers borne in clusters of two to four on the terminal shoot, subglobose ; scales dark purple, ovate with short incurved tips. Peduncles stout, short, covered with large, brown, ovate bracts.

Cones.—Lateral, one and one-half to two inches long, oblong-conical, oblique, incurved. Scales thin, stiff, thickened at apex and armed with small incurved often deciduous prickles. Persist for many years. Seeds nearly triangular, almost black ; wings pale, shining, one-third of an inch long. Cotyledons four to five.

The Gray Pine is the Scrub Pine of northern latitudes. In good soil it makes a fair tree, but in barren soils one finds miles and miles of scrub. The leaf is bluish green covered with so marked a gray bloom that the foliage mass is positively gray. The leaves are in clusters of two, short, recurved, and divergent. The staminate flowers are greenish yellow, more conspicuous than those of the White Pine, not so large as those of the Red Pine, and for the few days they are in bloom the tree is noticeable. Cones are small, twisted, and look not fully developed for they do not open evenly. They are light gray ; sometimes they shine almost silvery out of the grayish mass of foliage.

AUSTRIAN PINE

Pìnus larìcio austrìaca.

The Austrian Pine is extensively planted throughout the north in parks and lawns. The tree is native to the mountains of eastern Europe, and there reaches the height of one hundred and twenty feet. It bears our climate well, endures extremes of both heat and cold, will flourish in any fair soil, and always has a strong healthy look. Its leaves are not

Austrian Pine, *Pinus austriaca*.

Cones 2′ to 3′ long.

unlike those of the Red Pine, they are from three to five inches long borne in clusters of two, are a bright dark green, and appear tufted on the branches. The cones are very like those of the Red Pine, ovate, two to three inches long, and the scales are destitute of prickles.

SCOTCH PINE. SCOTCH FIR

Pìnus sylvéstris.

The Scotch Pine or Fir as it is called in England is perfectly hardy throughout the north, where it is planted both as an ornamental tree in parks and as a windbreak on the prairies. It is a tree of wide distribution throughout Europe and Asia, and is in fact, the principal timber pine of the eastern continent. But in the United States though beautiful when young, it is not long-lived, and succumbs to disease and insect enemies at the age of thirty or forty years.

The leaves are in clusters of two, an inch and a half to two and a half in length, stout, rigid, slightly twisted, bluish or grayish green. The cones are ovate, from an inch to an inch and a quarter long and abundant on the tree.

WHITE SPRUCE

Pìcea canadénsis. Pìcea álba.

A slender, conical, evergreen tree, usually sixty to seventy feet high, its greatest height one hundred and fifty feet. Resinous; foliage ill-smelling. Ranges from Newfoundland to Hudson Bay and Alaska, southward to Maine, New York, and Michigan, west to South Dakota, Montana, and British Columbia.

Bark.—Light grayish brown, separates into thin plate-like scales. Branchlets at first stout, pale gray green, smooth, during first winter orange brown, later become dark grayish brown.

Wood.—Light yellow; light, soft, weak, straight-grained, satiny surface. Used for construction, interior finish of houses, and wood pulp.

Winter Buds.—Light chestnut brown, ovate, obtuse, one-eighth to one-fourth of an inch long. Branch-buds usually three.

Scotch Pine, *Pinus sylvestris.*
Cones 1′ to 1¼′ long.

Leaves.—Spirally disposed, but crowded on the upper side of the branches by the twisting of those on the lower ; they point forward especially near the extremities of the branchlets. Linear, four-sided, jointed at the base to short persistent sterigmata, incurved, acute or acuminate at apex, with a rigid callous tip. Pale bluish-green, hoary at first, becoming dark blue green at maturity, one-third to three-fourths of an inch long.

Flowers.—April, May. Monœcious. Staminate flowers oblong-cylindrical, axillary, one-half to three-fourths of an inch long, pedicels half an inch long ; anthers pale red, becoming yellow from abundance of pollen. Pistillate flowers oblong-cylindrical ; scales broad, pale red or yellow green ; bracts nearly orbicular, denticulate. Ovules two, naked upon the base of each scale.

Cones.—Oblong-cylindrical, slender, narrowed at each end, about two inches long ; scales nearly orbicular, obscurely striate, margins entire, pale brown, thin, lustrous, falling in autumn or early winter. Seeds pale brown ; wings narrow, oblique at apex.

Three spruces are found east of the Rocky Mountains, the White, the Black and the Red. All are trees of a northern range belonging to regions of short summers and long winters, or in a southern latitude they seek high elevations. They are evergreen, cone-like trees with slender spiry tops, tall tapering trunks, and slender, whorled, horizontal branches with branchlets twice and three times divided, and in old trees pendent. The spiry tops of the spruces outlined against the sky is one of the characteristics of a northern landscape.

They differ from the pines in that their leaves are much shorter and placed singly upon the branches instead of being clustered in groups. The arrangement of the leaves is characteristic. They are set thickly on all sides of the branches. They are borne upon short, rhombic, woody bases called sterigmata, and falling when dry, they leave the bare twigs covered with low truncate projections.

The White Spruce attains the greatest height of any of the spruces, sometimes reaching one hundred and fifty feet, with a trunk three feet in diameter. In the northwest it touches the shore of the Arctic ocean and on the Atlantic coast it extends down to southern Maine ; often growing so close to the shore that it is bathed in the spray of the ocean. The foliage of the White Spruce is rich and beautiful but its

Sprays of White Spruce, *Picea canadensis.*
Cones 1½′ to 2′ long.

odor is rather unpleasant and this alone will often suffice to distinguish it from the Black Spruce. No other spruce grows more luxuriantly or is more ornamental in parks and lawns while in the vigor of youth, but as it becomes older it finds the mild climate of the northern states uncongenial and soon perishes or lives on in unsightly decrepitude. Resin exudes from cuts and gashes and hardens into a white gum.

RED SPRUCE

Picea rùbens.

A conical evergreen tree usually seventy to eighty feet high, occasionally one hundred feet, and upon its northern limit becoming a semi-prostrate shrub. Ranges from Nova Scotia to North Carolina and Tennessee. Grows slowly ; roots thick ; resinous.

Bark.—Reddish brown broken into thin irregular scales. Branchlets at first stout, pale green, pubescent, later become bright reddish-brown or orange brown, finally becoming dark and scaly.

Wood.—Pale, slightly tinged with red, sapwood paler; light, soft close-grained, with satiny surface. Used in construction and in production of wood pulp, also for sounding boards of musical instruments. Sp. gr., 0.4516 ; weight of cu. ft., 28.13 lbs.

Winter Buds.—Pale reddish brown, ovate, acute, one-fourth to one-third of an inch long.

Leaves.—Linear, four-sided, tipped at apex with callous point, pale bluish green at first, dark shining green when mature ; midrib prominent ; one-half to five-eighths of an inch long ; they stand out from all sides of the branch, point forward, and are more or less incurved ; jointed at the base to short, persistent sterigmata.

Flowers.—April, May. Monœcious. Staminate flowers oval, almost sessile, one-half inch long ; anther crests bright red, toothed. Pistillate flowers, oblong, cylindrical, three-quarters of an inch long. Scales rounded, thin, erose at margin ; bracts rounded and laciniate ; ovules two, naked on base of scale.

Cones.—Ovate-oblong, light reddish brown, shining, apex gradually acute, one and one-quarter to two inches long. Scales rounded, entire or slightly toothed, striate. Seeds dark brown ; wings short and broad.

The Red Spruce was for many years confounded with the Black Spruce ; Professor Sargent draws a wide distinction between them.

Fruiting Spray of Red Spruce, *Picea rubens*.
Leaves 1¼′ to 2′ long.

PINE FAMILY

The cones of the Red Spruce are large and fall during the first winter. Those of the Black Spruce are persistent for many years. Resinous exudations both of Red and Black Spruce are used as chewing gums ; and the branches of both are used in the domestic manufacture of beer.

Black Spruce is a tree of the far north existing but precariously south of the northern border of the United States, while the Red Spruce is an Appalachian tree attaining its greatest dimensions in northern New Hampshire and Pennsylvania.

BLACK SPRUCE.

Picea mariàna. Picea nigra.

An evergreen conical tree, maximum height one hundred feet, ordinary height fifty to eighty ; at the extreme north it dwarfs to a shrub. Branches slender, usually pendulous with upward curve forming an open and irregular head. Prefers a hilly and mountainous region with an altitude of 1,200 to 2,000 feet, but is also found in low swampy valleys. Resinous. Roots thick, wide spreading near the surface, rootlets long, flexible, tough. Ranges from Newfoundland to Hudson Bay and the Mackenzie River ; southward in Michigan, Wisconsin, Minnesota.

Bark.—Covered with thin, appressed, grayish brown scales. Branchlets at first pale green, pubescent, later they become cinnamon brown, finally dark brown. Bark has no commercial value.

Wood.—Pale, often with reddish tinge, sapwood pure white ; light, soft, weak. Used for wood pulp and house building, soundingboards for pianos ; fuel value slight. Sp. gr., 0.5272 ; weight of cu. ft., 32.86 lbs.

Winter Buds.—Branch buds usually three, light reddish-brown, ovate, one-eighth of an inch long.

Leaves.—Spirally disposed, thickly set and spreading in all directions ; jointed at the base to short, persistent, pubescent sterigmata on which they are sessile ; falling away in drying, the bare twigs appear covered with low truncate projections. Linear, one-fourth to three-fourths of an inch long, four-sided ; ribbed above and below, abruptly contracted at apex into a callous tip, slightly incurved above the middle. Pale blue green at first, dark bluish-green at maturity, hoary on lower surface, lustrous on the upper. Persistent for several years.

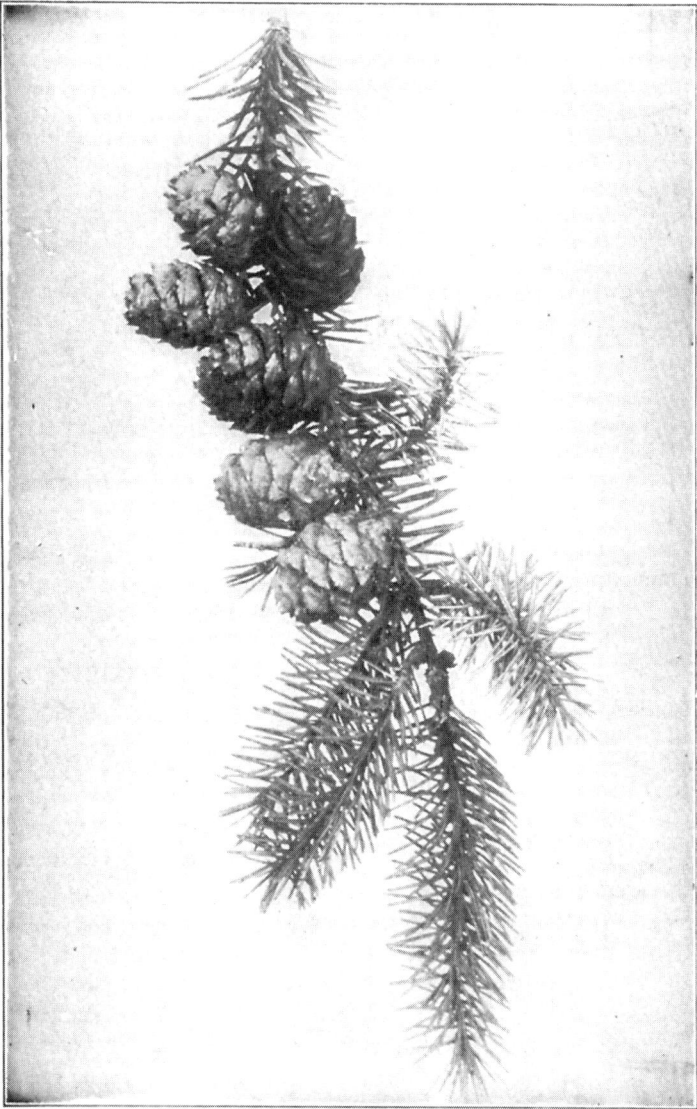

Fruiting Spray of Black Spruce, *Picea mariana*.

Cones 1' to 1½' long.

Flowers.—May, June ; monœcious. Staminate flowers one-eighth inch long, in subglobose axillary aments ; anthers dark red with nearly circular, toothed crests. Pistillate aments oblong-cylindrical with obovate purple scales ; bracts purple ; ovules two, naked on the base of each scale.

Cones.—Terminal on short branches, pale yellow brown, oval or ovate ; one to one and one-half inches long ; incurved at base, discharging their seeds slowly, and persistent for several years. Scales ridged, rounded at apex, margins pale, erose, or jagged. Seeds small, wings pale brown, shining, one-half inch long.

The Black Spruce is essentially a Canadian tree growing abundantly in the Labrador peninsula and forming great forests in Manitoba. Comparatively rare in the United States, it is found principally along the northern border of New England and New York and most abundantly on the lake-shores in Minnesota, Wisconsin, and Michigan. It has very little beauty except when young. Then the branches form a most regular and symmetrical outline, but as age comes on it loses its youthful vigor and beauty and becomes prematurely old, misshapen, and unsightly. In the forest all the lower branches fall off leaving a columnar shaft which is crowned by a small open irregular head.

The Black Spruce derives its name from the dark green of its foliage which when massed upon a mountain-side and in shadow is of so sombre a hue as to appear black rather than green. The name is given in distinction from the White Spruce whose leaves are of a paler color. In the early botanies the Black and the White Spruce were designated respectively as double and single spruce, for reasons which are not apparent, as the disposition of the leaves of each is the same. In fact, these two species bear such resemblance to each other that it is not always easy to distinguish them ; the cones furnish the principal distinctive feature when the flowering season is past. The cones of the Black Spruce are ovate-oblong, have great staying powers, are always on the trees at the flowering time and usually persist for several years. The cones of the White Spruce on the other hand are oblong or cylindrical and usually fall before the flowering time or during the heat of the second summer. The young leaves of the White Spruce are visible at flowering time, those of the Black Spruce are not. Resin flows freely from cuts and gashes and soon hardens into a thick white gum, which with slight preparation is sold as chewing gum. The odor of the leaves is pleasantly resinous aromatic.

A favorite domestic drink called Spruce Beer was formerly made by boiling the young branches in water and adding to the decoction molasses and yeast in certain fixed proportions, but its place has now been taken by other drinks.

One of the chief values of the wood is in the manufacture of wood pulp. The characteristics of good pulp wood are : long fibre to insure strength and felting property, light color to save bleaching, soft texture that it may be easily ground, and freedom from foreign matter such as resin, starch, and coloring material.

The wood of all the *Coniferæ* is rich in those long coarse fibres known as tracheids and contains relatively very few short cells ; consequently all are valuable as pulp woods unless they are more valuable for something else.

The Black Spruces of the Adirondacks fell victims a few years ago to a blight which destroyed one-half of the mature trees of the region. Expert investigation proved the cause of this destruction to be the work of a small beetle. The insects excavated a passage between the bark and the wood, eating away part of both and practically girdling the tree.

NORWAY SPRUCE

Picea excélsa.

This is a native of the northern part of Europe as its name denotes and consequently is hardy in the northern states. It is the most satisfactory spruce tree that can be planted in northern Ohio. It is a beautiful spiry-topped tree ; the branches sweep downward with a graceful curve and the branchlets, after the tree reaches the height of thirty feet or more, become pendulous. The cones are from four to six inches long, beautifully pendent from the tips of the branches. Take it, all in all, it is a very desirable tree, for ornament for hedge or for wind-break.

The Norway Spruce is the great tree of the Alps. It there reaches the height of one hundred and fifty feet, forms extensive forests, endures severe cold and reaches the elevation of 4,500 feet above the sea. Its wood is the white deal of Europe ; its resin, Burgundy pitch.

HEMLOCK

Tsùga canadénsis.

A conical evergreen tree, usually sixty or seventy feet high, maximum height one hundred feet. Loves steep rocky banks and narrow river gorges, often found on mountain sides. Bark rich in tannin. Grows slowly. Ranges from Nova Scotia to Minnesota and through Michigan and Wisconsin, southward to Georgia and Alabama, reaches its largest size on the mountains of North Carolina and Tennessee.

Bark.—Reddish brown or gray, deeply divided into ridges covered with closely appressed scales. Branchlets at first pale brown, pubescent, later become darker, finally dark gray brown with purple tinge.

Wood.—Light brown or white ; light, soft, brittle, coarse, crooked-grained, difficult to work, liable to splinter. Makes coarse lumber. Sp. gr., 0.4239 ; weight of cu. ft., 26.42 lbs.

Winter Buds.—Light brown, obtuse, one-sixteenth of an inch long.

Leaves.—Linear, flat, obtuse, rounded or emarginate at apex, entire or obscurely toothed above the middle, dark yellow green, shining above, hoary beneath, spirally arranged around the branch but appearing two-ranked by the twisting of their petioles, jointed to a very short sterigmata and falling away in drying. One-half to three-fourths of an inch long. Petiole short.

Flowers—April, May. Monœcious. Staminate flowers axillary, sub-globose, borne on slender stems, about three-eighths of an inch long ; anthers pale yellow, pistillate flowers one-eighth of an inch long, pale green. Scales short ; bracts broad, laciniate.

Cones.—Bright red brown, suspended on short peduncles, ovate—oblong, acute, three-fourths to one inch long. Remain on branches until spring. Seeds small wings short, broad.

Fruiting Spray of Norway Spruce, *Picea excelsa.*
Cones 4′ to 6′ long.

The Hemlock is one of the most beautiful of the cone bearing trees ; and although similar in general form to the spruces, rigidity has transformed itself into ease and formality into grace and beauty. The branches are slender and pliant, heavily clothed with foliage, drooping in habit and the lower sweep the ground. As the tree becomes older they become large and strong and stand out horizontally. The difference between youth and age is marked. The wood is not valuable, it has neither strength nor durability, but the bark is extensively used in tanning and is the chief commercial product of the tree.

TAMARACK. LARCH. HACMATACK

Làrix laricìna. Làrix americàna.

Fifty to sixty feet high, trunk eighteen to twenty inches in diameter, when young it forms a narrow pyramidal head and this continues in the forest, but in the open it loses its regular form and develops a broad, open, irregular and often picturesque head. It ranges northward to the arctic circle and its southern limit seems to be along the line of northern Pennsylvania, northern Indiana, northern Illinois, and central Minnesota. Prefers cold, deep swamps but is occasionally found on dry land.

Bark.—Bright reddish brown, separating into thin appressed scales. Branchlets pendulous, the young branches are green, smooth, and glaucous, later light orange brown, gradually they become darker and at last are dark brown.

Wood.—Light brown, very resinous, sapwood nearly white ; heavy, hard, strong, rather coarse-grained, durable in contact with the soil. Used for ship-timbers, fence posts, telegraph poles, and railway ties. Sp. gr., 0.6236 ; weight of cu. ft., 38.86 lbs.

Winter Buds.—Dark red, globose, lustrous, small.

Leaves.—Needle-shaped, rounded above keeled below, three-fourths to one and one-fourth inches long, at first bright green, later dark green. They turn pale yellow and fall in October. They are borne, either scattered on leading shoots, or in crowded fascicles on short lateral branchlets, each leaf in the axil of a minute, deciduous bud scale.

Flowers.—May, with the leaves. Monœcious. Staminate flowers subglobose, sessile, usually borne on branchlets one or two years old ; composed of many short-stalked anthers spirally arranged

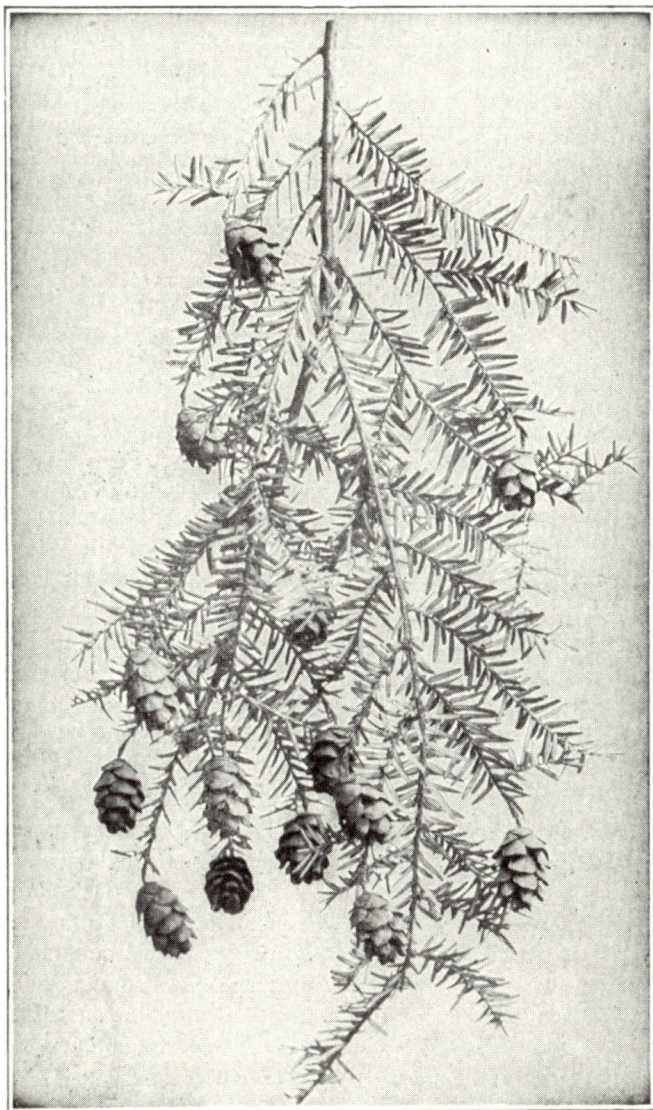

Fruiting Branch of Hemlock, *Tsuga canadensis.*
Leaves ½′ to ¾′ long. Cones ¾′ to 1′ long.

about a central axis ; anthers subglobose, pale yellow, two-celled ; connective pointed. Pistillate flowers oblong, pedunculate ; composed of many orbicular rose red scales spirally arranged about a central axis ; each scale in the axil of a pale rose colored bract with a long green tip. Upon each scale lie two naked ovules.

Cones.—Bright chestnut brown, oblong, obtuse, one half to three-fourths of an inch long and borne on a short, stout, incurved stem. Scales about twenty, the largest near the middle, the smaller at base and apex. Cone falls during second year. Seed one-eighth of an inch long, pale, with pale brown wings broadest in the middle.

> " Give me of your roots, O Tamarack!
> Of your fibrous roots, O Larch-Tree!
> My canoe to bind together
> So to bind the ends together
> That the water may not enter
> That the water may not wet me."
>   —HENRY W. LONGFELLOW.

One feature distinguishes the Tamarack from the other northern conifers, it sheds its leaves in the autumn of the year in which they are produced ; they turn a dull yellow and fall as do those of the poplar and the maple. This is a tree of the swamps and it serves a very valuable purpose in the economy of nature. When in those northern lands where it makes its home, a small lake has silted up from the surrounding country and so far dried that the rushes disappear from the margin and a coating of soil covers it ; the Tamarack creeps down and takes possession and the result is a Tamarack swamp. It is often possible to push a pole down ten feet into the mud about the roots of the trees of such a swamp. The roots developed there, long, tough, stringy are those Hiawatha needed for his canoe, those growing in dryer soil are not so flexible. The Tamarack will go up the hillside, it can live on dry land, but it loves the swamp and willingly yields the hillside to the spruces. In summer a Tamarack swamp is dark, cool, mossy ; in winter the appearance is somewhat desolate because the leaves are gone and one instinctively thinks of a leafless conifer as a dead tree.

The Tamarack and the Black Spruce go side by side toward the North Pole ; but at the ultimate boundary, at the very

Fruiting Spray of Tamarack, *Larix laricina*.
Leaves ¾′ to 1¼′ long.   Cones ½′ to ¾′ long.

edge of the treeless plain, the Tamarack is found standing a tiny tree, when its companion the Black Spruce is clinging to the ground, like a creeping plant, to escape being torn away by the force of the winds.

THE LARCH.

Làrix europæa.

The Larch which is extensively planted in parks and lawns is not the American species but the European. The European Larch is the finer tree in general appearance and as it naturally prefers loose well drained soil it flourishes where our native species would die. The leaves are longer, they clothe the branches more generously than those of the American species, the cones are larger and more abundant. It is a tree of the mid-temperate regions as well as of the north and is found in all the hill country of central Europe and forms large forests in the Alps of France and Switzerland.

BALSAM FIR. BALSAM.

Àbies balsàmea.

A conical evergreen tree, usually fifty to sixty feet in height, with trunk twelve to eighteen inches in diameter. On mountain tops and arctic regions reduced to a prostrate shrub. Northernmost limit yet observed is 62°; upon the Appalachians it ranges to southwestern Virginia. Loves moist alluvial land. Grows rapidly, is short-lived. Resinous.

Bark.—On young trees pale gray, thin, smooth and marked by swollen blisters filled with resin. On old trees reddish brown, broken into small, irregular, scaly plates. Branchlets pale yellow green, pubescent, later they become pale gray with reddish tinge, finally reddish brown.

Wood.—Pale brown often streaked with yellow, sapwood paler, light, soft, weak. Coarse-grained, not durable. Used for cheap lumber. Sp. gr., 0.3819; weight of cu. ft., 23.80 lbs.

Winter Buds.—Greenish brown, tinged with red, globose, very resinous.

Fruiting Branch of Larch, *Larix europæa.*

Leaves.—Linear, on young trees spreading at nearly right angles to the branch, remote or crowded. On old trees crowded, covering the upper side of branches. Dark green and shining above, pale below ; obtusely short-pointed and occasionally emarginate, and on fertile branches acute or acuminate ; vary from one-half to one and one-quarter of an inch in length and one-sixteenth of an inch wide. Persistent eight to ten years. Fragrant.

Flowers.—May, June. Monœcious. Staminate flowers oblong-cylindrical, one-quarter of an inch long. Anthers yellow, tinged with purple. Pistillate flowers oblong-cylindrical, one inch long ; scales orbicular, purple ; bracts oblong-obovate, serrulate, yellow green, contracted into long slender tips.

Cones.—Oblong-cylindrical, narrowed to the rounded apex, dark purple two to four inches long, three-quarters to one and one-quarter inches thick, upright ; scales broad, rounded ; bracts oblong, serrulate, mucronate at the apex, shorter or equal to the scales.

The Balsam Fir carries its resin, not scattered through the wood and under the bark as do the pines, flowing freely with gashes, but in superficial blisters in the bark itself. So characteristic is this that the New York Indians name the tree, Cho-koh-tung—" Blisters."

Whoever played as a child in northern woods remembers with what delight he punctured these blisters in order to see the clean limpid stream of resin flow out. As it comes from the tree it has the consistency of glycerine. Under the name of Canada Balsam it has been used in the *Materia medica* and it is the medium in which microscopic specimens are preserved upon the plates.

In form the Balsam Fir resembles the spruces. When young it is extremely beautiful, a slender symmetrical cone of shining, dark green foliage. In the forest the lower branches die but when the tree attains old age in the open, the head becomes sharp-pointed and spire-like, the lower limbs become pendulous sweeping the ground.

The leaves are flat, shining green above, a beautiful silvery color beneath, and very fragrant in drying. They are arranged spirally around the branch, but appear two-ranked because of a twist near the base ; occasionally they spread from all sides of the branch, this is especially true on the upper branches.

Balsam Fir, *Abies balsamea*.

Leaves ½′ to 1¼′ long.

The boughs of the Balsam Fir are sought by the northern hunter, fisherman, or tourist to make his wildwood bed. They possess an elastic quality which fits them for the purpose. The dried leaves are the material of which the much prized fir pillows are made.

The cones are produced in great numbers, they sit erect in rows on the upper side of the branches, are two to four inches long, an inch or more thick, cylindrical, with rounded ends. Bluish purple when young, they are often so abundant on the upper branches that they give a soft purple haze to the top of the tree.

In appearance the Balsam Fir resembles the Silver Fir of Europe which is a much finer tree.

BALD CYPRESS. DECIDUOUS CYPRESS

Taxòdium dìstichum.

The Bald Cypress is a southern tree growing in swamps and beside rivers, ranging from Delaware to Florida along the coast and in the Mississippi valley, growing as far north as southern Indiana. It is frequently planted in the parks and lawns of northern Ohio where it is perfectly hardy and becomes a tall, slender, spiry tree. Like the Tamarack its leaves are deciduous, falling in October. These are of two kinds ; the ordinary leaf is narrowly linear, flat, thin, one-half to three-fourths of an inch long, one-twelfth of an inch wide, apparently two-ranked ; when full grown is bright yellow green both above and below. In autumn they turn a dull orange brown before falling. The scale-like leaves appear on the flowering stem. The cones are globular or obovate, usually about an inch in diameter and appear irregularly along the branch.

This is the tree that when growing in the swamps forms the well-known cypress-knees. These are a development of the roots and appear in greatest size and numbers when the tree grows on submerged land. It seems to be an effort of the roots to get out of water and into the air.

Bald Cypress, *Taxodium distichum.*
Leaves ½′ to ¾′ long.

PINE FAMILY

The famous Cypress of Montezuma in the gardens of Che-
pultepec is a species of *Taxodium*. This was a noted tree
four centuries ago, and is believed to be about seven hundred
years old. It is one hundred and seventy feet high and about
fifteen feet in diameter.

ARBORVITÆ. WHITE CEDAR

Thuja occidentàlis.

Thuja is derived from a Greek word signifying, to sacrifice, the
wood having been used in sacrificial offerings because of its agreeable odor. *Occidentalis,* western. Arborvitæ, Tree of Life, is
supposed to have been given because the bark and twigs have
been used in medicine.

A narrow, conical, evergreen tree with flat frond-like foliage;
reaches the height of sixty feet. Inhabits wet soil along the banks
of streams and forms almost impenetrable forests northward; ranges
across the continent from New Brunswick to Manitoba and southward to Minnesota, Illinois and in the Atlantic region along the
mountains to North Carolina and Tennessee. Roots fibrous; juices
medicinal. Wood, bark, and foliage resinous, aromatic.

Bark.—Light reddish brown, slightly furrowed, on old trunks deciduous in ragged strips. Branchlets at first flat, disposed in one
horizontal plane, light yellow green, changing with the death of the
leaves during their second season to light cinnamon red, and growing darker the next year. Gradually becoming terete they are covered with dark yellow, coarse bark. Rich in tannin.

Wood.—Fragrant, light yellow brown, sapwood nearly white; light,
soft, brittle, coarse-grained and durable in contact with the soil.
Used for fence posts, rails, railway ties and shingles. Sp. gr.,
0.3164; weight of cu. ft., 19.72 lbs.

Leaves.—Opposite, imbricated in four ranks, scale-like, appressed.
The scale-like leaves of the ultimate branches are nearly orbicular,
or ovate, the two lateral rows keeled, the two other rows flat and
cause the twig to appear much flattened; many of the leaves bear a
raised glandular disk. When full grown are yellow green above
and below, in winter frequently become brown. The leaves of older
twigs are acute or acuminate and often remote. Leaves of seedlings
are lanceolate.

Flowers.—May. Monœcious, terminal, reddish brown, solitary.
Staminate and pistillate usually on different branchlets. Staminate

Fruiting Spray of Arborvitæ, *Thuja occidentalis*.

flowers minute, globose, consisting of four to six stamens arranged upon a short axis ; filaments scale-like, bearing anther cells. Pistillate flowers small, oblong, or ovoid ; scales eight to twelve, oblong, acute; reddish, the central or lower fertile, bearing two to four ovules.

Fruit.—Cone, ripening first season. Pale cinnamon brown, erect, oblong, one-third to one-half of an inch long ; scales six to twelve, obtuse. Seed one-eighth of an inch long, winged.

This tree is commonly called Arborvitæ, sometimes White Cedar, and the Indians of New York call it, Oo-soo-ha-tah— "Feather-leaf." The leaves are evergreen, arranged in four rows in alternately opposite pairs, completely covering and in fact seeming to make up the fan-like branchlets. They are scale-like, each lower pair covering the base of the pair above. The branchlets which they cover are arranged in a single plane as if they were parts of one large, flat, compound leaf. These planes are variously inclined to the horizon, often vertical, and form a marked peculiarity of the tree. The leaves when bruised exhale a very agreeable, aromatic, resinous odor.

The Arborvitæ has been extensively cultivated as an ornamental tree for at least a century, and nearly fifty varieties are recorded. The tree is so formal in outline that it rarely harmonizes with other trees. Its form seems the result of clipping shears but in reality it is its nature to look artificial. It has merits. Because of the density of its foliage, it will form a close leafy screen more effectually than any other evergreen. It is tolerant of many and diverse conditions of hot, cold, wet and dry, bears the knife well, and makes excellent hedges. During the early winter it stands up bright and green, during the weather changes of March and April it appears very brown, ragged, and discouraged, but all this is atoned for when the golden green spray starts from every leafy branch, and it responds to the influences of another spring.

WHITE CEDAR.

Cupréssus thyoídes.   Chamæcýparis sphæroídea.

Cupressus is the classical name of the cypress tree.   *Chamæcyparis* is of Greek derivation and means a low cypress.

A conical evergreen tree with open, flat, fan-shaped spray, reaches the maximum height of eighty feet.   Prefers deep swamps and in them forms impenetrable thickets.   Ranges from Maine to Mississippi along the coast ; endures salt water.   Roots fibrous.

Bark.—Light reddish brown, furrowed, ridges often twisted around the tree, scaly.   Branchlets compressed at first, later become terete ; slender, light green at first, then light reddish brown, finally dark brown.

Wood.—Light brown with rose tinge, sapwood pale ; light, soft, weak, close-grained, easily worked, very durable in contact with the soil, fragrant.   Used in boat building, cooperage, interior finish of houses, fence posts and railway ties.   Sp. gr., 0.3322 ; weight of cu. ft., 20.70 lbs.

Leaves.—Of ultimate branches opposite, imbricated in four rows, scale-like, small, ovate, acute or acuminate, closely appressed or, spreading at the apex, decurrent, often remote on vigorous shoots. Four-ranked, those of the lateral rows keeled, those on vertical rows slightly convex, each with a glandular disk on the back.   The young leaves are light bluish green, somewhat hoary below, when full grown they become a dark blue green.   During the winter in the north when exposed to the sun they become a rusty brown.

Flowers.—April.   Monœcious, minute.   Staminate flowers are oblong, four-sided, one-eighth of an inch long, consisting of several shield-shaped scale-like filaments bearing two to four anthers. Pistillate flowers globular, of about six shield-shaped scales, alternating in pairs and bearing generally two black ovules.

Fruit.—Woody, globular cone, ripens at end of first season ; about one-fourth of an inch in diameter, sessile on a short leafy branch.   Light green and covered with glaucous bloom when full grown, then bluish purple, very glaucous, finally dark red brown. Scales are thick, shield-shaped, each with a central point or knob. Seeds usually one or two under each fertile scale.

It is unfortunate that *Cupressus thyoides* and *Thuja occidentalis* are both popularly known as White Cedar.   *Thuja* is also known as Arborvitæ, but many who know it as Arborvitæ also know it as White Cedar.   This results in endless confusion in the popular mind concerning the two trees.

They have much in common ; both are evergreens of formal habit. The branchlets of each are disposed in one horizontal plane, and form an open, flat, fan-shaped spray. The spray of the White Cedar is closer than that of Arborvitæ. The leaves of both are scale-like, opposite in pairs, which makes them four-ranked, and so firmly pressed to the twig and so closely overlapping each other that they seem to be the twig itself. A tiny glandular disk is almost always present on the scales of the White Cedar, frequently present on those of the Arborvitæ. The width of the ultimate branchlets of the Arborvitæ is nearly an eighth of an inch, that of the White Cedar barely a sixteenth.

The cones are a marked and distinguishing difference between them. Those of the White Cedar are tiny round balls, ornamented with various points and knobs. Those of the Arborvitæ are oblong and consist of six or eight loose scales. White Cedar is the more southern tree. Arborvitæ has its chosen home in northern latitudes although both are hardy throughout the northern states. The White Cedar is especially a tree of the swamps, crowding as far into the water as is possible while retaining a foothold of earth. Cedar swamps as a rule are inaccessible except in midwinter on the ice ; or in midsummer when the water is reduced to its lowest stage. When the White Cedar and the Bald Cypress inhabit a swamp together, the former crowds to the centre and the latter grows about the edges. Notwithstanding its love of water it will grow in dry situations ; and twelve varieties are reported as in cultivation.

As an illustration of the durability of the wood it may be noted that the trunks of White Cedar, buried deep in the swamps of New Jersey and Pennsylvania, are found to be unchanged in character and to furnish excellent lumber.

Fruiting Spray of White Cedar, *Cupressus thyoides*. *Chamæcyparis sphæroidea.*

JUNIPER. GROUND CEDAR

Juníperus commúnis.

Evergreen, varying from a low tree to an erect, or a matted or a prostrate shrub. As a tree its maximum height is about twenty-five feet. Branches spreading, or erect, or drooping. Ranges from Greenland to Alaska, in the east southward to Pennsylvania and northern Nebraska, in the Rocky Mountains to Texas, Mexico and Arizona. Bark and fruit aromatic.

Bark.—Dark reddish brown, separating into loose papery scales. Branchlets slender, smooth, lustrous, three-angled between the nodes, at first pale reddish yellow growing gradually darker. By the third year the bark begins to scale.

Buds.—Ovate, acute, one-eighth of an inch long, covered with scale-like leaves.

Leaves.—Linear-lanceolate, free, jointed at the base, acute, rigid, spreading nearly at right angles to the branches, sometimes reflexed, tipped with sharp, rigid, cartilaginous points, verticillate in threes, often with smaller ones fascicled in their channels. One-half to three-fourths an inch long, channelled and hoary above, dark yellow green and shining below; persistent for many years. They have an unpleasant slightly astringent flavor, and during winter turn a dark bronze on lower surface.

Flowers.—April, May. Usually diœcious. From buds formed in the autumn in the axils of leaves of the year. The staminate flower consists of scales each bearing three stamens, verticillate on a central axis; anther-cells three or four. The pistillate, of numerous scales each bearing three ovules, arranged on a central axis.

Fruit.—Berry-like strobile, maturing the second year. Dark blue, glaucous, subglobose or oblong. Tipped with the remnants of the ovules. One-fourth of an inch in diameter; flesh soft, mealy, resinous, aromatic, sweet, persists one or two years after ripening.

The common Juniper or Ground Cedar is a most interesting plant. In the first place it is the most widely distributed tree of the northern hemisphere, ranging around the earth on the line of the arctic circle, and in America southward to the highlands of Pennsylvania in the east, and to northern California in the west. It spreads over northern, central, and eastern Asia, ranges to the Himalayas where it ascends 14,-000 feet above sea level. It is common throughout northern

Fruiting Branch of Common Juniper, *Juniperus communis*.
Berries ¼′ in diameter.

and central Europe. In North America though not abundant
it is generally distributed. It is evidently one of those trees
which has been driven from the better lands by more power-
ful competitors, for in its temperate habitat it is found on
dry, sterile, gravelly slopes, or worn-out pastures or upon high
mountain-sides. Because of its enormous geographical range
it naturally varies greatly in form, changing from a tree
twenty-five feet high with a trunk ten inches in diameter to a
prostrate shrub. Its remains occur in the tertiary rocks of
Europe.

The Juniper may be readily recognized among evergreens,
by its awl-like leaves, arranged in whorls of threes, spreading, sharp pointed, channelled and hoary above, shining
green below.

The fruit reaches maturity very slowly. The species is
diœcious and the flowers appear late in the spring. During
the first year the fruit does not enlarge, it looks during all
its first winter like a flower-bud, but at the blooming period
of the second year it feels the impulse of quickening life and
begins to grow, and by the second winter it has become a
hard, green, tiny sphere about three-quarters of its full size,
covered with white bloom. During the following season it
continues to develop and in early autumn becomes dark blue
or bluish black covered with a glaucous bloom, with soft,
mealy, aromatic flesh, and one to three seeds. This aromatic
fruit is gathered in large quantities and used in the manufacture of gin ; whose peculiar flavor and medicinal properties are due to the oil of Juniper berries, which is secured by
adding the crushed fruit to undistilled grain spirit, or by allowing the spirit vapor to pass over it before condensation.
The seeds of the Juniper are almost as slow to germinate as
they were to mature, requiring two years. Thirteen varieties
of *Juniperus communis* are reported in the Check List of the
Forest Trees of the United States and several foreign species
are also in cultivation. All are tolerant of the knife, and it
affords gardeners much pleasure to make them assume pecul
iar and fantastic shapes.

494

Fruiting Branch of Red Cedar, *Juniperus virginiana.* Leaves scale-like.
Berries ⅓′ to ¼′ in diameter.

RED CEDAR. SAVIN

Juníperus virginiána.

Evergreen, varying from a shrub to a tree one hundred feet high, which is conical when young but cylindrical or irregular in old age. Ranges from Nova Scotia south to Florida, westward to British Columbia and east of the Rocky Mountains to Mexico. Tolerant of many soils and varied locations. Roots fibrous.

Bark.—Light reddish brown, scaly or stringy. Branchlets slender and four-angled but after the disappearance of the leaves become terete and are covered with close, dark brown bark tinged with red or gray.

Wood.—Bright red, fading with exposure to air, sapwood nearly white; fragrant, light. soft, close-grained, weak, durable in contact with the soil. Largely used for posts, railway ties, interior finish of houses, chests and closets in which woollens are preserved against attack of moths, cabinet-making and lead pencils. Sp. gr., 0.4826; weight of cu. ft., 30.70 lbs.

Leaves.—Opposite, of two kinds; awl-shaped and loose, scale-shaped, appressed, imbricated, and crowded. The awl-shaped appear on young plants and vigorous branches, are linear-lanceolate, long-pointed, light yellow green, one-half to three-fourths an inch long. The scale-shaped are closely appressed, acute, occasionally obtuse, rounded, often glandular in the back, entire, about one-sixteenth of an inch long, dark blue green, glaucous, turning brownish during the winter at the north, beginning in the third season to grow hard and woody and persisting two or three years longer on the branches. They are four-ranked, making the twig appear quadrangular.

Flowers.—April, May; terminal on short axillary branches; diœcious rarely monœcious. Staminate flowers consist of four to six shield-like scales each bearing about four or five yellow pollen sacs. Pistillate flowers minute consisting of about three pairs of fleshy, oblong, bluish scales, united at base, and bearing two ovules. Scales are obliterated in the fruit.

Fruit.—Matures in first or second season. Berry-like strobile, subglobose, one-third to one-fourth of an inch in diameter, pale green covered with white bloom, when fully grown, dark blue and glaucous at maturity; flesh sweet, resinous; seeds two to three.

The Red Cedar grows throughout the United States. It reaches its largest size in the swamps and rich alluvial bottom lands of the southern and southwestern states, but in the

Red Cedar, *Juniperus virginiana.* Leaves awl-shaped.

northern states it grows abundantly on dry gravelly slopes and rocky ridges.

A distinctive characteristic of the tree is the variation in the form of its leaves. Variation of form occurs among the leaves of the Sassafras and the Mulberry ; the Pitch Pine sometimes bears two forms ; the Red Cedar does so habitually. These are the awl-shaped and the scale-shaped. There seems to be no law that determines their production except that the awl-shaped always appear upon the young plants, but on mature plants the different forms occur upon the same branchlet. The awl-shaped are rigid, long-pointed, channelled and white glaucous above, yellow green and convex below. They vary in length from one-fourth to three-fourths of an inch. The scale-shaped are minute, closely appressed, acute or obtuse, and usually bear a glandular disk on the back. They are opposite but are so closely ranked that they make the leafy twig appear quadrangular.

The wood of the Red Cedar is so valuable and has been used so lavishly that it has become extremely expensive. The present commercial supply is obtained chiefly from the swamps near the western coast of Florida.

Few insects attack the Junipers, but they are the hosts of numbers of very interesting fungi. These fungi belong to the Rust family and are popularly known as Cedar Apples. The common Cedar Apple, *Gymnosporangium macropus*, especially attacks the Red Cedar and forms tufts of bright yellow, jelly-like masses, from orifices in which long yellow spurs protrude. These cling to the smaller twigs and are frequently believed to be the flowers of the tree, or else an astonishing kind of fruit. They will appear in a single night during the rainy season ; and a Red Cedar covered with these bright yellow masses of waving tongues is a remarkable sight. When the weather becomes dry these gelatinous masses contract and they are then seen to arise from the changed tissue of very young twigs.

TAXACEÆ—YEW FAMILY

GINKGO

Salisbùria adiantifòlia.   Gìnkgo bilòba.

The Ginkgo is a Chinese tree which came to England by way of Japan and to the United States by way of England. It is proving itself to be perfectly hardy and is planted in greater numbers year by year.

That which astonishes the observer is the singular character of its leaves. There is nothing like them in the arborescent foliage of either America or Europe. Apparently they are fern leaves; they so closely resemble the leaves of the Maiden-hair fern, *Adiantum,* that one of the specific names of the tree is *adiantifolia.* They are not evergreen; they turn yellow and drop in late autumn, in that respect partaking of the character of the Larch and the Bald Cypress.

The fruit is a drupe about an inch long, oval in shape, very ill scented when ripe, and containing a nut which is highly esteemed in Japan. This nut resembles a large plump plum-stone. It is not palatable until roasted, but then it is considered a digestive and is very generally served at banquets.

The tree has been slow to fruit in this country, but it is becoming apparent that the reason has been that few trees have attained the requisite age. Trees thirty to forty years old are beginning to fruit quite generally.

The young trees are tall, slender and spiry with a tendency

in the branches to hug the stem. But after a time one branch or perhaps two will grow out horizontally, the others will loosen a little so that it becomes very evident that the type of the mature tree is not the Lombardy Poplar, but rather a spreading oak. The Ginkgo is said to attain enormous proportions in its native land ; and if the climate proves favorable it may become a valuable tree in the United States.

Ginkgo. *Ginkgo biloba.*

FORM AND STRUCTURE

OF

Roots, Stems, Leaves, Flowers, and Fruit

ROOTS.

THE **root** is that part of the plant axis which does not bear leaves. Normally it grows downward, is fixed in the soil and absorbs nourishment from the soil. True roots produce nothing but root branches and root hairs.

Roots differ from stems in the following particulars. They are simpler in internal structure, very irregular in their mode of branching, never directly bear leaves, and their growing point is placed just back of the tip of the root. This tip is

FIG. 1.—Showing Root-cap and Root-hairs.

covered with a protecting cap called the **root-cap** and this may push its way without injury to the growing point. The **root-hairs** are found on the ultimate branches just back of the growing point ; their function is to absorb nutriment from the soil. (Fig. 1.)

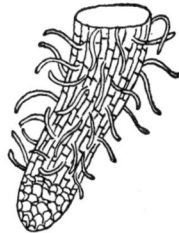

FIG. 2.—Tap Root.

When the main root is simple or the branches are small, it is called a **tap root.** (Fig. 2.)

When the main root divides very soon and is lost in its branches, the root is called **fibrous.**

The roots of the deciduous trees of North America are usually a modified form of the tap root, often a divided tap root with fibrous rootlets.

STEM.

The **stem** is that part of the plant axis which bears the leaves, flowers and fruit, and is the means of communication between them and the root. The stem differs from the root not only in that it is leaf-bearing but its branches are arranged regularly and the growing point is at the apex of the branches. A stem increases in length by the growth of a terminal bud and its branches normally originate from buds.

The points on the stem where the leaves appear are called **nodes.**

The parts of the stem between the nodes are called **internodes.**

The angle formed by the upper side of a leaf and the stem is called the **axil.**

LEAVES.

Leaves are stem-appendages and consist of expansions of the stem tissues. Foliage leaves are usually flat, bi-laterally symmetrical organs, green in color, and presenting a distinct upper and under surface. They are pre-eminently the assimilating organs of the plant; out of the crude sap under the influence of light and air they elaborate the plant food.

FIG. 3.—A Typical Leaf.

A **Typical Leaf** consists of three parts, the blade, the petiole, and the stipules; any one of these parts may be wanting. (Fig. 3.)

The **Blade** is the expanded portion of the leaf and the part to which the word leaf is usually applied. The **Petiole** is the leaf stalk. The **Stipules** are small leaf-like bodies, borne at the base of the petiole, usually one on each side. These are often united. Frequently they are wanting. The Sycamore and Black Willow afford excellent examples of stipules.

ARRANGEMENT.

When leaves are distributed singly at different heights on the stem, they are said to be **alternate.** When two stand opposite each other at the nodes, they are **opposite.** When more than two are borne at a node in a circle around the stem, they are **whorled.**

KINDS OF LEAVES.

Leaves are either simple or compound.

A **Simple Leaf** has but one blade. The leaves of the Elm are simple. A **Compound Leaf** has more than one blade ; each blade is then called a **leaflet.** The leaves of the Sumach are pinnately compound ; the leaves of the Horse-chestnut are palmately compound.

VERNATION OR PREFOLIATION.

In the study of the leaves of trees considerable attention is given to the way the leaves are folded in the bud ; this is

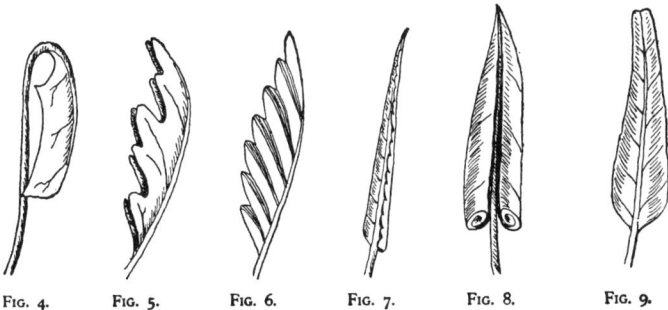

FIG. 4.   FIG. 5.   FIG. 6.   FIG. 7.   FIG. 8.   FIG. 9.

called **vernation.** It may be studied from two points of view ; how the leaves are arranged with reference to each other, or how the individual leaf is folded.

505

The following are the common forms of folding of the individual leaf :

Inflexed, bent inward toward the base. (Fig. 4.)

Conduplicate, two sides applied to each other, face to face. (Fig. 5.)

Plicate, when folded back and forth like the plaits of a fan. (Fig. 6.)

Convolute, when rolled inward from one margin to the other. (Fig. 7.)

Involute, rolled inward from each margin toward the midrib. (Fig. 8.)

Revolute, rolled outward from each margin toward the midrib. (Fig. 9.)

Botanically the inner surface of a leaf is that which in ordinary description is called the upper surface.

VENATION.

The **Venation** of a leaf is the arrangement of the **veins** or framework.

Three types are distinguished :

Forked-venation, seen in ferns.

Parallel-venation, seen in grasses and lilies.

Netted-venation, the form that prevails among deciduous trees. In the Netted-venation the veins branch repeatedly and the veinlets run together end to end, forming a more or less complicated network.

There are three modifications of this type :

Pinnate or **Feather-veined,** in which there is a midrib with lateral branches called primary veins which run toward the margin ; as in the leaves of the Elm, Beech, and Chestnut.

Palmate-veined, in which there are several ribs radiating from the petiole to the margin ; as in the leaves of the Maple and Sycamore.

Ribbed-netted-veined, in which there are several ribs running from petiole to apex with a network of small veins between.

FORMS OF LEAVES.

By **General Outline** we mean the outline form of the leaf, disregarding marginal indentations and slight irregularities.

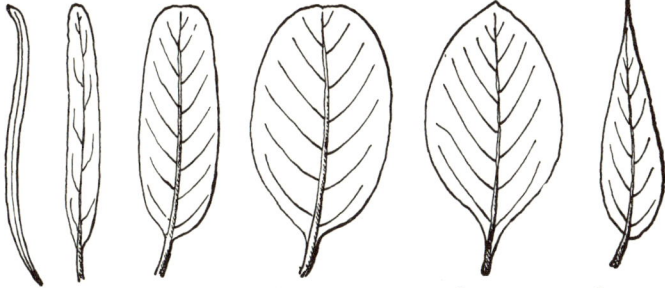

Fig. 10. Fig. 11. Fig. 12. Fig. 13. Fig. 14. Fig. 15.

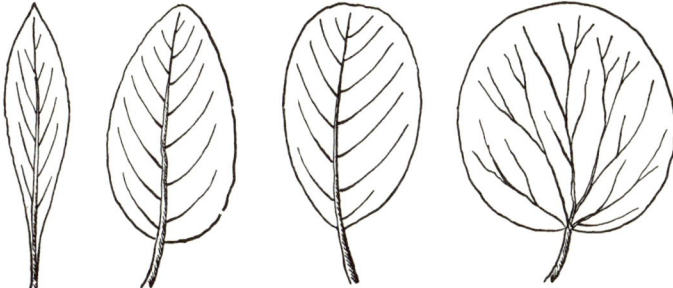

Fig. 16. Fig. 17. Fig. 18. Fig. 19.

The principal forms found in the leaves of trees are the following :

Needle-shaped, like the leaves of the Pine. (Fig. 10.)

Linear, a narrow elongated form. (Fig. 11.)

Oblong, two or three times longer than wide with sides nearly parallel. (Fig. 12)

Elliptical, oblong with a flowing outline, the two ends alike in width. (Fig. 13.)

Oval, broadly elliptical. (Fig. 14.)

Lanceolate, broader at base than apex, but narrow. (Fig. 15.)

Oblanceolate, the lanceolate reversed. (Fig. 16.)

Ovate, shaped like the longitudinal section of a hen's egg.
    (Fig. 17.)
Obovate, same form reversed, petiole at the smaller end.
    (Fig. 18.)
Orbicular, nearly circular in outline. (Fig. 19.)

The names are frequently used together in order to describe a leaf accurately.

APEX.

The **Apex** is the point of the leaf opposite the petiole.
The following forms prevail in the leaves of deciduous trees:

Acute, an apex which forms an acute angle. (Fig. 20.)
Acuminate, taper or long pointed. (Fig. 21.)
Obtuse, rounded or blunt. (Fig. 22.)
Truncate, cut off or terminating abruptly. (Fig. 23.)

FIG. 20. FIG. 21. FIG. 22.   FIG. 23.   FIG. 24.   FIG. 25.   FIG. 26.

Emarginate, with the rounded summit slightly indented
    forming a shallow notch. (Fig. 24.)
Mucronate, tipped with an abrupt short point. (Fig. 25.)
Bristle-pointed, tipped with a bristle. (Fig. 26.)

BASE.

The **Base** is the part of the leaf attached to the petiole or
stem. The following forms prevail in the leaves of deciduous
trees :

Rounded or **Obtuse,** as shown by the Black Cherry.
Cuneate or **Wedge-shaped**, as shown by the Papaw.
Cordate or **Heart-shaped,** as shown by the Balm of Gilead.
Oblique or unequal-sided, as shown by the Linden.

MARGINAL INDENTATIONS.

A distinction is made between indentations that are shallow and those that are deep. Of shallow indentations the following forms prevail in the leaves of deciduous trees :

Serrate, saw-toothed, with sharp teeth which incline toward the apex ; distinguished as fine and coarse. (Fig. 27.)

Bi-serrate, doubly serrate, with two sets of teeth one upon the other. (Fig. 28.)

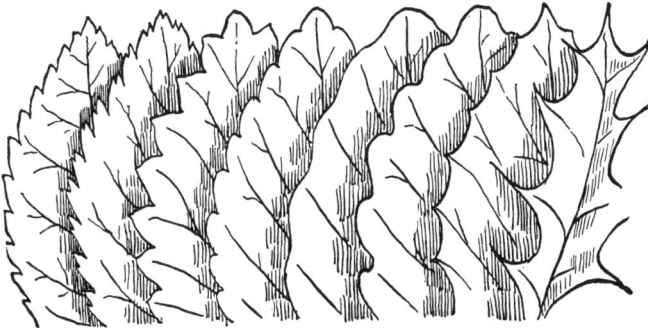

Figs. 27. 28. 29. 30. 31. 32. 33. 34.

Dentate, toothed with outwardly projecting teeth ; distinguished as fine and coarse. (Fig. 29.)

Crenate, scalloped, the teeth broad and rounded. (Fig. 30.)

Undulate, when the margin forms a wavy line. (Fig. 31.)

Sinuate, deeply wavy. (Fig. 32.)

Repand, margin like that of an opened umbrella. (Fig. 33.)

Spinose, margin spiny. (Fig. 34.)

The common forms of deeply indented margins found in the leaves of trees are **Lobed** and **Cleft.**

Lobed, when the indentations extend nearly half-way to the midrib or base, and the segments or sinuses or both may be either rounded or acute. The Oak and the Maple leaves are examples.

Cleft, when the sinuses are deep, narrow, and acute.

THE INDIVIDUAL FLOWER.

A complete flower consists of four sets of organs which botanists regard as modified leaves. These are **Calyx, Corolla, Andrœcium** the Stamens, and **Gynœcium** the pistils. They are borne on a short axis called the receptacle. (Fig. 35.)

The **Calyx** is the outer set. This is usually green though sometimes it is colored. It may consist of a number of separate parts called **Sepals**; these may be more or less united.

The **Corolla** is the second set. This is usually colored. It may consist of a number of separate parts called **petals**; these may be more or less united.

The calyx and corolla are called the **floral envelopes** because they surround and protect the stamens and pistils, which are the **essential organs** of the flower. They are called essential organs because together they produce the seed.

Fig. 35. Cherry Blossom, Showing Calyx (bud), Corolla, Stamens, and Pistil.

The **Stamens** constitute the third set. A stamen consists of two parts, the **filament** and the **anther.** The **Filament** is the anther stem. The **Anther** is the essential part and contains the **Pollen** which it discharges when mature. When the filament is wanting the anther is said to be sessile.

The Pistils are at the centre of the flower. It is not often that a number of pistils are found entirely separate ; as a rule they grow together and the parts unite or coalesce.

A single pistil consists of **ovary, style** and **stigma.** The **Ovary** is a hollow case which contains the ovules ; the **Stigma** is the upper part, usually flattened, which is covered by

FIG. 36.—Half a Cherry Blossom Showing Ovary, Style and Stigma.

an adhesive secretion and which receives the pollen ; the **Style** connects the ovary and the stigma. It may be wanting, the stigma is then said to be sessile. (Fig. 36.)

The **Ovules** are tiny sac-like bodies which after they receive the protoplasm of the pollen develop into seeds.

FIG. 37. — Raceme of Barberry Blossoms.

INFLORESCENCE.

Inflorescence is a term used to denote the arrangement of the flowers on the stem. Flowers may occur singly or in clusters ; they may be terminal or axillary.

Peduncle, is the stem of a solitary flower or of a flower cluster.

Pedicel, is the individual stem of each flower in a cluster.

Bract, is a small leaf found on a flower stem.

Involucre, is a collection of bracts around a flower cluster or around a single flower.

FLOWER CLUSTERS.

Raceme, is a cluster in which the flowers are arranged along the central axis upon pedicels nearly equal in length, those nearest the base blooming first (Fig. 37). The central axis is called a **rachis.** When the pedicels divide and subdivide the raceme becomes a **Panicle.** When a panicle stiffens and becomes rigid and

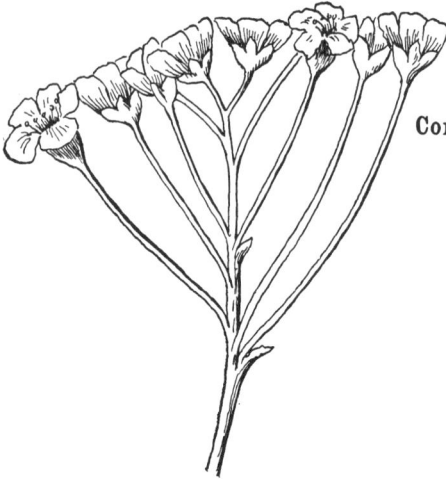

Fig. 38.—A Corymb.

erect it is called a **Thyrsus.** Flowers of Sourwood are borne in a raceme.

Corymb, is like a raceme except that the central axis is shorter and the lower pedicels are lengthened so as to bring all the flowers to nearly the same level. The oldest flowers are at the circumference (Fig. 38.) A flower cluster similar in form, but in which the oldest flowers are at the centre, is called a **Cyme.**

Umbel, resembles a raceme but the central axis is very short and the pedicels are nearly equal in length. (Fig. 39.)

Spike, is like a raceme except that the flowers are sessile ; they sit directly on the central axis.

Catkin or **Ament,** is like a spike except that its bracts are scales and the central axis is often drooping. Flowers of Poplar are examples.

Fig. 39.—Umbel of Cherry Blossoms.

Head, is like a spike except that the central axis is so short that the flowers form a compact cluster.

Strobile, is a compact cluster with large scales concealing the flowers.

FRUIT.

The **Fruit** consists essentially of the ripened pistil. After the ovaries have been fertilized the ovary is called a **Pericarp.** The following kinds of fruits are those most frequently borne by trees and are the products of a single flower :

Akene, is a one-seeded, dry, hard, seed-like fruit.

Samara, resembles an akene except that it has a wing-like appendage. The Ash, the Elm and the Maple produce samaras.

Glans or **Nut,** is a fruit with a thick hard pericarp, enclosed more or less in an involucre. The acorn is a nut.

Drupe, is often called a stone fruit. In it the wall of the pericarp is differentiated into three divisions—the outer or skin called exocarp, middle or fleshy portion called mesocarp, the inner wall enveloping the seed called endocarp. A cherry is a drupe.

Tryma, is a fruit structurally resembling the drupe, but the mesocarp is harder, more fibrous, and the outer husk ultimately splits open and comes off. A hickory nut is an example.

Berry, has a thin rind and all the rest of the pericarp is succulent. Berries may be one or many-celled. Grape and currant are examples.

Pome, is a fleshy fruit, the chief bulk of which consists of an adherent fleshy calyx. The apple is a pome.

Legume, is a dry one-carpelled fruit or pod that splits open front and back. The fruit of the Locust is a legume.

Capsule, consists of two or more united pistils which open and allow the seeds to escape.

Fruits that are the product of one flower but of more than one pistil are called **Aggregated Fruits.** Raspberry is an example. Fruits that are the products of flower clusters instead of single flowers are called **Multiple Fruits.**

Sorosis, is a multiple fruit of which the mulberry is an example.

Strobile or **Cone,** is a multiple fruit consisting of a scale-bearing axis, each scale enclosing one or more seeds. Pine cones are examples.

Galbulus, is a cone, the scales of which have become succulent. The juniper berry is an example.

The **Seed** is the fertilized and ripened ovule. It contains the embryo and usually more or less albumen. A well developed embryo possesses four parts : a tiny stem or **Caulicle,** at the lower end of which is the beginning of a root, called a **Radicle ;** and **Cotyledons,** which are two thickened bodies near the upper end of the caulicle, and between these is a small bud called a **Plumule.** These parts can be readily seen in the sprouting bean or pea. Some plants produce seeds bearing one cotyledon only ; such are called **Monocotyledones.** Others bear two cotyledons, they are called **Dicotyledones.**

THE TREE STEM OR TRUNK.

Stems are of two kinds, **Endogenous** and **Exogenous,** so named from the character of their growth. In an endogenous stem the wood is made up of separate threads scattered, here and there, throughout the whole diameter of the stem. In an exogenous stem the wood is collected to form a layer surrounding a central column of pith and is itself surrounded by bark.

A transverse section of a small twig of a tree shows the pith in the centre, around it a zone of wood, then a green inner bark, and finally the outer bark. All parts, except possibly the outer bark, are alive.

A transverse section of a mature tree exhibits a centre of heartwood or **Duramen** and a zone of sapwood or **Alburnum,** an inner bark and an outer bark. In addition are seen a series of concentric rings known as rings of annual growth, also a number of lines radiating from centre to circumference called **Medullary Rays.** The pith has disappeared but the medullary rays are composed of pith tissue and form a set

Transverse Section of Trunk of White Oak, *Quercus alba*, Showing Bark, Sapwood, Heartwood, Annual Rings and Medullary Rays.

of narrow plates which make the "silver grain" of the wood.

In the transverse section these appear as lines but when the wood is cut lengthwise parallel to them, "quartered," their faces show as glimmering plates which give a peculiar and beautiful appearance to the wood. Trees differ in the size and number of their medullary rays.

Each of the rings is supposed to mark a year's growth of the tree ; as a matter of fact it may or may not do so, but the number of concentric rings will give the approximate age of the tree.

The **heartwood** is the more valuable part of the trunk for timber. It is drier, harder, and more solid than the sapwood. The cells have been so filled by the deposition of hard matter that they are no longer able to take any part in the circulation of the tree ; the protoplasm has receded from them and they are virtually dead.

The zone of **sapwood** is a zone of living tissue. But the impulse of life is ever leaving the old and entering the new, and the cells of its inner circumference are continually being transformed into heartwood, and those of its outer circumference increased by new growth.

Between the sapwood and the bark, united to each, is a zone of growth called the **Cambium Layer.** This is a tissue of young and growing cells and it is here that the tree increases in diameter. Here is the newest wood and the newest bark, here new cells are formed, the inner ones adding to the wood, the outer to the bark, producing the annual layers of the two which are ever renewing and continuing the life of the tree.

The **Bark** is the outer covering of the trunk. At the surface it is made up of dead and dying tissue which is stretched and torn and shed in plates or scales as the wood beneath it increases in size and requires room to expand. The inner bark consists essentially of sieve-tissue or bast and forms a zone capable of rapidly conducting the fluids of the tree.

In all young bark is found a peculiar group of cells, called **Lenticels,** which protrude through the skin or epidermis. In some trees these lenticels disappear when the bark becomes older, in others they persist. The best opinion now is that they are openings for the purpose of admitting air to the living internal tissues.

SPECIES AND GENUS.

Under the term **Species** are included all individuals which possess in common such a number of constant characters that they may be considered to be descended from a common ancestral form. In the course of multiplication new peculiarities may arise and individuals characterized by these peculiarities are regarded in classification as **Varieties.**

When several species resemble each other so distinctly that their general characters indicate relationship they are grouped together in a **Genus.** Genera are not fixed, they vary with the views of botanists.

The **Scientific Name** of a plant consists of two words, the first indicating the genus, the second the species. If a third is added it indicates the variety.

GLOSSARY OF BOTANICAL TERMS.

ABNORMAL.—Differing from the usual structure.

ABORTION.—Imperfect development or non-development of an organ.

ABORTIVE.—Imperfectly developed or rudimentary.

ACUMINATE.—Tapering at the end.

ACUTE.—Forming a sharp angle.

ADHESION.—The union of members of different floral whorls.

ADNATE.—Grown together.

ADVENTITIOUS.—Occurring out of the regular order.

ÆSTIVATION.—The arrangement of floral organs in the bud.

AKENE.—A small, dry, hard, one-celled, one-seeded, indehiscent fruit.

ALBUMEN.—A name applied to the food store laid up outside the embryo in many seeds; also nitrogenous organic matter found in animals and plants.

ALBURNUM.—Sapwood.

ALTERNATE.—Applied to that form of leaf arrangement in which only one leaf occurs at a node.

AMENT.—A scaly spike or catkin.

ANGIOSPERMS.—Those plants which bear their seeds within a pericarp

ANTHER.—That part of the stamen which bears the pollen.

APETALOUS.—Having no petals.

APPRESSED.—Lying close and flat against.

ARBORESCENT.—A tree in size and habit of growth.

ARIL.—The exterior coat of some seeds.

AWL-SHAPED.—Narrowed upward from the base to a slender or rigid point.

AXIL.—The upper one of the two angles formed by the juncture of the leaf with the stem.

AXILLARY.—Situated in an axil.

BAST.—A name applied to the inner layer of the bark.

BEAKED.—Ending in a prolonged tip.

BERRY.—A fruit whose entire pericarp is succulent.

BI-PINNATE.—Applied to a leaf which is twice compounded on the pinnate plan.

BRACTLETS.—The smaller bracts borne on pedicels.

BRACTS.—The modified leaves borne on flower peduncles or at the base of flower stems.

519

GLOSSARY OF BOTANICAL TERMS

CADUCOUS.—Applied to the calyx of a flower when it falls off before the flower expands; also to the stipules of a leaf if they fall as the leaf appears.

CALYX.—The outer whorl of floral envelopes.

CAMPANULATE.—Bell-shaped.

CAPSULE.—A dry, usually dehiscent fruit, made up of two or more carpels.

CARPEL.—A simple pistil, or one member of a compound pistil.

CATKIN.—An ament.

CELLULOSE.—A primary cell-wall substance.

CHLOROPHYLL.—The green grains in the cells of plants.

CLAW.—The stalk or contracted base of a petal.

COHESION.—The union of members of the same floral whorl.

CONDUPLICATE.—Doubled together. The vernation of a leaf is conduplicate when the two sides are folded together lengthwise, face to face.

CONNATE.—Grown together.

CONNECTIVE.—That portion of the anther which connects the two lobes.

CONTORTED.—Twisted together.

CONVOLUTE.—Rolled up; applied to leaves that are rolled from one edge.

CORDATE.—Heart-shaped; applied to a leaf which has a deeply indented base.

CORIACEOUS.—Thickish and leathery in texture.

COROLLA.—The inner whorl of floral envelopes.

CORYMB.—A flower cluster in which the axis is shortened and the pedicels of the lower flowers lengthened, so as to form a flat-topped cluster.

CORYMBOSE.—Like a corymb.

COTYLEDON.—One of the parts of the embryo performing in part the functions of a leaf, but usually serving as a storehouse of food for the developing plant.

CRENATE.—Scalloped.

CRENULATE.—Finely crenate.

CROSS-FERTILIZATION.—When the stigma of one flower receives the pollen of a different flower.

CRUCIFORM.—Applied to corollas of four distinct petals arranged in form of a cross.

CUSPIDATE.—Tipped with a sharp and rigid point.

CYME.—A broad and flattish inflorescence with the central or terminal flowers blooming earliest.

DECIDUOUS.—Not persistent; applied to leaves that fall in autumn and to calyx and corolla when they fall off before the fruit develops.

DECURRENT.—Applied to leaves which are prolonged down the side of the petiole.

DEFINITE.—Limited or defined.

DEHISCENCE.—The act of splitting open.

DELTOID.—Triangular, somewhat like the Greek letter delta.

DENTATE.—Applied to leaves that have their margins toothed, with the teeth directed outward.

DIADELPHOUS.—In two brotherhoods. Applied to stamens when cohering by their filaments into two sets.

DICHOTOMOUS.—Forking; dividing into two equal branches.

DICOTYLEDON.—A plant whose embryo has two opposite cotyledons.

DIFFUSE.—Widely spreading.

DIGITATE.—Applied to a compound leaf in which all the leaflets radiate from the top of the petiole.

DIŒCIOUS.—In two households. With staminate and pistillate flowers separate and on separate plants.

DISCOID.—Having the form of a disc. Descriptive of the shapes of certain stigmas, glands, etc.

DISK.—A development of the receptacle at or around the base of the pistil.

DISSEPIMENT.—A partition in a fruit.

DRUPE.—A fleshy or pulpy fruit with the inner portion of the pericarp hard or stony. A stone fruit.

DURAMEN.—Heartwood.

ECHINATE.—Beset with prickles.

EMARGINATE.—Notched. Applied to a leaf which is notched at the apex.

EMBRYO.—Applied in botany to the tiny plant within the seed.

ENDOCARP.—The inner layer of the pericarp.

EPICARP.—The outer layer of the pericarp.

EPIGYNOUS.—Growing on the summit of the ovary, or apparently so.

EROSE.—Irregularly toothed, as if gnawed.

ETÆRIO.—A fruit, the product of a single flower, which consists of small aggregated drupes.

EXOCARP.—The outer layer of the pericarp.

EXSERTED.—Protruding; as stamens extending beyond the throat of a corolla.

EXTRORSE.—Facing outward. Applied to anthers which face away from the pistil.

FALCATE.—Curved or sickle-shaped.

FASCICLE.—A bundle. Applied to a compact cyme or a compact cluster of leaves.

FERTILIZATION.—The union which takes place when the contents of the pollen cell enters the ovule.

FIBRO-VASCULAR BUNDLES.—The bundles of vascular tissues of plants.

FILAMENT.—The stalk which supports the anther.

FILIFORM.—Thread-like.

FOLIACEOUS.—Leaf-like.

FUGACIOUS.—Soon falling off.

GALBULUS.—A berry-like cone, as the fruit of the Juniper.

GAMOPETALOUS.—Having the petals more or less united.

GAMOSEPALOUS.—Having the sepals more or less united.

GLOSSARY OF BOTANICAL TERMS

GERMINATION.—The sprouting of a seed.

GIBBOUS.—Swollen on one side.

GLABROUS.—Smooth ; destitute of hairs.

GLANDS.—A secreting surface or structure ; a protuberance having the appearance of such an organ.

GLANS.—A nut.

GLAUCOUS.—Covered or whitened with a bloom.

GLOBOSE.—Spherical or nearly so.

GYMNOSPERMS.—Plants bearing naked seeds ; without an ovary.

GYNŒCIUM.—The pistils of a flower taken as a whole.

HABITAT.—The geographical range of a plant.

HEAD.—A compact cluster of nearly sessile flowers.

HILUM.—The point of attachment of an ovule or seed.

HISPID.—Bristly.

HYBRID.—A cross between two species.

HYPOGYNOUS.—Situated on the receptacle, beneath the ovary and free from it and from the calyx. Applied to petals and stamens.

IMBRICATE.—Overlapping.

INCISED.—Cut sharply and deeply.

INCLUDED.—Applied to stamens or pistils that do not project beyond the corolla.

INDEFINITE.—Applied to petals or other organs when too numerous to be conveniently counted.

INDEHISCENT.—Not splitting open.

INDIGENOUS.—Native to the country.

INFERIOR.—Applied to an ovary which has an adherent calyx.

INFLORESCENCE.—The flowering part of a plant.

INNATE.—Applied to anthers which are attached by their base to the apex of the filament.

INSERTED.—Attached to or growing out of.

INTERNODE.—The portion of a stem between two nodes.

INTRORSE.—Facing inward ; applied to stamens that face toward the pistil.

INVOLUCEL.—A secondary involucre.

INVOLUCRE.—A collection of bracts at the base of a flower cluster or of a single flower.

INVOLUTE.—A form of vernation in which the leaf is rolled inward from its edges.

LANCEOLATE.—Applied to leaves which are slender, broadest near the base and narrowed to the apex.

LEAFLET.—A single division of a compound leaf.

LEGUME.—A fruit formed of a simple pistil and usually splitting open by both sutures.

LENTICELS.—Small oval dots which appear upon the branches.

LIBER.—The inner layer of the bark.

GLOSSARY OF BOTANICAL TERMS

LIGNEOUS.—Woody.

LIMB.—The spreading portion of a gamophyllus calyx or corolla.

LINEAR.—Applied to an organ with parallel margins that is many times longer than broad.

LOBE.—Any segment of an organ.

LOCULICIDALLY.—Dehiscent through the back of a cell of a capsule.

MEDULLA.—The pith.

MEDULLARY RAYS.—Rays of fundamental tissue which connect the pith with the bark.

MEMBRANOUS, MEMBRANACEOUS.—Thin and rather soft, more or less translucent.

MESOCARP.—The middle layer of the pericarp.

METABOLISM.—The oxydizing processes that go on in the living plant.

MIDRIB.—The central or main rib of a leaf.

MONADELPHOUS.—In one brotherhood. Applied to stamens which are united by their filaments into one set.

MONOCOTYLEDONOUS.—Possessing but one cotyledon or seed leaf.

MONŒCIOUS.—In one household. Applied to plants which have separate staminate and pistillate flowers, but both borne on the same plant.

MUCRONATE.—Tipped with a small soft point.

MULTIPLE FRUIT.—A fruit composed of numerous small fruits, each the product of a separate flower ; ex. mulberry.

NECTARY.—The honey gland or honey repository of a flower.

NERVED.—Veined.

NODE.—The point on a stem of a plant from which the leaf develops.

OBCONIC.—Conic with the point of attachment at the apex.

OBCORDATE.—Inversely heart-shaped.

OBLANCEOLATE.—Inversely lanceolate.

OBLONG.—Considerably longer than broad, with flowing outline.

OBTUSE.—Blunt, rounded.

OVAL.—Broadly elliptical.

OVARY.—The part of the pistil that contains the ovules.

OVOID.—Egg-shaped. Applied to solid bodies.

OVULE.—The rudimentary seed.

PANICLE.—A compound raceme.

PAPILIONACEOUS.—A term descriptive of such flowers as those of the Pea.

PARTED.—Cleft nearly but not quite to the base or midrib.

PEDICEL.—The stem of an individual flower of a cluster.

PEDUNCLE.—A flower stalk.

PERFECT.—Applied to a flower which has both pistil and stamens.

PERIANTH.—A term applied to the floral envelopes taken as a whole.

PARICARP.—The walls of the ripened ovary, the part of the fruit that encloses the seeds.

PERIGYNOUS.—Borne around the pistil instead of at its base. Applied to stamens and petals borne on the throat of the calyx.

GLOSSARY OF BOTANICAL TERMS

PERSISTENT.—Long continuous, applied to leaves that remain on the tree over winter and to a calyx that remains until the fruit ripens.

PETAL.—One of the leaves of the corolla.

PETIOLE.—The stem of a leaf.

PINNA (pl. pinnæ).—One of the primary divisions of a pinnately compound leaf.

PINNATE.—Applied to compound leaves where the leaflets are arranged on each side of a common petiole.

PISTIL.—The modified leaf or leaves which bear the ovules ; usually consisting of ovary, style and stigma.

PISTILLATE.—Applied to flowers that possess pistils but not stamens.

PLICATE.—Folded like a fan.

PLUMULE.—The primary bud of the embryo.

POLLEN.—The fertilizing powder produced by the anther.

POLYGAMOUS.—Applied to plants which produce staminate, pistillate, and perfect flowers all on the same plant.

PROTOPLASM.—The living matter of the cell.

PUBESCENT.—Downy, covered with soft hairs.

RACEME.—A simple inflorescence of pedicelled flowers upon a common, more or less, elongated axis.

RACHIS.—The axis of inflorescence.

RADICLE.—The primary root of the embryo.

RECEPTACLE.—The shortened stem on which the floral organs are inserted.

REDUPLICATE.—Doubled back.

REFLEXED.—Bent outward.

REPAND.—Leaf margin toothed like the margin of an umbrella.

REVOLUTE.—Rolled backward.

ROTATE.—Flat circular disk ; applied to corollas.

SAMARA.—An indehiscent dry fruit provided with a wing-like appendage.

SECUND.—Flowers arranged along one side of a lengthened axis.

SEPAL.—One of the leaves of the outer whorl of floral organs.

SERRATE.—Toothed, with sharp teeth projecting forward.

SINUATE.—Wavy.

SINUS.—The cleft between two lobes.

SPATULATE.—Resembling a spatula in outline.

SPIKE.—A form of simple inflorescence in which the flowers are sessile or nearly so, borne upon a lengthened axis. The lower flowers bloom first.

SPRAY.—The ultimate division of a branch.

STAMEN.—The pollen-bearing organ of the flower, usually consisting of filament and anther.

STAMINATE.—Applied to flowers which have stamens but not pistils.

STERIGMA. Pl. Sterigmata.—The woody base upon which the leaves of many of the evergreens are borne.

STIGMA.—That part of the pistil which receives the pollen.

STIPE.—The stalk possessed by some pistils.

STIPULE.—One of the blade-like bodies at the base of the petiole of leaves.

STOMA, pl. Stomata.—A breathing pore found in the epidermis of the higher plants.

STROBILE.—A compact flower cluster with large scales concealing the flowers. When this cluster matures and contains seeds it is still called a strobile.

STYLE.—That part of the pistil which connects the ovary with the stigma.

SUPERIOR.—Applied to an ovary that is not at all adherent to the calyx.

SYNCARP.—A multiple fruit.

TAPROOT.—The main root or downward continuation of the plant axis.

TERETE.—Nearly cylindrical.

TERMINAL.—Placed at the end.

THYRSE or THYRSUS.—A compact panicle.

TOMENTOSE.—Applied to surfaces which are covered with matted hairs.

TOMENTUM.—Matted hairs.

TORUS.—Another name for receptacle.

TRUNCATE.—Ending abruptly as if cut off.

TRYMA.—A drupe-like fruit which is commonly two-celled, has a bony nucleus and thick, fibrous epicarp.

TURBINATE.—Top-shaped.

UMBEL.—A flower cluster in which the axis is very short and the pedicels radiate from it.

UNDULATE.—Wavy.

VALVATE.—Meeting by the edges without overlapping.

VASCULAR.—Possessing vessels or ducts.

VEIN.—Thread of fibro-vascular tissue in a leaf.

VEINLET.—Small vein.

VENATION.—The system of veins as that of a leaf.

VERNATION.—The arrangement of the leaves in the bud.

VERSATILE.—Applied to an anther that turns freely on its support.

VILLOUS.—Covered with long, soft, shaggy hairs.

WHORL.—An arrangement of organs in a circle about a central axis.

INDEX OF LATIN NAMES

527

INDEX OF LATIN NAMES

INDEX OF COMMON NAMES

INDEX OF COMMON NAMES

INDEX OF COMMON NAMES